The Analysis of Structured Securities

SYLVAIN RAYNES AND ANN RUTLEDGE

The Analysis of Structured Securities

Precise Risk Measurement and Capital Allocation

OXFORD
UNIVERSITY PRESS

2003

OXFORD
UNIVERSITY PRESS

Oxford   New York
Auckland   Bangkok   Buenos Aires   Cape Town   Chennai
Dar es Salaam   Delhi   Hong Kong   Istanbul   Karachi   Kolkata
Kuala Lumpur   Madrid   Melbourne   Mexico City   Mumbai   Nairobi
Sao Paulo   Shanghai   Taipei   Tokyo   Toronto

Published by Oxford University Press, Inc.
198 Madison Avenue, New York, New York 10016

www.oup.com

Oxford is a registered trademark of Oxford University Press

Library of Congress Cataloging-in-Publication Data
Raynes, Sylvain.
The analysis of structured securities : precise risk measurement and capital allocation /
Sylvain Raynes and Ann Rutledge.
p. cm.
Includes bibliographical references and index.
ISBN 0-19-515273-5
1. Securities. 2. Asset-backed financing. 3. Mortgage-backed
securities 4. Investment analysis. I. Rutledge, Ann. II. Title.
HG4521 .R34 2003
332.63′2044—dc21   2003004691

9   8   7   6   5   4   3   2   1

Printed in the United States of America
on acid-free paper

To my two mentors—Professor S. I. Cheng of Princeton University and Manny

SRR

To Carroll Burrage Rutledge and Ivan Cate Rutledge, two lifelong seekers of knowledge.

AER

Preface

Structured securities are debt securities backed by the pooled receivables of existing loans, leases, trade financings, bonds, or other financial assets whose credit risk generally has been delinked from the credit of the originator or seller by sale, swap, or assignment. The result is a transaction governed by a set of documents with covenants crafted to achieve a unique profile of risk and return for one or more tranches of debt. The classic motivations for a corporation to raise funds in the structured market rather than the corporate credit market are lower funding costs, better placement ability, balance sheet restructuring, and arbitrage of interest rates, credit spreads, taxes, or regulatory conditions.

Structured securities were first introduced to the market as a type of corporate bond. In its credit essence, however, a structured security is actually the opposite of a corporate bond: it is a tabula rasa unencumbered by business policy, market position, sectoral risk, management capability, agency conflict, or any other variable of performance save its target risk-adjusted return. It has no intrinsic character that cannot be effectively altered or eliminated by changing the asset mix, redirecting cash flows under outright or contingent payment instructions, or adding more capital.

The flexibility of structured securities confers upon them some efficiency advantages over their corporate counterparts. First, repackaging allows borrowers and their bankers to seek out the most liquid market sectors for placement. This creates better information linkages between the demand for and supply of credit, increasing the economic efficiency of the debt market. Structured securities also allow borrowers to raise funds more cheaply than by issuing corporate bonds. The gain is not solely due to financial "alchemy." It has a sound credit basis. Ceteris paribus, if the procedures for creating cash securitizations are faithfully followed, investors have an investment in a pool of diversified assets of greater cash flow certainty than the credit of a single company; moreover, the structure of controls virtually eliminates discretionary uses of funds, increasing the certainty that cash collected will be used to pay investors. Also obvious, but frequently overlooked, is that the structuring process entails the disclosure of highly proprietary and potentially sensitive data. Historical asset-account-level data must be prepared in depth before origination and updated over the life of the structured transaction. Properly carried out, the due diligence process for a structured security yields a much richer data set than what is available from financial statement analysis. Moreover, the ability to synthesize expected loss behavior from pool data allows a structure of protection to be crafted that allocates precisely the right amount of capital for a quantum of risk. In this way, the "elusive" goal of capital optimality in portfolio management is *uniquely* achievable with structured securities—in theory. But not as structured finance is practiced today.

To a great extent, complacency has made the market for structured securities a victim of its own success. Bankers have mastered the routines of helping lower-rated companies arbitrage the rating of the firm by following published rating agency criteria, and they have honed the pitch that persuades firms to improve the execution by relinquishing ownership, control, and asset information advantages. For sellers operating on sufficient scale to absorb the fixed costs associated with securitization, the quid pro quo in funding cost savings can be substantial. But is it fair? Is the seller getting full value for his assets? In structured securities, there are no public benchmarks of structuring excellence. In the past decade a handful of highly efficient structures have emerged, like the Guiness Peat Aviation (GPA) aircraft lease securitization (see chapter 22) and the Platinum collateralized bond obligation (CBO), but the structuring details are not in the public domain. What incentive do the banks have to go the extra mile, analytically speaking, to create truly capital-efficient structures for their clients when there are no visible benchmarks?

We contend that there is still considerable inefficiency in today's framework of structured securities analysis. The contemporary framework is a resourceful reworking of company risk-analytic methods with some elements of portfolio analysis. Yet, as we noted above, the substance of company analysis is largely irrelevant to structured finance. A framework of analysis is finally like any other diagnostic tool: its output is only as good as its ability to probe in the right spots and give the user a result that is consistent and at least meaningful, if not precise. Not only is the current framework not designed to "probe in the right spots," but it yields inconsistent results.

There are actually three different rating agency approaches upon which the market relies. Referred to in this book as the *actuarial, default,* and *eclectic* methods, they were created to deal expediently with the main financing formats of structured finance. The actuarial method is an analysis of the fair value of a portfolio of mainly consumer loans, using account-level data. Monte Carlo simulation makes it possible to apply something akin to the actuarial method to collateralized debt, but the task is intensively quantitative. Hence the default method was created as an expedient alternative. Its strength is its simplicity. Its weaknesses are many—but the most glaring deficiency is that the results are inconsistent with the results of cash flow simulation in a Monte Carlo framework. For similar reasons, the eclectic method was created for the short-term market, to avoid the analytical complexity of analyzing asset-backed commercial paper (ABCP) conduits, which analytically are not dissimilar to collateralized debt or monoline insurance companies. Needless to say, the results of the eclectic method are also inconsistent with the results of cash flow simulation in a Monte Carlo framework.

Why would a rational market tolerate such inconsistency? Has the existence of multiple norms obscured the unity of the structured finance problem? Or do the sophisticated market players benefit from externalities that are simply too good to let go? These possibilities are not necessarily mutually exclusive. What is significant is that arbitrage behavior by market participants can motivate better convergence of norms. In the evolution of the structured market there have been many examples. As the games have become more sophisticated, so have the analytical responses of rating agencies. The authors believe that, presented with a capital-efficient, unified analytical approach, the market will find, in the intensity of competition and the amount of dollars at stake, the motivation to operate at higher standards of precision, making the prospect of real commodity credit risk management possible. That is the aim of our book.

We wrote parts I–III to demystify the contemporary framework and lay the foundation for the alternative approach laid out in parts IV and V.

Chapter 1 provides an introduction to the basic market conventions and institutions that influence the determination of value in structured securities. The remaining chapters of part I describe the contemporary framework of structured analysis, a hybrid of the corporate framework and a pure structured paradigm of analysis. It also systematically details and evaluates the methods of analysis used by the rating agencies in rating structured transactions based upon published literature and our experiences as former rating agency analysts. We freely acknowledge that this chapter has something to displease everyone. For seekers of a how-to book, the explanations may simply provoke more questions. We also anticipate that seasoned practitioners who come from the "if it ain't broke, don't fix it" school may be irritated by the implicit critiques of established methods. Rating analysts may feel (rightly) that our summary treatment does not do justice to all the work that goes into a real rating analysis. Finally, we expect that some readers, as consumers of ratings, will find themselves compelled to echo the late Peggy Lee in asking, "Is that all there is?"

Part II begins with a discussion of the elements we believe to be essential in a pure framework of structured analysis. What distinguishes the "pure" framework from the corporate or "hybrid" frameworks of today is the emphasis on the proper and improper uses of data rather than on dictums of value. A pure structured framework makes more rigorous analytical demands on the analyst while at the same time granting greater freedom to investigate more deeply the relationships between payment data and the payment process that are the basis of value in fixed income. In chapter 7, discussion then turns to a demonstration of the dynamic profile of risk in structured securities. Chapter 8 provides a comprehensive introduction to the mathematics of liability structures. Chapter 9 presents a theoretical introduction to the concept of average life as it applies to assets and liabilities. Chapters 10 and 11 analyze the mathematics of planned amortization classes and targeted amortization classes.

In part III we demonstrate selected numerical techniques that enable analysts to build cash flow models of sufficient granularity to achieve the degree of analytical precision permitted only in structured finance. The chapter begins on a philosophical note, with a case for synthesis over analysis (or process simulation rather than mere data fitting), then proceeds to a discussion of solutions to problems at the heart of the analysis of structured securities: common statistical distributions and techniques for sampling random deviates; eigenvalues and eigenvectors, without which loan-level modeling would not be feasible; the Markov formalism, which is highly applicable to the description of payment behavior and asset quality; nonlinear regressions to solve problems of an iterative nature (of which the structured security is itself a prime example); the Newton-Raphson nonlinear optimization method in particular; and finally correlation and the analysis of covariance matrices, supported by methods including Cholesky Decomposition and Tchebyshev Polynomials. Further illustration of select techniques is given in the appendices to chapter 4.

In part IV, we demonstrate the application of the methods presented in part III to analyzing structured transactions. Chapters 20–22 explore their application to three distinct asset types: automobile loan securitizations in chapter 20, collateralized bond obligations backed by asset-backed securities (ABS) in chapter 21, and aircraft securitizations in chapter 22. The analytical approach presented in chapter 20 builds on the rating agency method described in part I by demonstrating the technique of loan-by-loan analysis in a comprehensive cash flow model. Chapter 21 begins with a critique of the CBO method as it has been applied to ABS collateral, then moves on to a discussion of the development of a cash flow model for the CBO of ABS problem, and discusses implementing correlation analysis using the techniques of part III. Treatment of the revolving period is also touched upon. Chapter 22 is an in-depth discussion of risk and value in securitizations of aircraft collateral, a highly idiosyncratic asset type. The book concludes, in chapter 23, with a review of advanced liability structuring issues not previously covered and a discussion of whether structural optimization is really feasible or merely sleight-of-hand.

While the views and opinions expressed in this book are strictly those of the authors, we are indebted to many people who have given us the benefit of their knowledge and time. For their painstaking reviews and commentary on earlier drafts of this book, we would like to thank Perry D. Quick, Suresh Sundaresan, Ashish Garg, and Dennis F. Kraft. Thanks are also due to Kathleen and Howie for their inspired company at critical stages in the book's development, and to Kathleen Kopp for her unfailing support. We are especially grateful to Thomas J. McGuire, Doug Watson, Jerry Fons, Thomas G. Gillis, and Patrice Jordan for contributing generously to our understanding of the early structured finance market. We owe a special debt of gratitude to Lawrence J. White, for his early encouragement; to our editor, Paul Donnelly, for nurturing us with his good will and enthusiasm; and to our students at New York Univeristy. Finally, we would like to thank the Atlas pub in West Brompton for providing the atmosphere and "requisite liquidity" that allowed us to complete the first draft outline.

Contents

Part I

The Contemporary Framework

1

Market Basics

Macrostructures: The Frameworks of Law and Accountancy

From a handful of early mortgage deals in the 1970s, structured securities have evolved into a mainstream financing form, a permanent feature of U.S. public and private markets,[1] a significant source of alternative finance and investment for Europe, and, potentially, an important source of capital to Latin America and Asia. Yet despite their phenomenal growth record, it would be wrong to infer that structured securities are well suited to all markets. As engineered structures, they perform best in controlled environments.[2]

In addition to a framework of microcontrols to keep performance within an expected range (otherwise known as the transaction documents), structured deals rely on a framework of macro-level controls to mitigate the impact of the unexpected. In mature financial markets, stringent accounting rules and deep traditions of contracts, property, and judicial process are in place to create transparency of asset value, compel transaction parties to abide by their agreements, and enforce creditor claims when deals go awry. By contrast, the legal infrastructure of emerging markets is often incomplete: it has loopholes, or is long on rules but short on process, or lacks enforcement power. Thus, debt securities from emerging markets often carry large, sometimes incalculable downside risks. This tendency is more pronounced in structured securities, which rely on the possibility of precise risk measurement. And it is exacerbated by the multiplicity of "moving parts," which can actually increase the number of ways a deal can go wrong.[3] The benefits of capital preservation through careful structuring tend to elude those markets where capital efficiency is most needed.

Before the structuring or repackaging of debt securities can begin, professional legal, tax, and accounting input from securitization specialists is needed. Generally the transaction model is reviewed by lawyers, accountants, and tax specialists to ensure that the transaction is both legal and consistent with the transferor's financial goals. Accountants ensure that the financial assets have been correctly identified and accounted for. Securitization lawyers draft documents stating the rights and responsibilities of transaction parties. Cross-border transactions are often executed by multijurisdictional teams to ensure harmony with all applicable laws and regulations. In transactions from emerging markets, the advice of experienced local professionals with securitization expertise can be invaluable in preventing the transaction from running afoul of local policy, law, or regulation.

A transaction becomes a structured security only after a law firm of good standing and repute offers an opinion (or opinions) to that effect. Otherwise the transaction is not a *structured* financing but rather an *asset-based* financing, and no amount of structuring can make its propensity to default different from that of the transferor. The key legal document is the *true sale opinion*[4]: a reasoned argument as to why the mechanism of asset transfer is a sale, not a loan, and why the assets would *not* be part of a future bankruptcy filing of the transferor, if such bankruptcy were to occur.[5] A companion memo is the *non-consolidation opinion*, a reasoned opinion as to why a bankruptcy court would not order a consolidation of the transferee's assets with the estate of the transferor in bankruptcy in line with the doctrine of substantive consolidation. Legal review for the risk of preference or fraudulent conveyance may also be appropriate to defend the structure against other possible challenges from creditors of the transferor.

In addition to obtaining opinions, one must also observe certain legal procedures.[6] First, and foremost, control of the designated assets must be placed beyond the transferor's reach. In Anglo-Saxon countries, this is conventionally done by appointing a trustee to safeguard the assets belonging to the transferee and its investors. In civil code countries that expressly permit securitization, the procedure for asset separation is usually spelled out in a securitization law or its implementing guidelines. Second, the transferee, typically a special purpose entity (or SPE), must be shielded from risks of voluntary or involuntary bankruptcy through specific prohibitions in the incorporation and subscription documents, and from the likelihood of substantive consolidation. The latter is accomplished by creating a separateness between the transferee and the transferor that is not only operational but also physical, legal, managerial, and directorial.[7] Third, the assets must be *perfected*, or protected against the claims of creditors of the transferor. The mechanics of perfection vary by the type of asset backing the receivable and by the laws of the jurisdiction where the assets are held.

Large domestic and international boards of accountancy have also begun to assert their authority over the treatment off-balance-sheet financing generally. They have established explicit criteria for isolating assets (asset derecognition) and consolidating or giving off-balance-sheet treatment to the transferee, as well as publishing rules for reporting of transfers of assets, extinguishment of liabilities, recognition of residual income, and other securitization-related events previously unrecognized from an accounting perspective. In the United States, the Financial Accounting Standards Board (FASB), an independent body whose statements the Securities and Exchange Commission (SEC) recognizes as authoritative, has been primarily responsible for bringing securitization into the mainstream of U.S. generally accepted accounting principles (GAAP). The U.S. framework today is not entirely convergent with those of the International Accounting Standards Board, the U.K. Accounting Standards Board, the Canadian Institute of Chartered Accountants, or Japan's Business Accounting Deliberations Council, which have developed securitization accounting guidelines from within their distinct accounting own traditions.[8]

The foregoing survey of nonfinancial structural elements of structured finance glosses over many details; ignores the philosophical controversies, which are beyond the scope of this book; and leaves out the institutional discussion of regulatory policies on risk and capital. Capital reserving, properly speaking, is a complex problem of portfolio risk management whose solution has more to do with precision in measurement and modeling—the main topic of this book—than with accounting formalities or regulatory fiat.

The Anatomy of a Structured Security

Structured securities are said to have many "moving parts." Unlike corporate credits, where the company supplies all support functions and most if not all credit elements to the transaction, many operational and administrative functions are subcontracted to third parties, and the credit package is assembled from a variety of sources, internal and external. One would expect a high degree of individuation in transaction format with so many different pieces, but form follows function. There are fewer than two dozen structural variations in total, and all transaction structures conform in large degree to one of two types: a long-term and a short-term transaction model.

The Long-Term Transaction Model

The long-term transaction model applies to asset-backed, mortgage-backed, and collateralized debt issues with a maturity, or tenor, of one year or more.

In the long-term deal model, the ultimate borrower is referred to as the *originator/seller/servicer*, so called because the lending institution that generates the collateral is usually also the asset transferor and the operating platform that provides critical collections, documentary, and reporting functions. In most asset-backed and mortgage-backed transactions, that role goes to a single seller with special expertise in lending or leasing to a particular sector; in most collateralized debt transactions, the seller is a bank.[9]

The *issuer*, or transferee, is an intermediate borrower that purchases the collateral with proceeds from a (nearly) simultaneous sale of securities. Thereafter, all cash collections from the receivables are collected by the *servicer* (usually the same entity as the seller) and passed through to trust accounts in the name of the SPE held for the further benefit of *investors*. The issuer is almost always established as a bankruptcy-remote SPE with a narrowly defined business purpose to minimize the likelihood of an insolvency event that could land the SPE in bankruptcy court and cause cash flow or asset diversion.

The liability structure of the SPE has many possible variations. For simplicity's sake, Figure 1.1 features a transaction with two classes: *senior notes* and *junior certificates*. The issued amounts of notes and certificates are determined

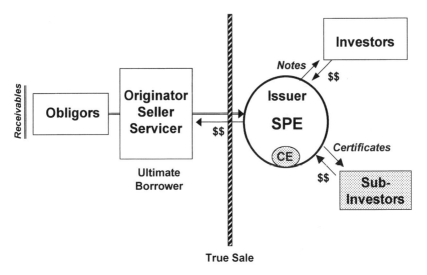

Figure 1.1. The Exchange of Value in a Term Securitization at Closing

via rating-agency analysis of the value of the collateral after losses and the sufficiency of the security package. There are many ways to enhance the security
package, depending on the cost and benefit analysis of different types of credit
enhancement (CE). In Figure 1.1 we include two potential sources:

• An unspecified type of CE in the collateral pool, which could be excess
  spread, a reserve fund, an insurance policy, and so on, or some combination thereof; and
• The *certificates*, purchased by the *sub-investors* whose claims on the SPE
  are subordinated to those of the noteholders, and which therefore represent CE for the latter in the form of subordination.

Note that this model is simpler than that of the *qualifying SPE* (QSPE) dictated under FASB 140, which entails a two-step process of removing the assets
from the control of the originator/seller/servicer. The assets are first purchased
by a bankruptcy-remote SPE wholly owned by the seller, which transfers them
to the second, issuing SPE. The first SPE receives true sale treatment under law;
this is not necessarily true of the issuing SPE. However, the issuer SPE is protected from bankruptcy by prohibitions in the charter of the first SPE.[10] Over
time, the note- and certificateholders receive interest and principal disburse-
ments in accordance with the instructions in the pooling and servicing agreement until the debt matures or is retired, as shown schematically in Figure 1.2.

Depending on the transaction, principal repayment may begin immediately as it mostly does in asset-backed securities (ABS) and mortgage-backed
securities (MBS). Alternatively, an initial revolving period may exist whereby
principal reimbursements to debt holders may be delayed temporarily while
principal payments made by the underlying obligors are simply reinvested in

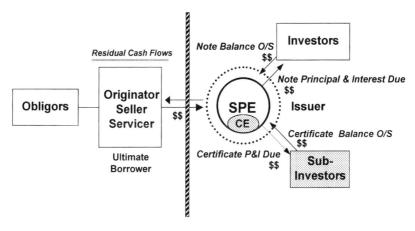

Figure 1.2. Repayment and Amortization of Debt after Closing

new eligible assets. This is the case, for instance, in most collateralized debt obligation (CDO) structures and credit card master trusts. Generally speaking, cash is distributed to investors at the same frequency it is received from obligors, in most cases monthly. (For more details on cash cycle mechanics, see chapter 3.)

The Short-Term Transaction Model

The short-term model applies to the *asset-backed commercial paper* (ABCP) market. The ABCP, a complex secured-lending form, should not be confused with *commercial paper* (CP), which is merely a form of unsecured, short-term finance to corporations. Most ABCP facilities (*conduits*) were established by commercial banks as a permanent, off-balance-sheet source of inexpensive funding for clients. A handful of industrial firms have also established their own, or "single-seller," ABCP facilities to finance their working capital needs, but these have never represented more than a fraction (0.002 basis points [or *bps*]) of the ABCP market's total authorized issuance.[11]

In this model, the *issuer*, or conduit, is a bankruptcy-remote SPE. It finances the acquisition of accounts receivable with funds raised through the sale of CP notes backed by the conduit's assets. The ultimate borrowers are the *sellers*, or clients of the lending institution, who may or may not have public ratings but are known to the ultimate lender, the *sponsoring bank*. The sponsoring bank usually performs multiple duties on behalf of the conduit, including the pivotal role of *conduit administrator*. The conduit administrator has overall responsibility for ensuring the proper functioning of the conduit throughout its daily operations, including services outsourced to the issuing and paying agent, which moves funds daily in accordance with the payment timetable and market custom. The broker-dealers' function is to distribute the notes to investors (see "CP Dealers" in Figure 1.3).

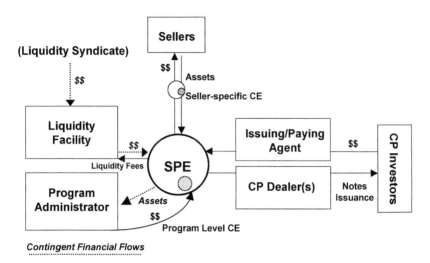

Figure 1.3. An ABCP Conduit Acquires an Asset: Operations and Value Exchange

An administrator's job is more than a list of duties in the program administration document; it also involves a large element of judgment and experience. Moreover, in every publicly rated ABCP conduit, there is always one entity, usually with deep pockets and high sensitivity to reputation risk, on the hook to indemnify investors against the impact of operational risk or other unforeseen risk of a non-credit nature. More often than not, that entity is the conduit administrator. Not surprisingly, most conduit administrators in the rated ABCP market are banks.

The sponsoring bank is usually also the *liquidity bank* or else the lead bank in a group of banks organized as a syndicate. The liquidity bank (or syndicate) provides interim funding in an amount specified under the liquidity-funding formula found in the documents. Liquidity is an important element in the short-term transaction model because unless the conduit's assets and liabilities are precisely matched, interim funds may be required in order to pay maturing CP. Unlike in the ABS market, where principal is repaid in stages and the legal final maturity date reaches far into the future, ABCP notes will come due with maturities of less than 270 days. Even when the paper is simply refinanced, or "rolled over," the pattern of rollovers can be highly variable. In addition, within a normal monthly collection cycle the issuing and paying agent is only required to effect a single cash distribution to the SPE, making it difficult to rely on collections alone for timely repayment.

Whenever collections plus sales proceeds are insufficient, the conduit can draw on its liquidity facility. The facility is typically sized to fund 100% of ABCP outstanding (or, equivalently, 102% of the facility amount including principal and interest). In conduits with full recourse to the sponsoring bank ("fully supported"),[12] the liquidity amount is unconditionally available. By

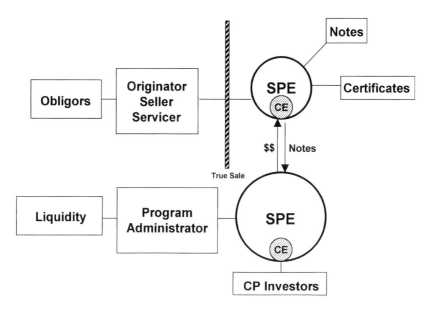

Figure 1.4. An ABCP Conduit Acquires A Structured Security

contrast, in partially supported transactions, liquidity is available only up to the amount of performing collateral; the latter is usually defined as the *borrowing base.* In loan-backed and market value programs, for instance, available liquidity is less than 100%. In such cases, the liquidity amount is sized based upon the inherent liquidity of the (usually highly rated) collateral, the expected amount of refunding, or some other statistically determined mechanism and restrictions are sometimes placed on the aggregate amount of allowable refunding. While the concept of relying on the intrinsic liquidity of the collateral has been around since the loan-backed programs of the early and mid 1990s, shortages in the liquidity market during the period 1998–1999 also sparked innovations in liquidity provision to ABCP structures.[13]

The security package for an ABCP conduit normally consists of two levels of credit enhancement: *seller-specific,*[14] evaluated and committed whenever the conduit adds new borrowers to the account, and *program-level,* committed when the conduit is established. The latter is designed to absorb risks not covered under the seller-specific facilities and small amounts of market risk that can cause yield erosion. Often, and unlike the long-term model, it is the liquidity bank that takes the security interest in the receivables instead of the ABCP investors. Such ownership arrangements do not necessarily weaken the investors' credit position, since the liquidity bank is liable for paying cash on the full value of performing collateral either way.

In Figure 1.4, as in the long-term model, the *investors* are purchasers of the senior notes. The absence of *sub-investors* in the diagram reflects the risk-averse preferences of ABCP investors. Activity between the sellers and the SPE (the vertical pair of arrows) illustrates the purchase of new accounts while the existing accounts amortize slowly. The main liability-side activity takes place along the horizontal axis between the SPE and CP investors as the CP matures or rolls over, with liquidity ready to step in to cover shortfalls.

The Composite Model

The purchase of structured securities as collateral destined for repackaging is becoming increasingly common. In 2001, over 25% of collateral purchased for ABCP conduits was repackaged.

Figure 1.4 shows how the short-term model adjusts to a conduit acquisition of a CDO tranche (cf. Figure 1.3). Note that this structure is similar to the two-step long-term model with the addition of an administrator and a liquidity bank.

Principal Markets: Their Character, Evolution, and Size

The growth of the principal structured securities markets (residential MBS [RMBS] and ABS) in the United States has been rapid since 1985, the year that the first ABS transaction came to market. From combined outstandings of $372 billion that year, level of outstandings in 2001 roughly equalled those of the U.S. corporate and municipal bond markets, at about $5.4 trillion.[15] During this same time frame, the short-term ABCP market grew to over $700 billion in outstandings, 1.0 to 1.5 times the level of outstandings of unsecured CP issued by prime corporate credits.[16]

Mortgage-Backed Markets

The earliest structured market and largest sector by issue volume, MBS began in 1968 with simple agency-insured transactions involving prime collateral. The story of the mortgage-backed bond market from inception through the mid-1980s encapsulates many great innovations in financial engineering, including the pass-through structure, cash flow stripping, and the valuation of embedded options. However, since much of that history is also particular to the conventions and the specific risks of mortgage collateral, we leave it for the experts in the field to tell.[17]

Today, private firms and special agencies created by the U.S. government to increase the supply of mortgage credit—Federal National Mortgage Association (FNMA, or Fannie Mae), Federal Home Loan Mortgage Corporation (FHLMC, or Freddie Mac), and Government National Mortgage Association (GNMA, or Ginnie Mae)—securitize primary and secondary mortgage collateral, prepayment penalties, and other strips of cash flow. The spectrum of representative collateral credit risk is wide and the geographic range is national.

The volume of combined agency and private-label residential MBS outstanding in the U.S. market for 2001 was $4.125 trillion, from a baseline of $372 billion in 1985.[18]

Commercial mortgage-backed securities, or CMBS, are securities collateralized by lease receivables of commercial real estate assets, which may include multifamily homes and retail, commercial, industrial, and entertainment properties. Commercial mortgage collateral frequently goes into CDOs and, less frequently, ABCP conduits. Once considered the exclusive purview of real estate analysis, the CMBS market has been subject to pressures for greater loan standardization and transparency, and it is viewed today as an apt subject for quantitative credit analysis.[19] Given the relationship between commercial real estate cycles and gross domestic product (GDP) evidenced in recent literature,[20] macroeconomic stress testing of the type described in the later chapters of this book has promising application to CMBS. On the other hand, in view of the potential for idiosyncratic location- or property-specific risks in the collateral, we believe that specialist asset knowledge must be carefully reflected in the assumptions of a CMBS model, if it is to be a credible representation of future performance.

The size of the CMBS market has grown from a reported $18.9 billion in 1995 to over $100 billion in third quarter of 2001.

Asset-Backed Markets

The ABS market began in 1985 with computer-lease and auto-loan securitizations. Even more than in the mortgage markets, which had large, public loss data sets, the creation of an ABS market initially raised unique legal, analytical, and marketing hurdles. Over time, solutions were developed by a handful of dedicated crusaders in the banks and by their counterparts at the rating agencies. Some fundamental elements of the solutions remain in the contemporary framework: the necessity of legal separation of the asset from the control of the borrower; the shift in focus from the credit of the whole company to the stand-alone payment strength of the asset pool, and from defaults to losses as the measure of relative collateral quality.[21] The analytical flexibility of the new ABS market made it amenable to "cloning" and thematic variation. Since the 1990s, new payment structures and asset types have proliferated and include aircraft leases, auto loans and leases, credit cards, equipment loans and leases, franchise loans, future flows of receivables, manufactured housing, medical claims, nonperforming loans, recreational vehicle loans, patent and entertainment royalties, structured settlements, synthetic ABS, tax liens, timeshares, trade receivables, and 12b-1 mutual fund fees, not to mention the proposed transactions that never saw the light of day.

The volume of ABS outstanding in the U.S. market at the end of 2001 was $1.3 trillion, from a baseline $900 million in 1985.[22]

Markets of Repackaged Collateralized Debt Obligations

In this book, all collateralized fixed income obligations are referred to as *CDOs*, regardless of whether they are backed by loans (CLOs), bonds (CBOs), or repackaged nonstandard debt instruments—for example, CBOs or RMBS, CBOs of CMBS, CBOs or ABS, CBOs of CDOs, or collateralized fund obligations (CFOs). Generally the collateral backing a CDO is more heterogeneous and more highly concentrated than in ABS or MBS. As mentioned earlier, a CDO typically has an initial three- to five-year revolving period during which principal payments made by the underlying obligors are used to purchase new eligible collateral, thus allowing bond balances to remain constant. The amortization period (sometimes referred to as an *interest-only period*) during which principal received is returned to investors follows the end of the revolving period. The design elements of CDOs borrow heavily from the credit card master trust structure, in particular the use of amortization triggers. However, these are similarities of form rather than credit substance. Credit card receivables issued by large consumer banks are intrinsically among the most well-diversified collateral in the securitization market. By contrast, CDO collateral has some of the highest concentrations. In addition, while early amortization triggers within credit card master trusts are conservatively set, the impact of such triggers in a CDO can vary from high impact to no impact at all. For more information on triggers in CDOs, please consult the "Default-Based Method" section in chapter 2.

The CDO market emerged in the late 1980s with a market value credit structure, with the prices of the underlying bonds serving as the main source of repayment. Before the end of the 1980s, the CDO market had shifted to a cash flow credit structure, which provided greater flexibility and probably higher ratings. Although market value CDOs have enjoyed a revival since the end of the 1990s and are a non-negligible percentage of today's market, cash flow structures predominate and are likely to outlast the market value structure, as they have in ABS and MBS.

Unlike ABS and MBS, for which the sellers are predictably specialty-market underwriters whose motivation is to arbitrage the rating of the firm, CDOs are issued from a variety of motivations, including restructuring of the seller's balance sheet (balance-sheet CDOs), capturing the arbitrage between the collateral net yield spread and the coupon using a leveraged investment vehicle (arbitrage CDOs), or financing an actively traded portfolio of exposures (market value CDOs). The authors consider the market value CDO to be closer to a hedge fund than a ratable credit product, not only in motivation but also in substance, because of the wide discretionary berth given to the asset manager. Another creative application of CDO method is that of the "origination" or "primary market" CDO in Japan (1998)[23] and Korea (2000), designed to allow groups of corporations to raise funds simultaneously so as to control the release of supply and establish a price floor in a buyer's market.[24]

Applied to a CDO, the term *synthetic* refers to the *form of risk transfer* rather than the *motivation*. With synthetics, the credit risk is transferred via a credit default swap without an actual sale of assets. A *credit default swap* is essentially an insurance policy provided to a party seeking to lay off credit risk, with the swap fee acting as the insurance premium. Synthetic transactions tend to be favored over cash transactions in markets (e.g., Europe) where the legal or tax consequences of asset sales in certain jurisdictions penalize the cash format.

The volume of total U.S. CDO outstanding at third quarter 2001 was estimated at $160 billion.[25]

Asset-Backed Commercial Paper

As described previously, ABCP is highly rated short-term paper issued by an ABCP conduit and backed by pools of heterogeneous collateral. The composition varies widely by program, in accordance with the funding strategy of the sponsoring bank and the current mood of the markets. Substantial changes have taken place in collateral composition between the mid-1990s, when approximately 50% of the collateral consisted of trade receivables, and today, with about 30% of collateral consisting of repackaged assets.

The distinctive ABCP risk-sharing arrangements described in the last section evolved from the sponsoring banks' initial ability to supply credit under the guise of "liquidity provision" without incurring regulatory capital charges. Banks also selectively absorb other non-credit-related cash flow shortfalls associated with assets in their conduits (e.g., dilution) that would be specifically measured and reserved against in a term structure. Since the mid-1990s, the imposition of regulatory capital controls on the banking system has driven program sponsors to be more selective and efficient in allocating liquidity. Paralleling the regulatory changes has been the decline of fully sponsored ABCP programs, which by early 1994 represented less than 30% of the market by program and less than 17% of CP outstanding. These proportions have remained fairly stable into the present.[26]

The volume of ABCP outstanding has grown from less than $500 million when the market began, in 1985,[27] to over $725 billion as of the third quarter of 2001. ABCP currently represents about 50% of the total secured and unsecured CP market.

Credit Structures: Cash Flow versus Market Value

Whereas the authors believe that too much credit significance has been ascribed to the institutional features of the different structured market segments, not enough critical attention has been paid to the differences between market value and cash flow credit structures.

The original cash flow structure was the pass-through security introduced in the mid-1970s. It is the quintessential structured financing and the subject of this book. Relying on interest and principal payments from the collateral as the main source of debt repayment, it is immune from the risk of asset price volatility, at least for the buy-and-hold investor. The analytical focus of cash flow structures is the determination of whether cash flows generated by the collateral are *ultimately* sufficient to repay liabilities according to the payment promise. By contrast, market value structures rely primarily on the market value of the collateral as the source of repayment. Conceived as a way of enhancing the value of industrial credits through additional collateral and structural protections to mitigate loss severity, the modern market value structure actually followed the invention of cash flow structure. In the modern context, the first market value structures were the mortgage-backed bonds of the early 1980s.[28]

Because portfolio liquidation value is the primary source of repayment, the analysis of credit quality in market value structures is based on the excess of asset over liability value at specified points in time in addition to the rigor of mark-to-market and liquidation covenants to cushion the impact of adverse price movements. As a result, a market value structure's credit strength is based on its ability to fulfill a *local* or periodic solvency condition at those points. Conversely, in the case of cash flow structures the requirement is merely for the cash flow value of the assets to equal or exceed the demands made by the liabilities by the legal final maturity. Thus, the creditworthiness of a cash flow structure is predicated on its ability to fulfill the sole *global* solvency condition imposed on it. In this context, logic dictates that there is greater capital efficiency associated with cash flow than with market value structures, since it is obviously easier to meet a single global condition than a set of local conditions.

Market value structures have never represented more than a fraction of total issuance in any sector. That trend has been true even in the surviving CDO and ABCP sectors. Moreover, in the brief history of the structured securities market, cash flow structures have shown a greater proclivity for "natural selection" than market value structures, perhaps due to their relative immunity to price risk and their greater capital efficiency. In fact, many ideas pioneered in cash flow structures, like true sale and asset-liability matching, have been copied into market value structures to raise their overall capital efficiency. Reverse experimentation with form has occurred to a lesser extent, with revolving cash flow credit structures with covenants aimed at replacing defaulted collateral (CDOs) as an example. In spite of some blurring in formal features, the line of demarcation between the two credit structures is drawn at discretion over the balance sheet.[29] The credit significance of reintroducing discretion in market value structures is, of course, not only increased price risk but also, in the extreme case, the dismantling of all the risk controls that make structured securities different from corporate credits.

Arbiters of Value: The Rating Agencies

Since the beginning of the structured finance market in the early 1980s, the rating agencies have been the sole arbiters of credit quality in structured securities. The uniqueness of their role in the structured finance market is due to a combination of historical, political, and economic factors. First and foremost, the agencies enjoy a unique Janus-like status within the capital markets in structured finance, as investment advisor to the "buy" side and structuring advisor to the "sell" side.

Second, rating agencies derive considerable power from assuming what an SEC commissioner has labeled their "quasi-public responsibilities" as Nationally Recognized Statistical Rating Organizations.[30] Economist Lawrence White describes these responsibilities as "help[ing] lenders pierce the fog of asymmetric information that surrounds lending relationships[31] and "delegat[ing] safety decisions about bonds to the rating firms."[32] Specifically, a 1975 amendment to the Securities and Exchange Act of 1934 (the Net Capital Rule) makes Moody's and Standard & Poor's (S&P) ratings the basis of broker-dealer calculations of their net capital positions, and a 1975 amendment to the Investment Company Act of 1940 limits money market funds (which hold over $2 trillion of U.S. investor assets) to investing in only high-quality short-term instruments, with Moody's and S&P ratings providing the minimum quality investment standards. More recently, U.S. banking regulatory agencies have also set capital requirements based on ratings, and the Basel Committee has proposed a similar ratings-based framework of regulation, although the details are still under discussion.

The third factor in rating-agency embeddedness in the structured market is their pivotal historical role. The rating agencies established credit standards for a market that had no prior norms—in contrast to the more usual role of the rating agency as credit "referee," and not rule maker, for traditional corporate credits. According to structured finance veteran Tom Gillis, Standard & Poor's played an active role in helping to establish the structured finance market:

> It was a completely different market from today—more nurturing. You had to gain consensus among the very few players. Since we were one of those players, we believe we played an essential and an important role. Everyone who was involved realized he was in an early market. To make the leap, you needed all of the key players to get involved. We needed to be on board with the concept that you could segregate the assets as cleanly as required to make the rating analysis work, and we got on board with the concept.[33]

Douglas Watson, the first structured finance group head at Moody's Investors Service, viewed Moody's contributions to the development of the structured market as very much in keeping with traditional roles of the rating agency, by adding to market understanding and transparency.

> I don't think Moody's role was one of "sponsorship," unless you consider having two ratings instead of just one as important to market development. In that sense, it may be seen as a sponsorship role. Lew Ranieri's role was formative. He felt strongly (as did Moody's) that the structured finance market would grow, and that we ought to have a published approach to the market. We published an approach in 1984, which Tom McGuire and I took around to the bankers. [McGuire was head of Corporate Ratings at the time, and Executive Vice President of Moody's when he retired in 1996.] It was well received, but Lew Ranieri was the most enthusiastic. He saw dual ratings as a way of deepening the market.[34]

To a great extent, the rating agencies still exercise a profound influence on the perception of credit quality in this market. While the players are far more sophisticated than in 1983, they still rely heavily on ratings for a "leg up" on the analysis. Ratings are also a critical element in the successful marketing of structured securities, as is evident from the decline in absolute terms of the unrated, private market while public transactions require not one, but two (and sometimes three) ratings. This is not true of the corporate bond market, where the supply of corporate credit skills is also more widely disseminated.

And it is not enough to obtain multiple ratings; the marketplace also pressures the agencies to strive for convergence. Consensus among the rating agencies brings a wider audience of investors to the table, while the failure of ratings to converge, known as *split ratings*, augurs poorly for deal placement and pricing because mixed signals can shrink the universe of potential investors.

Market dependence on ratings also has an economic dimension. It costs the market less to outsource as much of the structuring work to the rating agency as possible, so long as minimum standards of quality and independence are maintained. Moreover, outsourcing the analysis creates economies in time and training, for regulators no less than for bankers or investors. This is particularly true because, in any event, the rating agencies have the final say.

2

To Rate A Tabula Rasa

As prelude to the pure analysis of structured securities in part II, chapter 2 traces the origins of the contemporary credit-analytic framework for structured securities through its evolutionary stages as a special type of corporate rating to a portfolio analysis, and identifies the vestiges of corporate rating concepts still at work.[1]

As a matter of historical interest, both Moody's and Standard & Poor's declined to rate the first mortgage-backed security with which they were approached. Moody's objected that the underwriter's concept had not crystallized into a term sheet and was not concrete enough to be ratable.[2] (The fine line between *offering an opinion* on a structure and *creating* the structure is a distinction to which Moody's continues to adhere.) Standard & Poor's objected to the excessive concentrations of earthquake risk in the collateral particular to that first transaction.[3] Nevertheless, senior management in both agencies believed from the outset that structured finance was amenable to rating analysis, and they approached the task with a scientific spirit: *Apply what is known. Observe the results. Refine the method.* What the rating agencies knew was the meaning of credit quality. Their raison d'être was a standardization of the assessment of credit quality through systematic treatment of the fundamental elements in the analysis: the obligor, the term sheet, the supporting data, the analytical processes, the measure of performance, and the mapping of the measure to the rating.

How would these elements apply to the structured case? To a great extent, the initial answers appear to have been an exercise in finding the correspondence between the elements of the company analysis and their analogues in the structured world. Later, the rating agencies refined and extended their developing frameworks for structured securities as their experience and the supporting data deepened.

Obligor

In structured finance, the analogue of the obligor is the SPE. An SPE is a company only in the shallowest, formal sense of having a legal company registration and a balance sheet. It lacks the internal capacity to perform the duties essential to carry out its business mission and so must outsource all critical operations. As an issuer of amortizing, non-recourse debt, the SPE also lacks financial resources beyond its original endowment. Hence there are two ways to think about the obligor of a structured security. One is as a "disembodied company," with collateral and an operating platform made up of third parties, and with an investment profile that is otherwise like that of a company.[4] This is closer to the Standard & Poor's conception. The other is as a portfolio embedded in a documentary set of controls. As early as 1984, Moody's began to rate structured securities by analyzing the impact of pool-wide losses in a Monte Carlo framework.[5] This is a tacit if not express conceptualization of a structured security as a portfolio with controls. However, in practice, Moody's treatment of structured securities historically has been that of a hybrid, with both portfolio and company aspects. The company aspect, in particular, gives analysts a vocabulary with which to probe credit issues such as what happens when the structure falls apart, or when the seller goes bankrupt, or in the event of other risks that the control structure may not have addressed or anticipated.

From the ratings business perspective, both conceptions of the obligor conferred certain advantages. Finding the formalism to fit the problem gave Moody's an early edge in creating a more standardized product with the flexibility to fit many new applications. On the other hand, the disembodied company concept allowed Standard & Poor's to go on using a more experiential, case-by-case approach and even to set criteria. And, by asserting the relevancy of their corporate ratings experience to structured finance, both agencies were able to extend their authority to encompass the new market by their knowledge of corporate bond defaults, and to apply the existing corporate ratings machinery to the new market, with some modifications.

One such modification was to focus only on the range of the credit scale believed relevant to structured securities. The AAA range initially was considered out-of-bounds by the rating agencies, which were troubled by the seeming incomparability in the credit strength of an issue backed by a stand-alone portfolio of high credit quality which, nevertheless, lacked an institutional backstop, and that of an AAA-rated company. Clearly, an SPE did not have powers of taxation as the U.S. Treasury does, nor could it borrow funds, raise equity, or seek interim liquidity. Hence, for many years, the agencies maintained a AA ceiling on structured debt.[6] With time and experience, this concern abated, and the AA ceiling eventually disappeared in most asset types and structures, as did the market spread premium over comparably rated corporates. Similarly, there was initially little range below AAA because of the lack of demand. Although some investors understood risky *corporate* debt, the market as a whole had no experience with risky *structured* debt. The wholesale application of corporate ratings to structured debt gave yield-hungry investors a tool for taking calculated risks in an unfamiliar sector. By the middle of the 1990s, the range of obligor credit quality in structured transactions had been significantly extended, from AAA to B.

It is relevant to comment here that, analytically, the disembodied company concept has one very serious flaw. Real companies are going concerns in their business sectors. On the other hand, the sole business purpose of a structured "company" is to put itself out of business, literally, by following the payment rules and liquidating itself. This seemingly irreverent description turns out to be critically important to the assessment of structured credit quality in the secondary market. This distinction is at the essence of structured analysis, yet its significance becomes obvious only when the disembodied company assumption is dispensed with and the portfolio approach is fully adopted. We discuss the impact of seasoning and amortization on the credit profile of structured securities in much greater depth in chapter 6, "Towards A Science of Ratings."

The Term Sheet

Whether for structured security or industrial credit, a credit analysis entails an assessment of payment certainty in light of the payment promise. But the wording of the payment promise in a structured security merits close attention. The return on investment may not be primarily a function of creditworthiness, as is true for interest-only (IO) strips.[7] In that case, the rating will be a poor guide to the distribution of returns. Also, in structured securities, payment certainty depends on the quality of the collateral and the structure. All the elements of the analysis (the eligible collateral, covenants, third parties and their duties, and the payment promise) are contained in the term sheet. Customarily, the analyses of collateral and structural risks are performed separately because of the moving-parts problem, and a judgment about overall transaction quality is formed only after the risk elements have been "sized" in relation to the amount of protection.

Figures 2.1 and 2.2 illustrate the credit and non-credit contexts of risk in a cross-border securitization. Figure 2.1 is a graphic representation of the un-

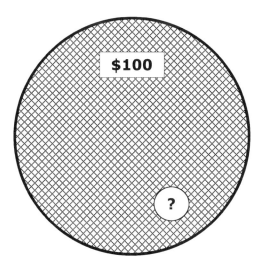

Figure 2.1. The Uncertain Value of a Nominal $100 Collateral Pool

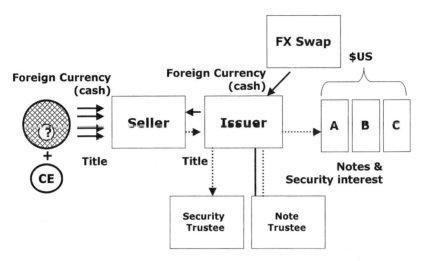

Figure 2.2. The Collateral Pool Repackaged in a Cross-Border Transaction

certainty, ex ante, of the loss amount in a fresh collateral pool. Figure 2.2 places the collateral pool in the context of the other risks in the transaction structure. The authors have depicted a typical cross-border securitization because of the variety of risks to which the deal may be exposed over its lifetime.

In Figure 2.1, a nominal $100 of receivables denominated in a foreign currency is sold to Xxxx-3. The focal analysis of collateral quality is that of the "expected loss," an evaluation of the fair value of the collateral, about which we say more below. Rating methods of expected loss analysis are described in detail, in steps 1–2 of chapter 3. The evaluation of the non-collateral risks is addressed in steps 2–4. To identify and assess all potential sources of risk that could impair security performance, it can be quite helpful to diagram the cash flows, as in Figure 2.2. The risks are often further segregated between credit and non-credit sources (see Figures 2.3 and 2.4) since market risk is typically quite different from credit risk and deserves separate treatment.

The identification of non-collateral-specific risks is conducted as a prelude to analyzing the protection given in the structure. The structural design will have some types of risk transferred to third-party specialist institutions that guarantee a range of performance for the right level of compensation. (Knowing the right level of compensation is the defining characteristic of the specialist.) Foreign exchange, price, interest, basis, and other commodity-type market risks are typically borne by banks, insurance or reinsurance companies, or derivative funds.[8] Those risks that cannot be transferred to third parties must be absorbed by the SPE, in addition to the expected effect of non-performing collateral. In mature markets, the most common source of unexpected loss is macroeconomic shock, whereas (as mentioned in the Introduction) the biggest source of uncertainty in emerging market securitizations may well be the changing landscape of legal, accounting, and tax policies. Es-

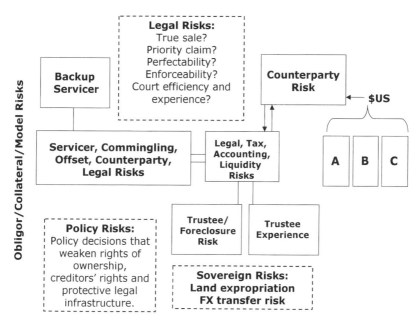

Figure 2.3. Sources of Credit Risk

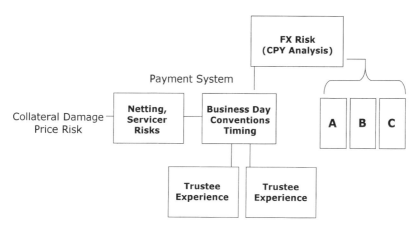

Figure 2.4. Non-Credit Causes of Cash Flow Disruption

timating the attrition in portfolio value due to environmental factors is perhaps the most complex aspect of the structured analysis.

Data and Measures

The early structured market could not have conceived (let alone analyzed) the complexity of today's security structures. The first transactions were simple

pass-through structures that relied, to a great extent, on third-party risk transfer mechanisms for support. Agency guarantees mainly backed MBS, while
bank letters of credit were widely used to support ABS structures; it is therefore not surprising that many of the first structured analysts inside the rating
agencies were research analysts pulled from their respective banking groups.
Because many or most of the early third-party guarantors were issuers of rated
debt, the data used to analyze such structured securities were mainly the rating of the guarantor and the analysis of coverage under the guarantee.

Risk-Sharing Concepts: Joint-and-Several or Weak-Link?

Initially, Moody's and Standard & Poor's embraced unlike methods of evaluating risk-sharing arrangements in these transactions. Moody's analysis was of
a *joint-and-several* nature, or the risk of falling between the cracks. In numerical terms, party A guarantees collateral pool B for transaction C.

For instance, assume the one-year default probability of A $[P_A]$ and
B $[P_B]$ is 0.58 bps and 17 bps (or Aa1 and Baa2), respectively. Moody's has articulated its joint-and-several approach to determining the default probability
of C as the following:

$$P(A \cap B) = P_A \cdot P_B + \rho_{AB} \sqrt{(1 - P_A) \cdot P_A} \cdot \sqrt{(1 - P_B) \cdot P_B} \qquad (2.1)$$

Given a (high) 70% correlation between A and B, the one-year, joint-and-
several default probability would be 11.28 bps.[9] By contrast, Standard &
Poor's initially adopted a weak-link approach. *Weak-link* refers to the assumption that overall credit quality is no stronger than the credit quality of the
weakest element. Under this approach, the default probability under the guarantee structure would be equivalent to B's default risk, or 17 bps.

By the mid-1990s, all players in the market, including Standard & Poor's,
had come to embrace the joint-and-several approach as being more correct on
technical grounds and, perhaps equally important, less punitive in capital
terms.

Stand-Alone Analysis

To analyze the creditworthiness of securities solely on the basis of supporting
assets and the structure (*stand-alone* structures), the rating agencies faced the
twin challenges of what types of data to use, and how to use them.

Concerning data, the reference measure of credit performance in the corporate framework was *default frequency*, defined as failure to pay timely interest or principal. The direct association between default and yield erosion as
well as its effectiveness as a warning sign of future obligor insolvency and further cash flow impairment under court-directed liquidation made it a useful

measure. However, since investors in structured securities had super-creditor-like claims over the assets, default was felt to be perhaps less useful as a measure of performance because it did not reflect the effect of loss severity and the impact of recoveries. Use of a default-based measure would cause credits with high frequency but low severity to be more punitively treated than credits with low frequency but high severity; both rating agencies considered the better metric to be the *expected loss* on the pool, which could be projected from the seller's net loss experience or calculated by multiplying the expected default frequency (EDF) given historical performance by the historical loss-given-default (LGD) statistics.

The Benchmark Pool

As with risk-sharing concepts, so with risk philosophies on stand-alone credits. Moody's and Standard & Poor's initially adopted somewhat opposed approaches. The primacy of cash flows through a pass-through structure was not lost on the early Moody's team (discussed in the "Obligor" section). From very early on, they chose to simulate cash flows in a Monte Carlo framework and analyze the variability of portfolio outcomes. At the other end of the risk-philosophical spectrum was Standard & Poor's focus on collateral ownership and liquidation analysis. Theory aside, however, secondary prices and recovery data were often scarce in the early ABS market, and in certain specialty MBS markets. To fill the vacuum, the *benchmark pool* was created as an expedient rating tool that did not require the volume of data that a mature rating approach would need. In point of fact, both rating agencies used benchmark pools to rate new markets, particularly in MBS.

A *benchmark pool analysis* is a variety of liquidation analysis employing a crude microeconomic model of the obligors in a collateral pool to simulate the financial impact of an economic downturn or depression. It is used to measure the increment of capital required to cushion the pool against economic shock, commensurate with the target rating level. To create a benchmark pool, certain economic variables or "factors" are identified as determinative in obligor credit quality, for example, the proportion of outstanding debt to the value of the asset (the *loan-to-value* or LTV ratio), the degree of borrower indebtedness, borrower income, and so on, and thresholds for each factor that are believed to assure payment reliability are set (for example, LTV < 50%).[10] Figure 2.5 presents the steps to rating a transaction using a benchmark pool. A simplified (hypothetical) factor analysis is shown in the following paragraphs.

Assume that a market for X-receivables exists, and that we agree that the break-even, single-A stress scenario gives rise to a 5% expected loss. If 3x coverage is necessary for a single-A rating, the total amount of required baseline credit enhancement is therefore 15%. Assume, further, that the benchmark pool for X typically has LTVs of 60%, an obligor debt-to-equity ratio of 40%, and an average property age of three years. Furthermore, we set the factor re-

Step 1	Disaggregate the key fundamental factors of the real portfolio to be rated.
Step 2	Compare the fundamental factors statistically to the benchmark pool, either on an average aggregate or loan-by-loan basis.
Step 3	Determine the need for additional cushion, based on the factor analysis.
Step 4	Set the rating level, based on the final structure and level of cushion.

Figure 2.5. Steps in Constructing a Benchmark Pool

Table 2.1
Factor Analysis for a Benchmark Pool (Hypothetical)

Loan-to-Value (%)	Adjustment (%)	Debt-to-Equity (%)	Adjustment (%)	Age (years)	Collateral Adjustment (%)
91–110	+2.0	71–90	+2.5	≥40	+1.0
76–90	+1.5	55–70	+1.5	26–39	+0.5
61–75	+1.0	41–54	+0.5	10–25	+0.0
≤60	+0.0	≤40	+0.0	≤10	−0.3

lationships in Table 2.1 for the aggregate pool.[11] A sample transaction with an average LTV of 72%, an average debt-to-equity ratio of 40%, and a property age of seven years would undergo the following factor adjustments:

> 15.0% baseline credit enhancement
> 1.0% addition for LTV of 61–75%
> 0.0% addition for debt-equity ratio of 40%
> 0.5% addition for average age of seven years
> 16.5% total required credit enhancement

Note the strong similarities between rating structured securities by a benchmark pool and rating corporate bonds. Both are essentially a form of peer comparison of factor variables on a scale of ordinal ranking but not on a ratio scale. (In other words, the intervals do not have one-to-one correspondence with the risk being measured.) Also, as is true in many cases with industrial credits, benchmark pools are frequently capped at some rating level below AAA. Capping reflects a presumption that stand-alone securitizations have an intrinsic default risk that structuring alone cannot overcome—a view carried over from the corporate approach.

Loss Curve–Based Approaches

The benchmark pool approach left a great deal of room for improvement. First, the benchmarks lacked analytical rigor. The microeconomic model was usually constructed ad hoc from internal sources and the assumptions usually remained empirically untested. It was more efficient for the agencies to adopt a security-specific approach given sufficient data to permit generalization about future performance. Second, the method was overly conservative from a capital-utilization standpoint: it demanded capital to cushion against exposures worse than the benchmark but did not provide offsetting relief for loans that were better than the benchmark. The justification for the conservatism relates to the first point, namely, the uncertain explanatory power of the model. By way of contrast, the "average loan" approach of the loss curve method offered the possibility of greater analytical precision and more capital efficiency.

For the mainstream residential MBS market, Standard & Poor's and Moody's tapped a rich vein of public mortgage data going back to the Depression era. From these data, they eventually developed norms of obligor payment behavior and ranges of recovery value on foreclosed residential real estate properties, and these norms facilitated more precise risk modeling.[12] An initial hurdle of the ABS market was that it did not have an analogous source of public data, but the agencies compiled performance profiles using private, issuer-level default and recovery data collected in connection with rating mandates. Gradually, they built up their own data warehouses from scratch to support the development of asset-specific norms. The new norms were industry and issuer loss curves—an advance over the hypothetical benchmark pool and a paradigm shift that added flexibility to the analysis of credit quality in individual transactions.

An *industry loss curve* is a generic profile of the cumulative principal losses likely incurred on a pool of loans backed by a particular type of asset. It tries to estimate how much principal the pool is likely to lose in total (the last point on the curve in Figure 2.6) and how much during each payment period. Like a benchmark pool, an industry loss curve is an idealization; however, the item of comparison (losses) has a direct, proportional bearing on performance. Industry loss curves can be further refined to reflect underwriting and collection policies of individual lenders on pool performance (issuer loss curves).

The shape of a loss curve depends on many factors, including the importance of the asset in the borrower's hierarchy of claims, borrower creditworthiness, the financial terms of the loan, the value of the collateral in the secondary market, and time-to-maturity.

A composite variable that can reflect many of these factors is the changing profile of the borrower's equity in the asset. As the ownership stake grows, the penalty of foreclosure becomes more onerous and the borrower's motivation to repay the loan increases. While not all borrowers are equally sensitive to the market value of their collateral, negative equity goes a long way toward explaining the changing pattern of aggregate loss performance. Since delinquent borrowers usually have a grace period before the lender writes off their accounts, loss recognition is delayed beyond time 0. However, once losses hit the books, the monthly percentage predictably increases steadily until it reaches a maximum, then decreases and tapers off, giving rise to the characteristic **S** shape of the cumulative loss curve of Figure 2.6.

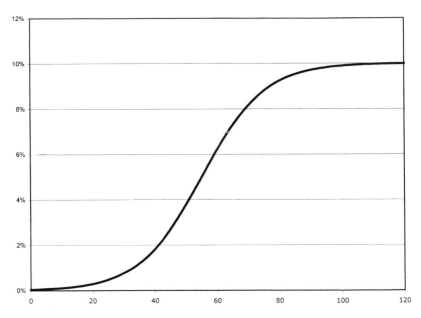

Figure 2.6. Automobile Loss Curve: Principal Losses at 10% (hypothetical)

The borrower's changing equity profile for a hypothetical ten-year secured auto loan is shown in Figure 2.7. The concave line is the principal balance outstanding of the loan from origination to the legal final maturity at the 120th month. The convex line is the time series of secondary market wholesale values of the automobile financed by the loan. While selection of the best price index to represent asset value depends very much on the asset and the conventions in the marketplace, wholesale values as reflected in official guides like that of the National Auto Dealers Association (NADA) are preferred for automobiles as the best representation of the arm's-length clearing price of repossessed collateral.

The dotted line at $t = 0$ shows the borrower initially with negative equity: the car is worth less on resale than the borrowed amount even though the retail price is higher (the difference is often the dealer's profit). The shortfall of collateral value relative to outstanding loan amount increases with the passage of time until it reaches a maximum at the 36th month. The borrower has the least to lose if he or she defaults at this point. Thereafter, the equity gap narrows until, at the 93rd month, the principal balance outstanding on the loan is equal to the value of the vehicle. From now on, the borrower has positive equity.

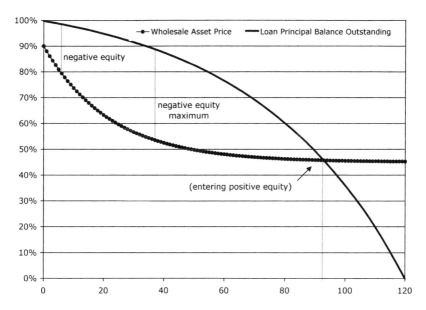

Figure 2.7. Hypothetical Curve Showing the Borrower's Equity Position

Modeling in Time and Probability Space

In the contemporary framework, loss curve analysis has become as fundamental to the analysis of credit quality in ABS and MBS (the actuarial approach) as financial statement and ratio analysis in company credit analysis. The issuer's historical loss curve is the basis for projecting the pattern of future pool losses of an originator in a particular asset type.

The simplest loss curve application is the estimation of the total loss amount (the endpoint) for new transactions. The estimate is called the *expected loss*: strictly speaking, the mean of a probability distribution. However, the rating agency expected loss is not the result of calculating $\sum x_i f(x_i)$ from the endpoints x_i of many loss curves but rather the result of a process described in greater detail in chapter 3 and vetted by the vote of a rating committee.

There is more to a loss curve than its endpoint. A loss curve evidences the physical process of repayment that is shaped by the psychology of the borrower and rights of the creditor. Process fundamentals impose limits on the shape of the curve. For example, a loss amount in t_n cannot reverse itself in t_{n+1} by more than the cumulative loss amount $\sum_0^n x_i$. There are maturity (T) constraints: for a new transaction XYZ, the endpoint on the *x*-axis is unlikely to be different from the T of recent deals, but if the loans in XYZ have a different maturity structure, it is very unlikely to be identical to that of recent deals. A loss curve also has a statistical dimension. It is impossible for losses to exceed 100% in any period. Large losses in any period $t_n - t_{n-1}$ (e.g., 30% of total principal of a long-term borrowing) are highly improbable. In sum, the points along the loss curve, while stochastic, are not haphazard; and the ensemble of points has meaning, not only the endpoint. Even with manipulation of loss data by the seller-servicer, analysts armed with knowledge about collection management and write-off policies can significantly fine-tune the periodic payment analysis by using the entire loss curve.

The Model behind the Rating

The structured rating is a measure of certainty ex ante that cash flows generated by the assets of the SPE will be sufficient to pay off its liabilities on or before the legal, final maturity. The greater the certainty, the higher the rating: that much is clear. But how is it done?

In the contemporary framework, ratings are implemented at one of approximately three levels of precision. We refer to the first level (most primitive, least granular rating implementation) as the *BOTE* (or *back-of-the-envelope*) approach: a credit snapshot of the transaction. All of the following inputs must be determined somehow independently:

A   Expected loss on the collateral
B   Weighted average coupon (WAC) of the collateral
C   Senior fees, including interest on the notes and servicing fee
D   Other reductions to spread, such as adverse prepayments
E   Average life (AL) of the notes
F   Sources of credit enhancement as defined in the term sheet

The output is a ratio, roughly $[E(B - C - D) + F]/A$. The rating is determined by the ratio, in lookup fashion from the schemata outlined above. (See Table 2.2.) This implementation is a classic "quick-and-dirty" approach. It does not reflect the effects of time, stochasticity, or asset composition.

The second level of precision embraces scenario analysis outside of an explicit view of probability. This is the Standard & Poor's approach. It relies heavily on the use of case-by-case stress assumptions to test the resistance of the transaction to losses in extreme situations. These stress scenarios are linked to various rating levels in similar fashion to the depression scenarios for the benchmark pool analysis above. For asset-specific details, interested readers should consult Standard & Poor's *Criteria* in various asset classes.

As an editorial aside, cash flow modeling is always better than a BOTE approach because it allows for the interaction of financial variables in time. However, a system of ratings that applies stresses outside a framework of probability lacks the discipline of consistency. What view of risk does the stress represent: does it occur at 1, 3, or 15 standard deviations from the expected loss? How much better is an AAA security that can sustain a 15–standard deviation event than one that can only sustain a 5–standard deviation event before defaulting? Knowledge of probability is not intuitive, it is empirical, but rating agencies do not collect volatility data. If at all, these data reside with issuers, intermediaries, clearinghouses, and economic research units. The best that an analyst can probably do is to make a reasoned assumption about the distribution of risk and run stresses using that assumption.

The third level of precision is the Moody's ideal of cash flows within a Monte Carlo simulation. Much depth is added to the analysis by examining the timing and amount of excess spread and reserve amounts on available funds. However, even within the contemporary framework, this procedure as currently implemented can still be improved upon in at least two ways:

- *Performing a loan-by-loan rather than an average-loan analysis.* Substituting a synthetic average loan for the real pool simplifies the analysis and shortens run times, but only at the expense of precision, as it rubs out some characteristic variability of the pool in the process.
- *Modeling the comprehensive liability structure (not just the senior tranche) and including the triggers.* Such features can have a decisive impact on performance in the secondary market.

Mapping the Measure to the Rating

The Meaning of the Rating

Originally ratings were simple, ordinal rankings of industrial credits. They were called *quality ratings*. By the late 1980s, rating agencies had begun to claim that the ratings corresponded to ranges of default probability, backing their claims with cohort studies of corporate bond ratings and historical bond performance. Severity was not a component of the meaning of ratings, because the recovery amount from bankruptcy proceedings was unpredictable, and the extent of yield erosion similarly difficult to estimate ex ante. But by the 1990s, Moody's thinking had begun to change. The first public indication was a footnote in the 1994 corporate bond default study otherwise dominated by default frequency analysis.[13] In 1999, Moody's "The Evolving Meaning of Moody's Ratings" justified the firm's increased emphasis on losses as opposed to defaults because of the "decline of [investor] market segmentation" and growing attention to "market efficiency" issues.[14] In 2001, the focus on losses became express with the name change of the bond default study to "Default and Recovery Rates of Corporate Bond Issuers 2000."[15]

By contrast, Standard & Poor's continues to make default frequency the basis of its corporate and structured ratings:

A traditional rating addresses the likelihood of full and timely payment of interest and principal to certificate holders. Therefore, a rating default is defined as nonpayment of interest in full and on time, and nonpayment of principal on securities by their legal final maturity date.[16]

In sum, rating agencies are reluctant to put the ratings of industrial credits and structured securities on a separate footing. Moody's solution is to make
losses the universal focus, even for corporate bonds, where the loss data are
poorer than the default data. Standard & Poor's meanwhile continues to keep
defaults as the universal measure, although technically, structured securities do
not default.

It follows that the two agencies' structured ratings have different mean-
ings. Moody's rating system is designed as security-level measure:

> In the most technical sense, a Moody's rating expresses Moody's opinion of
> the amount by which the internal rate of return (IRR) on a diversified portfo-
> lio of similarly rated securities would be reduced as a result of defaults on the
> securities, assuming that all the securities are held to maturity regardless of
> any changes in the ratings.[17]

One can obtain an estimate of the reduction of yield on a well-diversified portfolio by calculating the average yield on an individual security from many iterations of the cash flow model, usually in a Monte Carlo framework, and subtracting it from the payment promise. Any difference is a negative number—
a reduction of yield—that uniquely corresponds to a rating. For example, a
yield reduction of 0.05 basis points maps to a credit rating of Aaa. Because
credit rating scales are logarithmic, the absolute distance between the rating
cutoff points will increase going down the credit spectrum.

Standard & Poor's rating system is a measure of cushion, or safety margin,
which is much closer to a corporate rating concept: the more cushion, the safer
the credit. The S&P rating is usually determined as a multiple of the expected
loss. This is a *nonparametric* measure, meaning that it makes no assumption
about the form of the distribution from which the data are taken. There is also
a *parametric* formulation, refined by knowledge about the distribution, which
is sometimes used in ABCP conduits. It is usually based on a measure of dispersion, for example, the expected loss plus a certain number of multiples of
the standard deviation, which correspond to the rating. The rule of thumb on
coverage is stated as in Table 2.2.

Lifetime Ratings

By analogy with the corporate rating, which is designed to measure the steady-
state (or through-the-cycle) credit profile of company credit, the structured
rating is intended to be valid over the lifetime of the transaction. It is upgraded
or downgraded only when there is evidence that the profile of performance
is inconsistent with the rating. Despite recent debate on the matter, both
Moody's and Standard & Poor's structured ratings are still designed to be lifetime ratings.

Table 2.2
Ratings by Rule of Thumb

	Coverage Ratio	Corresponding Rating
	5x	AAA
	4x	AA
	3x	A
	1.5–2x	BBB
	<1.5x	Sub-IG

The Credit Scale

An S&P rating on a structured security signifies a likely range of default probabilities corresponding to the default probabilities on a portfolio of S&P corporate credits with the same rating. As we have shown, Moody's ratings on structured securities mean something quite different: a Moody's structured rating is a calibration of expected yield-reduction on the security. Thus, Moody's structured ratings are mapped not to the corporate credit scale but to a reduction-of-yield scale. An early version of this scale, based on the ten-year expected loss rates, was published in Table 5 of "Rating Cash Flow Transactions Backed by Corporate Debt 1995 Update," Appendix 4 of the working paper, "The Fourier Transform Method—Technical Document," published in January 2003 also contains a Moody's ten-year expected loss table. The scale used internally today for many consumer is based on securities of a five-year tenor.[18]

3

The Actuarial Method

The classic loss-based approach described in the first part of this chapter is typically implemented for ABS and MBS transactions but not for CDOs. It is called *actuarial* because it rests on an assumption that large, well-diversified, homogeneous, and mainly amortizing pools of receivables in the seller's portfolio give rise to stable, predictable loss distributions, and that representative loss and dispersion measures can be collected from sample data. The specifics of the actuarial approach depend on many factors: the rating agency doing the analysis; the experience, skill, and style of the analyst; and the quality and amount of data. The outcome is further subject to the socializing influence of committee members and to the committee chair, usually a managing director, whose role is both as guardian of institutional tradition and as business facilitator. Nevertheless, generalization about the framework of analysis is possible. Broadly, the steps are as shown in Figure 3.1.

Getting Started: The Information Packet

In general, the assets securitized in ABS and MBS are segregated by the time of origination. Portfolios thus organized are known as *static pools*. The exceptions are credit cards, discussed at the end of the "Actuarial Approach" section, and auto or mortgage collateral placed in ABCP conduits, discussed in "Eclectic Approach."

The analysis begins when the analyst receives a package of information provided by the bank on behalf of the seller. This information package becomes the property of the rating agency and provides additional data for the structured finance database. It typically contains a term sheet with basic information about the structure; information about the seller's underwriting and pricing policies; statistics on the entire servicer portfolio; and pool-specific asset summaries—loan level or, more often, a summary profile of key aggregate financial measures, such as the weighted average coupon, weighted average maturity, and seasoning, as well as obligor-related data like credit scores and place of origination (diversification) and collateral-related data, as appropriate. This summary is commonly referred to as a *pool cut*. The analyst also receives and reviews underwriting and collection policy information for clues about possible improvement or deterioration of this collateral vis-à-vis past transactions.

Step 1	Estimate the cumulative credit loss distribution function (loss curve) arising from obligor default in the collateral pool.
Step 2	Given the distribution derived in Step 1, determine how much credit enhancement will be required to make the performance of the senior-most security consistent with its rating.
Step 3	Identify and measure other sources of risk that could further diminish cash flow, and adjust credit enhancement accordingly.
Step 4	Check that the structure apportions and retains the enhancement determined in Step 2 (above) with a degree of certainty implied by the rating.

Figure 3.1   Steps in an Actuarial (ABS) Analysis

In this information packet, the two most important sets of data in the static loss analysis are the following:

- The pool cut that provides inputs for a cash flow model (the method of Step 2)
- Pool losses on previous vintages by the same seller (or sellers with similar underwriting criteria)

Actuarial Method, Step 1: Static Loss Analysis

As we observed previously, static pool marginal losses are nonlinear. First they accelerate, until they reach a maximum over some characteristic range, and then they decelerate until finally tapering off. If the pool is not static—if it revolves with new collateral coming in and old collateral winding down—this pattern of marginal periodic losses will lose its characteristic bell-curve shape.

Table 3.1 profiles a rapidly growing portfolio of consumer loans. Given that the underwriter's policy is to write off loans that are 120 days or more past due, column (7) represents uncollectible loans. Note the decreasing trend, from 2.28% in the first period to 1.32% after eighteen months. This is not due to improving credit quality. Rather, it is because the growth in total loans masks the losses. Expressing aggregate credit losses as an annualized percentage of current balances will understate the true level of losses in a growing portfolio; only in the later stages will the true extent of the loss "toxicity" materialize.

It is very difficult to interpret performance when the numbers are presented in the aggregate without reflecting the effects of seasoning. Simply adjusting for the ballooning denominator effect by backing out the ratio of total loans at each period (column [1]) to the number in the initial batch of loans, as in Table 3.2, is incorrect because write-offs from other periods will be counted together with the write-offs from the first period. This will cause an overstatement of the losses in the first batch and indeterminate results for every

Table 3.1
Servicing Portfolio of an Aggressive Consumer Lender

N	Total Balance Due ($) (1)	Current (%) (2)	25–30 days (%) (3)	31–60 days (%) (4)	61–90 days (%) (5)	91–120 days (%) (6)	>120 days (%) (7)
1	119,381	69.05	10.09	13.48	3.24	1.86	2.28
2	153,609	73.05	12.72	5.52	6.06	1.73	0.92
3	209,994	82.73	5.89	5.12	1.93	3.45	0.88
4	238,096	81.62	7.22	4.59	3.86	0.60	2.10
5	252,993	79.11	8.85	5.86	2.39	2.73	1.05
6	286,823	82.53	6.88	3.64	4.63	0.94	1.38
7	303,001	83.35	6.67	4.23	2.96	1.27	1.51
8	355,542	84.12	7.74	3.26	2.11	1.06	1.70
9	409,032	86.30	6.51	2.55	2.01	0.90	1.73
10	465,295	86.13	7.68	1.47	2.38	0.70	1.64
11	523,528	85.64	7.75	2.39	1.77	0.83	1.63
12	608,242	84.33	9.32	2.93	1.62	0.25	1.55
13	694,017	80.65	11.35	3.16	2.63	0.80	1.40
14	832,432	79.19	12.73	3.09	2.39	1.14	1.46
15	967,259	86.20	5.77	4.08	1.52	0.80	1.63
16	1,061,974	85.32	6.95	3.68	1.54	0.70	1.81
17	1,203,110	85.28	7.27	3.63	1.26	0.88	1.68
18	1,475,739	86.34	6.90	2.83	1.83	0.78	1.32

other batch. Segregating collateral by time of origination, or "vintage," is thus necessary to prevent the masking of performance trends and to make evident the possible changes in underwriting policy or collection effort.

The Loss Curve Method

As discussed earlier in this chapter, a loss curve is a generic cumulative loss profile for a pool or pools of a particular receivable type underwritten by a particular lender. The rationale for using loss curves as the basis for predicting future performance of new transactions is an assumption that each lender's unique underwriting guidelines and collection practices give rise to characteristic loss and recovery patterns that are somewhat stable over time.

Whenever a new transaction is evaluated, the analyst will build a new loss curve as a projection of actual historical loss curves. As stated previously, loss curves on individual transactions generally are constructed using static pool (vintage) loss data. When no prior static pool history is available for a particular lender, loss curves are constructed using the static pool history of other lenders judged to have similar underwriting and collection characteristics (peers).

Table 3.2
Misguided Attempt to Restate Write-Offs

N	Balance Due (1)	>120 Days (%) (2)	Restated (%) (3)
1	119,381	2.28	2.28
2	153,609	0.92	1.19
3	209,994	0.88	1.54
4	238,096	2.10	4.18
5	252,993	1.05	2.23
6	286,823	1.38	3.32
7	303,001	1.51	3.83
8	355,542	1.70	5.07
9	409,032	1.73	5.94
10	465,295	1.64	6.40
11	523,528	1.63	7.13
12	608,242	1.55	7.92
13	694,017	1.40	8.14
14	832,432	1.46	10.16
15	967,259	1.63	13.22
16	1,061,974	1.81	16.10
17	1,203,110	1.68	16.95
18	1,475,739	1.32	16.29

The loss curve analysis is generally performed inside a spreadsheet by arraying cumulative loss data in separate columns by vintage and in ascending temporal order by row, each row representing a single month or quarter. In this way apples are always compared to apples and the problem of averaging across time is avoided. To create a new loss curve, the analyst selects a consecutive series of vintage curves believed to be representative of how the new transaction will perform and, from this series, computes an average curve, which becomes a *base curve*. The base curve is normalized between 0 and 1. Each point on the curve is thus interpreted as the time-dependent ratio of current to ultimate losses. The normalized curve becomes the basis of the expected loss projection for the new transaction.

Table 3.3 shows the construction of a base curve from a loss curve that has been completed, using hypothetical vintage data on a pool, which we will call SMRF 2xxx-2. The SPE name follows the typical formula for naming securitizations, with an acronym followed by the year and quarter of issuance (in this case, second quarter, sometime in the twenty-first century). Not all historical loss curves will show the entire range of results as this one does; the newer the pool, the less complete the data sets. Because the loss curve procedure entails an averaging over ranges of completed loss curves, the analyst will need to "complete" more recent curves by projecting cumulative losses over the missing data. Generally this is done one of two ways, as described next.

Table 3.3
Normalizing A (hypothetical) Base Curve

Base Curve (%)	Normalized (%)
0.25	9.03
0.79	28.36
1.07	38.47
1.40	50.00
1.61	57.66
1.87	66.97
2.10	75.20
2.30	82.36
2.50	89.44
2.63	94.30
2.69	96.36
2.73	97.73
2.79	99.91
2.80	100.27
2.80	100.27
2.79	100.00

Additive Method

This method is a simple shifting algorithm whereby each new datum is simply set equal to the previous point plus the difference between the previous and the target point for the base curve. If the base curve is defined by y_i, $i = 1, 2, 3, \ldots N$, the target curve by g_i, $i = 1, 2, 3$, and the target curve data stop at $i = n$, then for the point g_i, $i = n + 1, n + 2, n + 3, \ldots \ldots N$, the rule is

$$g_i = g_{i-1} + (y_i - y_{i-1}). \tag{3.1}$$

In this case, the new cumulative expected loss estimate for the pool is

$$E(L) \equiv g_N = g_n + (y_N - y_n). \tag{3.2}$$

Multiplicative Method

This method is a ratio method whereby each new datum is simply set equal to the previous data point multiplied by the ratio of the target and previous data points for the base curve. Using the identical nomenclature, this rule is

$$g_i = g_{i-1} \frac{y_i}{y_{i-1}}. \tag{3.3}$$

In that case, the new cumulative expected loss estimate for the pool is

$$E(L) \equiv g_N = g_n \prod_{n+1}^{N} \frac{y_i}{y_{i-1}}. \tag{3.4}$$

Illustration of the Loss Curve Method

Table 3.4 illustrates three vintages from the issuer of SMRF 2xxx-2, which we can imagine from their compressed profile as perhaps quarterly results. It is impossible to know a priori whether a loss curve is complete except by inspection. Even after inspection, there is always a risk of misjudging the endpoint of the curve. Needless to say, when the loss curve is prematurely truncated, the loss estimate will turn out to be inaccurate and the loss likelihood will turn out to be higher than the rating would imply.

However, as advertised, 2xxx-2 is complete, as is evident in the tapering of the curve in the last few periods. The slight downturn in period 16 is most likely due to trailing cash flows arising from recoveries on previously defaulted receivables. By the same logic, 2xx2-1 and 2xx2-2 are still outstanding.

To project a loss curve for SMRF 2xx2-2 (a SMRF pool issued in the second quarter, two years after 2xxx-2), the only data available are the static pool data of 2xxx-2 alone or an average constructed from the two pools. Since 2xxx-2 is used to derive the tail of 2xx2-1, it would make no sense to base the construction of 2xx2-2 on 2xx2-1 alone. An argument might be made that only the 2xxx-2 curve should be used because early losses in 2xx2-1 trend higher earlier, whereas early 2xx2-2 has the lowest losses of all. However, losses

Table 3.4
Projecting (hypothetical) Loss Curves

N	2xxx-2 (%)	2xx2-1 (%)	2xx2-2 (%)	Multiplicative Method (%) y_t/y_{t-1}	Multiplicative Method (%) 2xx2-1	Additive Method (%) $y_t - (y_{t-1})$	Additive Method (%) 2xx2-1
1	0.25	0.37	0.19	0.32	0.37	0.00	0.37
2	0.79	0.90	0.67	1.00	0.90	0.54	0.90
3	1.07	1.23	—	1.36	1.23	0.28	1.23
4	1.40	1.65	—	1.30	1.65	0.32	1.65
5	1.61	1.95	—	1.15	1.95	0.21	1.95
6	1.87	2.15	—	1.16	2.15	0.26	2.15
7	2.10	2.47	—	1.12	2.47	0.23	2.47
8	2.30	2.66	—	1.10	2.66	0.20	2.66
9	2.50	2.78	—	1.09	2.78	0.20	2.78
10	2.63	—	—	1.05	2.93	0.14	2.92
11	2.69	—	—	1.02	3.00	0.06	2.98
12	2.73	—	—	1.01	3.04	0.04	3.01
13	2.79	—	—	1.02	3.11	0.06	3.08
14	2.80	—	—	1.00	3.12	0.01	3.09
15	2.80	—	—	1.00	3.12	0.00	3.09
16	2.79	—	—	1.00	3.11	−0.01	3.08

recorded in the early period do not carry as much significance as later-period results, or the overall trend. Moreover, 2xx2-2 is closer to 2xx2-1 in time and may be somewhat more representative of loss performance for 2xx2-2 than 2xxx-2. Hence an average of the two curves would not be inappropriate.

To compute the composite base curve, the first task is to complete the curve for the 2xx2-1 vintage. It is always a good idea to check the results of both the additive and the multiplicative methods to verify that they are in the same range. Large discrepancies, especially in the multiplicative case, are symptomatic of fundamental differences in the character of the two vintages and hence in the timing and amount of their respective losses. Following through, the multiplicative method produces an expected loss of 3.11% while the additive method yields 3.08%, a negligible difference.

Note that using 2xxx-2 as a base curve yields an expected loss of 2.93% to 2.95%, which is not far off the 3.1% estimate produced by the composite base curve. This is further evidence that the SMRF static data provide a reasonably convergent picture of obligor default risk—a happy situation. Sometimes the expected loss from the data set is a moving target from vintage to vintage. If this is the case, the analyst must judge based on the totality of available data on the issuer and the market whether the pools are approximately from the same distribution, or whether they represent different loss distributions. To average loss curves of fundamentally different risk profiles (the fact that they are from the same the lender notwithstanding) can be perilous to the health of the structured transaction. It can lead to the sort of loss estimation errors that the static pool analysis, as a comparison of like to like, was designed to avoid.

For spotting trends or irregularities that may not be apparent from the raw data, graphing the loss curves and "eyeballing" them can be helpful. Loss curves for this issuer are presented in Figure 3.2. Aside from the overall shape of the curve, which resembles the top half only of the characteristic S curve, the shape of the three curves is unexceptional and relatively convergent, which is what we would expect.

Reflections on the Loss Curve Method

As mentioned before, when constructing a loss curve the analyst must decide how much performance history is relevant. Old history has the advantage of completeness but may not capture current credit dynamics; recent history is more germane but requires extrapolation and entails subjective data points. Analyst judgment in constructing the base curve can influence the expected loss outcome significantly.

The analyst must also interpret the data; sometimes, reporting errors creep in. In addition, issuers have different ways of organizing and presenting data. For example, losses are sometimes reported on a cash basis, with gross losses recorded when incurred and recoveries added back as realized. Alternatively, gross losses can be restated with recoveries added back in the period they were written off. Other times, losses are reported net of estimated recoveries

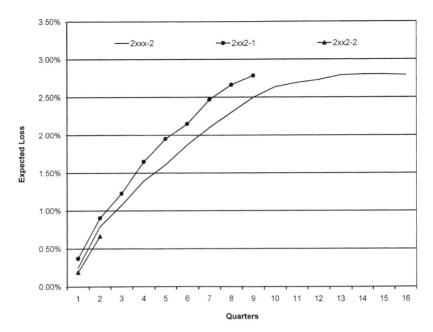

Figure 3.2. Issuer's (hypothetical) Loss Curve History

with a true-up when the real recovery amount is known. These are managed data. Managed data sometimes hide adverse information, so it is important to verify whether the data are real or estimated and, if estimated, the true-up method. Eyeballing the data sometimes leads to clues about which method is used. For example, the decline in losses on 2xxx-2 from period 15 to period 16 suggests that the reporting is cash basis. Studying the data set is a good starting point for discussions with the banker or issuer.

Loss curve analysis is based on the assumption that historical data are a guide to the future. This is a fair assumption. However, to jump from this to the assertion that issuers have characteristic loss curves is more dubious. Issuers competing for market share in a niche underwrite to the standards that enable them to stay in business, and when facing stiff competition, they will go down-market. In general, the reliance on loss history to project future losses creates a lagging signal of change that is bidirectional: the analyst will be slow to recognize credit deterioration and slow also to recognize credit improvement.

Also, as mentioned in the first half of the chapter, the average-loan approach is not the ideal basis for loss analysis. Each static pool has a unique payment profile that becomes increasingly pronounced as its pool balance pays down. While it may be computationally much simpler to work with averages than with an array of hundreds or thousands of loans, averaging blunts the idiosyncratic contours of risk in different vintages. Pools that resemble each other on an aggregate basis might not seem to be cohorts in a more granular framework of analysis. Generally, a data set that is richer with respect not only to losses but to prepayments and delinquencies will yield a more precise analysis.

Finally, garden varieties of human error such as the following may also lead to mistakes in loss curve construction:

- Failure to review and understand what the data represent
- Failure to consider all the sources of data when forming judgments
- Inappropriate or inaccurate techniques of extrapolation
- Analytical inconsistencies

Loss Analysis for Composite Pools

Some ABS transactions are issued backed by pools consisting of multiple sellers of the same asset. While it is technically possible to build a composite curve, the re-aggregation of static pool information is cumbersome and to some extent defeats the purpose of vintage analysis. If there are data to construct individual loss curves, cumulative expected losses for the portfolio may be calculated as the weighted sum of expected losses on each pool. Portfolio variance, calculated as the sum of the variance on each pool and their covariances (which will probably be high for related issuers in the same market), is likely to be higher than for homogeneous single pools.[1]

Actuarial Method, Step 2: Measuring Credit Enhancement

There is no uniform implementation of step 2. Many variations exist as a result of both institutional and individual styles of analysis. A certain degree of uniformity will arise from the use of *groupware*, which is to say models developed internally that, over time, have become a standard for a particular type of analysis. It is typical for rating analysts to supplement their analyses or double-check the results with alternatives using more than one of these standard models—a commendable practice.

The calculation of credit enhancement normally consists of the following steps:

- Identify the deterministic components of credit enhancement in the transaction. These components may include reserve funds, initial overcollateralization amounts, subordinated tranches, and most other forms of credit enhancement as given in the term sheet.
- Calculate the total amount of deterministic credit enhancement.
- Estimate the stochastic component, primarily excess spread, and add it to total credit enhancement. Estimating excess spread any way other than in a comprehensive cash flow model is haphazard. The standard

method used by rating agencies to estimate excess spread is discussed in the next section.

- Identify the noncash forms of credit enhancement, such as third-party guarantees and swaps. In Step 3, the analyst will determine whether their credit quality is commensurate with the rating.

To illustrate the BOTE calculation of excess spread, consider the basic structural terms of the hypothetical transaction, SMRF 2xx2-1 LLC, displayed in Figure 3.3. Advance rates on the Class A notes are 90.5%, versus 9.5% on the Class B notes. From excess spread the reserve account builds to 1% of the outstanding balance and stays there for the remainder of the transaction. The total Class A note security package is the sum of the subordination amount, the reserve floor amount, and the yet-undetermined amount of excess spread as displayed in Table 3.5. For the Class B notes, the security package consists of the 1% reserve amount and excess spread.

Estimating Excess Spread

Assuming that the total principal balance of the liabilities is always equal to the aggregate principal balance of the trust, the *excess spread* or excess servicing (XS) is defined as the residual of interest collections flowing through the trust in excess of the amount required to service liabilities.

To calculate excess spread, rating agencies first make a static determination of maximum available excess spread and then apply internally determined stresses and haircuts to this result to compensate for the imprecision of the static computation.

On an annual basis, *gross excess spread* is the difference between income due to the weighted average coupon (WAC) of the pool and the sum of these *annualized* deductions from interest income:

SMRF LLC issue amount	$300,000,000
Principal balance amounts	
Class A notes	$271,500,000
Class B notes	$28,500,000
Class A percentage	90.5%
Class B percentage	9.5%
Reserve fund for Class A and Class B	
Initial reserve (% total balance)	0.0%
Maximum reserve	1.0%
Reserve floor (% total balance)	1.0%
Other credit support	—
Expected loss (from 2xx2.1)	3.1%
Recoveries (% of defaulted assets)	N.A.

Figure 3.3   SMRF 2xx2-1 LLC Hypothetical Transaction Parameters

Table 3.5
SMRF-2xx2-1 LLC Class A Credit Support

	Percentage
Total CE for Class A notes	10.5
Reserve fund	1.0
Subordination	9.5
Excess spread	?
Over-collateralization	0.0
Other	0.0

- The weighted average interest of the liabilities (WAI)
- Servicing and other senior fees expressed as a percentage of the pool's outstanding principal balance (S)

Although precise security coupon rates cannot be known until the transaction closes, the analyst can make a reasonable estimate by proxy with similar deals recently in the market. Given the senior fees reported in Figure 3.4, parameters, annualized gross excess spread (XS) for SMRF LLC would be computed as

$$XS = WAC - WAI - S$$

$$XS - 12.33\% - (90.5\%)(4.75\%) + (8.5\%)(6.25\%) - 1.925\% = 5.513\%.$$
$$(3.5)$$

Unless SMRF LLC matures in one year, the annualized XS amount will underestimate the total amount of XS produced over the lifetime of the transaction. To find total XS, multiply annualized XS by the average life of the pool, L_a. The average life of the pool is the number of months it would take an equivalent pool to amortize fully if the principal balance were paid out in bullet maturity instead of amortizing gradually.

___ The average life can be illustrated graphically as the point intersected by BE on the *x*-axis in Figure 3.5. There, the area of rectangle ABEF (representing the point in time in which principal would be repaid in bullet form) equals the area ADF under the curve ACD (the actual pattern of principal repayment), and the area of the triangle $\triangle$ABC (the amount of principal payments

Class A interest rate (assumed)	4.75%
Class B interest rate (assumed)	6.25%
Weighted average coupon (WAC)	12.33%
Weighted average note interest (WAI)	4.94%
Servicing and other fees (S)	1.925%

Figure 3.4   SMRF-2xx2-1 LLC Senior Fees

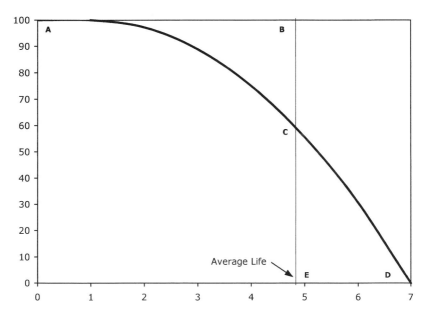

Figure 3.5. Average Life Definition

received after the average life under the actual repayment schedule) exactly equals the area of ΔDEC (the amount of principal under accelerated repayment at the average life under an equivalent bullet repayment schema).

Rating analysts typically compute the average life as an output of a cash flow model. Their outputs will reflect the analyst's assumptions about prepayment speeds and defaults and their impact on principal repayment. Average life may also be calculated with reference to equation (3.6), where T is the weighted average maturity (WAM) of the loans in the pool, dp the expected principal amortization over the time interval dt, and B_0 the initial pool balance:

$$L_a = \frac{1}{B_0} \int_0^T t \, dp \qquad (3.6)$$

Due to the importance of average life calculations in pricing and rating ABS securities, we will return to the topic in greater detail in chapter 9. To bring the calculation of gross XS to a close, if L_a is estimated at 2.0 years, the amount of gross XS is twice that of annual XS, or 11.03%.

Stressing Excess Spread

To the gross XS calculation, rating agencies apply haircuts. Justifications for haircutting XS include principal prepayment behavior and the dynamics of credit losses. Principal prepayment considerations are as follows:

1. Relatively high prepayments reduce the duration of the pool and hence total interest collections.
2. Even if prepayment speeds are consistent with expectations, the weighted average collateral coupon may be reduced if obligors with high interest rates prepay first.

To adjust for the first effect, prepayment speeds are raised to above their expected value to cause the average life to decrease. The adjustment is computed as the average life difference in years times the annualized total XS. By market convention, the ABS prepayment assumption is measured as the percentage of the current aggregate pool balance that prepays in a single period, excluding regularly scheduled amortization. For instance, 1.00 ABS means that 1% of the pool's principal balance prepays per month. As an example, Figure 3.6 shows that increasing prepayments from 1.50 ABS to 2.50 ABS produces a 0.4-year reduction in average life, which has the effect of reducing excess spread by 2.59%.

To adjust for the second effect, rating agencies assume that a certain proportion of the highest coupon obligors will prepay preferentially and calculate the resulting loss of interest income using the stratified sample of coupon rates in the prospectus or from issuer data. That proportion typically ranges from 10% for transactions with relatively low expected losses to 20% for transactions whose expected losses are relatively high. Adjustments due to adverse prepayments per Table 3.6 reduce excess spread by 66 basis points per annum.

A third type of haircut reflects the potential timing-mismatch risk between spread availability and credit losses. A significant amount of excess spread may already have been released from the structure back to the issuer as residual income before losses materialize. The amount of spread leakage is difficult to estimate ex ante but can generally be sized by reference to the loss curve. The analyst measures the time required for losses to become significant enough to absorb sizable XS, and reduces the credit for spread by the amount of excess servicing presumed to have leaked from the trust up to that time. This estimation process is ad hoc and subject to analyst discretion, and thus we do not illustrate spread leakage here.

Finally, care is exerted to ensure against double-counting sources of spread. For example, the reserve account is designed to build up from 0% to 1% from XS. The same spread clearly cannot be counted again as incremental enhancement. To avoid double-counting, the analyst would reduce credit for XS by that 1%, or give credit only for the initial 1% reserve deposit. These

Average life at 1.50 ABS	2.0 years
Average life at 2.50 ABS	1.6 years

Figure 3.6   Impact of Accelerated Prepayments

Table 3.6
Agency Adjustment for Adverse Prepayments

APR (≥, <)	Original			Haircut		
	Balance ($)	%	WAC (%)	Balance ($)	%	WAC (%)
19.5%	0	0.00	0.00	0	0.00	0.00
18.5%, 19.5%	0	0.00	0.00	0	0.00	0.00
17.5%, 18.5%	0	0.00	0.00	0	0.00	0.00
16.5%, 17.5%	0	0.00	0.00	0	0.00	0.00
15.5%, 16.5%	9,279,051	3.03	0.48	0	0.00	0.00
14.5%, 15.5%	15,387,995	5.02	0.75	0	0.00	0.00
13.5%, 14.5%	38,656,474	12.62	1.77	1,900,604	0.62	0.09
12.5%, 13.5%	65,896,474	21.51	2.80	65,896,474	26.91	3.50
11.5%, 12.5%	99,898,689	32.61	3.91	99,898,689	40.80	4.90
10.5%, 11.5%	42,028,122	13.72	1.51	42,028,122	17.16	1.89
9.5%, 10.5%	23,000,087	7.51	0.75	23,000,087	9.39	0.94
8.5%, 9.5%	12,152,049	3.97	0.36	12,152,049	4.96	0.45
7.5%, 8.5%	0	0.00	0.00	0	0.00	0.00
6.5%, 7.5%	0	0.00	0.00	0	0.00	0.00
5.5%, 6.5%	0	0.00	0.00	0	0.00	0.00
4.5%, 5.5%	0	0.00	0.00	0	0.00	0.00
Total	306,298,941	100.00	12.33	244,876,022	80.00	11.67

various stresses and haircuts are combined in Figure 3.7 to yield the total credit given by the rating analyst for XS.

Table 3.7 displays the total credit enhancement available to support each of the Class A and Class B notes. From the loss curve analysis (see Table 3.4) the analyst determined net losses on SMRF LLC as 3.1%. This provides a 5.71x cushion to absorb losses before the Class A notes are affected and a 1.71x cushion before Class B noteholders would suffer a loss. By the BOTE or cushion method in Table 3.8, these ratios are roughly consistent with strong AAA and low-investment-grade ratings on the Class A and Class B notes, respectively.

Reflections on Credit Enhancement Estimation Methods

Excess spread is perhaps the most determinative and volatile element of structured analysis. One of the main attractions of a structured financing is the spread differential between the interest income and the interest expense. Investor and seller alike covet it; the way it flows through the structure and what happens to it along the way are of vital interest to both parties. Yet XS calculations are often mishandled. Inexperienced analysts may ignore it altogether. When it is performed outside of a cash flow analysis, the results are often arbitrary and misleading. Back-of-the-envelope stresses like the ones performed

Weighted average collateral coupon	12.330%
Weighted average security coupon	4.893%
Servicing fees	1.925%
Annualized gross excess spread	5.513%
Average life at 1.50 ABS	2.0 years
Average life at 2.25 ABS	1.7 years
Total gross excess spread	11.03%
High prepayment reduction (0.4 × 6.48)	3.70%
Adverse prepayment reduction (2 × 3.12)	1.32%
Reserve fund double counting	1.00%
Spread leakage	0.00%
Total credit for excess spread	5.01%

Figure 3.7   Credit-for-Spread Calculation Demonstrated

in the preceding section are not a replacement for cash flow analysis. The reader may already have developed a feel for how applying some of these stresses without regard for the pool's particular prepayment and default patterns can assume away a significant portion of XS, rightly or wrongly.

The deterministic components of credit enhancement are more straight-forward; but if there are trigger mechanisms to make the structure more dynamic and cost efficient, the deterministic elements become contingent to some degree. Just as XS is difficult to evaluate without the ability to model time, contingent payment mechanisms cannot be properly evaluated except by stochastic cash flow modeling.

Cash Flow Analysis on the Senior Class

Cash flow models that allow for the interaction of key variables in time are superior to BOTE approaches. By and large, Moody's and Standard & Poor's have progressed well beyond the BOTE approach (the first level, mentioned previously) for analyzing most transactions of a familiar nature. Both rating agencies have many spreadsheet-based cash models to assess the performance

Table 3.7
Credit Enhancement for Class A and Class B Notes

	Class A Notes	Class B Notes
Total credit enhancement	15.51%	6.01%
Reserve fund	1.00%	1.00%
Subordination	9.50%	—
Excess spread	5.01%	5.01%
Over-collateralization	—	—
Other	—	—

Table 3.8
"BOTE" Ratings on Hypothetical Class A and Class B Notes of SMRF LLC

Scale of Ratios	Coverage	Tranches	Rating
5x	15.51/3.1 = 5.00x	Class A	AAA
4x	—	—	AA
3x	—	—	A
1.5–2x	6.01/3.1 = 1.94x	—	BBB+
<1.5x	—	—	Sub-IG

of the senior class. In most cases, these models consist of a single-loan analysis of cash flows based on average statistics in the pool cut. In some cases, the single-loan model is more intricate and includes a loss modulation derived from the loss curve. The asset analysis is joined to a simplified version of the liabilities structure. Typically only the senior class is analyzed, and mechanisms of contingent cash flow diversion are generally not modeled. The differences in risk philosophy between Moody's and Standard & Poor's, as described at some length earlier, govern to some extent whether credit losses are applied ad hoc as stresses to contractual cash flows or whether a spreadsheet-based Monte Carlo simulation package is used to introduce stochastic variations in the amount and timing of credit losses, as is Moody's stated approach. Sophistication in use of the cash flow model also depends upon the skills of the individual credit analyst.

Reflections on Senior-Tranche Cash Flow Modeling Methods

Spreadsheet-based cash flow models are not built to yield infallible answers but to support the analyst's conclusions. What will persuade a rating committee is to a great extent a matter of custom and practice within the rating agency. Standard & Poor's, relying more heavily on the use of stress cases, is also more forthcoming in publishing scenario-building guidelines. At Moody's, the baseline simulation is based on an assumed probability distribution, to which ad hoc stresses may also be added.

In reality, many aspects of asset analysis cannot be realistically modeled in a spreadsheet, and significant distortions of pool performance do occur in many of the ways suggested before. Single-loan models are artificial. Even models with modulated losses or Monte Carlo simulation give the false impression that the dynamics of default have been fairly represented when the result, in fact, may be as far away from the transaction's real risk profile than are results using a BOTE approach, as each distortion adds to the suboptimality of the transaction.

On the liability side, certain liberties are also taken. Due to the constraints of spreadsheet-based analysis, realistic structural features such as triggers or over-collateralization tests are not modeled but are given, at best, nominal credit on a case-by-case basis. The structural features that are not modeled are often decisive in determining the effective credit quality of asset-backed securities.

Analyzing Subordinated Classes

Under the cushion method favored by Standard & Poor's, subordinated tranches are analyzed within a stress-case cash flow framework alongside the senior tranche. A consistent application of Moody's method to subordinated tranches would be an identical reduction-of-yield method in a cash flow framework, but this is not what is done. Rather, all Moody's analysts use a static spreadsheet-based analytical tool, which this book will refer to as the *subordinated tranche analysis model*, to determine ratings on subordinated tranches. It has been revised and fine-tuned after many years of use and now exists in several versions. All versions take in pool-level factors (expected loss, credit loss standard deviation, external enhancement, available XS) and class-specific factors (advance rate, coupons, weighted-average life, credit enhancement). Some assume that the loss distribution is lognormal;[2] others use a normal assumption.

The model works broadly as follows. After the Aaa credit enhancement has been determined via the previously mentioned steps for the senior tranche, the collateral cumulative credit-loss distribution is derived by assuming the functional form of the loss distribution; taking the mean of the distribution as the pool's expected loss; and calibrating the standard deviation so the reduction of yield on the senior tranche corresponds to the ideal reduction of yield on an Aaa security using Moody's reduction-of-yield scale.

In practice, the target reduction of yield is usually the midpoint of the Aaa range, or approximately 0.025 bps. Ratings on each of the subordinated classes are determined by calculating the reduction of yield on each sub-tranche using a static liquidation model, which nets collateral losses against security-level credit enhancement. Security losses that result are deemed to occur on the last payment date of a hypothetical transaction with a maturity equal to the target transaction's average life (only integers are allowed). The internal rate of return (IRR) that results is calculated and weighted by the probability of the corresponding loss obtained from the selected loss distribution. The difference between the IRR and the payment promise (i.e., the reduction of yield) is averaged over the entire loss distribution and mapped to a letter-grade rating. This process is shown in Figure 3.8.

Under the subordinated tranche analysis model, the expected security loss $E(L)$ is equal to the integrated product of the credit loss (net of enhancement) and its probability of occurrence. Security losses occur where risk coverage is not available, in the shaded area of Figure 3.8. In other words,

$$E(L) = \int_{CE}^{1} f(L)(L - CE) dL \tag{3.7}$$

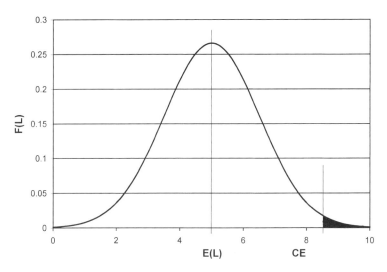

Figure 3.8. Distribution of Normal Losses

In equation (3.7), $f(L)$ is the probability density function of credit losses and CE is the total credit enhancement available to the relevant security. This expected security loss is then compared to fixed criteria to determine the rating.

Alternatively, the expected security loss computed above can also be expressed as an average reduction of yield as follows. The internal rate of return $IRR(L)$ on a security with a principal balance measured as a percentage of the pool, an average life of n years, a coupon rate r, available security credit enhancement CE (also expressed as a percentage of the pool), ratio of pool to security balance A, and resulting from credit losses L, expressed as a percentage of the pool, can be computed as the solution of the following equation:

$$0 = -1 + \frac{r}{1 + IRR(L)}$$
$$+ \frac{r}{(1 + IRR(L))^2} + \ldots \frac{r + 1 - A \max(0, L - CE)}{(1 + IRR(L))^n} \quad (3.8)$$

Readers will recall that the yield on a fixed income security is bounded from below by -1 and from above by its coupon rate r. The reduction of yield corresponding to this credit loss scenario is

$$\Delta IRR(L) = r - IRR(L).$$

The average reduction of yield is therefore calculated as

$$\Delta IRR_{avg} = \int_{CE}^{1} f(L) \Delta IRR(L) dL. \quad (3.9)$$

This expected reduction of yield is then compared to a fixed scale to determine the appropriate rating.

Reflections on Subordinated Tranche Analysis

The Moody's subordinated tranche analysis model is not a replacement for basic cash flow modeling, which, even in its simplest form, sheds light on how average pools of collateral perform within specific structures. It is not as powerful as a comprehensive cash flow model displaying the credit dynamics of the subordinated tranches, an analysis largely ignored under the contemporary framework. Its chief advantages are those of any static equilibrium model, namely expediency and the ability to handle any problem generically. But by simplifying the problem it can also distort the true picture of risk.

Normally, one would expect the loss distribution to be determined independently of credit enhancement, and not through what is essentially a self-fulfilling prophecy. Choosing the distribution presents another issue. The lognormal is a standard assumption for stock, interest rate, and other security prices in the market. This is its chief advantage; whether credit losses behave this way remains an open question. In any case, there is a nontrivial technical problem associated with choosing a lognormal probability distribution for losses in a model with volatility as an independent parameter (namely, the relationship of standard deviation to expected loss is offsetting: an increase in volatility shifts the bulk of the probability mass toward lower values while the tail is simply made a little fatter). The distribution becomes more singular (more sharply peaked, with less dispersion around the mean) and the percentage of zero security-loss scenarios is involuntarily increased at the expense of very few high-loss occurrences. Although mathematically speaking, expected loss has not changed, it has lost much of its intuitive character. This is not what most users would want to accomplish by increasing volatility.[3] The assumption of a normal distribution does not have this flaw. However, it suffers from another kind of limitation: that the allowable domain of the independent variable does not exclude negative values. Although there is no theoretical bar against negative credit losses, when the expected loss is close to zero, this may create a distortion that can result in an understatement of risk.

Another issue is the allocation of losses to the last payment period and limitation of the maturity to integer values. Most average lives turn out to have fractional components. For short-lived assets, the matter of months can be significant in real credit terms. Moreover, although applying losses to the last period is not an unreasonable decision rule under a liquidation scenario, it does make the rating improve artificially with longer weighted-average lives. In other words, if a tranche with a three-year average life is non-investment-grade, the rating can be artificially improved by slowing down the rate of repayment in the cash flow model. Thus a long-term transaction is seen as less risky than a short-term one with the same parameters—hardly an intuitively appealing result.

Liquidation Analysis for Credit Card Portfolios

Credit card–backed securities, issued within revolving master trust structures, are an asset-class exception to the loss curve credit enhancement sizing method described here. A static loss curve would be inappropriate for all the reasons discussed previously. A dynamic loss curve is feasible and perhaps desirable for the sake of consistency with other ABS and MBS methods, but it has not been contemplated by the rating agencies. Instead, cash flow–based liquidation analyses are used to size enhancement on senior credit card obligations. For example, a typical Moody's liquidation scenario would assume that, on a run-rate basis, credit losses would double immediately after early amortization has been triggered, only to double again in linear fashion from the second to the twelfth month thereafter, after which they would remain constant. Senior tranche credit enhancement is then sized such that senior noteholders are made whole under this stress scenario. In other words, in this case Moody's uses the Standard & Poor's approach to rating asset-backed securities.

Liquidation analysis not only suffers from static treatment under a stress-case assumption, it is also inherently more conservative than the loss curve method. Credit card–backed structured securities are thus generally of stronger credit quality at a given rating level than other asset classes. Spreads over treasuries for AAA credit card ABS are perennially thinner than for other asset types, reflecting the additional degree of security. The natural inference is that subordinated tranches issued from credit card master trusts are generally undervalued.

Cash Flow Analysis When Asset Performance Data Are Unavailable

By definition, there is no standard approach to creating new ABS models in asset classes for which the static pool model is inappropriate. In order to rate new complex assets that have limited or nonexistent loss data, rating agencies will often build fundamental models of cash flow generation, taking inputs from experienced analysts in relevant sectors. For example, Moody's developed an approach to tax lien securitizations from a statistical analysis of the underlying phenomenon—the behavior of delinquent taxpayers in respect of property taxes owed under tax liens. Taking another example, the analysis of mutual fund 12b-1 fee securitizations is driven by a fundamental model that simulates the impact of stock market volatility on mutual fund price levels to determine the level of recoverable fees, given that they are capped at some percentage of the fund's net asset value. Interested readers are invited to read part III, which discusses an array of numerical methods appropriate for building cash flow engines powerful enough to resolve the dynamics of individual assets, obviating the use of single-loan modeling approaches.

Actuarial Method, Step 3: Moving-Parts Analysis

Whereas steps 1 and 2 involve the application of models and procedures for estimating credit losses and sizing credit enhancement, step 3 addresses the unexpected sources of risk—more of a qualitative analysis, but no less important. Here, the robustness of the risk-transfer mechanisms is evaluated within the structure: letters of credit, surety bonds, total-return swaps, and credit default swaps as mechanisms of wholesale risk transfer. At this time, operational risk is also assessed by an evaluation of the servicer, a topic beyond the scope of this book. This is also the time to identify special environmental risks (often of a policy nature) that cannot be quantified solely by reference to ratings on the institutions taking the risk. Possible changes in tax policy or financial rules that could cause the structure to incur costs unforeseen at the time of issue, or that could otherwise prevent the moving parties from fulfilling their contractual obligations under the structure, are an example. Sovereign or other specialists within the rating agency often play a large role in evaluating special policy-related risks, where the only satisfactory resolution may be that of formal acknowledgment and reassurances by representatives of the responsible institutions that such actions will not be taken. Such risks can also be "deal-breakers."

Due to the broad and qualitative nature of operational and specialty risks, we confine our remarks to the risk-transfer analysis. It generally has three components, all bearing on the willingness and the ability of the counterparty to perform:

- *Payment mechanics.* Do the formula and the mechanism of payment by the counterparty produce payments of sufficient size and timeliness to be consistent with the target rating on the security?
- *Counterparty creditworthiness.* Does the counterparty have sufficient credit to carry out its guarantees under contingent contracts, such as swaps?
- *Economic motivation.* Does the counterparty have sufficient economic interest in the current arrangement, more often than not a swap, such that the likelihood of default will not be inconsistent with the security rating if the market moves adversely?

The Payment Promise

The external credit enhancement should perform as intended when needed. Many of the structured market's spectacular failures have arisen from failure to understand the substance of the indemnification. Such analysis is tedious but critically important. To determine that the logic of the risk-transfer mechanism works, the analyst must read the documents to gain an understanding of where it could break down. At a minimum, the analyst must be reasonably certain that the following legal and financial items are addressed formally in third-party credit enhancement[4] documents:

- The arrangement is for the benefit of the investors in the structured security.
- The contract amount is not less than the required coverage.
- The credit event to trigger payment is unambiguously defined.
- There are no exceptions (conditions or outs-to-payment) that vitiate the value of the contract.
- The timing of payment concords with the issuer's payment schedule down to the details of draw-down mechanics.
- Termination arrangements do not expose the structure to avoidance risk without adequate contingency arrangements.

The degree and type of scrutiny over the contractual language also vary with the form of enhancement. The following paragraphs briefly explain some of the most basic forms of external credit enhancement.

Surety bonds are the most straightforward. This type of contract follows a standard form for each issuing institution, with contract terms conforming closely to the structured market's payment conventions and requirements. Moreover, monoline insurers who wish to remain active have considerable disincentive against writing tricky policies because their business is based on a rating agency–sanctioned arbitrage. They must continually purchase low-investment-grade structured deals in order to achieve the required earnings and degree of portfolio diversification for a high-investment-grade rating. They can do this only by building and maintaining relationships of trust with issuers, investors, and the rating agencies that closely monitor their portfolios. Hence, in monoline insured transactions, the structured rating analyst's focus is on the substance of the transaction (i.e., the scope of indemnified risk and the credit of the security) rather than on the form of the guaranty.

At the other end of the spectrum are insurance contracts from diversified insurance companies seeking opportunistic sources of income. They typically are not written for the value of the structured security but for specific risks to the SPE. These contracts must be read literally and in laborious detail, with special attention given to the conditions of payment, as they may have been crafted to avoid the assumption of risk.

Letters of credit (LOCs) were once the mainstay of external enhancement to the structured finance market but now are mainly used in commercial paper only. The thrust of the analysis is to ascertain that the LOC bank is sufficiently creditworthy (as measured by its financial strength rating) to support the risk, that draw-down mechanics permit timely payment, and that preference risk is adequately addressed in the mechanics of reimbursement and LOC termination.

Swaps are flexible ways to transfer risk without transfer of title. Due to tax or legal restrictions, they may be an attractive alternative to an asset sale in many jurisdictions. Wholesale transfer of risk exposures can be achieved through total return and credit default swaps, whereas limited non–credit risk transfer arrangements are common under interest rate, basis, and market value swaps.

The first task of an analyst reading swap documentation is to confirm that the SPE is liable to pay the swap counterparty only when there is sufficient cash available, to prevent technical payment defaults. As with LOCs, the analyst must work through the payment mechanics to make sure that timing mismatches do not occur, or that the investors are protected against their occurrence by some form of interim liquidity.

Use of the standard form swap indenture (the International Swap Dealers Association [ISDA] Master Agreement) poses a range of presettlement and settlement risks to structured transactions. First and foremost, the credit analyst must identify the conditions under which the swap counterparty may terminate the swap. Events of default should be narrow in scope and, in particular, consistent with the intent of the transaction. For instance, the risk that the swap is designed to assume should not itself be an event of default. Termination events need to be similarly reviewed.[5]

The ISDA Master Agreement is frequently revised. In recent years, ISDA members have sought to broaden the definition of default to include events not addressed in rating agencies' definitions, and to expand the swap providers' power of avoidance in termination scenarios. Such changes highlight the credit analyst's ongoing challenge of identifying, mitigating, and quantifying new sources of counterparty risk in deals where swaps provide a significant sources of credit enhancement or interest rate risk mitigation.

Market value risks in credit default swaps add another layer of complexity. In addition to the other caveats, the analyst needs to determine that the reference asset is clearly identified and that the mechanism for determining the loss on the reference credit, including the timing of the valuation, is clearly spelled out. The two main mechanisms are a bidding process by independent third parties and a workout process.[6]

Counterparty Creditworthiness

The credit of the enhancement provider must be consistent with the transaction rating. As discussed, Moody's generally evaluates this in a joint-and-several framework (see equation [2.1]). Standard & Poor's evaluates the counterparty credit on a case-by-case basis, taking the short-term rating into consideration as a key factor, and requires the posting of collateral by counterparties whose credit is judged insufficient for the rating on the transaction. In general, where N is the notional amount of the swap, σ is an appropriate market-volatility factor obtained from published S&P tables, and A is the in-the-money dollar amount of the swap (if any), the amount C of collateral to be posted is determined by the following relationship.[7]

$$C = N(1 + \sigma) - A \qquad (3.10)$$

Economic Motivation of the Swap Counterparty

Determining the adequacy of coverage can be particularly tricky for long-term exposures in volatile environments. It is important to model transaction cash flows based on amortization schedules under different payment-speed and interest-rate assumptions to determine cash flow sustainability. Although swap modeling in the cash flow is a discretionary item for rating analysts, it is a commonplace requirement for the banker as part of the rating agency package. Separately, contingency arrangements need to be in place to deal with counterparty downgrades and swap breakage or termination costs.

Reflections on the Analysis of Swaps as Risk-Transfer Mechanisms

Human error and inattention are the main causes of error in step 3 as it is implemented today. Because the current method stops short of analyzing swap payments within a comprehensive cash flow framework with a consistent probabilistic view, it always stands outside the analysis of expected loss where, conceptually, it belongs. There are also some well-known drawbacks to using counterparty ratings as indicators of performance. Anecdotally, the way that counterparties perform in specialty markets where their bread-and-butter business is transacted is not necessarily captured by their ratings, which refer to their payment capacity in relation to senior obligations. In such cases, for example, where the swap counterparty is also a dealer in the risk market where the swap is undertaken, the ratings may be too conservative as a proxy of performance. Also, the willingness of a counterparty to perform under a given swap obligation may be strongly related to the importance of the underlying business relationship, which is not addressed in a generic rating. In terms of how well counterparty and short-term ratings have stood up under the validation process of the corporate bond default study, they have been evaluated only within the broader context of corporate bond defaults—sector-specific bond default studies have not been carried out. Hence the usefulness of counterparty ratings as a proxy for default is more assumption than fact.

All Methods, Step 4: Reviewing the Logic of the Structure and Its Protections

Step 4 begins with a reading of the summary of terms in the offering memorandum or prospectus. While not legally binding, this marketing document is a quick introduction to the transaction's structure. After gaining an understanding of how the structure is intended to work, the rating analyst is ready to review and confirm that the rules spelled out in the documents agree with the concept of the structure. In ABS and MBS transactions, the document that contains detailed payment instructions, credit enhancement, and other structural mechanics is the *Pooling and Servicing Agreement* (P&S). The focus of the work at this stage is to identify and correct potential errors or inconsistencies in the P&S, some of which may appear insignificant. Drafting errors can become incorporated into documents through either errors of logic or ambiguous wording.

A classic error in logic is the mistaken use of *and* instead of *or* in the definition of triggers (triggers are discussed fully in chapter 23). *Or* is the operator for several independent conditions; it is more stringent than *and*, which is the operator for simultaneous conditions. For example, a condition worded "If > 60 + delinquencies exceed 5% or losses exceed 1%" is comprehensive and prevents deterioration as measured by losses or delinquencies. This dual condition is particularly useful in situations where the servicer is accounting for delinquent accounts but failing to write them off. By contrast, the wording "If 60+ delinquencies exceed 5% and losses exceed 1%" is much less effective and gives the servicer a way out that can significantly weaken investor protection. It is entirely possible that losses would greatly exceed 1% before delinquencies reached 5%.

Many different types of errors can appear in formulas. They are sometimes difficult to ferret out when the document is drafted in convoluted "legalese." While it is impossible to speak of characteristic mistakes, the analyst should be aware of trigger index definitions that, for instance, fail to annualize periodic values to reflect the basis of the trigger level. For example, the following wording is taken from a transaction currently outstanding:

> Default Level for any Due Period is equal to the sum of the Loan Balances of [Originator] Loans that became Defaulted [Originator] Loans during such Due Period divided by the Aggregate Loan Balance on the last day of such Due Period.

In this definition, which is critical to investor protection in advance of real trouble, the rules fails to annualize defaulted loan balances while the trigger level is defined on an annual basis. This trigger is completely ineffective as drafted.

Another common error is to mistake the adverse credit event for the trigger level. The following abridged wording is an instance of such confusion:

> The Reserve Fund Floor is 6% of the Current Pool Balance. . . . To the extent funds are available on each Payment Date during a Reserve Fund Trigger Event, the Trustee shall make the following distributions in the following order of priority: [after senior fees, pro-rata interest and senior principal] to the Reserve Fund. . . . The Reserve Fund Trigger Event shall exist if the balance of the Reserve Fund drops below 6%.

Here, the reserve fund is funded exclusively from excess spread. The amount of excess spread available at the level of the reserve fund when the transaction is in trouble will most likely be minimal. In order to maintain a floor of 6%, the trigger level causing XS capture should be set above the required floor, to begin refunding the reserve fund anticipatorily.

Where the Structural Review Can Fail

Step 4 is critically important to the smooth functioning of the transaction because it insures that the decision rules work as intended. When deals go awry, contractual parties are bound by the literal wording of the documents, not by the parties' stated intentions at closing. The choice of *and* when what was meant was *or* can sink a transaction. The significance of language increases in proportion to the degree of reliance by the investor on structure rather than collateral alone. The review of how triggers are worded is absolutely critical in the CDO transaction—a much more volatile type of security that relies more extensively on triggers (strings of conditions) to maintain stability of performance over time. Anecdotally, the wording of triggers may not always receive the quality of oversight and review it deserves. As in step 3, human error and inattention are important causes of review failure in this step.

However, the main shortcoming of step 4 implementation arises from the failure to quantify the impact of structure on cash flow availability. It is impossible to judge the dollar-effectiveness of triggers and payment rules without modeling them probabilistically and interactively inside a cash flow framework; yet the analysis of triggers is usually done qualitatively and intuitively.

4

The Default Method

The default (CDO) method applies to portfolios containing smaller numbers of heterogeneous debt collateral: bonds, loans, and nonstandard debt, including structured securities. From chapter 1, the credit structure of CDOs is based either on their market value or on the quality of their cash flows. Market value CDOs tend to be actively traded. Investors rely on the cushion inherent in over-collateralized portfolios for value: the higher the collateral value relative to par, the better the credit. Cash flow CDOs are designed as buy-and-hold investments. Investors in cash flow CDOs depend on the return of interest and principal from the underlying collateral for repayment. The main source of data for the cash flow analysis is corporate bond default and recovery data. Issuer-specific loss and recovery data used in ABS and MBS analysis are not used in CBOs generally—not even for CBOs of ABS—although price volatility data are used in determining collateral levels of market value structures.

The CDO method works by transforming portfolios backed by real collateral into *benchmark pools* of independent, synthetic exposures whose credit quality equals the sum of the weighted-average ratings on constituent securities, with ad hoc adjustments for correlation and other factors bearing on security performance. The process is roughly the same for market value and cash flow CDOs, but implementations at step 2 are different. For this reason, we treat the credit structures separately. We defer the discussion of steps 3 and 4, which apply to all three methods, until the end of the chapter.

The steps in the CDO method are shown in Figure 4.1.

Default Method, Step 1: Constructing the Portfolio

Remarks concerning the difference between *benchmark* and *eligible* pools in the section "Benchmark Pool" apply also to the CDO collateral pool: if the rating agency dictates what goes into the pool, it is an eligible pool. If the rating agency places minimal constraints on collateral eligibility prior to finding its benchmark equivalent, it is a benchmark pool.

Here are a few highlights of the Standard & Poor's approach in relation to step 1:[1]

1(a) Assemble a collateral pool that conforms to Standard & Poor's criteria (eligible pool).

1(b) Audit the pool.

1(c) Assign ratings based on Standard & Poor's issuer ratings, or approved rating proxies, to each security in the pool and generate an average rating on the collateral.

1(d) Address correlation by selecting the appropriate cash flow model: currently, the single-jurisdictional or the global cash flow model, which deals with emerging market exposures.

1(e) For a single-jurisdiction pool, determine intermarket correlations from a list of thirty-nine independent industries and percentage concentrations of pool exposures in each category.

The Moody's CDO approach is similar:[2]

1(a) Assemble the collateral pool.

1(b) Audit the pool.

1(c) Assign ratings based on Moody's issuer ratings or approved rating proxies to each security.

1(d) Determine the weighted average rating and maturity of the pool based on the percentage composition of exposures.

1(e) Address correlation by transforming the portfolio into a synthetic portfolio of independently distributed securities chosen from a list of thirty-two independent industries. This procedure leads to the computation of a diversity score for the pool.

The main differences between the Moody's and the Standard & Poor's approaches are in the degree of flexibility in choosing collateral, and in the treatment of diversity in step 1(e).

Poolwide Default Probability and Maturity

The default probability corresponding to the rating on each security at its maturity (rounded up to the next integer) is assumed to be the probability of default for that security. Exposures with fractional maturities are considered as

---

Step 1	Classify the securities in the initial pool by sector and obtain their parameters (terms, ratings or other default measure, recoveries).
Step 2	Size the expected loss. Determine how much credit enhancement is required for a level of performance consistent with target security ratings, especially the senior class.
Step 3	Identify and measure other sources of risk that could further diminish cash flow, and adjust credit enhancement accordingly. Establish security-specific or pool-wide criteria for purchases in the revolving period.
Step 4	Review the structure to determine that it works as intended to sustain the target rating level.

Figure 4.1 Steps in a Default (CBO) Analysis

Table 4.1
Compiling and Profiting the Collateral of a Hypothetical CDO Portfolio

Collateral	Size (mm)	% Pool	Default (%)	Collateral Rating	Term (month)	Term (year)	Industry
A	30.2	3.73	2.3800	Baa3	47.4	4.0	2
D	22.2	2.74	0.3450	A2	51.6	4.0	3
E	7.3	0.90	0.3600	A3	40.5	3.0	6
N	15.9	1.96	0.4670	A2	61.0	5.0	6
R	14.8	1.83	1.2000	Baa2	51.1	4.0	6
S	27.2	3.35	1.5800	Baa2	62.1	5.0	6
B	1.4	0.17	0.0900	Baa1	15.7	1.0	6
K	14.2	1.76	1.0500	Baa3	21.5	2.0	11
L	16.5	2.03	2.3800	Baa3	45.3	4.0	11
I	1.6	0.20	3.0500	Baa3	54.4	5.0	14
P	20.2	2.50	0.1010	Aa3	44.7	4.0	14
H	18.6	2.29	0.4200	Baa3	12.1	1.0	18
C	5.7	0.70	0.4670	A2	64.6	5.0	21
O	9.8	1.21	0.5400	A3	27.7	2.0	21
J	10.4	1.29	1.7100	Baa3	34.9	3.0	27
M	22.8	2.82	0.0030	Aa3	9.3	1.0	27
Q	11.5	1.42	0.1700	Baa2	6.2	1.0	27
F	17.5	2.17	0.2800	Baa1	24.3	2.0	27
G	21.1	2.61	0.0900	Baa1	11.6	1.0	31
T	21.1	2.60	0.8300	Baa2	40.7	3.0	31
+38	500.0	61.73	0.3600	A3	38.0	3.0	+6
	14.0						
	810.0	100.00	0.5600	Baa1	37.5	3.0	

having a one-year default horizon. The poolwide maturity and default probability are equal to the weighted average of the ratings and maturities of the constituent collateral, as shown in Table 4.1. For ease of display, we have made two adjustments to a more realistic situation:

1. The collateral pool consists solely of senior investment-grade debt from investment-grade countries, and
2. We show details of the analysis for 38% of the pool only and summarize the profile of the remaining 62%. The poolwide average collateral maturity turns out to be three years, with an average rating of Baa1, corresponding to a default probability of 56 basis points. The recovery-rate assumption is the standard Moody's corporate recovery rate of 30%.

Diversity Score

Moody's diversity score method transforms the debt exposures in the pool to equivalent, independent and identically distributed exposures, by which pool

Table 4.2
Counting Rules for Treating Sector Correlations

Number of Same-Sector Securities	Number of Synthetic Exposures	Number of Same-Sector Securities	Number of Synthetic Exposures
1.0	1.00	5.0	2.67
1.5	1.20	5.5	2.80
2.0	1.50	6.0	3.00
2.5	1.80	7.0	3.25
3.0	2.00	8.0	3.50
3.5	2.20	9.0	3.75
4.0	2.33	10.0	4.00
4.5	2.50	>10.0	Committee decision

default risk may be calculated by assuming a binomial distribution and summing the probabilities of one or more constituent securities' defaulting.

To calculate the diversity score, Moody's segregates and counts industry exposures using a counting rule based on a 30% correlation assumption. The counting rules have been summarized in Table 4.2. For example, three obligors from the aerospace industry would be counted as two independent exposures. To adjust for differences in issue size, the average exposure amount is calculated (here, $14 million) and compared to each exposure. Securities smaller than the average size are counted as a fractional synthetic exposure, but the adjustment is not symmetrical: securities equal to or larger than the average size are capped at unity.

The results of the diversity calculation on the first twenty securities in the sample deal appear in the column labeled "Grouped" of Table 4.3. The diversity score for the remaining $500 million of collateral (whose industry exposures do not overlap with the first twenty credits) is 6, and was calculated separately. This is added to the diversity score of 12 on the first twenty credits, for a total score diversity score of 18.

Global CDOs

The method just described applies to CDOs for which most or all of the collateral is originated in the United States or Organization for Economic Cooperation and Development (OECD) countries. For global CDOs, Moody's uses elements of this and its emerging market approaches for step 1. Rather than counting industries, the diversity count is based on the number of countries. Credits from non-investment-grade countries are stressed more severely: they are grouped by region rather than by country, and a more severe correlation assumption is applied by multiplying the raw score by the factor (1 +

Table 4.3
Calculating the Diversity Score on the Hypothetical Portfolio

Security	MM	Term (year)	Industry	Fractional	Grouped	Diversity
A	30.2	4.0	2	1.0	1.0	1.0
D	22.2	4.0	3	1.0	1.0	1.0
E	7.3	3.0	6	0.5	3.6	2.0
N	15.9	5.0	6	1.0	—	—
R	14.8	4.0	6	1.0	—	—
S	27.2	5.0	6	1.0	—	—
B	1.4	1.0	6	0.1	—	—
K	14.2	2.0	11	1.0	2.0	1.5
L	16.5	4.0	11	1.0	—	—
I	1.6	5.0	14	0.1	1.1	1.0
P	20.2	4.0	14	1.0	—	—
H	18.6	1.0	18	1.0	1.0	1.0
C	5.7	5.0	21	0.4	1.1	1.0
O	9.8	2.0	21	0.7	—	—
J	10.4	3.0	27	0.7	3.6	2.0
M	22.8	1.0	27	1.0	—	—
Q	11.5	1.0	27	0.8	—	—
F	17.5	2.0	27	1.0	—	—
G	21.1	1.0	31	1.0	2.0	1.5
T	21.1	3.0	31	1.0		6.0
38	500.0	3.0			Total	18.0
Average	14.0					

[number of synthetic exposures − 1] × 0.05) to yield a much smaller diversity score. Standard & Poor's has a different model that applies different stress assumptions for global CDOs.

Default-Based Method, Step 2: Calculating the Expected Loss and Sizing Credit Enhancement

As mentioned, the CDO method is a sophisticated variant of the benchmark pool concept whereby idiosyncratic portfolios of credit exposures are transformed into standardized pools with a default probability that can be modeled using the *binomial expansion theorem* (BET). Thus, the method falls short of comprehensive modeling within a cash flow simulation framework, but it is more involved than loss modeling based on single-event or selective stress scenarios. The implementation of the CDO method is to determine the loss on a portfolio of N identically and independently distributed securities (equal to the diversity score) by calculating loss severities on the pool for the range $[1, N]$ in a cash flow model and weighting these losses by their probability of occurrence under the BET.

Here are some of the highlights of the Standard & Poor's approach to sizing credit enhancement with respect to a given pool of collateral:[3]

2(a) Select the appropriate Standard & Poor's default model (single-jurisdictional or expanded multijurisdictional) and apply the Standard & Poor's ratings haircuts based on percentage concentrations.

2(b) Determine the expected level of collateral defaults (D) using the Standard & Poor's model, which is a version of the BET with some adjustments.

2(c) Multiply this amount by an idealized percentage recovery rate (R) on each asset type. The expected loss is then defined as $D(1 - R)$.

2(d) Perform a cash flow analysis of the structure using the results from this model in combination with over-collateralization (OC) and interest coverage (IC) test levels and apply the type of stresses the rating agency deems appropriate to the transaction.

2(e) Using the cushion method, determine the sufficiency of credit enhancement for the target ratings. Keep iterating until the target ratings are reached.

Highlights of the Moody's approach for sizing credit enhancement on cash flow CDOs[4] are as follows:

2(a) Based on the term of the transaction, the five-year default probability, a ratings-determined default stress, the appropriate recovery rate, and the diversity score, apply the BET or the double BET (DBET) method to determine the expected loss.

2(b) Perform a cash flow analysis of the structure using the results of the BET (or DBET) model and OC and IC test levels, and apply the type of stresses deemed appropriate to the transaction.

2(c) Calculate the average reduction of yield to determine the sufficiency of credit enhancement for the target rating on the senior tranche and apply the multiclass model (see above) to determine ratings on subordinated tranches. Iterate until the target ratings are obtained on subordinated tranches.

To apply the BET method, we must transform real portfolio exposures via the method described in step 1 to produce a theoretical pool consisting of identical securities as measured by their average rating and average term exposure. Once this is done, the probability that n defaults will occur simultaneously in a set of N binomially distributed and independent securities with unique default probability p is given by

$$P(n) = \binom{N}{n} p^n (1 - p)^{N-n}. \tag{4.1}$$

In the Moody's method, N is set equal to the diversity score, and p is the average default probability computed from the average security rating. Non-defaulted securities are deemed to provide cash flows at the known weighted-average security coupon rate. These parameters can be stressed in various ways. For instance, the average default probability may be stressed in proportion to the rigor demanded by the desired rating.[5] The percentage and timing of recoveries also may be stressed in the cash flow model. These stressed defaults are then allocated in the cash flow model based upon results of the bond default study, which show that 66% of all defaults in a ten-year period happen in the first six years, and 35% of six-year cumulative losses happen in the first year. For a six-year maturity transaction, this technique usually causes 50% of losses to be deemed to occur in the first year and 10% each year thereafter for five years. Periodic net cash flows to each tranche under each default scenario in $[1, N]$ are discounted back to present and divided by the initial principal amount of each security. The results are recorded as the loss percentage incurred for that default scenario. Each loss amount is then multiplied by the appropriate probability generated by the above formula. The expected loss on each security is defined as the sum of these products.

As we have shown above when discussing the Moody's subordinated tranche analysis model, this expected loss could also be expressed as a reduction of yield. Although the outputs would be numerically different, they would be mutually consistent and could be used interchangeably.

To illustrate step 2, let us place the hypothetical pool above, with an average rating of Baa1 and a diversity score of 18 and embedded within a senior-subordinated structure, into a cash flow model. Assume structural parameters as follows: $900 million in Class A notes, with a coupon at 40 over London Interbank Offer Rate (LIBOR); $100 million in Class B certificates, with a coupon at 120 over LIBOR; a 4% reserve fund; and an estimated 320 basis points of excess spread.

The scenarios that produce the loss analysis are shown in Table 4.4. The leftmost column displays the number of simultaneous defaults. Adjacent columns show the probabilities associated with each default scenario according to equation (4.1), the loss percentages on the pool as a result, the loss percentage on the Class A notes, the loss percentage on the Class B certificates, and the respective weighted average maturities of the notes and certificates, respectively. All losses were assumed to occur within the first two years—a typical front-loaded severity stress.

The rating analysis shown in Table 4.5 yields a poolwide net expected loss of 28 bps. The Class A average life is 2.25 years, with an expected loss of 0.0%, which is consistent with a Aaa rating. Since the reduction of yield is below the midpoint of 0.06 bps, which means tranche sizing is not optimal, more Class A notes could have been issued. The average life of the Class B certificates is 6.38 years, and the expected loss is 1.48%, giving them an A rating. These are severe results generated by severe assumptions about the timing of losses.

Table 4.4
Loss Analysis on the Hypothetical CDO

No. of Defaults	Probability of Default (%)	Loss of Pool (%)	Loss on Notes (%)	Loss of Subloan (%)	AL Notes	AL Subloan
0	88.0043	0.00	0.00	0.00	2.24	6.35
1	11.2856	2.22	0.00	11.51	2.30	6.58
2	0.6834	4.44	0.00	25.12	2.36	6.86
3	0.0260	6.65	0.00	41.53	2.44	7.26
4	0.0007	8.87	0.00	58.63	2.52	7.95
5	0.0000	11.09	0.54	71.38	2.59	9.50
6	0.0000	13.31	1.89	77.71	2.57	9.50
7	0.0000	15.53	3.25	82.27	2.56	9.50
8	0.0000	17.74	4.61	85.31	2.54	9.50
9	0.0000	19.96	5.96	87.60	2.52	9.50
10	0.0000	22.18	7.32	89.26	2.50	9.50
11	0.0000	24.40	9.30	90.37	2.48	9.50
12	0.0000	26.62	11.48	91.77	2.46	9.50
13	0.0000	28.83	13.64	93.24	2.44	9.50
14	0.0000	31.05	15.85	94.17	2.42	9.50
15	0.0000	33.27	18.24	94.25	2.39	9.50
16	0.0000	35.49	20.53	94.32	2.37	9.50
17	0.0000	37.70	22.90	94.39	2.34	9.50
18	0.0000	39.92	25.26	94.47	2.31	9.50

Market Value CDOs

Although the collateral of market value CDOs is a pool of rated fixed-income securities, this does not change the fact that the essential risk of market value CDOs is asset price volatility (i.e., market, and not credit risk). In substance, they have more in common with hedge funds than with structured securities; therefore, the treatment here is superficial.

Both Standard & Poor's and Moody's use their own simulation methods to determine how much over-collateralization is required to protect the structure from losing market value over its lifetime, given the price volatility of its particular assets.[6] Generally these market value CDO simulations recognize a

Table 4.5
Rating Analysis on the Hypothetical CDO

	Pool	Notes	Certificates
Expected loss	0.282%	0.000%	1.482%
Maturity	5.68	2.25	6.38
Rating	Baa1	Aaa	A3

loss on a security if, on a collateral test date, the amount of liabilities out-standing exceeds the portfolio's market value during the preceding period after subtracting the value of securities senior to it. Normally the rating agencies include portfolio earnings for market value calculation purposes and set prin-cipal balances equal to the product of price (not par value) and a predeter-mined advance rate. The expected loss is the average of losses net of enhance-ment, across all scenarios of the simulation. Our reservations about the method for CDOs generally apply to market value and cash flow credit struc-tures. It is difficult to comment specifically on the implementation of price-volatility simulation methods when the data and the stresses applied to them by the rating agencies are not a matter of public record.

Default Method, Step 3: Moving Parts Analysis

All remarks with respect to step 3 of the actuarial method also apply to the de-fault-based method. It is important to point out that for synthetic (noncash) CDOs, while the risk analysis of steps 1 and 2 *presumably* is performed for the various counterparties whose guarantees make up the credit structure, the public analysis is focused on step 3: do the mechanics of risk transfer work, and will the counterparties assume their obligations? The recent rapid growth of the synthetic market and the trend toward risk transfer via the swap market instead of the cash market raises the level of concern about the reliability of rat-ings that have not been historically validated—particularly if there is any doubt as to the capacity of the counterparties to value the structured exposures they are in fact booking.

Default-Based Method, Step 4: Standard Covenants and Triggers

This is the step in which the analyst must "test-drive" the structure to insure that it works as advertised. The general remarks of the actuarial method step 4 apply here as well. CDOs tend to exhibit even greater structural intensity. Ab-sent comprehensive valuation techniques to yield precise estimates of relative credit quality in CDOs, standard covenants and triggers have been developed as periodic tests of whether a CDO is "in the range" and to protect it from dra-matic value declines. Key tests include over-collateralization coverage and in-terest coverage applied prior to each coupon payment and when new collateral is purchased. The latter are based on the after-purchase portfolio. If the struc-ture breaches any of these or other tests on any payment date, steps must be taken to cure the breach—for example, contributing additional collateral, sell-ing collateral to pay down debt, or substituting collateral. The choice of mea-sure usually rests with the collateral manager.

Key CDO Triggers and Coverage Tests

For *cash flow CDOs*, the interest coverage test is based on the ratio of interest receipts, plus scheduled interest on performing collateral in the current payment period, to the current coupon on the security plus the coupon on each security senior to it. For a two-tranche transaction we would then have

$$\text{Class A IC Test} = \text{Coll Aggr Interest/Cl A Interest} \qquad (4.2)$$

$$\text{Class B IC Test} = \text{Coll Aggr Interest/(Cl A Interest + Cl B Interest)} \qquad (4.3)$$

The cash flow CDO over-collateralization test is calculated as the ratio of collateral pool par value to the sum of the par values of the security and each security to which it is subordinate. Collateral aggregate par value is based on the aggregate par value of the non-defaulted securities plus an assumed recovery percentage on defaulted securities:

$$\text{Class A OC Test} = \text{Coll Aggr Par Value/Cl A Prin Balance} \qquad (4.4)$$

$$\text{Class B OC Test} = \text{Coll Aggr Par Value/(Cl A + Cl B Prin Balances)} \qquad (4.5)$$

For *market value CDOs*, the collateral market value OC test compares the sum of the products of current market values of collateral securities times their advance rate to the cumulative sum of par values and accrued interests on each liability tranche. For instance, tranche k ($k = 1$ means Class A, etc.) would be subject to the following market value test with trigger ratio r_k (trigger ratios decrease as k increases):

$$\text{Market Value Test} \equiv \sum P_i \cdot \text{AR}_i \geq r_k \cdot \sum_{j=1}^{k} \text{ParValue}_j + \text{AccrInterest}_j, \qquad (4.6)$$

where

P_i = price of each collateral asset,

AR_i = advance rate on each collateral asset, and

$\text{ParValue}_j + \text{AccrInterest}_j$ = par value and accrued interest on the CDO tranche.

The OC covenant is often paired with an average-rating covenant to discourage OC compliance merely by swapping current assets for deeply discounted collateral. If the average rating test does not cause early amortization, as is often the case, the effectiveness of that trigger is extremely limited.

Reflections on the Default Method

The logarithmic nature of the credit scale creates opportunities for issuers to game the BET method by assembling a pool of generally high-credit-quality securities sprinkled with relatively few lower-quality credits, thus raising the portfolio's expected default frequency but without any change in the ratings of the associated securities. The real impact of those few exposures on the portfolio will become evident only as the portfolio unwinds in time. To address this weakness, Moody's developed the ("double") DBET method as a refinement of the binomial method. The DBET method mandates the segregation of collateral of disparate credit quality before implementing steps 1 and 2, and combining the results.[7]

That the default method can easily be manipulated in CDOs speaks to deeper methodological problems. It does not reflect the propensities of the real collateral to default. Moreover, it is a one-time analysis that does not show the impact of time on revolving pools of collateral. The correlation adjustments are also problematic. There is no research to support the notion that downgrading structures because they have excess concentrations captures the real dynamics of correlation; nor is there reason to find the diversity-score method representative. Both methods treat all portfolios the same way—but given the unique attributes of each collateral pool, there is no guarantee of consistent results. The remedy is granular, comprehensive cash flow analysis using collateral-specific data.

5

The Eclectic Method

The hybrid aspect of structured securities (as both quasi-corporations and portfolios) in the contemporary framework carries over to the analysis of ABCP and their conduits. As a permanently revolving financing facility for commercial banks and a handful of industrial companies, an ABCP conduit is very close in substance to a corporate credit. It is also very similar analytically to a CDO that has a very long revolving period as well as amortization triggers. However, unlike ABS and CDOs, ABCP credit quality is measured on the short-term credit scale, which both agencies define as a measure of default frequency: the traditional metric for corporate ratings.

The Meaning of the Short-Term Rating Scale

Rating agencies view short-term and long-term ratings as closely correlated (see Figure 5.1). To a great extent, the short-term rating can be inferred from the long-term rating; for instance, at the time of publication, Standard & Poor's cutoff for its highest prime rating is a notch or two lower than the Moody's cutoff. Certain industrial sectors are characteristically more liquid and enjoy higher short-term ratings than what the long-term rating would predict. Financial institutions that have special access to payment system liquidity, like the access of U.S. banks to the Federal Reserve discount window, are one example. Other businesses with strong, predictable cash flows from receivables are another.

Ratings: On the Conduit or the Notes?

ABCP ratings are actually ratings on the conduit issuing the notes. In general, all ABCPs target the highest rating level on the short-term rating scale (in Moody's nomenclature, "Prime-1," and in Standard & Poor's, "A-1" or "A-1+") and the rating exercise revolves around achieving and maintaining the highest prime rating. Unlike for ABS, MBS, and CDOs, the ABCP rating is implemented in two distinct phases.

The first phase establishes the conduit's fundamental credit quality. Global in scope, the goal of this phase is to confirm that the conduit structure is consistent with the highest prime rating. At that point, the conduit is still only a blueprint. Each time a new receivable purchase is contemplated, the

Non-Prime		Least-Prime		Medium-Prime		Highest Prime
< BBB	BBB-	BBB+	A-	A	A+	AAA

Figure 5.1. Relationship of Short-Term Ratings to Long-Term Ratings

"high-primeness" of the conduit rating must be reevaluated in light of the effect of purchasing the new receivables.

The second phase is a local analysis that focuses on the two components of prime quality, liquidity and collateral quality, as governed by the liquidity and receivables purchase documents. Except in fully supported transactions, the method of analyzing the credit quality of the new purchase is either actuarially or default-based, depending on the type of asset—hence the name *eclectic approach*. Rating agencies currently require that, in general, all new account purchases should also carry ratings that are long-term equivalents of high prime, which generally corresponds to a minimum of A or A+. The step-by-step credit rating process for ABCPs is detailed in Figure 5.2.

Eclectic Method, Step 1: Analysis of the Conduit Blueprint

Along with the establishment of an ABCP program, a half-dozen or more program documents are created that define the permissible activities of the conduit. Key documents typically include a private placement memorandum for the investor; administration and management agreements for the program administrator; possibly an investment-advisor agreement for special collateral or risk management functions; a collection agreement governing the collection of funds; a security agreement establishing the security interest in the asset; depository, issuing, and paying agent agreements governing custody and the

Global	Step 1	In setting up the conduit, determine that the rules governing borrowing facilities and structural features are initially consistent with the rating.
Local	Step 2	Analyze the standalone credit quality of new account additions using actuarial or default methods. Confirm the original rating if (i) the analysis is consistent with a minimum A-1 or Prime-1; and (ii) payment mechanics allow for ample liquidity.
G/L	Step 3	Monitor account-level performance. Probe or take action on unsatisfactory performance as required. Evaluate requests to change the structure based on qualitative and quantitative performance elements, and peer conduit analysis.

Figure 5.2. Steps in an Eclectic (ABCP) Analysis

movement of funds; one or more liquidity support (or asset purchase) agreements that govern when and how much support will be made available from the liquidity bank; and receivables (or note) purchase agreements that govern the purchase of eligible collateral.

If collateral repurchase arrangements are involved in the management of liquidity, there will also be repurchase agreements. Swing-line loan documentation may be found as an additional source of liquidity. There may well be credit enhancement–related documents, for example, if a monoline insurance company is providing program credit enhancement in the form of a surety bond, or a bank is providing a letter of credit. Swap documentation for swaps covering credit or market-related risks will also be part of the package. The credit and investment manual must also be reviewed, for insight into the quality of managerial judgment.

In the global phase, the first challenge is familiarity with the "architecture" of the program documents, as the organization of documentary information varies significantly by program administrator. Also, unlike ABS documentation, where the P&S contains the information most critical to the credit analysis, ABCP documents must be read closely for loopholes and omissions. The documents must be read again in ensemble, to attain an integrated understanding of conduit functioning, including the investment policy and investment controls; the capital structure; the interplay between credit enhancement and liquidity at the program- and pool-specific levels; and the protective qualities of program covenants and triggers. Conduit mechanics must be reviewed to determine that essential custody and payment operations will run smoothly without over-reliance on managerial intervention. Qualitative assessments of the suitability of the participating institutions for their roles in the conduit must be formed. In particular, because highly rated conduits depend on liquidity from the sponsoring bank to administer their operations and maintain their high ratings, the integrity and capacity of the sponsoring banks (and their subcontractors) to stand behind their commitments must be evaluated.

To support the analyst's final recommendation on the conduit rating, a thorough global analysis will address the following perennial ABCP concerns:[1]

- Experience and financial resources of the program administrator and its subcontractors
- Bankruptcy = remoteness of the conduit
- Market mechanics
  - How much commercial paper is the conduit allowed to issue?
  - When does it issue?
  - Under what conditions does the program terminate?
  - What procedures will the conduit follow in case of a market disruption?
  - Drafting consistency: do the procedures that are detailed in different documents governing the operations of different parties—for

example, the conduit and the depository, or the conduit and the issuing and paying agent—mirror each other?
- Asset quality
  — Are the credit and investment guidelines readable, comprehensive, consistent, and prudent?
  — What quality of underwriting experience do they reflect?
  — For conduits that purchase only rated collateral of a minimum rating threshold (highly rated collateral), what is the threshold and what is the entitlement of such collateral to seller-specific or program-level credit enhancement?
  — How are concentration risks to be handled?
  — How is ongoing seller performance to be measured?
  — How are sub-performing assets dealt with in the program?
  — If the conduit is mainly designed to warehouse the receivables of a single seller, how will the takeout of assets be handled, and what will be the credit impact on the remaining pool?
- Liquidity facility mechanics
  — Does liquidity fund as it is intended?
  — Are the documents clearly worded to prevent misinterpretation?
  — Is a timely mechanism in place to replace a liquidity bank that is downgraded?
  — If liquidity is structured, does the proposed structure work, or are investors subject to risks unintended by the rating?
- Credit enhancement structure and mechanics
  — Is program credit enhancement adequately sized?
  — Is it liquid?
  — Does it cover all sellers?
  — What profile of seller does it exclude, and how are they covered?
  — Does it cover non-credit risks?
  — What profile of non-credit risks does it exclude, and how are they covered?
  — Is the seller-specific credit enhancement provided at arm's length, or through recourse to the sponsoring bank?
- Risk allocation between the liquidity facility and the credit enhancement facilities
  — Is the program designed to be fully supported or partially supported?
  — How is performing collateral (the *borrowing base*) defined?
  — What, if any, risks of technical default are absorbed by liquidity?
  — Are there gaps between the two that would expose the conduit to risks inconsistent with the prime rating?
- Swaps (many items have their counterparts in step 3 for the actuarial and CDO methods)
  — Can the counterparty put the conduit into bankruptcy? (Has the counterparty signed a non-petition agreement with the conduit? Is

there "excess-funds" language, so that the counterparty liabilities
are paid only to the extent there are funds to make payment?)
— Can the liabilities to the conduit be offset by the liabilities of the
counterparty, or have netting and other offset provisions been
waived?
— Is the conduit responsible for charges that are typically the assumed
by the party entering into the swap, for example, swap termination
fees, breakage costs, and withholding taxes?
— Can the swaps be prematurely terminated by events that have not
been addressed in the structure?

Finally, the analyst must know not only how the conduit works but how
it compares to other conduits of similar structure or strategy that are already
in existence. As can be expected, the bulk of this analysis is legal and addresses
merely the documentary aspects. Quantitative, portfolio-level analysis is generally de-emphasized. Quantitative analysis has been attempted for conduit
innovations, for example, evaluating the feasibility of structured liquidity, but
such models have been developed only on a case-by-case basis. A unified
model, such as might be developed to address the risks common to CDOs,
monoline insurance companies, and ABCP (that of debt backed by revolving
asset pools) has yet to be developed, although in Moody's case, the multisector
CDO approach is a starting point.[2]

Eclectic Method, Step 2: Local Analysis of Account Additions

In step 2, the focus is on the account addition. From chapter 1, ABCP conduits characteristically are fully supported by the liquidity provisions of the
liquidity bank, or they are partially supported to the extent that the collateral
is performing. The content of the analysis thus depends essentially on the nature of the support structure.

Fully Supported Structures

By definition, fully supported transactions have the same profile of risk and
carry the same rating as the liquidity bank. The rating on the conduit is therefore subject to the downgrade risk of the liquidity bank. The key question in
the determining the support structure is what liquidity funds. A funding formula that answers

"Outstanding note + accrued yield"
or, for discount paper, "The full face value of CP"

is always a fully supported transaction.

In some cases, full support is also achieved surreptitiously by structuring
the liquidity to effectively wrap the entire asset pool and by giving the appear-

Eligible Receivables	Capital
− Defaulted receivables	− Defaulted receivables in excess of loss reserves
+ ABCP yield	+ ABCP yield
+ Deemed collections	
+ Cash collected, unremitted to issuer	

Figure 5.3.   Receivables- and Capital-Based Funding Formulas

ance of funding only performing assets. Certain banks make greater use of structured liquidity than others. To determine whether a transaction uses structured liquidity, the analyst must work through the funding formula.[3]

Partially Supported Structures

The rating on a partially supported transaction has two main components: the analysis of liquidity and the analysis of credit quality. The liquidity analysis begins with the question "What does liquidity fund?" Whatever risks liquidity does not fund must be picked up by the credit enhancement, with sufficient cushion to keep the transaction consistent with the highest prime rating.

The funding formula appears in the liquidity document. There are two variations on the funding formula. Some conduits account for receivables by unit (eligible receivables) and some by dollars (capital). Figure 5.3 shows an example of each type of formula. Table 5.1 shows that the differences are a matter of convention and do not alter the fundamental structure of coverage.

The term *deemed collections* includes payment shortfalls due to dilution or breaches of representations and warranties on receivables. *Cash collected but not remitted* refers to payments that have been collected but not yet for-

Table 5.1
Receivables- and Capital-Based Funding Formulas Applied

Formula	Funded Amount
Eligible receivables	$100
−Defaulted receivables	22
+ABCP yield	2
+Deemed collections	15
+Cash collected, unremitted to issuer	7
Total	$102
Capital	$100
−Defaulted receivables in excess of loss reserves	(22 − 22)
+ABCP yield	2
Total	$102

warded to the distribution account. These are non-credit risks that can result in a technical payment default that the sponsoring bank is willing to absorb as an extension of its routine banking business. Some of the other risks that sponsoring banks may assume include interest rate mismatch, currency risk, withholding taxes, residual values, seller bankruptcy, and preference payments. Such items appear in the loss reserves column under the capital-based formula, whereas they are broken out in the asset-based formula.

When alternative liquidity (an LOC, a joint liquidity facility by lower-rated banks, a total return swap, or other structural device) is involved, the relevant questions in a moving-parts analysis must also be considered.

The analysis of receivables credit quality is based on performance data. An analyst on the CDO or ABS team (depending on the asset type) usually conducts the analysis using the actuarial or the default method outlined earlier in this chapter. In some cases, the account addition may be a high-grade structured security. In this case, the credit will already have been rated, but the ABCP analyst must also review the payment mechanics on the notes purchased, to ensure that there are no latent timing mismatches that could cause a missed payment; and if such exist, to recommend an effective solution. This review is particularly important for conduit structures that are built to purchase highly rated assets only and do not have an available cushioning mechanism to absorb unplanned yield erosion.

Following such analysis, if the long-term rating on the target purchase is consistent with the highest short-term rating, the conduit's rating will be reconfirmed at A-1 or Prime-1. In general, rating agencies consider the eligibility threshold to be a long-term rating in the middle-investment-grade range. Furthermore, program-level credit enhancement may be viewed as additional comfort when the rating of the planned account addition is borderline or in the low-A range, but this is a qualitative (not a quantitative) determination.

Postreview Conduits

Exemptions from the local analysis may be offered to certain large conduits for account additions of a certain maximum size. Such exemptions may be granted only after careful review.

Eclectic Method, Step 3: Performance Review and Revisiting the Structure

The rating analyst reviews monthly remittance reports for trigger violations and other issues related to account performance. Rating analysts are also responsible for monitoring the health of the conduit on a medium-term basis. The guidelines for review are not a matter of public record, and none of the rating agencies have disclosed their procedures beyond the monthly review monitoring. Oversight quality may depend more on the acuity of the analyst and the program administrator's level of involvement than on a philosophy of oversight.

From time to time, the sponsoring bank may initiate requests for changes to the conduit structure—usually decreases in the commitment of capital without rating impairment. The following requests are particularly common:

- Lowering or changing the composition of program credit enhancement
- Allowing the conduit postreview status, whereby the conduit is permitted to acquire new assets up to a certain credit limit without the rating agency's prior approval
- Approving changes to the credit and investment policy.

The analyst responsible for the conduit responds to such requests by evaluating recent conduit performance and ascertaining how the requested change could affect conduit credit quality. How the quantitative analysis is implemented, and what threshold of statistical significance the postaddition conduit must meet, are matters of conjecture.

Reflections on the ABCP "Eclectic" Method

ABCP may be viewed from a corporate credit perspective as a structured financial institution analysis where the degree of transparency surrounding the asset-liability structure is exceptionally high. Viewed from the structured credit perspective, ABCP is short-term paper backed by a permanently revolving CDO of ABS fortified with bank liquidity.

In the latter regard, ABCP may be seen to be one of the least structured financing forms. It is the one area where the weak-link philosophy still has credibility. Any conduit that permits the sharing of risks across the portfolio may be said to have some element of weak-link analysis, and most conduits do. In most cases, there is a small portion of program credit enhancement (5–10%) that is fungible across all accounts. In many cases, there is program-level liquidity; and in a few cases, cross-collateralization of seller-level credit enhancement is permitted under certain conditions. Structures that allow global risk sharing also inherently benefit from a sizable amount of diversification, particularly the large conduits authorized to purchase $15 billion or more in receivables and whose account purchases tend to be highly diversified consumer or trade-related assets. Thus, ABCP's two-phase rating process is inherently inefficient because it does not give proper credit to structural enhancement.

In fact, ABCP is the only market segment where the standard analytic method does not yield a direct, global measure of credit quality based on the reduction of yield. The imprecision of the quantitative analysis compounds the problem of spotty investor reporting to make relative value determinations in ABCP exceedingly difficult. There really is no way to tell how close paper from a particular conduit is to the boundaries of prime. In truth, it could be anywhere from low-investment-grade to hyper-Aaa.

Part II
Analyzing Structured Securities

6

Toward a Science of Ratings

Bond ratings have been a measure of relative value in the fixed income market since their invention by John Moody in 1909. From the first corporate ratings to today's structured ratings, the meaning of the rating has evolved as the claims for the measurement power of ratings have expanded: from *relative quality* (quality or safety ratings) to *payment certainty* (default frequency) to *risk-adjusted yield* as we discuss in chapter 2. However, as part 1 shows, many different applications of the corporate framework have been applied to structured securities, which has opened the door to inconsistent rating results. One is compelled to ask whether the expanded claims of ratings precision and power in structured finance are justifiable. In this chapter, we put forth a critique of the corporate rating model itself, on fundamental grounds. Our critique takes a closer look at basis for treating ratings as numerical measures, by examining the statistical research (rating agency bond default studies) by which they are validated.

To make our argument clear to the general reader, some preliminary comments on the semantics of the word *probability* are in order. Probability has three rather different interpretations: *a priori, a posteriori,* and *a priori linked to a posteriori* in a feedback capacity. The a priori interpretation, associated with the work of the French scientist Pierre-Simon de Laplace (1749–1827), postulates an identity between the probability and the phenomenon to be measured that can be derived mathematically without reference to the physical world or empirical data. Examples are tossing dice or flipping coins. The a posteriori interpretation, associated with the work of the German engineer Richard von Mises (1883–1953), is empirical and refers to outcomes of the following process:

- Identify the proper *collective* for the phenomenon whose probability of occurrence is sought.
- Form a sample on the collective by collecting data over time.
- Measure the limiting frequency of the phenomenon via the sample or by a mathematically defined process inspired by the sample.

The linked interpretation, associated with the work of Englishman Thomas Bayes (1701–1761), is partly theoretical and partly empirical. It works as follows:

- Obtain a first, a priori estimate of the probability somehow—perhaps by the Laplace method. This is the theoretical part.

- Collect data on the collective from the field. This is the empirical part.
- Examine the data and adjust the original, a priori estimate in light of them. The adjusted estimate is the a posteriori estimate of probability, which changes constantly as new data become available. The way the a priori estimate is modified in light of new data is given by the celebrated Bayes' theorem (see below).

The first and the second interpretations are the two poles of the debate. Theoretically, the main difference between them is that only the latter, a posteriori interpretation allows real events to be deemed "impossible," whereas an a priori interpretation does not. To demonstrate how possible events can be assigned zero probability, consider the sequence of points (6.1) for a data universe of two possibilities A and B, where the probability $P(A)$ of event A is required:

$$\text{B A B B A B B B A B B B B A} \ldots \tag{6.1}$$

Sequence (6.1) has a repeating pattern of n instances of B for each instance of A, starting with $n = 1$ to $n = \infty$. Now, the von Mises definition of probability $P(X)$ of some event X is the limiting frequency with which X occurs. Applied to event B, we have

$$P(B) = \lim_{N \to \infty} \frac{N(B)}{N} \tag{6.2}$$

In equation (6.2), $N(B)$ is the number of instances of B in a sequence of arbitrary length N, the remaining instances being those of event A. We refer to each such arrangement of events A and B as a pattern. In other words, the first pattern is simply B A, the second is B B A, and so on. In view of this assumed structure, we can write for a sub-sequence consisting of n patterns as follows:

$$\frac{N(B)}{N} = \frac{\frac{1}{2}n(n + 1)}{\frac{1}{2}n(n + 1) + n} = \frac{1}{1 + \frac{2}{n + 1}}$$

Therefore, the probability $P(B)$ is simply

$$P(B) = \lim_{n \to \infty} \frac{1}{1 + \frac{2}{n + 1}} = 1. \tag{6.3}$$

Since the probability of event B is unity and there are only two possible events in this data universe, it follows that $P(A) = 1 - P(B) = 0$. Thus, although event A clearly occurs at some (increasingly rare) positions in the sequence, event A has been assigned a zero probability according to the von Mises framework.

Of the three interpretations, the a posteriori is the closest to the corporate model, which has no general theory of credit risk other than empirically founded, conventionally accepted data relationships. Thus it can happen, for example, in an otherwise respectable Monte Carlo simulation of a few thousand scenarios, that the difference between "rarely" and "never" hinges on the semantics of probability. In the next section, we demonstrate how the same biased treatment of nonconforming data in long-run averages can work against the information content of the rating.

The "Naive" Rating Agency

The *through-the-cycle* rating agency rating has a limiting frequency interpretation, as the numerical meaning of the rating is constantly updated in light of the entire body of default experience available since its foundation. But investors do not want to know that a portfolio of securities similar to each security they hold will default with a 2% annual frequency; they want to know specifically the risk of their own holdings. It is entirely possible that one or even several of their investment-grade securities default without weakening rating agency claims of validity, which are based on the a posteriori interpretation. However, the investor and the rating agency will not see eye to eye on what those defaults signify about the rating—unless one side decides to adopt the other's interpretation of "probability."

In the following pages we show by a simple, hypothetical model of a posteriori ratings how the predictive quality of ratings can deteriorate, even as the weight of historical data solidifies rating agency claims.

The Model

In this hypothetical model, statisticians have decided to start a rating agency and to base all their rating decisions on the available default data. The rating agency being initially naive, the statisticians have no idea about the actual default rates of companies with various ratings, and as a result they initially assume a uniform distribution across all ratings. But the agency is not irrational: regardless of any subjective impressions of corporate quality, they will update the default probability estimate for each company they rate based solely on Bayes' theorem. Our naive statisticians are confident that whatever errors are contained in their initial estimates of default probabilities will be corrected by repeated use of Bayes' theorem. There is no reason to believe this would not happen.

Bayes' theorem can be stated as follows:

$$P(X\,|\,Y) = \frac{P(Y\,|\,X)P(X)}{P(Y)},$$

where X and Y are two events under consideration.   (6.4)

In this case, X will be interpreted as a default event and Y as a rating category that will be defined by a set of attributes such as financial ratios and other objective and subjective criteria, for example, an attribute entitled *management quality*. Any company should be ratable on those attributes. The agency is new, so the founders have established three rating categories (D1, D2, and D3) and have classified each company they rate as belonging to one of the three. We further assume that the universe of rated companies remains constant in size: when a company defaults in one rating category, another company replaces it without altering the original distribution. This is approximately correct in practice because defaults are infrequent events.

Unknown to our rating agency, the disposition of default rates in the world is such that, moving up the credit spectrum, the default propensity goes down by half. In other words,

D1 = 1

D2 = 0.5

D3 = 0.25

Moreover, there are alternating periods of recession and expansion, with an overall peak default rate of 5% during a recessionary period, and an overall trough default rate of 1% during an expansionary period. In other words, in a recession the maximum total number of defaults is 0.05 times the rated universe, and during an expansion, the minimum total number of defaults is 0.01 times the rated universe. Finally, a complete credit cycle is assumed to last eight years and our naive agency is founded arbitrarily somewhere in the middle of a cycle.

The rated universe is made of 1,000 companies, split as follows across the categories:

D1 = 600 companies

D2 = 300 companies

D3 = 100 companies

We have partitioned them thus to highlight the fact that better credits tend to be larger corporations, and there tend to be fewer of them. In any case, our conclusions hold whatever the distributions of firms across ratings.

In keeping with our naive-agency assumption, our statisticians assume that the probability of defaulting is invariant across rating category, and therefore, that a default is just as likely to have come from any one company. This means the prior default estimates are as follows:

$$P(D_1|X) = \frac{1}{3} \tag{6.5}$$

$$P(D_2|X) = \frac{1}{3}$$

$$P(D_3 \vert X) = \frac{1}{3}$$

That is, given that there has been a default, the probability that it came from a D1-, D2-, D3-rated company is the same and thus equal to 1/3 each.

Figure 6.1 shows roughly the first half-century of the agency's history for D1-rated companies given that this model is strictly followed and the world unfolds as described before. Data labeled "Actuals" are the actual default rates incurred, and those labeled "Agency" show rating agency estimates through Bayesian updates. The ratings are published at the beginning of the year and the estimates are compared with actual performance. Therefore, the two lines show predicted default rates versus actual default history for the D1 rating category. The equivalent graph could also be given for the other two rating categories but would show a similar pattern.

Outcomes

The initial naive assumption of equal propensity to default is indeed quickly corrected by actual performance. Year 1, January 1 estimates are completely wrong, and are in the "wrong" direction. At the end of that year, the agency commissioned a bond default study to revise these ratings. The results are shown along Year 2, and the agreement is clearly better. As advertised, the agency was only completely "wrong" in the year after founding (see Figure 6.1).

In the first few years, except for the usual rating agency lag in response time, the comparison between actuals and rating estimate is not bad at all. Remember that the agency uses all of the available default evidence since incep-

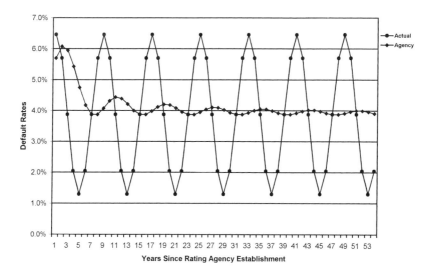

Figure 6.1. Actual versus Estimated Defaults for Naive Agency D1-Rated Firms

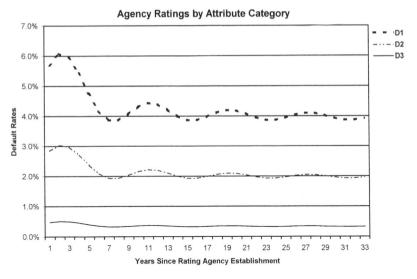

Figure 6.2. Naive Rating Agency Default Estimates, by Rating Category

tion to estimate default rates, and its definition of a rating is through-the-cycle performance (see Figure 6.1).

Our third observation is that, if comparison versus actuals is the measure of performance, the first few years are truly the golden years at the agency. The reason is obvious: as time passes, the influence of the cyclical nature of the world matters less and less to the rating estimate. The entire body of default experience quickly begins to overwhelm the current default experience in each category so that the discrepancy between agency rating and current default data starts to increase.

From the agency's standpoint there is absolutely nothing wrong since the difference between the default estimate and the "truth" becomes smaller and smaller. For instance, in category D1 the long-term average is 4.0%. At Year 5, the rating agency declares a default rate of 5.4%. By Year Ten, it is down to an impressive 4.1%, a mere 10 bps away from the "truth." This process continues forever, as shown in Figure 6.2.

The weight of evidence is clearly on the agency's side *if the a posteriori meaning of a rating is accepted.* With time, as the agency's rating definition approaches the limiting frequency value, the natural conclusion is that agency ratings become more and more accurate. Investors, having learned to rely fairly consistently on the agency's ratings during its first five years of existence, will find a growing disparity between ratings and performance.

Moral: The Importance of Hypothesis

Recall that what makes the corporate credit rating a posteriori in nature is the intensive reliance on data in the absence of an accompanying hypothesis. With or without a theory of default, through-the-cycle ratings will work most of the time, at least in mature markets, because default is a relatively rare event. But without a working hypothesis, no one ever knows how far any credit is from actually defaulting until it defaults.

An example of a credit rating backed by an underlying theory of default is the expected default frequency (EDF) under the Merton default paradigm, where value is a function of solvency that has been defined as assets less liabilities using market data to calculate asset values.[1] There have been many implementations of this paradigm, some more successful than others. Perhaps the best known is that of the KMV Corporation, now a subsidiary of Moody's Investors Service. Some arguments have been made to the effect that EDFs are based on only one measure (solvency) whereas traditional ratings reflect more information; hence ratings should be no less, or should perhaps be more, accurate.

However, the relevant point here is that a rating ceases to be a mere posterior probability and becomes a self-correcting forecast only with continuous mapping to actual default experience and continuous refinement. Absent a theory of default, ratings cannot systematically predict defaults, nor can they improve.

Framework for a "Pure" Structured Rating

Thus far we have indicated heuristically how the corporate rating framework is essentially nonanalytic—a bundle of conventions that work reasonably well under static conditions but have less certain outcomes under situations of volatility and change. We now proceed from a discussion of the shortcomings of corporate ratings to a discussion of the desiderata for a structured ratings framework. In order to improve upon the shortcomings of the corporate framework, we propose an analytic framework, one that seeks to identify the hypotheses on which the structured framework rests and accepts the discipline imposed by them, rather than encouraging repetitive application of methods sanctioned by the dons of corporate credit research. At once more rigorous and more noncommittal, the pure framework gives the analyst the freedom to "make music" by using the tools of part III.

The Measure

For ratings to work as a consistent signal of relative credit quality in structured transactions we must be able to assume the possibility of equilibrium; otherwise, price and risk will not converge and valuation will not be stable. For our purposes, the *Fisher separation theorem* is a sufficient condition. It says that, absent material transaction costs (taxes and bankruptcy in particular), an objective criterion exists for the production-consumption decision without regard for individual preference. That criterion is *wealth maximization*. A corollary, the *unanimity principle*, says that all shareholders (investors) will make the same (wealth-maximizing) choice. The assumptions underlying the separation theorem are not onerous, given that the issuing SPE has been structured so as to avoid taxes and bankruptcy.

However, not every measure is equally well appointed as an objective criterion of an investment's wealth-maximizing properties. The traditional corporate rating measures the likelihood that cash flows will be interrupted, but payment certainty is a weak measure of wealth maximization. By contrast, the *reduction of yield*, which is essentially a rate-of-return measure, is more on point. However, the lack of secondary market liquidity in structured securities offers some empirical evidence that the market does not consider structured ratings as a strong measure of credit quality after the initial pricing, nor does it have a good replacement measure.

The Continuum Hypothesis

The formal mathematical definition of the *continuum hypothesis* may not make much sense to the non-mathematician, but it presents a clean solution to a common physical problem that can be stated thus: if two measuring devices with different scales of finite resolution are used to measure the same phenomenon, or if the scale of resolution of a single device is somehow suddenly improved, then logical contradictions will emerge at the margins. If nothing is done to resolve the contradictions, disagreements will arise that can be ultimately resolved only by human interference, and the entire framework collapses.

To see the problem in simple terms, imagine that you are asked to judge the distance between points on a line.[2] Imagine further that the data fall on a scale of finite resolution (the eye, the ear, the quarterly servicer reports, etc.). Define Δ as the resolution of the measurement scale in appropriate units. Figure 6.3 depicts the situation as it presents itself.

Assume now that A is separated from B by a distance less than Δ, while C is separated from A by a distance greater than Δ. Now suppose that the phe-

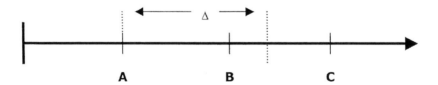

Figure 6.3. Explanation of the Continuum Hypothesis

nomenon under review, initially located at A, moves to B. Since the magnitude of the move is below your resolution (or that of the measuring device), your judgment will not change: the wall is still five feet away, the note is still E, and the firm is still BBB.

By the same token, the judgment will not change if the phenomenon moves from C to B. However, were the phenomenon to shift from A to C or from C to A, the judgment would change, since the distance between A and C now exceeds the scale's resolution Δ. The situation can be summarized by the following three logical identities:

$$A = B \qquad B = C \qquad A \neq C$$

Hence an obvious logical contradiction arises. The solution is to increase the resolution of the measuring apparatus so that $|A - B| > \Delta$ and $|C - B| > \Delta$. But this merely creates the same problem across an interval further down, as sharpening the resolution of the scale brings on new cycles of inconsistency. The interposition of such imaginary alphanumeric boundaries leads to a cascading series of distortions (optical illusions, false intervals, arbitrage opportunities) in an otherwise objective measurement process. At some point, a human arbiter would have to intervene, to decide whether B = A or B = C. In structured finance this is an everyday occurrence, especially at the border between investment-grade and non-investment-grade ratings.

The solution reached by mathematicians long ago was to assume that a third value could always be inserted between any two values, thereby preventing the contradiction from ever arising in the first place. The idea that the scale of resolution of a measuring apparatus can always be increased, ad infinitum, is the only way to remove the requirement for human arbitrage. This is the origin of the continuum hypothesis.

Adopting the continuum hypothesis does not imply that a *difference* is also a *distinction*. Rather, it removes the emphasis on artificial boundaries that create distortions and arbitrage opportunities. In a world where market risk is measured in fractional basis points, the only workable means of reconciling credit to market risk is by a "passage to the limit" and the adoption of a numerical credit scale to replace the current alphanumeric scale.[3] Today the business of manipulating and massaging empirical evidence to achieve investment-grade status thrives because of the artificial importance attached to achieving a low BBB rather than a high BB rating. The investment-grade fetish may have a legitimate place in corporate finance, where it could be argued that investment grade is more a matter of kind than of degree, but it is entirely misplaced in a structured world where credit ratings are manufactured. Similar abuses of the finite credit scale at other rating levels are rampant in CDOs.

To replace the alphanumeric with a numeric credit scale would enable the "meat-axe" world of credit structuring to be raised to a level of objectivity perfectly compatibility with the "scalpel" world of market risk. From that moment on, the unification of credit and market risks would be only a matter of time.

The Ergodic Hypothesis

In analyzing economic processes that are dynamic, the problem arises of how to link the initial statistical estimates of a portfolio's credit losses (*ensemble average*) with subsequent statistical estimates of performance (*time average*) derived from time integration. The ensemble average may be obtained via Monte Carlo simulation and is usually amenable to a consensus among analysts. The time average is less amenable to consensus, as it amounts to knowledge of the future. Asserting the equality of the two averages, known as the *ergodic hypothesis*, allows us to make meaningful statements about a deal's performance over its remaining lifetime.

The ergodic hypothesis says, in essence, that the spectrum of losses over a transaction's remaining life can be known today by analyzing the impact of a potential universe of evolving credit conditions on the same transaction. This universe may be derived by proxy from a long-term study of structured securities, or from a macroeconomic consensus of market observers and analysts. The second alternative, while not as well grounded in empiricism as the first one, is more on point because what happened a century ago has little relevance to today's situation.

The ergodic hypothesis is important in a framework for analyzing structured securities because it gives the Monte Carlo simulation meaning—provided that the structure of the transaction is modeled precisely. Properly constructed structured ratings do tell investors about the risk profile of their *own* investments, not generic ones, and assess the current credit quality of each security in response to a changing environment.

The Efficient-Markets Hypothesis and the Markov Formalism

We have reasoned that issuer loss curves and corporate default rates cannot be used to model the formation of losses within structured pools because rather than explain behavior they merely describe it. In general, default behavior is believed to occur according to an unknown stochastic process. Thus, to explain this behavior, some type of stochastic process needs to be specified or at least some assumption about the functional form of such process needs to be made.

Of all the readily available stochastic frameworks, the *Markov process* and its associated formalism is the closest in spirit to the credit essence of structured securities. Co-opting the Markovian formalism is accomplished by an assumption that the Markov property holds at the account level. Owing to its critical importance in the analysis of structured securities, some bare-bones introduction to stochastic processes and the Markov property is warranted.

Stochastic processes are processes that can be described by a random variable x, which depends on a discrete or continuous parameter t, usually taken to represent time. In this treatment, structured finance stochastic processes will be characterized by a predefined set of states that generally correspond to stages of delinquency and that economic agents (or *obligors*) will be allowed to occupy. In general, x will refer to arbitrary values assigned to these states. For an N-state stochastic process $x(t)$, $t = 0, 1, 2, \ldots, T$, $x \in [1, 2, 3, \ldots, N]$, the Markov property is said to hold in the absence of a memory effect. Mathematically, this is equivalent to the statement that the conditional probability of finding the system in a given state over the next time increment Δt depends only on its current state:

$$p[x(t + \Delta t) \mid x(t), x(t - \Delta t), x(t - 2\Delta t), \ldots] = p[x(t + \Delta t) \mid x(t)] \quad (6.6)$$

By asserting the absence of a memory effect at the account level, we are assuming that all the information about the dynamics of obligor-level defaults at any future time step is entirely contained in their present. Intuitively, this cannot be exactly true. In consumer credit, for instance, an obligor's delinquency history is known to contain valuable information about its future credit behavior, information that is in fact put to use daily by large U.S. commercial banks when computing behavior scores. But recognizing that a phenomenon is true and doing something about it are two different things. To incorporate the impact of each obligor's actual delinquency history on a structured pool would demand a level of individualized knowledge that is unavailable and uneconomical. More importantly, the credit quality of a structured security is based on aggregate pool measures. More often than not, the aggregate statistical measures of structured pools hold up fairly well despite the lack of attention paid to the microstructure, or path dependency, of obligor-level default events. Therefore, the analytic simplification that results from assuming the Markov property is both a tacit admission of the state of our current knowledge and a reasonable model of obligor behavior. One day, perhaps, enhanced data-acquisition methods may allow us to analyze obligor microstructure more fully through the introduction of more general stochastic processes. Until then, the Markov property appears to be the best compromise available.

Interestingly, it turns out that market risk practitioners have already encountered the Markov property as *the efficient market hypothesis*. A fuller discussion of loss estimation by delinquency matrix modeling (an outgrowth of the Markov property) and its relationship to the efficient market hypothesis may be found in the Appendix C.

Partitioning and Synthesizing the Components of Risk

One of the complications of explaining loss behavior is that cash flow performance is influenced not only by the microstructures of risk but also by macroeconomic factors. Micro-level risks are captured by the Markov property at the account level. Macroenvironmental factors are responsible for destabilizing and systematic effects that affect all the obligors within a pool. To be relevant, a comprehensive credit analysis of structured securities should partition and address both the micro- and macroeconomic components of risk.

A microanalysis of individual assets and their default propensity produces an *expected loss*, defined as the mean of a relatively narrow microstructure credit-loss distribution arising spontaneously from pool dynamics and calibrated to a portfolio data set of an issuer's managed exposures, if such exists, or else to the best proxy. That is the method of this book.

To compute the expected loss and give it a precise meaning requires a fairly detailed asset-side cash flow analysis. As a natural consequence of the inherent micro-level diversification of the pool, the variance of the microdistribution for most structured pools is relatively small and brings significant stability to the analysis of large asset pools. The lack of such stability now plagues much of structured analysis. For instance, it is incorrect to change the expected loss estimate every time a new static-pool cumulative credit loss figure becomes available. The probability with which a static pool will produce a cumulative credit loss equal to its expected loss is zero because, like all statistical measures, expected loss is a theoretical concept. Instead of thinking of it as a number to be achieved by some ethereal, undefined static pool, one should instead use the measure as a calibration factor inside a cash flow model. Only then does it acquire its analytical meaning: the intrinsic measure of an issuer's underwriting standards under a universe of likely economic conditions.

By overlaying the macroeconomic conjecture onto the microstructure loss distribution, the analyst achieves the pool's full credit loss distribution. Professional macroeconomic forecasts and outlooks are a straightforward source of macroeconomic conjecture and represent a convenient probability distribution of macroeconomic views. Comparing forecasted conjectures to the macroconditions known to exist when static pool data were collected also simplifies the task of modifying the original unconditional probability distribution of macroenvironments to better reflect the likely future influence of the macroeconomy.[4] The qualification and judgment that go into the synthesis of the loss distribution constitute a significant portion of the credit analysis.

The hallmark of an efficient market is not whether all risks have been eliminated but how quickly the market adjusts to changing conditions. In structured finance, as the range of potential macroeconomic outcomes reveals itself over time, a properly constructed analytical framework should respond likewise by effectively reducing the macro-level universe that gave birth to the credit enhancement to a narrower range, leaving as a residual a much more predictable microeconomic default process in which the level of risk facing security-holders would become a virtual certainty. The main cause of inefficiency in structured markets today is the failure to explicitly recognize and separate the two levels of risk. As a result, cash is too often held "hostage" inside seasoned structured transactions for reasons that have long since disappeared.

Calculating the Effect of Time

By no means are we claiming reliable knowledge from the joint analysis of micro-macro process—only greater verisimilitude. Moreover, a credit rating can only address known and measurable risks when issued. Furthermore, as the object of nonstationary forces, it can rarely be expected to last until maturity. By the ergodic hypothesis, we are justified in linking initial rating estimates to subsequent estimates, and through a Markov process modulated for macroeconomic instabilities, we can then visualize the full distribution of risk to a structured security.

When the assets begin to amortize, their essential credit quality reveals itself incrementally through time. Let us not forget that a structured security is a portfolio embedded in a system of controls: as the pool exposure and the time-to-maturity wind down, the current expected loss may have changed in relation to the original expected loss, but the ultimate loss number becomes increasingly certain as the likelihood of a disturbance to the pool payment trend becomes increasingly remote. The credit quality of securities backed by *performing* pools therefore will always strengthen vis-à-vis the initial expectation, while the credit quality of securities backed by *nonperforming* pools will deteriorate, according to an irreversible logic that we explore more fully below with worked examples using a simple model of stochastic credit loss behavior.

The Nonlinearity of Structured Ratings

The pricing of structured securities is largely determined by their credit ratings; but because the excess spread generated by the difference between the WAC and the weighted average interest on the bonds is also a part of the security structure, pricing can also directly affect the credit of a structured security. Unlike corporate bonds, structured debt cannot be rated and priced in two independent steps. Because rating and pricing are inextricably linked, both must be derived simultaneously within an iterative (and, ideally, convergent) process. To know the rating, one must know the promised yield; but to know the yield, one must know the rating. This inseparable relationship is why credit ratings arise as the solution to an essentially nonlinear problem.

If the basic structure is known a priori, this conundrum may be resolved by starting with a "guesstimate" of the credit rating. Prior experience with similar structures simplifies the estimation of average life so that the coupon rate can be estimated based on current credit spreads. When taken into a cash flow "engine," these initial estimates produce new average lives and reductions of yield on the securities. The output values in turn correspond to interest rates on the yield curve, which may or may not match the input rates. The key to the proper credit analysis is to use differences between the two, if any, to derive an update rule for the coupon rates. Properly done, coupon rates and credit ratings then converge pairwise toward a consistent solution.

It is of course artificial and incorrect to assume the structure to be known a priori, since the "right" structure is precisely what is being sought to achieve optimal funding costs. The essence of structured finance is precisely the ability to design structures ex nihilo. If, in addition to computing credit ratings and coupon rates, the problem requires the simultaneous design of liability structures, the convergence processes just described will invariably include additional elements reflecting possible structural variations. Adding structure as an unknown significantly increases the labor involved in fairly pricing structured securities.

Without an explicit recognition of the interdependence between structural elements and credit ratings within a nonlinear framework, resulting structures will almost certainly be suboptimal, with either the sell side or the buy side paying for this suboptimality.

The Possibility of Structural Optimization

In the marketplace and in academic literature, considerable confusion exists over the difference in meaning between value creation and optimization. In one sense, they are related. *Optimization* increases average wealth by redistributing the margins of risk and return locally; *value creation* increases total wealth. However, in an important sense, these concepts are also opposed, or orthogonal. True optimization becomes possible only when total value has been determined. This is the lesson we draw from the Modigliani-Miller proposition 1 (MM-1) which states the following:

> The average cost of capital to any firm is completely independent of its capital structure and is given by capitalizing its expected return at the rate ρ appropriate to its risk class.

In the context of structured finance, MM-1 asserts the independence of the value of assets of the SPE from the structure of the SPE liabilities. If MM-1 did not obtain, it would be possible to boost asset valuation by making changes to the capital structure. There are rating games (to which we have alluded in the section on the continuum hypothesis) that create the illusion of "finding" more cash flow by tranching the liabilities so that the junior tranche rating is just above, not just below, the investment-grade cutoff point. But this is not true value creation. It is a zero-sum game inadvertently tolerated within an alphanumeric rating system at the expense of the investor.

The lesson to be drawn from MM-1 is the importance of not confusing the SPE's assets with its liabilities. The asset cash flow analysis needs to be made first, followed by an analysis of the liabilities given the amount and timing of cash flows. In the next two chapters, we approach the analysis of assets and liabilities of the SPE in greater detail.

7

Dynamic Asset Analysis

The assertion that the risk profile of a structured security changes over time is not new. In fact, the key conclusion of Moody's pioneering study of MBS rating upgrades and downgrades, known as *rating transitions*, is that "rating revisions are correlated with the aging of underlying asset pools." The study describes the changing credit contour of MBS based on performance data from 1987 to 1994 as follows:

> [V]ery few rating changes occur within two years of issuance. By the third year, the pace of rating changes increases, with downgrades exceeding upgrades by more than two to one when weighted by the distance of the rating movement. Interestingly, upgrades outnumber downgrades through the sixth year following issuance, but when weighted by the distance of the movement, average rating quality is still shifted downwards. Again, this is due in part to the initial ratings being predominantly in the highest rating categories, with only downward rating changes available to them.[1]

Moody's followup 1996 study reconfirms these tendencies but shows less negative drift.[2]

Standard & Poor's study of RMBS rating transitions in 2001 draws very definitive conclusions about stability and positive drift. A comparison of performance results done in 2000 with rating transitions of RMBS for the period 1978–1999 shows the credit ratings of RMBS at the one-, three-, five-, ten-, and fifteen-year transition periods to be "remarkably more stable than corporate bonds," and attributes the results to good collateral and good structures. In particular, the ratio of downgrades (588) to upgrades (162) in corporate bonds was nearly exactly reversed in RMBS, with 164 downgrades and 556 upgrades in 2000.[3]

Nor is the observed difference versus corporate securities strictly an MBS phenomenon. The first ABS rating transition study, published by Moody's in 1996, concludes that "the overall rating volatility in the asset-backed securities market since its inception has been comparable to that of the mortgage-backed securities market but lower than that of the traditional corporate bond market during the same period."[4]

While not new, the implication runs counter to the assumption of corporate equivalency underlying the use of the corporate rating as a metric of structured performance. Indeed, in the early days of the market, senior managers in Moody's believed strongly that, despite the relative emphasis on loss rather than default, the performance characteristics of structured deals would roughly converge with those of corporate bonds.[5]

The point is explicitly made in Moody's 2001 transition study, *Rating Changes in the U.S. Asset-Backed Securities Market: First-Ever Transition Matrix Indicates Ratings Stability . . . To Date,* which considers U.S. dollar–denominated securities backed by CDOs, home equity loans, and most other traditional ABS collateral but excluding ABCP, CMBS, and most RMBS, from the public, private, and 144A markets:

> Asset-backed security ratings have experienced lower transition rates than corporate ratings since 1986. However, over the long run, we expect asset-backed transitions to lead to credit losses roughly equal to those of corporate securities.[6]

Standard & Poor's ABS rating transition study of 2001, which is based on a comparable deal population, offers different insights. It documents how the spreads on less highly rated ABS deals tightened vis-à-vis the spreads on comparably rated corporate credits in 2000, reversing a long-standing trend and reflecting an expectation of less negative volatility. The same study confirms the positive relationship between seasoning and positive ABS ratings drift from 1985 to 2000 first identified in the 1995 RMBS transition study:

> The pattern of a positive association between the length of the transition period and the significance of the transition is clearly demonstrated by the average five-year transition ratio. Even "AAA"s experienced 0.85% downgrades. It is remarkable that only 0.95% of "BBB"s experienced downgrades, to "BB." All other transitions were upgrades, with 8.57% moving all the way to "AAA."[7]

The Standard & Poor's study also candidly addresses the discrepancies between ratings volatility and real volatility—credit events resulting in security default or loss. Single-A-rated structured debt had fewer rating changes and showed a slight negative drift but experienced the highest historical level of real default, 0.45%. All transitions of single-B-rated debt were downgrades, yet the securities have experienced no actual defaults to date. Ratings on BBB and BB classes showed an upward drift, yet the BB range has a one-year average default of 0.38%.

These findings are significant. First, they highlight the subjective element in rating transition. Second, they underscore the difference between rating transitions and credit risk volatility. Rating transitions are the outcome of a human process by which a committee of analysts decides to raise or lower the rating. Many factors can intervene in the accuracy or timely implementation of a revised rating judgment, and it is difficult to gauge how accurately the rating transitions reflect essential volatility—particularly because the rating agencies publish studies of ratings volatility only as a proxy for credit risk volatility, and moreover, the exact process underlying credit rating modifications is not transparent. To date, no evidence has ever been marshaled to dismiss the hypothesis that observed rating stability, in reality, is an artifact of the static rating.

Seasoning and the Theoretical Credit Curve

All structured securities have a dimension of statistical certainty unfolding through time that sets them apart from corporate bonds. Even though, at closing, the exact maturity value of the loss distribution on a structured security is unknown, over time its ability to meet the payment promise becomes increasingly certain—and on average, most securities will perform to expectation. The studies in the previous section offer empirical evidence that the returns of structured securities have a characteristic positive drift. This section presents a formal exposition of the drift phenomenon by replicating the process by which losses might develop in actual structured pools.

Transaction Model

The following simplified asset-behavior/transaction model will now be used to highlight the essential features of structured securities:

- Collateral with stochastic losses determined by geometric Brownian motion
- A case-specific amount of credit enhancement
- A case-specific security interest rate
- Excess spread leaked from the transaction and returned to the issuer at each payment period
- A single tranche of liabilities with a bullet principal repayment, annual interest payments, and a seven-year maturity
- A bid-ask spread of 10 bps
- Collateral liquidated in the market at maturity to repay the principal balance outstanding
- Obligor defaults modeled as secular downward trend in the market value of the collateral, with some defaults occurring even in performing pools due to random effects
- Defaults that occur according to a stochastic process resulting in pool losses (loss amount capped at 100% of the initial pool principal balance)
- A transaction rating based on the security's reduction of yield

The structure does not have excess spread capture, dynamic reserving, early amortization of the principal balance, or any of the other commonplace capital-redirecting mechanisms that enhance performance and thus temper the volatility of security losses over time. Thus, this streamlined market-value model provides the purest and, in some sense, most basic example of drift in structured securities due to decreasing portfolio loss volatility.

Default Process

Geometric Brownian motion is selected as the default process paradigm because it is non-negative and well understood by most finance professionals, having been used repeatedly as a paradigm of stock price behavior. Because the theory has been presented in comprehensive detail by several other authors,[8] this section presents only as much of the derivation as is required. Any reader not familiar with the derivation of equation (7.2) should consult the above reference.

For an index $x(t)$, geometric Brownian motion is defined by the following equation:

$$\frac{dx}{x} = \mu dt + \sigma dz \qquad (7.1)$$

where μ is the drift, σ is the volatility, and dz is a Wiener process. That is, we have $E(dz) = 0$ and $E([dz]^2) = dt$ ($E[\cdot]$ is the mathematical expectation operator).

Using Ito's lemma for stochastic differentials and setting $y = \ln x$, we have

$$dy = \left[\left(\frac{d\ln x}{dx}\right)\mu x + \frac{1}{2}\left(\frac{d^2 \ln x}{dx^2}\right)\sigma^2 x^2\right] dt + \left(\frac{d\ln x}{dx}\right)\sigma x dz$$

Simplification yields

$$dy = \left(\mu - \frac{1}{2}\sigma^2\right) dt + \sigma dz. \qquad (7.2)$$

Equation (7.2) implies a normal stochastic process for $y(t)$ with the following parameters:

$$\text{Mean of } y(t)[m(t)] = y(t_0) + \left(\mu - \frac{1}{2}\sigma^2\right)(t - t_0) \qquad (7.3)$$

$$\text{Variance of } y(t)[sd^2(t)] = \sigma^2(t - t_0) \qquad (7.4)$$

Reduction of Yield

At the maturity of the transaction, the expected reduction of yield must be calculated. Pool performance variables may be taken as the following:

I_0 = Initial balance of the security

R = Annual rate of interest on the security

$L(T)$ = Brownian motion loss index value at the maturity of the transaction

CE = Credit enhancement as subordination

$T =$ Years to maturity

$t_0 = 0$

Given the parameters μ and σ of the default process expressed in equation (7.2), imagine now that $(\mu - 1/2 \cdot \sigma^2)(t - t_0)$ is the average logarithmic rate of credit loss formation and that $\ln[L(t_0)] + (\mu - 1/2 \cdot \sigma^2)(t - t_0)$ is thus the average logarithm of credit loss at any point from $t = t_0$ to $t = T$.

Assuming interest is paid until liquidation from available spread, the yield IRR(L) on the asset-backed security is the solution to the following equation:

$$I_0 = R \cdot I_0 \sum_{i=1}^{T}\left[\frac{1}{1 + \text{IRR}(L)}\right]^i + \frac{I_0 - \max(L - CE,0)}{[1 + \text{IRR}(L)]^T} \qquad (7.5)$$

By construction, $P_0 = I_0 + CE$ holds at closing, where P_0 is the initial balance of the collateral pool. Given the structure presented above, the yield on the security is then only a function of $L(T)$, the loss index at maturity assumed to behave according to the stochastic loss process in equation (7.2).

Neglecting values of $L(T)$ greater than P_0, the average yield reduction ΔIRR can be computed from equation (7.2):

$$\Delta\text{IRR} = R - \frac{1}{sd(T) \cdot \sqrt{2\pi}} \int_0^1 e^{-[\{\ln L(T) - m(T)\}/sd(T)]^2} \text{IRR}[L(T)]d \ln L(T) \quad (7.6)$$

In equation (7.6), $m(T)$ and $sd(T)$ are the mean and standard deviation, respectively, of the normal distribution of $\ln[L(T)]$ at time $t = T$.

The only remaining unknown parameter is the starting value $\ln(L[t_0])$. It is safe to assume that $\ln(L[t_0])$ will be at least as large as the bid-ask spread on a similar pool of collateral; how much larger depends on relative liquidity. Once $\ln(L[t_0])$ has been determined, equation (7.6) allows ABS credit ratings for this security to be computed at various times from closing to maturity.

Scenarios

The basic structured rating model discussed previously is applied to three separate situations:

1. Well-performing collateral
2. Poorly performing collateral
3. An offsetting relationship between credit losses and the passage of time in which the rating is left unchanged (a case that is of largely academic interest)

Case 1: Performing Pool

In this case, we assume that losses build up according to the mean value of the index $m(t)$ given by equation (7.3). The associated structured rating will therefore change according to the distribution of remaining losses from t to T.

Table 7.1
Point Estimate Reductions of Yield: Case 1, Seven-Year Bullet, 8% Coupon

Time	Rating	ΔIRR
0	BBB	25.89
1	BBB	24.80
2	BBB+	22.82
3	BBB+	20.06
4	BBB+	16.93
5	A−	13.86
6	A	10.45
7	AAA	0.00

To concretize this example, assume the security coupon is 8% and that it has already been structured at closing by the rating agencies to a BB level of payment certainty. This translates roughly into a loss coverage ratio between 1.0 and 1.5, and the midpoint (i.e., 1.25) is chosen arbitrarily. To find the values of parameters μ and σ, we also assume that the bid-ask spread is 10 bps, the coefficient of variation (σ/μ) is 0.5, subordination is 10%, and the initial bullet maturity is seven years.

Using these parameters, we have the following system:

$$\log\left(\frac{0.10}{1.25}\right) = \log 0.001 + \left(\mu - \frac{1}{2}\sigma^2\right) \cdot 7 \qquad (7.7)$$

$$0.5 = \frac{\sigma}{\mu} \qquad (7.8)$$

The solution is the smallest positive root of $\mu^2 - 8\mu + 5.008 = 0$. This yields $\mu = 0.6846$ and, using equation (7.7), we obtain $\sigma = 0.3423$.

In order to compute the average reduction of yield expected on this security at closing, we also need $m(7) = \ln(0.08)$ and $sd(7) = 0.3423 \cdot \sqrt{7} = 0.9056$. In this case, equation (7.6) results in an average reduction of yield (ΔIRR) of 25.89 bps.

This maps to a Moody's structured rating of Baa2[9] or to BBB in the Standard & Poor's nomenclature. Note that, according to Moody's, a BB structured security should lose approximately 70–100 bps on average, given its 1.25x cushion. From the agency point of view, our default model therefore appears to underestimate expected losses at closing. The remaining entries in Table 7.1 were likewise computed by assuming that the loss index's actual path follows its expected value throughout. Time is calculated in years from closing, and ΔIRR is in basis points. Figure 7.1 shows the same data graphically.

With all the shortcomings of the model, the previous analysis nevertheless shows that the transaction warrants upgrades at the beginning of years 3

Figure 7.1. Credit Curve for Case 1, Seven-Year Bullet, 8% Coupon

(BBB to BBB+), 5 (BBB+ to A−), 6 (A− to A), and 7 (A to AAA). Real transactions, which are generally much more complex than simple bullet-repayment structures, tend to have performance-stabilizing features such as excess spread capture and early amortization of their principal balance. Such features would force the rate of credit improvement to begin earlier and occur more evenly over time, smoothing out the sharp drop-off in the last period.

Table 7.2 presents the same scenario with a 5% coupon to highlight the early beneficial yield effect of higher interest rates for long-dated transactions. Note that the reduction of yield in the 5% coupon case is higher than in the

Table 7.2
Point Estimate Reductions of Yield: Case 1, Seven-Year Bullet, 5% Coupon

Time	Rating	ΔIRR
0	BBB−	29.20
1	BBB	27.34
2	BBB	24.58
3	BBB	21.14
4	A−	17.49
5	A−	14.07
6	A	10.45
7	AAA	0.00

Table 7.3
Point Estimate Reductions of Yield: Case 1, Six-Year Bullet, 8% Coupon

Time	Rating	ΔIRR
0	A+	4.84
1	A+	3.74
2	AA−	2.65
3	AA−	1.65
4	AA	0.76
5	AA+	0.11
6	AAA	0.00

8% case early on but loses that disadvantage as the maturity draws nearer and liquidation becomes the major driver.

To demonstrate the impact of extension risk, Table 7.3 shows one last case of a performing deal with a shorter, six-year maturity at 8%. In this case, the deal closes at the high single-A level and steadily progresses to AAA. Based on this model, we conclude that regardless of interest rate or maturity, when the underlying collateral is performing, the credit rating of a structured security should always improve with seasoning.

Case 2: Nonperforming Pool

In this case, assume for argument's sake that performance data indicate that run-rate losses on the deal are actually 25% worse than expected on a logarithmic basis. In terms of the model, this can be expressed by saying that the mean value of $\ln(L[t])$ is 25% higher than the original forecast from $t = 0$ to the present. The model simulates this fact by computing the mean of the loss index as

$$\text{mean of } \log[L(t)] = \log[L(0)] + 1.25\left(\mu - \frac{1}{2}\sigma^2\right)(t - t_0) \qquad (7.9)$$

Table 7.4
Point Estimate Reductions of Yield: Case 2, Seven-Year Bullet, 8% Coupon

Time	Rating	ΔIRR
0	BBB	25.89
1	BBB−	35.42
2	BB+	49.32
3	BB+	70.42
4	BB	104.65
5	B+	168.90
6	CCC+	347.13
7	Default	1,547.55

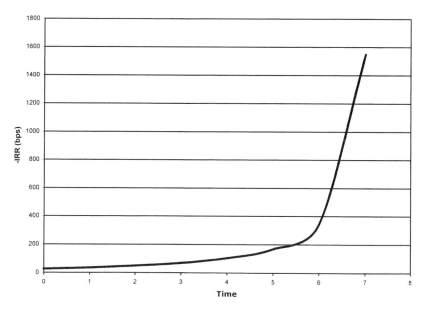

Figure 7.2. Credit Curve for Case 2, Seven-Year Bullet, 8% Coupon

The remaining calculations are identical to those in case 1. Table 7.4 and Figure 7.2 show the corresponding history of this transaction's credit rating from inception to maturity. In this case, although the actual loss will not be recognized until maturity, the certainty of loss increases with each period. Tables 7.5 and 7.6 correspond to the additional runs presented in case 1. The outcome for a six-year transaction shown here is much less traumatic, the final loss being on the order of 1% instead of the 15% bloodbath for the first two cases. Nevertheless, the conclusion is the same. Regardless of interest rates or the maturities, the credit quality of ABS securities backed by pools of nonperforming collateral gradually deteriorates over time until default.

If the ratings of transactions with performing collateral improve (case 1) and those of nonperforming deals deteriorate (case 2) there must be intermediate cases where the rating remains constant. The next (rather academic) example demonstrates how a static ABS rating might occur.

Case 3: The Academic Case of a Static ABS Rating

Through trial and error, we can determine the value of the loss adjustment factor (it was 25% in case 2) such that the average reduction of yield on the security remains approximately constant. When the loss adjustment factor on the above transaction is set to 5%, the credit rating history shown in Table 7.7 results.

Note that since ultimate losses fall below the 10% available credit enhancement, the security's credit rating still telescopes to AAA at maturity, but

Table 7.5
Point Estimate Reductions of Yield: Case 2, Seven-Year Bullet, 5% Coupon

Time	Rating	ΔIRR
0	BBB−	29.20
1	BBB−	39.12
2	BB+	53.36
3	BB	74.61
4	BB−	108.61
5	B+	171.90
6	CCC+	347.13
7	Default	1,547.55

remains essentially constant from closing till maturity. We include this contrived case here to illustrate the practical absurdity of a theoretical case for static structured ratings. In the main, transactions either perform fairly well or do not perform at all. The historical evidence, as reported by the rating agencies,[10] is that they mostly perform. The *rate* at which ratings improve depends on specific deal parameters, but the improvement will always be monotonic for continuously performing deals. The data feed that evidences improvement or deterioration is the periodic remittance report, which provides all the data required to calculate the effect of drift on ratings.

This transaction model is clearly a simplification of reality whereby collateral behaves according to a basic lognormal stochastic loss process and deteriorates monotonically.[11] Actual collateral performance would be much more chaotic given the influences of changing collection practices or the inevitable "balance-sheet management" effect at year end. But real-life performance effects do not change fundamental dynamics. Excess spread availability and early amortization, for example, would tend to increase the rate at which ratings improve by shortening the average life. For deals with multiple tranches, the analysis would see a differential rate of improvement or deterio-

Table 7.6
Point Estimate Reductions of Yield: Case 2, Six-Year Bullet, 8% Coupon

Time	Rating	ΔIRR
0	A+	4.84
1	A	6.08
2	A	7.69
3	A−	10.00
4	BBB+	13.86
5	BBB	22.99
6	Default	104.57

Table 7.7
Point Estimate Reductions of Yield: Case 3, Seven-Year Bullet, 8% Coupon

Time	Rating	ΔIRR
0	BBB	25.89
1	BBB	26.68
2	BBB	26.81
3	BBB	26.23
4	BBB	25.22
5	BBB	24.70
6	BBB	26.56
7	AAA	0.00

ration depending on the investor's position within the capital structure—tranching being a mechanism for reapportioning risk among different classes of investors. Across some range of collateral performance, including nonperforming collateral, triggers stabilize the ratings of nonperforming ABS transactions, but nothing can save a portfolio that is short on cash from defaulting. In the end, the statistical weight of performing or nonperforming collateral on the changing credit profile of structured transactions will always prevail.

Dynamic Overenhancement

The credit rating of structured transactions is linked to the certainty and sufficiency of capital in various forms (credit enhancement) to absorb credit losses: the more excess capital available, the higher the rating. However, as indicated in the last section, a static corporate rating on a structured transaction will generally fail to accurately reflect the true dynamics of structured credit quality. In a few cases, agency ratings overstate the amount of investor protection in the transaction, but in the majority of cases they understate it. In the latter case, some portion of credit enhancement must therefore be redundant in most transactions as they mature. An approximation of the level of such waste is offered via the following simplified analysis.

Assume that, with respect to some transaction, Class A notes have been issued and rated at closing by a rating agency. The transaction is performing and, as a result of its particular structure, the average reduction of yield on the Class A notes can be approximated fairly consistently over time by a quadratic function $f(t)$ starting from its initial value $f(0) = b$. In other words, we have

$$f(t) = \Delta\text{IRR}(t) = -at^2 + b, \, a > 0, \, t \geq 0 \qquad (7.10)$$

By construction, the average reduction of yield given by the curve in equation (7.10) will fall to zero at some time t_0 given by the solution to

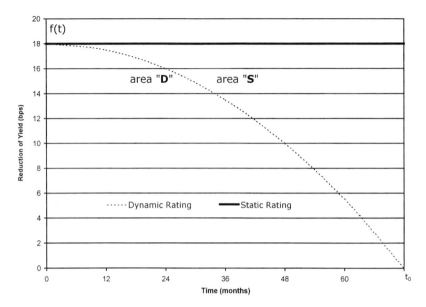

Figure 7.3. Illustration of Redundant Capital

$$f(t_0) = 0 \qquad (7.11)$$

Assume also that initial capital reserved against this ABS exposure is a multiple of the average reduction of yield as determined by the initial agency rating (a fairly good approximation to a consistent method) and that, as is customary, the agency rating remains static throughout the life of this transaction. The problem is to determine what percentage of capital is wasted over the life of this transaction assumed to be outstanding from $t = 0$ to $t = t_0$ for convenience, as a result of the static rating.

Graphically, the situation can be represented as in Figure 7.3. The horizontal line intersecting $f(t)$ at time zero represents the static agency rating while the curve $f(t)$ is the actual transaction rating, in view of its credit quality, assumed to behave quadratically. If we define S as the area between $f(t)$ and the static rating line, and D as that below the dynamic curve $f(t)$, then on a constant principal balance outstanding, the amount of wasted capital (%) is $S/(S + D)$. By definition, the area under $f(t)$ is

$$\int_0^{t_0}(-at^2 + b)\,dt = bt_0 - \frac{1}{3}\,at_0^3. \qquad (7.12)$$

We also have by definition $S = (S + D) - D = bt_0 - (bt_0 - [1/3]at_0^3) = (1/3)at_0^3$. But since, by equation (7.11), we have $a = b/t_0^2$ and $S + D = bt_0$, we finally arrive at our rough estimate for wasted capital:

$$\text{Redundant Capital} = \frac{S}{S + D} = \frac{1}{3} \qquad (7.13)$$

Under this simple model, about 33% of the capital reserved over its lifetime against this performing tranche is being squandered by measuring required capital using static ratings. As posited, the model applies to any invested amount and to all initial average reductions of yield, hence to all initial ratings. Further, if the transaction remains outstanding beyond $t = t_o$, redundant capital is greater than 1/3 by definition.

One can punch many holes in this argument. For one, there is no guarantee that reductions of yield will behave quadratically. However, under any rational choice, although the precise amount of relative over-enhancement would change, the transaction would still be wasting some capital. Our own stochastic model shows a more or less linear improvement early on followed by a quasi-exponential drop-off in the last period; however, that model largely understates the credit situation in realistic transactions. Real deals are equipped with many credit features such as unconditional excess spread captures and early amortization that would increase the rate of improvement beyond the quasi-linear regime. Moreover, credit losses do not occur linearly according to the default process given in this model but rather, as explained in chapter 2, follow a characteristic loss curve. This loss behavior would tend to accelerate the rate of improvement in the middle of a transaction, bringing it closer to the postulated quadratic form.

Although these arguments by no means amount to a proof, they tend to indicate that a significant portion of capital originally reserved against performing ABS exposures will continue to cover essentially nonexistent risks. Were this capital re-deployed intelligently and efficiently, it would more than offset investor losses on the few transactions that in fact do not perform. By their nature, investors like additional security; but they might feel differently if the capital now being wasted on good deals were selectively re-allocated to cover excessive losses on nonperforming deals they, in fact, own. Capital inefficiency obviously benefits some market participants in the short term, but it will benefit no one in the long term.

8

Liabilities Analysis and Structuring

Until now our focus has been mainly to critique the contemporary framework for rating structured securities and propose a replacement framework. In this section, we introduce some basic concepts related to the cash flow modeling of liability structures—the "structure" of structured finance. We will return to this topic in our concluding remarks.

There are two reasons for this book's emphasis on asset analysis. The first is the priority of complexity. Because bond structures are logical constructs rather than statistical estimates, liability modeling involves the application of simple rules of logic to the distribution of periodic cash collections. It is relatively straightforward. By contrast, faithful replication of asset behavior is less straightforward, and requires the knowledge and use of numerical methods, such as those introduced in part III and demonstrated in chapters 20 through 22.

The second is a matter of value for effort. Much of the current suboptimality in the cash flow analysis of structured securities arises from shortcuts taken in analyzing the assets, not the liabilities. Moreover, structural design is largely dictated by market convention rather than capital optimality. In most asset classes, investors have grown comfortable with a restricted set of structural alternatives that they feel adequately address their concerns and their need for downside protection. For instance, the complex bond structure of the first global aircraft portfolio lease securitization (Guinness Peat Aviation) reflects certain idiosyncratic operating constraints of the seller. Nevertheless, most aircraft lease securitizations since then have copied the GPA structure, even though the risks and challenges are very different. GPA is still considered "the only way to do" aircraft leases. It is perhaps regrettable that the preferences of today's investor reduce the motivation to seek structural optimality.

Liability structures may be simple, but they are not dull, and it should never be assumed from the simple, intuitive nature of the payment rules that the impact of the structure on the credit quality of a structured security will also be simple and intuitive; quite the contrary. Particularly when structural features are imported wholesale from unrelated transactions, frequently unwanted rating implications might be dramatic. The impact of such features often can be quantified only by modeling the precise liability structure within a cash flow engine. How to model the structure to understand its credit impact is the main topic of this chapter.

The Payment Rules (Waterfall)

The rules that govern the collection and distribution of cash to various parties during the course of the transaction are normally contained in the pooling and servicing agreement (P&S, first mentioned in chapter 2). The P&S is a legally binding document, in contrast to the prospectus or offering memorandum, which the SEC treats as marketing material. In addition to a variety of other legal, operational, and regulatory stipulations, the P&S contains a set of payment instructions commonly referred to as the *waterfall*.[1] These instructions represent the priority of liability claims against the assets of the trust. The P&S also typically includes contingent instructions for when and how the rules may be altered if conditions change.

In the remainder of this chapter, the terms *waterfall* and *structure* are used interchangeably. Although the principles of payment waterfall mechanics are the same regardless of how many tranches of debt are created, in order to concretize our description we will restrict our discussion to a two-tranche structure (A and B).

To ease the reader into the rather specialized waterfall-related vocabulary, we first review some basic terminology:

Waterfall	Rules contained in the P&S that specify the order of priority in which cash will be distributed to the various stakeholders in funds collected by the SPE. Each item in the distribution list is referred to as a *level*. A waterfall may have any number of levels.
Collection period	Within a structured financing, the minimum time span in which cash accumulates in a segregated account for future distribution. A collection period is normally sandwiched between two record dates.
Record Date	The date that marks the end of one collection period and the beginning of the next.
Determination Date	The date on which funds available for distribution are precisely determined. In practice, this determination is largely a reconciliation process by the servicer handling the collection system.
Calculation Date	The date on which all fund allocations are computed, either by the trustee or by some other designated party.
Distribution Date	The date on which cash is transferred to the various stakeholder accounts established at closing.
Payment Date	The date on which the funds, previously distributed, are transferred to the target stakeholder accounts.

Class	A rung in the hierarchy of payments within the waterfall. Classes usually bear alphabetical designations (A, B, etc.). Seniority normally is denoted by alphabetical order, beginning with A as the most senior class.
Bond structure	In its most basic meaning, both the principal allocation method and the relative percentage issued in each bond class. There are two main types of bond structures: *sequential* and *pro rata*. Otherwise, it refers to the entire allocation method used in the waterfall, which may involve features like insurance policies and special allocation mechanisms such as planned and targeted amortization classes (see later sections).
Pari passu	An expression whereby two separate stakeholders having the same priority of claim on cash flow proceeds in the waterfall are said to rank pari passu.
Available Funds	The aggregate amount of cash readily available to pay trust liabilities on any given payment date. Although the primary source of Available Funds is the collection account, other ready forms of credit enhancement, including the reserve account, the spread account, and distributions from surety bonds, are always included in Available Funds.
Total Principal Due	Aggregate amount of principal amount due to investors each payment date, generally counted as the periodic reduction in the asset pool's outstanding principal balance.
Reserve Account	Cash deposited into a segregated account at closing for the benefit of the trustee to pay future trust liabilities. The reserve account is usually funded at closing from proceeds.
Spread Account	A kind of reserve account that builds to its stated amount from an initial deposit using excess spread rather than proceeds. The initial deposit is often zero.
Cumulative Principal Due	Cumulative principal amounts due to investors as measured from closing to the current payment date. This amount is generally equal to the difference between the original pool balance and the current pool balance.
Sequential	A term describing a structure in which total principal amounts due are fully allocated to the most sen-

ior class outstanding until the principal balance of that class is reduced to zero, before any principal is allocated to a more junior class.

Pro Rata

A term describing a structure in which total principal due is allocated strictly in proportion to the initial principal balance of each class.

Trustee

The natural or legal person tasked with the safekeeping of the funds owed to stakeholders in the SPE. A trustee makes distributions to investors and others (stakeholders) out of trust accounts on each payment date. A trustee must carry liability insurance and have a contractually determined minimum net worth. As a matter of market practice, trustees are usually commercial banks or their subsidiaries.

Servicer

The organization that will perform various collection and administrative functions on behalf of the trustee during the course of the transaction. In most cases, the servicer is the originator of the receivables transferred to the SPE at closing. Many transactions are equipped with a backup servicer to replace the original servicer if it proves unable to acquit itself of its obligations for whatever reason (mainly bankruptcy). Backup servicers can be "hot" or "cold." A *cold backup servicer* stands by in the event of a primary servicer failure. A *hot backup servicer* acts as a shadow-servicer by receiving monthly reports and performing many of the operations of the primary servicer so that it can spring into action immediately upon primary servicer failure.

Surety bond

An insurance policy issued by special-purpose insurers that guarantees required interest and principal payments to bond holders should insufficient funds be available from regular collections and other sources of credit enhancement. Because this is their sole line of business, such institutions are normally referred to as *monoline* insurers. The bonds they guarantee are given the same rating as the insurer (generally AAA but sometimes also A). Structured bonds promise timely interest but ultimate principal only, leaving monolines with significant flexibility in how to fulfill their obligations under the surety agreement. A surety bond is an insurance policy on the liabilities, not the assets, and should never be confused with other forms of credit enhancement that offer protection against individual obligor defaults (e.g., default insurance).

Amortization period   A predefined period of time in which principal received is to be distributed to investors as a partial repayment of the original investment. In amortizing transactions, the amortization period spans the entire length of the transaction.

Revolving period   A predefined period of time in which principal collections, rather than being repaid to investors, are to be reinvested in new eligible receivables. During the revolving period, Total Principal Due has the same value as during the amortization period, but principal amounts due on individual classes of securities are zero.

Trigger   Generally, a predefined, contingent modification in the operation of a structured transaction that is caused or "triggered" by the truth of a certain prestipulated condition. Triggers may be local, affecting only specific portions of a transaction, or global, resulting in a fundamental transactional change up to and including immediate termination. Triggers are further partitioned into two main types: curable and noncurable. *Curable triggers* may be reversed if the relevant condition becomes false, either within a given time period or at any time. *Noncurable triggers* are irrevocable. Analytically, the most interesting triggers are cash flow triggers: contingent cash reallocation mechanisms based on predefined indices. The philosophy underlying such triggers is the diversion of funds from certain stakeholders (to whom they were originally allocated) to other stakeholders, to increase the amount of credit protection due to the latter at the expense of the former.

Cash Cycle of the SPE

Before discussing the waterfall, it should be noted that payments for certain professional services are not reflected in the waterfall since they are paid from transaction proceeds. Such services, which substantively terminate at closing, usually include legal, accounting, and rating services, but may also include specialized services like appraisals and background checks. The waterfall consists exclusively of ongoing liabilities. Although there are many variations, we present the most common schemes.

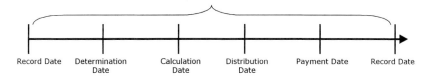

| Record Date | Determination
Date | Calculation
Date | Distribution
Date | Payment Date | Record Date |

Figure 8.1. The Cash Collection Cycle

Figure 8.1 is a schematic of the cash inflow-outflow cycle of a structured deal. A typical transaction consists of multiple nonoverlapping intervals or "collection period," each usually lasting one calendar month. However, collection periods are not limited to this or any other time interval.

During the inflow phase of any cycle, collections received from the underlying obligors are deposited into a segregated, liquid account (the *collection account*) over which the trustee has control at all times. Earnings on the collection account may or may not be part of trust's corpus. The inflow phase of a cycle corresponds to any collection period, while the outflow phase of the same cycle takes place, in real time, during the inflow phase of the next cycle, beginning on the next record date. Figure 8.1 shows the superposition of the cash inflow phase of one cycle with the cash outflow phase of the preceding cycle. Operationally, the issuer allocates its obligor cash receipts according to the definition of each collection period, which may vary slightly from month to month due to holidays and special circumstances.

The outflow phase of a cash cycle is separated into the following four distinct operations:

1. *Determination* of Available Funds (funds to be distributed) based on the precise contents of the collection account and other accounts and credit lines representing available credit enhancement, on the Determination Date.
2. *Calculation* by the trustee of the exact cash amounts distributable to all transaction participants from available funds, according to the priority of payments (waterfall), on the Calculation Date.
3. *Distribution* of the amounts computed in step 2 by transfer of funds to the various trust accounts and sub-accounts established at closing, on the Distribution Date.
4. *Payment*, or disbursement of the amounts deposited in step 3, to the stakeholders, on the Payment Date.

Regardless of whether these precise names are used, each of the previous four steps must be performed in this order to transfer funds out of trust accounts. The four dates are usually scheduled on different days to stagger the operations so as to take the timing of funds transfer into consideration and ensure timely distribution on the payment date. Realism in the timetable is of particular issue in cross-border transactions, where funds require multiple days to transfer and settle even under ordinary circumstances, and where consideration needs to be given to the possibility of payment-system issues that could delay the delivery of funds.

The cycle is repeated

- For as many collection periods as there are debt securities outstanding;
- Until cash has, for all intents and purposes, run out and the trust must be liquidated; or
- Until the legal final maturity of the transaction where liquidation normally takes place.

In the event that all trust liabilities are extinguished in the normal course or upon liquidation, the indenture is released and equity investors may deal with the corpus as they see fit. In the opposite case, bankruptcy courts will eventually decide on the fate of each class of investor.

Anatomy of the Waterfall

Strictly speaking, the term *waterfall* addresses merely the priority of payments out of available funds and does not necessarily stipulate how funds are to be allocated. Allocation mechanics of most types of liability are self-evident. However, when it comes to principal allocations, several alternatives are possible. The same section of the P&S that stipulates the waterfall usually contains an explicit description of the principal allocation method to be used as well. In some asset classes, the principal allocation method may also depend on related legal documents. For instance, it may differ among transactions that are related to the same master trust.

In order to illustrate basic payment mechanics, the following definitions will be used with respect to a hypothetical, fully collateralized two-tranche structure in the remainder of this section. We may not explicitly illustrate structural features that affect only Available Funds without introducing any additional conceptual difficulty. Reserve accounts, surety bonds, and other forms of outside credit enhancement are found under this rubric. For the sake of clarity, we assume they are not relevant to our hypothetical transaction.

Basic Transaction Parameters

$t \equiv$ The reference time index of any cash input-output cycle; by definition, t is an integer.

$r_A \equiv$ Class A periodic interest rate[2]

$r_A^p \equiv$ Class A periodic past-due rate

$r_B \equiv$ Class B periodic interest rate

$r_B^p \equiv$ Class B periodic past-due rate

$s_f \equiv$ Servicing periodic rate

$s_r \equiv$ Servicing periodic shortfall rate

$M(0) = A(0) + B(0)$ (see below)

$\alpha \equiv A(0)/M(0) = $ Class A advance rate, $\alpha \le 1$

Asset-Side Parameters

$M(t) \equiv$ Outstanding Pool Balance at time t

$D(t) \equiv$ Defaulted Receivable Balances at t

$PP(t) \equiv$ Prepaid Receivable Balances at t

$P_R(t) \equiv$ Regular Principal Collections at t

$I(t) \equiv$ Interest Collections at t

$P(t) \equiv$ Total Principal Due at t

$C(t) \equiv$ Cumulative Principal Due at t, $C(0) = 0$

Liability-Side Parameters

$A(t) \equiv$ Class A Principal Balance at t

$B(t) \equiv$ Class B Principal Balance at t

$I_A(t) \equiv$ Class A Interest Due at t

$I_B(t) \equiv$ Class B Interest Due at t

$P_A(t) \equiv$ Class A Principal Due at t

$P_B(t) \equiv$ Class B Principal Due at t

$F_i(t) \equiv$ Remaining Available Funds at time t and level i in the waterfall

$S(t) \equiv$ Servicing Fee Due at t

$R(t) \equiv$ Residual Payment Due to SPE stockholders at t

Quantities Ascertained on the Determination Date

Available Funds: $F_0(t) \equiv P_R(t) + PP(t) + I(t)$

Total Principal Due: $P(t) \equiv D(t) + P_R(t) + PP(t) = M(t-1) - M(t)$

Starting Class A Principal Balance: $A(t-1)$

Starting Class B Principal Balance: $B(t-1)$

Cumulative Principal Due: $C(t) = P(t) + C(t-1)$

As always, the shortfall amount with respect to any quantity is simply the amount due less the amount paid. Amounts paid are always subject to Available Funds.

Our standard two-tranche waterfall usually consists of the following six levels:

1. Servicing and other fees
2. Class A interest
3. Class B interest
4. Class A principal
5. Class B principal
6. Residual amount to SPE stockholders

In some (rare) cases, junior interest payments are subordinated to senior principal payments as follows:

1. Servicing and other fees
2. Class A interest
3. Class A principal
4. Class B interest
5. Class B principal
6. Residual amount to SPE stockholders

However, when this type of subordinated junior interest waterfall is used, the principal allocation method is usually a hybrid between the basic pro rata and sequential schemes since current junior interest payments must somehow be made attractive to buyers seeking higher yield. In the following pages we discuss the first three levels of the standard waterfall and then the principal allocation schemes. Most of the variability among waterfalls is associated with differences in principal allocation methods.

Senior Fees: Waterfall Level 1

The first position in the waterfall is typically reserved for essential services without which the transaction would not function at all. In addition to the normal servicing fees, claims in this category may include repayments of interim liquidity provided by the primary servicer (known as *servicer advances*), fees to collateral managers (*management fee*), and fees to the trustee. If investors benefit from a surety bond provided by a monoline insurer, the surety bond fee would come either at this first level or immediately after, ahead of Class A interest. Although there is a technical difference between paying surety fees pari passu with servicing fees or not, there is little practical difference because Available Funds are normally more than sufficient to pay all fees senior to interest payments. It is the norm for all fees found in first position in the waterfall to be paid pro rata.

Referencing the previous definitions, fees owed to the servicer and paid in arrears would be computed thus on any Calculation Date:

$$S(t) = s_f M(t-1) + S_S(t-1)(1 + s_r) \tag{8.1}$$

Here, the quantity $S_S(t-1)$ is the cumulative servicing fee shortfall[3] from previous periods. Note that the shortfall rate (s_r) on unpaid amounts, although compounding at the same frequency as the accrual rate (s_f), need not be equal to the latter. The servicing fee normally constitutes the bulk of distributions made at the first level of the waterfall. Note that the same formula with different rates normally applies to trustee and other fees.

Interest Payments: Waterfall Levels 2 and 3

In general, interest owed to bondholders consists of two components: current interest and past due interest, whose sum is the class interest due. In terms of the previous definitions, the respective interest amounts due on each class can be written as follows:

$$\text{Class A Interest Due: } I_A(t) = r_A A(t-1) + I_{AS}(t-1)(1 + r_A^p) \quad (8.2)$$

$$\text{Class B Interest Due: } I_B(t) = r_B B(t-1) + I_{BS}(t-1)(1 + r_B^p) \quad (8.3)$$

As was the case with servicing fees, the amounts $I_{AS}(t-1)$ and $I_{BS}(t-1)$ are the classwise cumulative interest shortfalls from previous periods.

In most transactions, recoveries on defaulted receivables are treated as interest collections. An amount equal to the aggregate principal balance of such defaulted receivables presumably was already applied to decrease the pool's outstanding balance at the time these defaults were recognized. In cases where earnings from any reserve or spread account are part of the trust's corpus, such amounts are also included in interest collections. In other words, interest collections are defined negatively, as what are not principal collections, rather than positively.

Principal Allocation Schemes: Pro Rata and Sequential

As indicated before, the bulk of the work involved in waterfall design is concerned with the various ways principal may be allocated dynamically to individual classes of bonds. The two chief methods of allocation, *pro rata* and *sequential*, are discussed in this section, while hybrid schemes such as Targeted Amortization Classes are discussed in chapter 10.

In all principal allocations schemes, the fundamental rationale is the same: to maintain equality between aggregate liabilities and aggregate assets throughout the life of the transaction. In order to fulfill this condition, the periodic reduction in aggregate liabilities must equal the periodic amortization of the assets arising from a combination of regular principal payments, prepayments, and defaulted receivables. Because defaults are a noncash item, the funds needed to effect an equivalent reduction will have to come from another source. Generically speaking, this source is credit enhancement.

In the main, credit enhancement usually consists of interest collections over and above those needed to pay periodic fees and make interest payments on the liabilities, the so-called *excess spread*. This excess spread can be used to make up the amount of defaulted receivables, and thus enable the aggregate liability balance to remain on par with the pool balance. In the simple case under study here, excess spread is the only source of credit enhancement. As explained before, in reality other sources will come into play.

Once an amount equal to defaulted receivables has been allocated using excess spread on every calculation date, there may still be funds remaining in the collection account. This might happen, for instance, because defaults were zero or simply less than the amount of excess interest collections for the most recent collection period. These funds, referred to as the *residual amount*, can be dealt with in any way acceptable to the parties. Normally, they would become the property of SPE stockholders and be distributed as a dividend on the next payment date. If the structure is equipped with a spread account feature, the money could also be used to fund it up to its required amount. In yet other cases, it could be used to further reduce the outstanding principal balance of a given class of securities, usually the senior-most class, beyond what is needed to maintain aggregate par with the assets. This is the *turbo concept* whereby the trust soon becomes over-collateralized at the expense of SPE stockholders.

The possibility that excess spread might leak out of a structure in the absence of defaults creates a strong incentive on the part of the trustee to ensure that accounts be written off on a timely basis. Any delay in default recognition will cause more excess spread to escape and be unavailable when the default is eventually recognized. However, the incentive not to recognize defaults will be strongest precisely when they are excessive, hence the need for close monitoring of transaction covenants. It is one of the chief tasks of a credit analyst to ensure via triggers[4] that the P&S does not contain a black hole where delinquent accounts may be parked without being written off, thus allowing excess spread to escape back to the seller.

Pro Rata Schemes: Waterfall Levels 4 and 5

Pro rata comes from the Latin for *according to proportions*. In a pro rata principal allocation scheme, Total Principal Due is allocated to each class of investor based on that investor's original contribution to the total investment, which amount is measured by the advance rate α[5] defined earlier. Here, as well, the principal amount due to each class of investor consists of the sum of current and past due components. Of these, only the first one is allocated pro rata. Using our list of definitions, these amounts would be computed as follows:

$$\text{Class A Principal Due: } P_A(t) = \alpha P(t) + P_{AS}(t-1) \qquad (8.4)$$

$$\text{Class B Principal Due: } P_B(t) = (1-\alpha)P(t) + P_{BS}(t-1) \qquad (8.5)$$

In these formulas, the quantities $P_{AS}(t-1)$ and $P_{BS}(t-1)$ represent the cumulative principal shortfalls from previous periods on Class A and Class B, respectively. As can be surmised, these amounts are much more likely to be different from zero than the equivalent amounts on interest or servicing fees.

The critical point to understand about principal allocation methods is that they refer merely to allocations and not to fund distributions. For example, if $10 of Available Funds is left after Class A and Class B interest amounts have been paid, $\alpha = 0.8$, and Total Principal Due is indeed $10, then Class A investors will receive $8 and Class B investors $2. With $10 of Available Funds and Total Principal Due of $8, Class A would receive a payment of $6.4 and Class B $1.6, with $2 left as the residual amount flowing back to the seller.

The structure becomes interesting only when insufficient funds are available to make the required distributions. To illustrate, if Class A investors are currently in a shortfall position, Available Funds will be used first to cover such shortfalls according to the above formula before any payment is made to Class B investors. Otherwise, the pro rata structure would effectively undermine the subordination of Class B to Class A investors. Even assuming zero shortfalls, if excessive defaults have caused Total Principal Due [$P(t)$] to exceed the $10 of Available Funds with no cash compensation, the allocation to Class A investors will be greater than $8 and will infringe on the expected receipts of Class B investors. A simple example should clarify this point:

$$F_2(t) = \$10$$
$$P(t) = \$12$$
$$P_{AS}(t-1) = P_{BS}(t-1) = 0$$
$$P_A(t) = 0.8 \times 12 = \$9.60$$
$$P_B(t) = (1 - 0.8) \times 12 = \$2.40$$
$$P_{BS}(t) = \$2.00$$
$$F_3(t) = \$0.00$$

As a result of this situation, Class A investors would receive $9.60 while Class B investors would receive only $0.40 out of their $2.40 allocation. The $2.00 difference would be recorded, as shown, as a principal shortfall on the Class B in this period with no shortfall on the Class A. However, even Class A investors would have suffered a shortfall if Available Funds [$F(t)$] had fallen below $9.60.

If $P_A(t)$ and $P_B(t)$ had been paid pari passu as well as pro rata, the situation would have been quite different. Both classes would have suffered proportional shortfalls, making them effectively the same class in their vulnerability to credit risk. In that case, the results would have been the following:

$$\text{Class A principal paid: } \frac{9.60}{12} \times \$10 = \$8.00$$

$$\text{Class B principal paid: } \frac{2.40}{12} \times \$10 = \$2.00$$

$$\text{Class A principal shortfall: } P_{AS}(t) = \$9.60 - \$8.00 = \$1.60$$

Class B principal shortfall: $P_{BS}(t) = \$2.40 - \$2.00 = \$0.40$

$$F_3(t) = \$0.00$$

In general, assuming that the condition $F_2(t) \geq P(t)$ holds at all times, the net effect of a pro rata structure is obviously to keep the ratio $[A(t)/B(t)]$ constant and equal to its initial value throughout the transaction. This condition is expected to hold in all performing securitizations. Clearly, the key to structural design is the management of what happens when the transaction is underperforming.

Note that in this fully collateralized example, if any class of security suffers a shortfall, then by definition the trust is insolvent since the aggregate principal balance of both classes now exceeds the pool's outstanding principal balance. However, since the promise of a securitized debt is only ultimate principal reimbursement by the legal final maturity date (rather than timely, scheduled principal and interest) this insolvency does not cause a bankruptcy. Recoveries and excess spread in later periods are then expected to reduce accumulated shortfalls to zero, thereby restoring the trust to solvency.

Sequential Schemes: Waterfall Levels 4 and 5

In a sequential principal allocation scheme, Total Principal Due is allocated to the most senior class to reduce its principal balance to zero before any principal is allocated to a more junior class. Here, too, the principal amount due to each class of investors is the sum of current and past due components. When Cumulative Principal Due $[C(t)]$ is less than the initial outstanding principal balance of the senior-most class, principal due on more junior classes is zero. With the previous definitions, these amounts would be computed as follows for our simple two-tranche structure:

Class A Prin Due: $P_A(t) = \min[A(t-1), P(t) + P_{AS}(t-1)]$

Class B Prin Due: $P_B(t) = \max\{0, C(t) - \max[A(0), C(t-1)]\} + P_{BS}(t-1)$

As before, the quantities $P_{AS}(t-1)$ and $P_{BS}(t-1)$ are the cumulative principal shortfalls from previous periods on Class A and Class B, respectively.

Consistent with these formulas, Class B investors will suffer shortfalls if Class A bonds are still outstanding when $C(t) \geq A(0)$. Through the shortfall mechanism, Class B bonds will not receive any principal payments until Class A bonds are fully retired.

Final Comments and Two Examples

In general, a pro rata structure is more advantageous to subordinated investors than a sequential scheme since such investors are scheduled to receive principal as well as interest throughout the life of the deal, thereby reducing the risk they will bear should receivables start under-performing toward the end of the transaction. This is referred to as *extension risk*. As a result, it will be more difficult at a given advance rate for Class B to achieve the same credit rating under a sequential as under a pro rata structure. Conversely, under a sequential scheme it will be easier for Class A to beat the rating it received under a pro rata allocation.

On the other hand, from the standpoint of the trust the pro rata structure is better because it pays down the higher coupon class immediately instead of having to support its initial principal balance until the Class A balance is reduced to zero. However, Class B investors might in fact be more interested in maintaining their relatively high current yield than in the danger of extension risk. In other words, while the pro rata structure has the advantage of maintaining the trust's weighted average liability coupon at its initial value, under a sequential allocation scheme this average would monotonically increase toward the Class B coupon as Class A slowly amortizes. In the end, all these factors will have to be weighted against each other to arrive at the final structure. In most instances, structural optimality will lie somewhere between purely sequential and purely pro rata allocations.

To firm up the distinction between the pro rata and sequential principal allocations, we present an example of each for a representative deal. Table 8.1 illustrates a transaction with a pro rata payment regime. It shows a single realization of a twenty-four period transaction with front-loaded credit losses of 6.2% and two-month average lagged recoveries of 47%. The total invested amount is $300 million, consisting of a 92% Class A tranche bearing 6% interest and an 8% subordinated tranche bearing 8% interest. The WAC on the underlying assets is a little less than 11%. The reductions of yield, indicated in the footnotes a and b, are negligible for the Class A notes and 57 bps for the Class B notes.

By contrast, Table 8.2 illustrates a single realization of the same transaction with a sequential payment regime. Note how, in this case, the more deeply subordinated Class B noteholder experiences a higher reduction of yield: 1.25% (equivalent to low BB or high B). The Class B noteholder receives more in interest (8% against the entire Class B principal balance for twenty-one periods), but this income is offset by a greater proportionate loss of principal in period 24.

Hybrid Payment Regimes

Over the years, some transactions have displayed hybrid structures with like-rated tranches of debt paying down pro rata while the rest are paid down sequentially. More commonly however, like-rated tranches of staggered maturities pay down sequentially.

Table 8.1
Pro Rata Principal Amortization

t	Class A Notes Ending Balance	Class B Notes Ending Balance	Servicing Fee Paid	Class A Interest Paid	Class B Interest Paid	Class A Principal Balance Paid[a]	Class B Principal Balance Paid[b]
0	276,000,000	24,000,000	—	—	—	—	—
1	260,237,171	23,285,219	325,000	1,380,000	160,000	15,762,829	714,781
2	244,771,298	21,909,338	307,149	1,301,186	155,235	15,465,874	1,375,882
3	229,607,659	20,609,598	288,904	1,223,857	146,062	15,163,639	1,299,739
4	214,751,743	19,385,886	271,069	1,148,038	137,397	14,855,916	1,223,712
5	200,209,278	18,238,083	253,649	1,073,759	129,239	14,542,465	1,147,802
6	185,986,265	17,166,075	236,651	1,001,046	121,587	14,223,012	1,072,009
7	172,089,027	16,169,747	220,082	929,931	114,440	13,897,238	996,328
8	158,524,260	15,248,993	203,947	860,445	107,798	13,564,767	920,753
9	145,299,106	14,403,720	188,254	792,621	101,660	13,225,154	845,273
10	132,421,245	13,633,850	173,011	726,496	96,025	12,877,861	769,870
11	119,899,013	12,939,335	158,226	662,106	90,892	12,522,232	694,516
12	107,741,561	12,320,161	143,908	599,495	86,262	12,157,452	619,173
13	97,385,068	10,350,372	130,067	538,708	82,134	10,356,493	1,969,790
14	87,266,881	9,169,637	116,713	486,925	69,002	10,118,187	1,180,734
15	77,390,570	8,040,382	104,473	436,334	61,131	9,876,311	1,129,256
16	67,759,750	6,962,371	92,550	386,953	53,603	9,630,819	1,078,010
17	58,378,083	5,935,361	80,949	338,799	46,416	9,381,667	1,027,010
18	49,249,276	4,959,094	69,673	291,890	39,569	9,128,808	976,267
19	40,377,081	4,033,299	58,726	246,246	33,061	8,872,195	925,795
20	31,765,299	3,157,695	48,111	201,885	26,889	8,611,782	875,604
21	23,417,779	2,331,985	37,833	158,826	21,051	8,347,520	825,710
22	15,338,418	1,555,861	27,896	117,089	15,547	8,079,362	776,124
23	7,531,160	829,002	18,302	76,692	10,372	7,807,258	726,860
24	0	151,071	9,057	37,656	5,527	7,531,160	677,931

[a] 0.00%
[b] 0.57%

Table 8.2
Sequential Principal Amortization

t	Class A Notes Ending Balance	Class B Notes Ending Balance	Servicing Fee Paid	Class A Interest Paid	Class B Interest Paid	Class A Principal Balance Paid[a]	Class B Principal Balance Paid[b]
0	276,000,000	24,000,000	—	—	—	—	—
1	259,522,391	24,000,000	325,000	1,380,000	160,000	16,477,609	0
2	242,681,826	24,000,000	307,149	1,297,612	160,000	16,840,564	0
3	226,221,940	24,000,000	288,905	1,213,409	160,000	16,459,887	0
4	210,147,991	24,000,000	271,074	1,131,110	160,000	16,073,949	0
5	194,465,476	24,000,000	253,660	1,050,740	160,000	15,682,514	0
6	179,180,169	24,000,000	236,671	972,327	160,000	15,285,308	0
7	164,298,162	24,000,000	220,112	895,901	160,000	14,882,007	0
8	149,825,931	24,000,000	203,990	821,491	160,000	14,472,231	0
9	135,770,409	24,000,000	188,311	749,130	160,000	14,055,522	0
10	122,139,084	24,000,000	173,085	678,852	160,000	13,631,326	0
11	108,940,124	24,000,000	158,317	610,695	160,000	13,198,960	0
12	96,182,552	24,000,000	144,018	544,701	160,000	12,757,572	0
13	83,876,470	24,000,000	130,198	480,913	160,000	12,306,081	0
14	72,601,156	24,000,000	116,866	419,382	160,000	11,275,314	0
15	61,621,309	24,000,000	104,651	363,006	160,000	10,979,848	0
16	50,940,236	24,000,000	92,756	308,107	160,000	10,681,072	0
17	40,561,282	24,000,000	81,185	254,701	160,000	10,378,954	0
18	30,487,822	24,000,000	69,941	202,806	160,000	10,073,460	0
19	20,723,267	24,000,000	59,028	152,439	160,000	9,764,555	0
20	11,271,063	24,000,000	48,450	103,616	160,000	9,452,205	0
21	2,134,688	24,000,000	38,210	56,355	160,000	9,136,375	0
22	0	17,317,658	28,313	10,673	160,000	2,134,688	6,682,342
23	0	8,812,385	18,761	0	115,451	0	8,505,272
24	0	619,351	9,547	0	58,749	0	8,193,034

[a]0.00%

[b]1.25%

Revolving Structures

We will not discuss the modeling of revolving structures in any detail. They are conceptually simple, but the modeling implementation is not straightforward and may unnecessarily cloud basic issues. The essential difference between amortizing and revolving structures depends on what happens to Total Principal Due in the revolving period, which usually falls at the beginning of the transaction. In amortizing structures, Total Principal Due is returned to investors as partial repayment of their initial investment. In revolving structures, it is applied to the purchase of additional eligible receivables, so that the pool balance is maintained at its original level until the scheduled termination of the revolving period, or sooner if insufficient funds are available to effect such purchases. This recycling of cash into new receivables is the meaning of the term *revolving*.

To illustrate, suppose the pool balance has been reduced by $10 through a combination of prepayments, regular principal collections, and defaulted receivables. During the amortization period, $10 of aggregate principal collections normally would be allocated to investors on the next payment date as partial repayments. If, instead, this amount is used to purchase new, eligible receivables from the originator, the pool balance and the principal balance of each liability tranche remain unchanged. Furthermore, if the portion of the $10 corresponding to defaulted receivables could not be covered from excess spread, the trust would then be forced to eat into outside credit enhancement to cover such shortfall. Under most structures, this type of shortfall would cause the declaration of an early amortization event within the indenture, and the revolving period would cease immediately in order to protect investors.

In terms of modeling effort, a revolving period involves some nontrivial complications. First, instead of a single, relatively large static pool to reckon with, there are a number of "mini" static pools to be considered (one for each collection period in the revolving period) consisting of the loans purchased during such monthly collection periods. After the pool has been revolving for a year or so, the default propensity of the total pool will be the combination of the interaction of twelve or thirteen static pools at different points in their default history.

Second, to properly analyze revolving structures, credit analysts must synthesize new receivables from the original pool and insert them seamlessly inside the trust. Since each account is now potentially at a different point in its default-propensity cycle, all accounts must be treated individually and followed through their delinquency history. This requirement increases the modeling effort by an order of magnitude, and makes the use of the Markovian techniques a sine qua non of asset analysis.

Third, because the precise description of the additional receivables that will be purchased after the closing date cannot be known a priori with certainty, structures with revolving periods are inherently riskier than strictly amortizing structures. Generally, the statistical distribution of these new accounts is assumed to replicate substantially the initially securitized pool.

Finally, although all amortizing structures and asset classes have the potential to revolve, only credit cards and a large portion of CBOs have made it a standard transaction feature. Inexplicably, rating agency analysis is typically insensitive to the existence of a revolving period in sizing required credit enhancement on a transaction.

9

The Average Life of Assets and Liabilities

The average life of assets or liabilities is an essential concept of structured finance that addresses the fact that principal repayments on the underlying loans do not come all at once, as would those of bullet maturity bonds, but rather trickle in over time. The ideal analytical method would be to value each cash flow according to its exact maturity date, but this would be next to impossible given their essentially unpredictable repayment characteristics; the random nature of prepayments and defaults usually plays havoc with a theoretical forecast of principal repayments. Because liabilities can carry only a single rate of interest, investors must choose some measure of debt maturity that best captures the expected repayment process. This measure should replicate as closely as possible the desired bullet maturity concept on which the yield curve is built. To do this, an aggregate measure is used under which the series of individual periodic principal amortizations is transformed into an equivalent principal repayment of the entire pool balance at some unique, "average" maturity, thereby synthetically simulating an obligation with the corresponding bullet maturity. The maturity thus obtained is defined as the *average life* of the pool. For convenience, a more detailed version of Figure 3.5 in chapter 3 is reproduced here for a loan with initial principal $10,000 maturing in sixty months.

In effect, we are attempting to find the time value t^a at which the area of rectangle $P_0 t^a$ in Figure 9.1 is equal to the area under the smooth curve representing the loan's theoretical amortization and extending from $t = 0$ to $t = T$, where T is the loan's expected maturity (here $T =$ sixty months).[1]

Mathematically, the average life of the loan t^a is thus defined by the equation

$$t^a P_0 = \int_0^T t \, dp. \tag{9.1}$$

In equation (9.1), we have denoted by dp the principal amortization schedule of the loan. The latter will usually be different in particular cases and the challenge behind computing the average life of assets will normally consist in finding suitable expressions for dp. Equation 9.1 yields the formal definition of the average life of a loan or a pool of identical loans with initial principal balance P_0:

$$t^a = \frac{1}{P_0} \int_0^T t \, dp \tag{9.2}$$

124

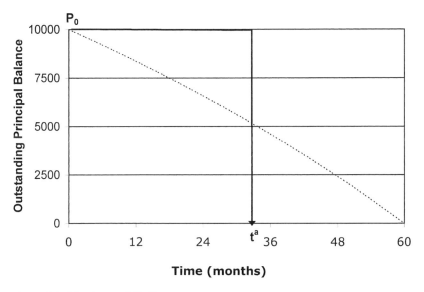

Figure 9.1. The Average Life Concept

In the case of pools of loans rather than single assets, the schedule dp corresponds to the amortization schedule of the pool, regardless of whether such write-downs were actually received as either principal reimbursements or prepayments, or else resulted from defaulted exposures and thus were never received.

Note in passing that the average life can obviously be derived via the following alternative formulation:

$$t^a = \frac{1}{P_0} \int_0^T p \, dt \qquad (9.3)$$

Under equation (9.3), we would be integrating by taking vertical slices through time instead of the horizontal slices implied by equation (9.2). However, we will stick to equation (9.2) in what follows because it explicitly shows the "life" character of the average life concept.

An Example in Continuous Time

To firm-up the average life concept in a simple case, let us compute the theoretical average life of a single loan having maturity T and paying down according to its originally scheduled amortization curve.

We begin our analysis by deriving an equation for the outstanding principal balance $p(t)$ of this loan as a function of time.

First, the defining condition of a *level-pay loan* is for the sum of interest and principal payments to remain invariant as a function of time. This allows us to immediately write down

$$M\,dt = rp\,dt - dp. \tag{9.4}$$

In equation (9.4), $M\,dt$ the payment made during a small time interval dt, measured in years for a loan paying at the annualized rate M; $rp\,dt$ is the interest payment for a loan with balance p carrying an annualized interest rate r; and dp is the decrease in principal balance during dt. The negative sign on the right-hand side of equation (9.4) expresses the fact that the principal balance decreases with time and that, therefore, dp is negative.

After dividing through by dt and rearranging, we arrive at

$$M = rp - \frac{dp}{dt}. \tag{9.5}$$

The general solution to this first-order, linear, ordinary differential equation is the superposition of the solution in the case $M = 0$, the homogeneous solution, with any particular solution of equation (9.5).

By inspection, we find the homogeneous solution of equation (9.5) as $p_h = Ae^{rt}$ (subscript h meaning "homogeneous"), and for the particular solution (subscript p), we choose the constant solution $p_p = M/r$. The general solution is then

$$p(t) = p_h + p_p$$

$$p(t) = \frac{M}{r} + Ae^{rt}. \tag{9.6}$$

To find the values of the unknown parameters M and A, we make use of the following two boundary conditions:

$$p(0) = P_0 \tag{9.7}$$

$$p(T) = 0 \tag{9.8}$$

Substituting equation (9.7) into (9.6) yields

$$A = P_0 - \frac{M}{r}. \tag{9.9}$$

Substitution of equation (9.8) into (9.6) then gives

$$P_0 = \frac{M}{r}\,e^{-rT}[e^{rT} - 1]. \tag{9.10}$$

Substitution of equations (9.9) and (9.10) back into (9.6) and rearranging then yields

$$p(t) = \frac{M}{r}\{1 + [e^{-rT}(e^{rT} - 1) - 1]e^{rt}\} = \frac{M}{r}[1 - e^{r(t-T)}]. \tag{9.11}$$

Equation (9.11) is the desired continuous compounding principal amortization schedule. To obtain the equivalent equation for discrete compounding, we note the identity

$$\lim_{n \to \infty} \left(1 + \frac{r}{n}\right)^n = e^r.$$ (9.12)

Equation (9.12) implies that in order to derive the requested discrete time-compounding principal amortization schedule, one needs merely to substitute $(1 + [r/n])$ in place of the exponential factor e^r in equation (9.11) where n is the annual compounding frequency. If time is measured in months instead of years, M becomes the monthly payment to be made by the obligor and r/n is the periodic (i.e., monthly) rate.

Doing this leads to the following form:

$$p(t) = \frac{M}{r} \frac{[(1 + r)^{T-t} - 1]}{(1 + r)^{T-t}}.$$ (9.13)

In equation (9.13), the rate r is now the periodic rate for the relevant period. For instance, in the case of a 12% loan with monthly payments, r would be numerically equal to $0.12/12 = 0.01$.

If a transaction involves leases instead of loans, the relevant notional initial principal balance will in general not pay down to zero by the term of the lease due to the latter's relatively smaller periodic payment. In such cases, we need to derive an alternative formula to describe the implicit principal amortization schedule that corresponds to lease cash flows once the implied interest rate is available. To do this, we simply replace the original boundary condition $P(T) = 0$ with the new condition $P(T) = R_v P_0$ where we have defined R_v as the residual percentage at lease maturity $t = T$, and where $R_v \in [0, 1]$ by construction.

Skipping the trivial algebra, the solution to equation (9.4) given this modified boundary condition along with the standard $P(0) = P_0$ is easily found to be

$$p(t) = \frac{P_0}{1 - (1 + r)^{-T}}\{1 - (1 + r)^{t-T}(1 - R_v) - R_v(1 + r)^{-T}\}.$$ (9.14)

We are now ready to derive a formula for the average life of our amortizing, level-pay loan. After dropping the minus sign on the cash flow, differentiation of equation (9.13) yields

$$dp = \frac{M}{r} \ln(1 + r)(1 + r)^{t-T} dt.$$ (9.15)

Insertion of equation (9.15) into equation (9.2) then gives

$$t^a = \frac{M \ln(1 + r)}{rP_0} \int_0^T t(1 + r)^{t-T} dt.$$ (9.16)

Integrating by parts, we easily find

$$\int_0^T t(1+r)^{t-T}\,dt = \frac{t(1+r)^{t-T}}{\ln(1+r)}\Big|_0^T - \frac{1}{\ln(1+r)}\int_0^T (1+r)^{t-T}\,dt$$

$$\int_0^T t(1+r)^{t-T}\,dt = \frac{T}{\ln(1+r)} - \frac{[1-(1+r)^{-T}]}{[\ln(1+r)]^2}. \tag{9.17}$$

Combining equations (9.16) and (9.17), we arrive at

$$t^a = \frac{M}{rP_0}\left\{T - \frac{1-(1+r)^{-T}}{\ln(1+r)}\right\}. \tag{9.18}$$

Rearrangement of equation (9.10) gives the original principal balance of the loan as

$$P_0 = \frac{M}{r}\{1 - (1+r)^{-T}\}. \tag{9.19}$$

Finally, combining equations (9.18) and (9.19) yields

$$t^a = \frac{T}{1-(1+r)^{-T}} - \frac{1}{\ln(1+r)}. \tag{9.20}$$

In keeping with equation (9.12), the continuous time-compounding analogue of equation (9.20) would simply be

$$t^a = \frac{T}{1-e^{-rT}} - \frac{1}{r}. \tag{9.21}$$

For instance, a sixty-month loan with an annualized interest rate of 12% would have an average life of

$$t^a = \frac{60}{1-(1+0.01)^{-60}} - \frac{1}{\ln(1+0.01)} = 32.97 \text{ months} \approx 2.75 \text{ years}.$$

An entire pool of such identical loans would also have this average life if it paid down according to its scheduled amortization. In realistic settings, the average life of a pool with a WAM of sixty months and a WAC of 12% will be less than 2.75 years due to prepayments and defaults. Thus, the value $t^a = 2.75$ years can be considered an upper limit for the average life of such pools.

Starting from equations (9.20) and (9.21), more complicated but generally straightforward analytical formulas can be derived for the average life of homogeneous or non-homogeneous pools with specified prepayment and default schedules. For instance, consider a pool of N identical loans with maturity T, annualized interest rate r, and a hypothetical combined default and prepayment history[2] $d(t)$ given by

$$d(t) = \sum_{i=1}^m \delta(t - t_i^d)n_i. \tag{9.22}$$

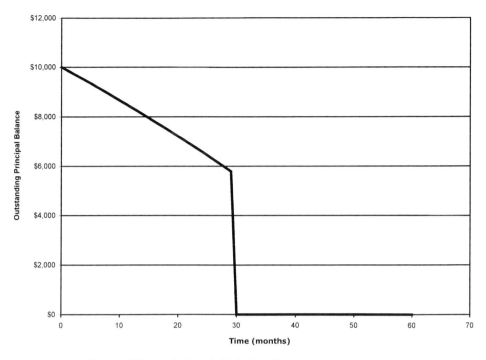

Figure 9.2. Balance History of a Loan in Default or Prepayment

In equation (9.22), n_i is the number of loans defaulting or prepaying at time t_i^d and $\delta(\cdot)$ is a convenience delta function satisfying

$$\delta(x) = \begin{cases} 1, x = 0 \\ 0, x \neq 0. \end{cases}$$

We also require a boundary condition limiting the total number of defaulted and prepaid loans to the original number of loans in the pool:

$$\sum_i n_i = M \leq N$$

Formally, the average life of any loan described above with an initial principal balance P_0 but defaulting or prepaying at time t_i^d can be defined by

$$t_i^a = \frac{1}{P_0} \left\{ \int_0^{t_i^d} t \, dp + t_i^d \, p(t_i^d) \right\}. \tag{9.23}$$

The principal balance history for such a loan is shown in Figure 9.2 for an initial principal balance of $10,000. After some algebra, the solution to equation (9.23) is found to be

$$
t_i^a = \frac{(1+r)^{t_i^d} - 1}{(1+r)^T - 1} \left[\frac{t_i^d}{1 - (1+r)^{-t_i^d}} - \frac{1}{\ln(1+r)} \right]
$$
$$
+ t_i^d \left[\frac{1 - (1+r)^{t_i^d - T}}{1 - (1+r)^{-T}} \right]. \tag{9.24}
$$

The average life t_p^a of the pool of N identical loans subject to the default process given by equation (9.22) can now be written as the weighted average of the average lives of its constituent loans, both defaulting (t_i^a) and non-defaulting (t^a):

$$
t_p^a = \frac{1}{N} \left\{ \sum_{i=1}^m n_i \, t_i^a + (N - M) t^a \right\} \tag{9.25}
$$

If, on the other hand, defaults and prepayments were regarded as a continuous phenomenon, the procedure above would have to be slightly modified as follows. First, postulate an account-wise cumulative default distribution function $F(t)$. Next, define the associated marginal account-wise density function $f(t)$ as

$$
f(t) \equiv \frac{\partial F(t)}{\partial t}.
$$

The logistic curve discussed in detail in chapters 14 and 20 is a fairly useful approximation of the default behavior of many asset pools, although in general suitable forms for $F(t)$ are asset specific.

Then, for a pool of N identical loans subject to the default process given by $F(t)$, $t \in [0, T]$ and a cumulative account-wise default rate D_r, the average life of the pool would be given by

$$
t_p^a = \frac{1}{N} \left\{ N(1 - D_r) t^a + \int_0^T f(t) t^a(t) \, dt \right\}. \tag{9.25a}
$$

In equation (9.25a), $t^a(t)$ is the right-hand side of equation (9.24) with t replacing t_i^d. Any integrable functional form can be used for the function $f(t)$. If analytical integration is not possible, an approximate solution can always be found using asymptotic expansions or Taylor series.

This continuous time formalism can clearly be extended to derive more complicated formulas applicable to non-homogeneous pools containing loans with different balances, interest rates, and maturities. In all cases, however, equations (9.22) and (9.24) are the basic building blocks needed to carry out these manipulations. Again, we should mention that these formulas should be viewed as rough guides and benchmarks to which actual figures can be compared, and not as inputs to pricing calculations. For the latter purpose, a more intensive cash flow simulation must be performed.

An Example in Discrete Time

In reality, obligors do not pay down their loans under a continuous time regime. Rather, principal repayments come in the form of discrete monthly or otherwise periodic cash flows from inception to maturity. Thus, the actual repayment curve of a non-defaulting loan looks more like the staircase pattern shown in Figure 9.3 for the same $10,000 loan as before.

To calculate the average life of this more realistic loan, we must consider a discrete sum of monthly principal payments $\Delta p(t_i)$ and associate with them the time t_i at which they are received. Therefore, the average life of a "real loan" can be defined as

$$t_r^a = \frac{1}{P_0} \sum_{n=1}^{T} t_n \Delta p(t_n). \tag{9.26}$$

Using equation (9.13), we can derive the values $\Delta p(n)$ as

$$\Delta p(n) = \frac{M}{r}\{(1 + r)^{n-1-T} - (1 + r)^{n-T}\}$$

$$\Delta p(n) = \frac{M}{(1 + r)^{T+1-n}}. \tag{9.27}$$

Substitution of equations (9.27) and (9.19) into equation (9.26) yields

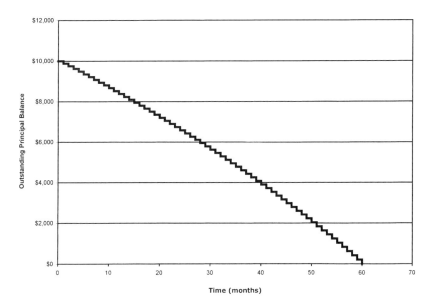

Figure 9.3. Balance History of a Timely Loan Repayment

$$t_r^a = \frac{r}{(1 + r)[(1 + r)^T - 1]} \sum_{n=1}^{T} n(1 + r)^n. \qquad (9.28)$$

The arithmetic-geometric series on the right-hand side of equation (9.28) can be summed (any mathematical formula handbook[3] can be used to look up the answer) as follows:

$$t_r^a = 1 + \frac{1 + r}{(1 + r)^T - 1} \left[\frac{1 - T(1 + r)^{(T-1)} + (T - 1)(1 + r)^T}{r} \right] \qquad (9.29)$$

Taking the same 12%, sixty-month loan used in our first numerical example, we find

$$t_r^a = 1 + \frac{1.01}{1.01^{60} - 1} \left[\frac{1 - 60(1.01)^{59} + 59(1.01)^{60}}{0.01} \right]$$

$$t_r^a = 33.46 \text{ months} \approx 2.79 \text{ years}$$

The positive difference of approximately 0.04 years between the discrete and the continuous time cases can be non-negligible in some cases, and would increase as either the maturity of the loan decreases, the interest rate increases, or both. In practical applications, individual loan maturities will obviously vary and credit analysts should compute the magnitude of errors they might make when using equation (9.20) instead of equation (9.29).

The Average Life of Liabilities

The foregoing calculations of the average life of individual assets, and by extension of corresponding asset pools, were a necessary preamble to those leading to the average life of structured liabilities.

The average life of the *assets* should not be confused with the average life of the *liabilities*. Although the average life of the former will always be finite, that of the latter may be infinite if insufficient cash is received as a result of excessive losses; an infinite average life will translate into some reduction of yield on the liabilities after taking into account how much of the initial principal balance of the notes or certificates is still outstanding after the pool's cash payments have run out. Thus, an infinite average life is just another way of expressing the "default" of a structured security without reference to the severity of such default. Theoretically speaking, in each instance where the average life of a structured liability is infinite, the severity of the default might be different. However, even when enough cash is on hand to cover losses, the average life of the liabilities will be structurally determined.

In a simple, two-tranche, *performing* transaction under a purely pro rata regime, the average life of both classes will be identical and equal to that of the assets calculated previously. Conversely, for the same performing transaction under a strictly sequential structure paying down in alphabetical order, the average life of the Class A notes will be smaller than that of the Class B notes, but their weighted average will nevertheless remain equal to the average life of the assets.

The reason for this equality, which we term the *parity condition*, is the fact that the defining equation for the average life (equation [9.2]) is a linear integral operator. As a result, the average life of a tranche from a performing transaction is constrained by the requirement that the weighted average life of all tranches, using the initial tranche principal balances as weights, must equal the average life of the asset pool since the pool's total amortization may somehow be partitioned among its liabilities. It follows that in a two-tranche sequential structure, the Class A average life t_A^a will satisfy $t_A^a \leq t^a$ while the Class B average life t_B^a will satisfy $t_B^a \geq t^a$.

For instance, in a plain-vanilla sequential structure the average life of the Class A notes with an initial principal balance A_0 would be defined by

$$t_A^a = \frac{1}{A_0} \int_0^{T^*} t\,dp. \qquad (9.30)$$

To solve equation (9.30), equation (9.13) is used to yield an implicit definition of T^* via the boundary condition

$$p(T^*) = P_0 - A_0. \qquad (9.31)$$

Insertion of equation (9.31) into equation (9.13) yields

$$T^* = T + \frac{\ln\{1 - [1 - (1+r)^{-T}](1-\alpha)\}}{\ln(1+r)}. \qquad (9.32)$$

For convenience, we have introduced the advance rate $\alpha = A_0/P_0$ in equation (9.32).

Using the previous continuous time result given by equation (9.20), we can compute t_A^a with the help of equation (9.32) as

$$t_A^a = \left\{ \frac{T^*}{1 - (1+r)^{-T^*}} - \frac{1}{\ln(1+r)} \right\}. \qquad (9.33)$$

Next, from the fact that the weighted average life of both classes must be that of the assets (the parity condition), we find for t_B^a

$$t_B^a = \frac{t^a - \alpha\, t_A^a}{1 - \alpha}. \qquad (9.34)$$

Assuming an advance rate of 80%, these formulas would yield the following results.

First, T^* is calculated as

$$T^* = 60 + \frac{\ln\{1 - [1 - (1.01)^{-60}]\, 0.2\}}{\ln(1.01)} \approx 50.5 \text{ months.}$$

Then, equation (9.33) yields

$$t_A^a = \left\{ \frac{50.5}{1 - 1.01^{-50.5}} - \frac{1}{\ln(1.01)} \right\} = 27.35 \text{ months} \approx 2.28 \text{ years}.$$

Last, the average life of the Class B notes is calculated from equation (9.34):

$$t_B^a = \frac{2.75 - 0.8(2.28)}{0.2} \approx 4.63 \text{ years}$$

As expected, the average life of the Class A notes satisfies $t_A^a \leq t^a$ while that of the Class B notes satisfies $t_B^a \geq t^a$.

There is, of course, an infinite array of intermediate possibilities within structures that are neither strictly sequential nor pro rata. Generally, such structures will include, either implicitly or explicitly, the concept of a *Targeted Amortization Class* (or TAC) whereby an arbitrary amortization schedule will be created at closing.

Sometimes, for instance in mortgage-backed securities, TAC schedules may refer initially to notional balances as opposed to physical balances, but the concept will not change. Assuming cash availability, the TAC schedule then becomes the path dp required to solve equation (9.1) for the average life of each class. From an implementation standpoint, however, TACs would correspond to some deterministic specification of $d(t)$ as described by equation (9.22). Mechanics of TACs are discussed in detail in the following pages.

This game may obviously be played with more than two classes of securities. In fact, the process is formally identical from three to N, where N is the total number of classes. As a result, we present here the basic ideas for the case of three securities only. The numerical calculations are identical to the two-tranche case and are therefore skipped.

Consider first Figure 9.4 depicting the amortization schedule of a three-tranche sequential structure backed by a pool of identical of level-pay loans of five-year maturities wherein sufficient cash is received for the liabilities to pay down according to the pool's original amortization schedule. The triangular regions labeled A, B, and C show the time intervals where Classes A, B, and C (respectively) amortize according to the sequential pay-down schedule. The parity condition still holds, but this time with three classes:

$$t^a = \alpha_1 \, t_A^a + \alpha_2 \, t_B^a + \alpha_3 \, t_C^a \tag{9.35}$$

In equation (9.35), we have defined the various classwise advance rates in a way similar to our earlier two-tranche deal (subscripted letters refer to initial balances of the corresponding class):

$$\alpha_1 = \frac{A_0}{P_0}, \alpha_2 = \frac{B_0}{P_0}, \alpha_3 = \frac{C_0}{P_0}$$

Let's assume that tranche A is paid down completely at time T_A (approximately thirty-six months in Figure 3.10) and that tranche B pays down to zero at time T_B (approximately fifty months in Figure 3.10). The values of T_A and

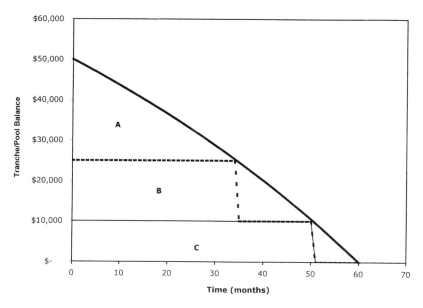

Figure 9.4. Amortization of a Hypothetical Three-Tranche Sequential Structure

T_B are found analogously to the two-tranche case (i.e., we have $p^{-1}[P_0 - A_0]$ $= T_A$ and $p^{-1}[P_0 - \{A_0 + B_0\}] = T_B$). Once these two values are found, we may apply the same formalism to find

$$t_A^a = \left\{ \frac{T_A}{1 - (1 + r)^{-T_A}} - \frac{1}{\ln(1 + r)} \right\} \tag{9.36}$$

$$t_B^a = T_A + \left\{ \frac{T_B - T_A}{1 - (1 + r)^{-(T_B - T_A)}} - \frac{1}{\ln(1 + r)} \right\}. \tag{9.37}$$

Equation (9.37) stems from the fact that from the average-life point of view, Class B is fully outstanding until T_A, at which point it simply starts amortizing according to the pool's amortization schedule $p(t)$. This is equivalent to shifting the time origin by an amount T_A and having the initial balance B_0 amortize to zero in a time frame $T_B - T_A$.

Once t_A^a and t_B^a are available, t_C^a can be computed using the three-tranche parity condition, equation (9.35):

$$t_C^a = \frac{t^a - \alpha_1 t_A^a - \alpha_2 t_B^a}{\alpha_3} \tag{9.38}$$

The Case of Principal Shortfalls

The parity formulas derived earlier implicitly assumed that sufficient cash was on hand on each payment date to retire liabilities according to the pool's amortization schedule. However, when insufficient cash is available to pay such allocated principal amounts on schedule, equation (9.34) may no longer be used to express the relationship between the average life of asset pools and that of their corresponding liabilities.

In that case, the above parity condition needs to be slightly modified via the incorporation of the complete cash balance between assets and liabilities under shortfall conditions. We derive the new formula for the two-tranche structure below, other cases proceeding completely analogously.

Recall that the original parity condition in equation (9.34) arose from the fact that dollar-for-dollar liability reductions were assumed on a current basis within our basic two-tranche transaction. As a result, any reduction dp in the pool's outstanding principal balance was partitioned between both classes according to the deal's allocation structure (i.e., sequential, pro rata, or some combination thereof) in such a way as to reduce the aggregate principal balance of the liabilities by the same amount. In other words, in that simple case, the parity formula stemmed from the fact that the following condition was assumed to hold at all times:

$$dp = dp_A + dp_B \qquad (9.39)$$

In equation (9.39), the quantities dp_A and dp_B stand for the principal reimbursement to classes A and B, respectively. However, when available funds' shortfalls occur, perhaps due to excessive defaults, equality (9.39) no longer holds. Instead, a cash balance applied to the transaction on a periodic basis would lead to the inequality

$$dp \geq dp_A + dp_B. \qquad (9.40)$$

The difference between the right- and left-hand sides of equation (9.40) is known as the *aggregate shortfall* and can therefore be obtained as the schedule $S(t)$ of such differences for all collection periods from closing ($t = 0$) to maturity ($t = T$). The schedule $S(t)$, satisfying $S(t) \leq 0$ by construction, is the key to the modification of the parity condition (9.34). To see this, proceed as follows.

First, define the shortfall average life t_s^a, a negative quantity by construction, as

$$t_s^a = \frac{1}{P_0} \int_0^T t\, ds. \qquad (9.41)$$

In equation (9.41), we have defined $ds = [\partial S(t)]/\partial t$ and equipped it with boundary conditions guaranteeing that principal shortfalls are eventually made up in later periods should they accumulate in any current period. These two normalizing conditions are clearly as follows:

$$S(0) = 0 \qquad (9.42)$$

$$S(T) = 0 \qquad (9.42')$$

In essence, we are asserting that no aggregate shortfall can exist at closing, which is true by definition, and that any shortfall developing during the life of the transaction must eventually be eliminated from available funds by the maturity date such that none remains at time T. Thus for conditions (9.42) and (9.42') to hold, both the pool and aggregate liability balances would vanish at maturity no matter what differences might have existed between the two during the transaction's lifetime.

With these definitions in mind and remembering that principal shortfalls and principal payments carry opposite signs, we can replace inequality (9.40) with the following equality:

$$dp = dp_A + dp_B - ds \qquad (9.43)$$

Finally, substitution of equation (9.43) into our basic average life formalism, consisting of equation (9.22), we arrive at the following modified parity condition for any two-tranche transaction experiencing principal shortfalls during its lifetime, but recovering from them:

$$t^a = \alpha t_A^a + (1 - \alpha)\, t_B^a + t_s^a \qquad (9.44)$$

As mentioned previously, failure to satisfy equation (9.42') would lead to an infinite average life for some subset of liability classes. In other words, if $S(T) \neq 0$ turned out to be the case, we would have either $t_A^a \to \infty$ or $t_B^a \to \infty$, or both, depending on the particular structure, thereby invalidating equation (9.44). As already mentioned, although the average lives of assets are always finite, those of liabilities may not be.

Last but not least, since ABS are normally priced based on average life, accurate determination of the latter is of paramount importance. In actual cases, statistical methods will usually be necessary to estimate the mean average life of securities in complicated structures within a statistical universe of possible repayment and default scenarios. Therefore, in practice the average life will itself be subject to a meta-level of averaging stemming from such statistical behavior. Merely using the "best" or "expected" repayment case is unlikely to yield an estimate sufficiently accurate for pricing purposes. Because the yield curve is normally upward sloping, and since average life estimates will tend to err on the low side, this issue will affect investors much more than issuers.

10

PACs and TACs

Planned Amortization Classes

As we have alluded, while the purely pro rata or sequential allocation schemes may be said to form the two ends of the risk allocation spectrum, infinitely many intermediate structures can be devised through the introduction of the TAC and Planned Amortization Class (PAC) concepts. These operate on the basis of a preestablished schedule of theoretical principal allocations in an attempt to accommodate the varieties of investor appetite for credit risk and prepayment speculation. Their popularity having increased significantly over the past twenty years, we feel a fuller treatment is warranted. This section is concerned exclusively with PACs while the next addresses TACs.

The concept of the PAC was invented for the benefit of mortgage investors and later transplanted with varying degrees of success to other ABS asset classes. Today, PACs are fairly common structural features of mortgage- and some auto-loan-backed structured financings. By their nature, PACs are more difficult to use in high- than in low-credit-loss environments, such as MBS. For this reason, it is unlikely that they will become de rigueur in many other ABS asset classes in the foreseeable future. As plays on interest rates, they are also unlikely to be attractive in environments where interest rate–related cash flow sensitivity is weak, which is the case in most liquid ABS asset classes.

The next few paragraphs discuss the philosophy of PACs and their mechanics as they relate to prepayment protection. Because PAC interest-only (IO) strips are more germane to ABS than are standard PAC bonds, this is the focus of our remarks. Interested readers can find a more detailed treatment of other types of PAC bonds in standard textbooks on MBS.

To round out the discussion, the section ends with a worked example taken from a hypothetical pool. Readers should keep in mind that this bare-bones summary is intended merely to convey concepts, not to address the full spectrum of implementable variations, nor to investigate specific transaction modalities.

The Philosophy of the PAC

Essentially, PACs were conceived to give prepayment protection to certain classes of investors who would either suffer severe yield erosion or experience unexpected reinvestment risk should prepayment speeds exceed worst-case historical norms. This may arise many different ways, but a paradigm example is that of the buyer of an IO class in a pool of mortgages. Since the buyer's cash flows stem exclusively from interest payments, in the extreme scenario whereby the entire pool were to prepay on day 1, interest cash flows would amount to zero and the return on the IO would be -100% (i.e., the entire investment would be lost). Furthermore, this unfortunate situation would not result from any default or credit event, and could happen with unspecified probability despite the fact that the IO itself may have been given a Aaa rating by a major rating agency. The flip side of this argument would obviously apply to the Principal-Only (PO) buyer who would receive all of his or her cash flows on day 1 and thus realize an unexpected windfall from this extreme prepayment speed.

Although academic, these extreme cases illustrate why an investor exposed to such high yield volatility would usually demand some modicum of downside protection. It may be argued that the downside risk of the IO is counterbalanced by the opportunity of perhaps equally probable (but lower than expected) prepayment speed, causing the IO to receive the windfall gain instead of the PO. Unfortunately, the predictive power of most prepayment models, which are essentially interest rate prediction models,[1] is low and the Wall Street fear index usually exceeds its greed index by a wide margin. Therefore, this sort of "opportunity" argument is unlikely to be well received by investors, whose risk aversion usually creates an asymmetry around an otherwise risk-neutral pricing scenario. As a result, given equal low and high prepayment-speed probability masses on either side of the pricing curve, IO investors will nevertheless require additional security against the risk of excessive prepayments. Achieving this security was why the PAC was conceived.

IO class buyers are clearly aware that their investment entails prepayment risk, but they have grown comfortable over time with a certain universe of prepayment speeds—a universe derived from actual prepayment history with similar collateral. Regardless of the fact that the price of the IO was negotiated freely between a buyer and a seller with diverging views on prepayments, these views were strongly influenced by historical patterns and the current thinking about interest rate fluctuations over the life of the pool. If interest rate volatility were to take the pool outside the prepayment universe initially contemplated, the IO buyer would have no recourse. The PAC mechanism is not supposed to remove *all* downside risk from the IO, just that portion of prepayment risk that could arise from prepayment speeds in excess of most conceivable historical norms. In the end, nothing can save an IO buyer from the cash flow consequences of the doomsday scenario described earlier.

The Mechanics of the PAC

The basic technique at the heart of the PAC is the partitioning of the pool's outstanding principal balance $B(t)$ into two components: the PAC $[P(t)]$ and the companion $[C(t)]$ class. At all times the following condition holds:

$$B(t) = P(t) + C(t) \tag{10.1}$$

Forgetting cash availability considerations for the sake of argument, the IO buyer would receive the following periodic allocations $F(t)$:

$$F(t) = rP(t-1), 0 < r \le R \tag{10.2}$$

In equation (10.2), r is the IO periodic rate and R is approximately the pool's weighted average asset coupon. The next step is the crux of PAC mechanics.

Based on prepayment speeds considered high given historical norms, a PAC schedule $S(t)$ is established at closing. The schedule $S(t)$ may be derived in a number of ways, but for our purposes we will assume that it represents some fixed percentage α of the pool's outstanding principal balance under an extreme (historically speaking) prepayment scenario. In other words, $S(t)$ is computed based on the highest historical prepayment speeds seen on similar collateral over a comparable period. Once the ratio $\alpha = [P(t)/B(t)]$ is decided upon, the IO price is negotiated between buyer and seller based on expected cash flows allocated solely to the PAC component as per equation (10.2).

Finally, the PAC balance $P(t)$ required as input to equation (10.2) is computed for each period according to the following schema. First, the companion class balance $C(t)$ is calculated from

$$C(t) = \max\{0, (1-\alpha)B(t) - \max[0, S(t) - \alpha B(t)]\}. \tag{10.3}$$

Then the PAC balance $P(t)$ is computed from equation (10.1).

Remembering that IO cash flows are based on $P(t)$ only, this technique offers investors the following prepayment regimes:

1. For prepayment speeds between zero and the speed at which $B(t) \ge [S(t)]/\alpha$, $P(t) = \alpha B(t)$. In such cases, the IO holder is taking prepayment risk within the universe originally contemplated and is receiving a nominal return presumably in line with those risks.
2. For prepayment speeds such that $B(t) \le [S(t)]/\alpha$ and $C(t) > 0$, then $P(t) = S(t)$. This is the chief prepayment protection feature of the PAC feature. In essence, over a range of prepayment speeds in excess of extreme historical norms the IO buyer is locked into a known balance for purposes of IO cash flow allocations. Obviously, this range depends entirely on the value of α. Historically, this particular range of prepayment speeds has been referred to as the *PAC structuring band* or *PAC range*. We will henceforth adhere to this naming convention.
3. For prepayment speed such that $B(t) \le [S(t)]/\alpha$ and $C(t) = 0$, $P(t) = B(t)$. In other words, in this case IO investors would suffer a dollar-for-dollar reduction in the basis of their cash flow allocation formula. This regime would be considered extreme by any measure and completely outside even the highest conceivable prepayment speeds.

It can be readily seen that equations (10.1) and (10.3) satisfy the above requirements. For instance, under the first regime, equation (10.3) yields

$$C(t) = (1 - \alpha)B(t) \tag{10.4}$$

Insertion of equation (10.4) into (10.1) yields

$$P(t) = B(t) - (1 - \alpha)B(t) = \alpha B(t) \tag{10.5}$$

Under the second regime, we have the following from equation (10.3):

$$C(t) = (1 - \alpha)B(t) - [S(t) - \alpha B(t)] = B(t) - S(t) \tag{10.6}$$

Insertion of equation (10.6) into equation (10.1) now yields

$$P(t) = B(t) - [B(t) - S(t)] = S(t).$$

Finally, under regime 3, equation (10.2) leads to

$$C(t) = 0. \tag{10.7}$$

Insertion of equation (10.7) into equation (10.1) gives

$$P(t) = B(t) - 0 = B(t).$$

As mentioned earlier, the value of α dictates the amount of downside protection the investor will receive under regime 2, since the companion class is nominally sized as $(1 - \alpha)B(t)$. Thus, the lower the α, the higher the corresponding PAC protection region defined by $0 < C(t) \leq (1 - \alpha)B(t)$. Clearly, a smaller α can always be compensated by a lower price for the IO, and vice versa.

Note that since investors' prepayment views may deviate from historical norms, arbitrage profits are definitely possible. Moreover, the credit risk of the IO would only enter the fray should there be insufficient cash to make the promised payment to IO holders (equation (10.2)) as a result of high defaults or delinquencies. In certain asset classes (e.g., autos) the probability that this will happen may in fact be non-negligible and such IO buyers would need to consider credit risk as well as market risk. However, in most cases IO investors will be betting indirectly and exclusively on interest rates via the associated pool's prepayment behavior. Needless to say, to do this is inherently risky.

Although PACs are a viable market risk protection mechanism available to investors especially vulnerable to prepayment risk, they can sometimes distract investor attention from the credit risk that may be peripherally entailed. Those accustomed to thinking of PACs in a mortgage-backed context may be lulled into a false sense of security, and may be surprised to find that PACs in other ABS asset classes can display unexpected credit-linked features that should have some influence on pricing once these are properly assessed. As always in finance, the extension of a concept successful in one environment to a completely different one should initially be viewed with skepticism.

In general, however, in instances where an investor purchases a standard PAC bond rather than a PAC IO (i.e., one that includes both interest and principal components), and where credit risk is not an issue, the idea of prepayment protection over the PAC range might be essential, since such an investor may in fact be looking to duration-match a specific liability on the balance sheet, and thus would be highly concerned about reinvestment risk protection. In that case, investing in a PAC might make perfect sense. Conversely, some other investor merely hungry for raw return might purchase the corresponding companion class and, given its structural imperatives, receive an attractive yield incentive to do so. Thus, although the practical utility of a PAC IO may have been oversold, that of standard PAC and companion bonds in the right context is significant.

Let us now take a few moments to see how the structure of the PAC reduces the duration impact of interest rate volatility for an investor. To see this, recall from basic fixed income arithmetic that the price P of a bond may be set equal to the discounted present value of the cash flows C_t, $t \in [1, T]$ to which its holder is entitled over the remaining life of the bond:

$$P = \sum_{t=1}^{T} \frac{C_t}{(1 + r)^t} \qquad (10.8)$$

In equation (10.8), r is defined as the bond's periodic yield to maturity or simply yield, and as is well known, is a critical parameter in pricing any type of fixed income security. In circumstances where the cash flows C_t are independent of interest rates—a condition covering much of corporate finance—the duration D of the bond, defined as the first derivative of its price with respect to yield, may simply be written as

$$D \equiv \frac{\partial P}{\partial r} = \frac{-1}{(1 + r)} \sum_{t=1}^{T} \frac{tC_t}{(1 + r)^t}. \qquad (10.9)$$

Conversely, in instances where C_t are dependent on prepayment rates and hence on interest rates—that is, we have $C_t(r)$—duration is no longer given by equation (10.9). Rather, we must go back to the middle term in equation (10.9) and include such cash flow dependence on yield:

$$D = \sum_{t=1}^{T} \frac{(1 + r)^t \dfrac{\partial C_t(r)}{\partial r} - t(1 + r)^{t-1} C_t(r)}{(1 + r)^{2t}} \qquad (10.10)^2$$

As a rule, the acceleration of cash flows stemming from a reduction in the level of interest rates vis-à-vis their original benchmark, and thus from a corresponding increase in prepayment rates, also increases the absolute value of duration since in general, the condition $\partial C_t(r)/\partial r \leq 0$ will hold for values of r (see Figure 10.1) in some target range. Normal PAC buyers will usually be more interested in cash flow stability than capital gains, and so will seek to become comfortable with the fact that $\partial C_t(r)/\partial r$ should be fairly benign over the same range. The latter will usually consist mostly of the PAC band where the condition $\partial C_t(r)/\partial r = 0$ holds throughout.

The good news here is that although the prediction of absolute prepayment rates (being an attempt to indirectly forecast interest rates) is notoriously inaccurate, *conditional prepayment rate* (CPR) models provide respectable results over a wide range of yields. Some of the major Wall Street investment banking firms have developed fairly reliable models of prepayment behavior given interest rates, which models are thus crucial inputs to structured bond pricing models.

In general, however, being the result of statistical analyses, such yield-dependent cash flows will be given as point-sets rather than continuous functions and will therefore be (at best) piecewise continuous in r. Unfortunately, in order to compute first- and higher-order derivatives, continuity of the approximations to $C_t(r)$ and of its derivatives will be paramount. However, in practice, the calculation of derivatives beyond $\partial^2 C_t(r)/\partial r^2$ will usually not be necessary, the latter being required to compute the bond's convexity.

For example, consider Figure 10.1 as the output of some conditional prepayment model giving the interest rate sensitivity of some arbitrary cash flow $C_t(r)$ accruing to the owner of a PAC bond.

As expected, an investor would experience little price volatility solely from the time-dependent distribution of cash flows in an improving (i.e., decreasing) interest rate environment. In this hypothetical example, the PAC band corresponds approximately to the yield range $r \in [4.5\%, 6.5\%]$ and is therefore the range of prepayment speeds during which the companion class would be slowly eaten away to protect the PAC. Unfortunately, albeit continuous in r per se, the above approximation to $C_t(r)$ is discontinuous in its higher order derivatives at both ends of the PAC range.

As a result (and contrary to what some readers might conclude from our remarks on splines in Appendix G), this is one of the few instances where we definitely advocate the use of cubic splines as approximating functions to the discrete sets $C_t(r)$. The reason is that spline polynomials strictly enforce continuity of first and second derivatives as well as that of functional values over the relevant range. Once such approximations are derived, they can be substituted into equation (10.10) to calculate duration or its next of kin, convexity.

Structured analysts can certainly make the game more interesting by partitioning a standard PAC bond into a sequential array of sub-PACs, thus adding further effective prepayment protection to holders of the senior-most tranches in the sequence. This super-protection stems from the fact that for a given single-month mortality path, the senior tranches in the sequence would most likely have sufficient time to be paid off according to their original schedule, despite the existence of prepayment rates above the upper limit of the PAC band, before the exhaustion of the companion class. Therefore, in a dynamic sense, the effective subordination of the more junior sequential sub-tranches in a multi-tranche PAC effectively creates enhanced prepayment protection for the senior sub-tranches vis-à-vis the standard one-tranche PAC, especially in view of the fact that, from a prepayment standpoint, the most predictable part of a transaction's prepayment history is clearly its initial phase. In practice, the optimization of a PAC structure is largely a matter of interest rate speculation and more of an art than a science—that is, something better left alone.

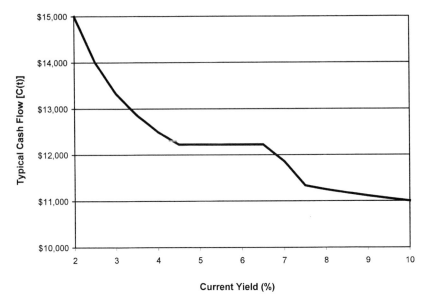

Figure 10.1. Interest Rate Sensitivity of PAC Cash Flows

An Example of PAC IO Mechanics

The following simple example should further clarify the PAC concept. Consider Figure 10.2, showing three amortization scenarios for a $10,000 pool. The top curve represents zero prepayment speeds, the middle curve is the base-case prepayment scenario given historical norms and expected interest rates, while the bottom curve is the highest observed prepayment environment over a comparable period in this asset class. As explained above, the PAC would be priced based, more or less, on the middle curve.

Now assume the following pricing parameters:

Period length = one month

$R = 10\%$ (APR)

$r = 5\%$ (APR)

α = (see below)

WAM = sixty periods

Pricing yield = 12% (APR)

Starting from these parameters, we can derive the price of the IO as the net present value of base-case cash flows discounted at an annual rate of 12%, yielding a basic price of

IO price ($\alpha = 0.8$): $810.39,

IO price ($\alpha = 0.9$): $911.69.

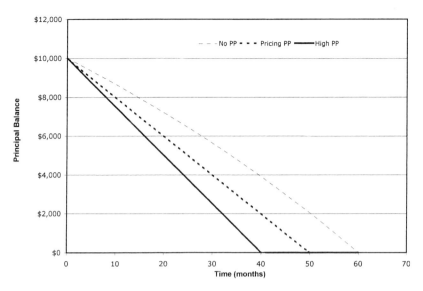

Figure 10.2. An Example of PAC Mechanics

Essentially, an IO strip of 5% is being structured into this transaction. The question is what will happen to the return on the IO under various prepayment scenarios. The 12% return on this investment is clearly realized only if prepayments cause the pool to amortize exactly according to the "Pricing PP" curve in Figure 10.2 an unlikely result despite the best of intentions. Before buying, the IO investor will want to see the distribution of returns across the entire spectrum of prepayment scenarios and attach probability estimates to these scenarios. The hypothetical distribution of returns is presented in Table 10.1 for a range of prepayment speeds measured by a single parameter, δ. By definition, zero prepayment means $\delta = 1$ and corresponds to the maximum return achievable on this investment. (In prepayment analysis, defaults and prepayments are not distinguished.) For pricing purposes, $\delta = 0.9$ is assumed, while the PAC schedule $S(t)$ is defined using $\delta = 0.8$. In other words, either a 10% or a 20% prepayment protection cushion has been created as measured by the value of α.

As expected, the IO with $\alpha = 0.8$ is afforded a wider protection region compared to the holder of the second IO, with only a 10% cushion. Also, note that both IO holders are exposed to the same return profile up to speeds corresponding to the beginning of the PAC Structuring Band (i.e., for $\delta = 0.8$).

Although this analysis can form the basis of a purchase in some sense, it is more interesting to investigate risk-adjusted returns in both cases. To do this, a probability distribution of prepayment speeds is postulated via the parameter δ.

Assume prepayments are ruled by a *gamma process* (for more on gamma processes, please see chapter 12) defined by a distribution function $F(\delta)$ with

Table 10.1
Hypothetical Distribution of Returns for an IO Strip

PP Speeds: δ Parameter	IO Strip Returns (%)	
	$\alpha = 0.8$	$\alpha = 0.9$
1.000	18.49	18.49
0.975	16.90	16.90
0.950	15.29	15.29
0.925	13.65	13.65
0.900	12.00	12.00
0.875	10.32	10.32
0.850	8.62	8.62
0.825	6.90	6.90
0.800	5.14	5.14
0.775	5.14	5.14
0.750	5.14	5.14
0.725	5.14	5.14
0.700	5.14	3.56
0.675	5.14	1.55
0.650	5.14	−0.50
0.625	3.81	−2.60
0.600	1.55	−4.74
0.575	−0.76	−6.93
0.550	−3.13	−9.18
0.525	−5.56	11.49
0.500	−8.05	−13.87

a mean $E(\delta) = 0.9$ and a standard deviation such that $F^{-1}(0.99) = 0.8$. In other words, prepayment speeds used as a basis for the schedule $S(t)$ exceed 99% of all historical experience. The resulting probability distribution is shown in Figure 10.3. Surprisingly, when the risk-adjusted return is computed for the first and the second IO, one finds essentially the same value: approximately 12% in both cases. Although the first IO had significantly more downside protection due to the 20% cushion, the overall risk profile is in fact similar on a probabilistic and historical basis.

Of course, an investor might assign a higher probability to severe prepayment scenarios than those implied by the Gamma process assumed here, but the basis for such an assumption should be examined. The authors believe that the attribution of equal probabilities to increasingly remote outcomes is the source of much suboptimality in structured analysis and in rating-agency work in general. We conclude that in the absence of better prepayment or yield curve models, the perception of added investor security that seems to be associated with the PAC IO feature is perhaps misguided.

Finally, it should be noted that ABS investment bankers have, over the years, shown much creativity in defining PAC schedules for IO cash flow allo-

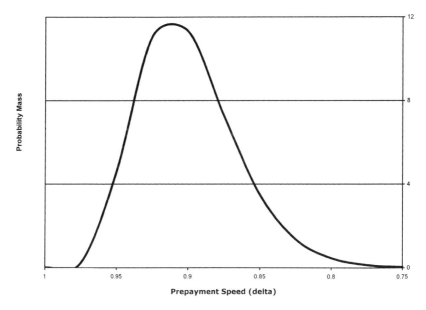

Figure 10.3. Sample Prepayment Speed Distribution

cation purposes. Unfortunately, it cannot generally be said that such offerings in the ABS universe have met with the success they once encountered in MBS. To be sure, this is in large measure related to the issue of credit risk; but it is also related to the fact that investors have yet to develop the confidence required to allow the design envelope to be pushed out to a sophistication level where the special features of the PAC can emerge and reach maturity. Until that day, PAC IO classes will remain largely marginal features of most non-MBS transactions.

Targeted Amortization Classes

In ABS generally, TACs are usually created as a compromise between purely pro rata and purely sequential principal allocation schemes. The TAC usually consists of a targeted class balance to be potentially achieved at every period pending fund availability. Here, the goal is not necessarily prepayment protection but the attempt to strike a balance between the extremes of sequential versus pro rata structures; TACs represent a family of intermediate structures available between such extremes.

In some asset classes, TACs are simply schedules of targeted amortization without any prepayment protection intent. For instance, this is the case in aircraft ABS whereby minimum, scheduled, and supplemental schedules are defined and used at various locations throughout the waterfall. In such cases,

TACs are designed merely to introduce additional principal protection to junior or senior classes and to effectively undermine a nominally sequential bond structure that would otherwise create excessive extension risk to junior security holders. The main impact of such TACs is an improvement in junior security credit ratings at the expense of the senior debt. While this might sometimes be undesirable, senior securities might in fact be initially rated above minimally acceptable levels such that the credit arbitrage induced by the TAC becomes a simple way to optimize the structure at essentially no cost

From a pricing standpoint, the consequences of introducing a TAC to an otherwise purely sequential two-tranche structure are clear. It extends the average life of the senior security and correspondingly shortens that of the junior security so that it pays down faster than under the purely sequential regime. The credit consequences are less clear. In fact, depending on the cash flow universe to which such structures are exposed, the credit impact of introducing a TAC can be both severe and counterintuitive. The reasons for this are obvious when one considers the mechanics of structured finance, which are distinct from those of corporate finance. Since the credit rating of a structured security is proportional to its average reduction of yield, it is heavily and disproportionately dependent on cases where this reduction is non-zero—at the tail of the cash flow probability distribution. Unfortunately, the introduction of a TAC may severely affect yield outcomes at the tail. Consequently, because such extreme scenarios are precisely those that matter to the assignment of credit ratings, TACs may have a profound impact on the latter. While the maturity impact may be favorable on average, the credit impact may be surprising. This non-linear behavior is especially harsh when the TAC schedule is inserted between senior and junior interest in the standard waterfall (see levels 2 and 3, discussed earlier). Doing this causes cash to be diverted for principal payments on senior obligations at the expense of junior interest payments. In a stress case, the impact on the junior bond's reduction of yield may be devastating, and its credit rating thus severely reduced.

The situation is far more favorable to the junior class when the senior principal TAC schedule is inserted after junior interest but ahead of junior principal. Here, junior bond-holders would still receive a full interest allocation before cash would be diverted to pay senior principal, thereby significantly increasing their yield owing to the difference between junior and senior coupons. This improved reduction-of-yield environment in a stress case would help to raise the junior tranche credit rating.

To solidify the latter argument, we simulated the rating process on a hypothetical transaction using the following structures:

1. Pro rata principal allocation
2. Sequential principal allocation
3. TAC 1 structure (Class A interest, Class B interest, Class A TAC principal schedule, and Class B principal with all remaining available funds)

4. TAC 2 structure (Class A interest, Class A TAC principal schedule, Class B interest, and Class B principal with all remaining available funds)

The TAC structures were computed using the midpoint between purely sequential and purely pro rata amortizations, respectively. In other words, if P_t is the expected Class A principal balance for a pro rata structure at time t and S_t is the corresponding value for the sequential structure, then the TAC balance T_t is simply computed as

$$T_t = \frac{1}{2}(P_t + S_t). \tag{10.11}$$

The difference between the TAC 1 and TAC 2 structures is that Class A principal distributions come ahead of Class B Interest distributions under TAC 2 but after Class B Interest under TAC 1. We consider both cases to demonstrate clearly the significant impact that senior principal distributions ahead of junior interest may have on ratings. This feature is commonly seen in aircraft ABS, for instance. The basic deal parameters are as follows:

Initial pool balance = $10,000

WAC = 10%

WAM = sixty months

A class = $8,000

B class = $2,000

A coupon = 6%

B coupon = 8%

For this simple exercise, we assumed that prepayments resulted solely from defaults and measured the default process using a logistic curve as we have done before. We then postulated a normal distribution for the default curve's critical parameter (a) and computed the average reduction of yield on the liabilities stemming from this particular asset behavior. To make it easier to grasp, we expressed these reductions of yield as Moody's letter-grade ratings. Table 10.2 shows the resulting senior and junior credit ratings for various values of the coefficient of variation (COV) used for the default process.

Before we discuss these rather surprising results, consider what happens if the maturity of the pool is extended to twenty years instead of five. Table 10.3 is the analogue of Table 10.2 for a twenty-year transaction but with slightly different liability interest rates (6.5% and 9.0% for Class A and Class B, respectively) and slightly different coefficients of variation. The rates were increased simply to reflect the longer maturity of the deal and the COV was adjusted for convenience. In any event, our conclusions are neither dependent on the particular interest rates nor on the COV values.

Table 10.2
Ratings Impact of the Payment Regime (five-year transaction)

	COV									
	5.40%		8.00%		10.67%		16.00%		20.00%	
Tranche	A	B	A	B	A	B	A	B	A	B
Pro Rata	Aa3	Aa3	A3	A3	Baa3	Baa3	Ba2	Ba2	Ba3	Ba3
Sequential	Aaa	A3	Aaa	Baa3	Aaa	Ba3	Aaa	B3	Aaa	Caa2
TAC 1	Aaa	A3	Aaa	Ba1	Aaa	Ba3	Aa3	Caa1	A1	Caa2
TAC 2	Aaa	A3	Aaa	Ba1	Aaa	Ba3	Aaa	Caa1	Aaa	Caa2

Those who were wondering how much of a difference the structure can make should now be convinced that ignoring it can lead to serious misconceptions about credit risk. Even for a single volatility level (e.g., 4.35% in Table 10.3), the junior rating ranges anywhere from Aaa in the pro rata structure to A2 in the second TAC case. This is a sizable difference, attributable purely to structural effects.

Next, consider TAC 1 and TAC 2 in Table 10.2 under the most severe environment (COV = 20%). While the two TAC structures give essentially identical results at lower volatility values, it can be readily seen that, with respect to the senior class, TAC 1 is significantly worse than TAC 2 in such extreme cases. How rating agencies view volatility is therefore important in the assessment of which structure is in fact optimal in practice. Selection of a structure simply cannot be done without initial rating agency consultation to set basic asset behavior assumptions.

If the interaction between the assets and the liabilities is ignored when one is deciding on a structure, the rating outcomes can be severely distorted. In the end, there are minor deficiencies in asset performance that can best be addressed structurally without any requirement for a fundamental change of views on asset quality. In order to do this however, the paramount role of the

Table 10.3
Ratings Impact of the Payment Regime (twenty-year transaction)

	COV									
	4.35%		6.52%		10.87%		17.39%		21.74%	
Tranches	A	B	A	B	A	B	A	B	A	B
Pro Rata	Aaa	Aaa	Aa3	Aa2	A3	A2	Baa3	Baa3	Baa3	Baa3
Sequential	Aaa	Aa3	Aa1	A3	A1	Baa3	Baa2	Ba1	Baa3	Ba2
TAC 1	Aaa	Aa3	Aa1	A3	A1	Baa3	Baa2	Ba1	Baa3	Ba2
TAC 2	Aaa	A2	Aaa	Baa2	Aaa	Ba1	Aaa	Ba3	Aaa	B2

bond structure needs to be explicitly recognized and incorporated into the modeling.

TACs are an extremely difficult and tricky structural feature to use effectively without detailed knowledge of asset-behavioral assumptions and without being intimately cognizant of the interactions and correlations that exist between transaction parameters. As Tables 10.2 and 10.3 clearly demonstrate, the wanton introduction of a TAC into a structure, possibly from a naive desire to emulate other transactions or sellers, can actually cause the junior bond to fall below Baa3 and the senior tranche to rise to Aaa. An example of this type of nonlinear effect between TAC 1 and TAC 2 is given in Table 10.3 for the case COV = 10.87%.

Finally, it may be seen from Table 10.2 that in certain cases (e.g., COV = 8.00%) the TAC 1 structure may in fact be worse than the sequential structure due to the "interest rate" effect. This counterintuitive phenomenon stems from the fact that under a sequential structure, the junior class will receive interest on its full initial principal balance rather than on a decreasing balance. Unfortunately, when heavy losses show up much later, the relatively small increase in principal distributions arising from TAC 1 will, on average, be unable to make up for lost interest distributions. As a result, the reduction of yield is actually lower for the sequential than for the TAC 1 structure. Although the improvement is usually in the one-notch range, it can still make a difference depending on the precise position of the tranche along the credit spectrum. From Table 10.3, note also that this phenomenon seems to disappear in a longer maturity but otherwise identical transaction. In that case, the TAC 1 and the sequential structures are "optically" identical throughout the range of volatilities investigated. By this we mean that letter-grade ratings are indistinguishable although the associated reduction of yields are definitely not. This aberration is yet another rationale for the use of a continuous scale in structured finance.

Part III

*Applications of Numerical
Methods to Structured Finance*

11

The Art of Mathematical Modeling

When the pianist Van Cliburn was still a student at the Juilliard School of Music, the legendary Arthur Rubenstein overheard him practicing one day and declared, "Now that you can play the piano so well, maybe you could start to make some music!"

As strange as it may seem, this exchange reflects the essence of financial analysis. Good analysis, like good music, has a quality not contained in the building blocks, a quality that can only be judged from the final result. Just as making music is more than playing the right notes in sequence, so is the difference between a bad and a good model more than a matter of applying stock solutions. It is the result of the analyst's skillful selection and combination of methods to suit the context. An analyst must be free to choose the most appropriate technique at will; achieving this freedom will enable the analyst to "make music": to express the truth locked up in the data. Without some "virtuosity" in model building, the credit analysis of ABS is sure to fall short of the mark.

A major goal of this book is to demonstrate the art of mathematical modeling as it pertains to repackaging and analyzing the credit quality of structured securities. Here the ability to build cash flow models in sufficient detail to address the intrinsic granularity of the assets is paramount in importance. Granular modeling brings out the intensely statistical nature of asset portfolios and encourages the analyst to pay proper respect to such issues as diversification and correlation.

On the other hand, a credit analyst should not come to rely exclusively on the outputs of statistical models or be lulled into a false sense of comfort that these outputs are the unimpeachable truth. Models should be viewed as a way to organize our thoughts so that influence factors can be looked at rationally. John Maynard Keynes expressed this caveat insightfully when he stated,

> The object of our analysis is not to provide us with a machine or method of blind manipulation which will furnish an infallible answer, but to provide ourselves with an organized and orderly method of thinking out particular problems; and after we have reached a provisional conclusion by isolating the complicating factors one by one, we then have to go back on ourselves and allow as well as we can for the proper interaction of the factors amongst themselves. This is the nature of economic thinking.[1]

In what follows, we review just enough theory to solve problems in structured finance. Individually, the methods described in these chapters are straightforward. But combined into a structural analysis model, they may interact in

unexpected and counterintuitive ways that can ultimately defeat the original intention: knowing the limits of each method is also a part of "making music"
instead of cacophony. We prove very few theorems except where the proof illustrates a fundamental truth or guides the practitioner through the many pitfalls
that can occur. The reason we leave the proofs out is that whereas these techniques are not new (and a complete theoretical treatment can be found in many
scholarly textbooks), the emphasis of this book is on understanding the fundamentals and achieving useful analytical results. The emphasis on practical application rather than theoretical knowledge is critical: the application of statistical
techniques to real data is not trivial since empirical data often do not cooperate
with the goals of the analyst! Yet without results, the entire effort is wasted. Analysts struggling with a method that does not seem to work out have no choice
but to go back to fundamental principles and understand the problem anew in
order to find closure. There are no shortcuts to a deeper understanding of these
securities and their credit dynamics. Time taken at the front end to learn the
tools of the structured trade will be amply rewarded at the back end with more
efficient structures and better fundamental credit understanding.

Notation and Some Basic Concepts

Table 11.1 is a short summary of our conventions along with some algebraic
background, with the notation on the left and the definition or comment on
the right. This notation will be used throughout the remainder of the book.

Analysis and Synthesis: Two Philosophies of Mathematical Modeling

In this section, we present the two essential philosophies of numerical analysis.
Structured credit analysts need to be aware of the essential trade-offs between
them so they can make better use of the time allocated to a solution and have
realistic expectations about the quality of results under field conditions. In a
mathematical context, the words *analysis* and *synthesis* have a fairly precise
meaning. Analysis is the taking apart of a phenomenon into its constituent
units, while synthesis is its reconstitution therefrom. For instance, the Fourier
analysis and synthesis of a function $f(x)$ are found in the following way:

$$\text{Fourier analysis: } a_n = \left(\frac{1}{\pi}\right)\int_{-\pi}^{\pi} f(x)\cos(nx)\,dx$$

$$\text{Fourier synthesis: } f(x) = \sum_{n=1}^{\infty} a_n \cos(nx)$$

Here, the coefficients a_n are the constituent units. Therefore, in general, analysis and synthesis are inverse operations.

Table 11.1
Conventional Notation

Notation	Definition
a A	Parameters, variables, or scalar functions are in lower- and uppercase, non-boldface Latin alphabet letters.
$\mathbf{f}$	Vectors or vector functions are in small, boldface, Latin alphabet letters (by *vector* we mean a column vector unless otherwise specified).
λ	Parameters of probability distribution functions or specially defined parameters are usually denoted by lowercase Greek letters.
$\bar{x}$	A quantity with an overstrike will normally designate the mean value of that quantity over some defined region.
$\mathbf{M}$	Capital, boldface Latin alphabet letters will denote matrices.
f_i, m_{ij}	Elements of a vector $\mathbf{f}$ and of a matrix $\mathbf{M}$ are denoted as shown, with i as the row index and j as the column index.
Note:	The rank of square matrix $\mathbf{M}$ is the order of the smallest nonzero determinant constructed from $\mathbf{M}$. The rank of a square matrix with N rows is an integer between 1 and N and is equal to the size of the largest nonzero determinant of the matrix.
$\mathbf{I}$	The identity matrix of rank N is a square matrix with unity along the main diagonal and zeros elsewhere. The rank of this matrix will always be understood from the context without specifying it.
$\mathbf{M^T}$	The transpose of a matrix $\mathbf{M}$. It is defined by $m_{ij}^T = m_{ji}$. Transposing a matrix is equivalent to "turning" it 90° clockwise (or counterclockwise). The transpose of a column vector is a row vector.
$\mathbf{M}^{-1}$	The inverse of an N-dimensional matrix $\mathbf{M}$ of rank N is defined by the equation $\mathbf{MM}^{-1} = \mathbf{I}$. An $[N \times N]$ square matrix with a rank less than N cannot be inverted. We will call these matrices *singular*.
Note:	A matrix $\mathbf{M}$ will be referred to as positive semi-definite or nonnegative definite if, for any vector $\mathbf{f}$, the following holds: $\mathbf{f}^T \mathbf{M} \mathbf{f} \geq 0$. All the eigenvalues of a positive semi-definite matrix are nonnegative.
$\lvert x \rvert$	This refers to the norm of a quantity x. If x is a scalar, its norm will be equal to its absolute value, i.e., $\lvert x \rvert = \text{abs}(x)$.
Note:	The norm of complex number $c = a + ib$ is given by: $\lvert c \rvert = = \sqrt{a^2 + b^2}$. If x is a vector $\mathbf{x}$, its norm will be the norm of its largest element: $\lvert x \rvert = \max \lvert x_i \rvert$. If x is a matrix $\mathbf{M}$, its norm can be defined in a few ways. In this book, we will refer to its row-sum norm $\lvert \mathbf{M} \rvert = \max_i \sum_k \lvert m_{ik} \rvert$. Matrix norms satisfy four basic properties. If $\mathbf{x}$ and $\mathbf{y}$ are matrices and a is any constant, we have 1. $\lvert x \rvert \geq 0$ 2. $\lvert xy \rvert \leq \lvert x \rvert \lvert y \rvert$ 3. $\lvert x + y \rvert \leq \lvert x \rvert + \lvert y \rvert$ 4. $\lvert ax \rvert = \lvert a \rvert \lvert x \rvert$
Note:	Vector spaces in which norms have been defined are called *normed spaces*. In this book, we will be concerned exclusively with such spaces.

In the context of this section, however, they refer to two different methods of data processing with a view to forecasting. By *analysis*, we mean the assumption that the given data represent the appropriate level of granularity from which to begin the synthetic process, and that the analyst's task is simply to synthesize the true process from that level. The raw data per se are assumed to contain the most fundamental truth, and the search for answers stays at that level. This philosophy underlies the use of regression techniques.

Synthesis represents a philosophy that views raw data as mere evidence of yet-to-be-understood processes, which we must deconstruct. As soon as we have extracted the process, we can proceed in the reverse direction and reconstruct the basic data going forward. Synthesis is thus an express modeling of the phenomenon. In practice, synthesis involves a search for invariants of the data field around which models will be constructed. These invariants are then seen as representing the true phenomenon underlying the data. This search will usually lead to a deeper understanding of data structures than is possible with analysis alone. That is because the invariants we will discover normally represent causal relationships between data elements, rather than accidental circumstances. Paradoxically, perhaps, the goal of analysis is synthesis, and the goal of synthesis is analysis.

In this chapter, we introduce numerical techniques that facilitate data synthesis and promote a deeper understanding of intrinsic data relationships. Statistics alone can never let us attach meaning to correlation; only physics can do that. Synthesis allows a physical understanding that is difficult to achieve with analysis. There are many instances in financial analysis where synthetic methods lead to more powerful and precise results because the physics of the process have been extracted by invariance metrics. Although the discovery of causal relationships often entails considerable investigation and hard work, the improvements in the predictive power of the results are well worth the effort.

Going from philosophy to praxis, we illustrate below how the same data set would be handled using both methods and compare the predictive accuracy of the outcomes. Consider the credit card master trust receivable data for a hypothetical small issuer, shown in Table 11.2. The goal of the modeling exercise is to forecast the next six months of default data given the last twelve months of actuals. Only current balances and thirty-day delinquencies are given a priori. The other columns will be explained shortly. Although current balances and delinquencies are also important, most credit analysts prefer to focus on defaulted balances to gauge the short-term creditworthiness of credit card master trusts. We neither agree nor disagree with this proposition.

Column (4) of Table 11.2 shows the seasonal factors computed using a model of the form

$$y = y_0 + at + b\cos\left(\frac{2\pi ct}{12}\right). \tag{11.1}$$

In this model, a, b, and c were constants to be evaluated. A positive seasonal factor means that the actual value is above the trend while a negative factor

Table 11.2
A Comparison between Analysis and Synthesis

Issuer X Credit Card Master Trust Data

Month	Current ($)	30 Days Past Due ($)	Factors	Deseasonal ($)	Default ($)	Invariant
Jan-98	370,093,924	53,342,850	0.195	44,585,043	1,567,934	—
Feb-98	350,746,385	52,005,706	0.079	48,461,307	1,789,344	—
Mar-98	369,061,509	53,777,377	0.087	49,843,190	1,968,673	—
Apr-98	352,763,458	52,179,690	0.018	51,383,437	1,988,945	—
May-98	347,032,096	48,628,962	−0.082	52,336,145	2,078,909	—
Jun-98	356,799,990	49,957,581	−0.095	54,254,695	2,273,837	0.0510
Jul-98	367,503,341	51,185,405	−0.121	56,619,572	2,544,219	0.0525
Aug-98	378,553,574	51,482,638	−0.082	55,180,875	2,437,332	0.0489
Sep-98	396,571,745	59,857,149	0.013	59,255,707	2,535,773	0.0494
Oct-98	465,095,012	63,653,119	0.057	61,068,262	2,605,325	0.0498
Nov-98	485,529,966	64,831,775	0.089	60,813,918	2,731,724	0.0504
Dec-98	493,420,220	70,986,798	0.122	65,499,856	2,898,922	0.0512
Jan-99				**69,314,930**		

means it is below the trend. To save space, the intermediate results are not displayed.

The workhorse forecasting method of analysis is *regression*, and a regression line can be fitted to any data set in no time. By contrast, synthesis involves the search for invariants that may not even exist. As a result, there is no infallible scheme to find them. To achieve results within a reasonable time frame, experience and knowledge are therefore invaluable.

For the task at hand, we first define the following two quantities:

- Current defaulted balances $d(t)$
- Thirty-day delinquent and deseasonalized balances $d30(t)$

After many trials and dead ends, we discover the following relationship:

$$\frac{d(t)}{d30(t-5)} \approx K \tag{11.2}$$

To see that this is so, plot the ratio of column (6) to column (5) five months prior to obtain the data shown in column (7). Given the usual instability of credit card master trust receivable data, the pattern might appear remarkable at first, but in fact it makes perfect sense, for it says that a constant portion of thirty-day delinquent balances will write off contractually five months later. The reason we must de-seasonalize the raw data is that a significant proportion of these thirty-day accounts represent "sloppy payors" (rather than poor credits) whose balances will cure the following month.

Once an invariant has been discovered, the rest is straightforward. The forecast equation is simply given by

$$d(t) = K \cdot d30(t-5). \tag{11.3}$$

In practice, an "invariant" is allowed to vary somewhat, but with a variance much smaller than that of the raw data. For instance, if the average variance of raw data is 10% we could consider something invariant if its variance remained below 1%. Note also that the invariant need not be a constant. It can come in the form of a smooth and parametric invariant relationship—for instance, if instead of equation (11.2), we had found

$$\frac{d(t)}{d30(t-5)} \approx Kt. \tag{11.4}$$

The forecasting equation would change, but the method would not. For that matter, any analytical function of time will do as an invariant.

The discovery of this invariant (11.2) is fortuitous because, in order to obtain the required half-year default forecast, we simply need to forecast the next data point of thirty-day balances, since the other five months are found automatically by equation (11.3) using existing data. The extra data point, shown in bold at the bottom of Table 11.2, was derived from equation (11.1) using $t = 13$.

Table 11.3
Analysis versus Synthesis of the Hypothetical Credit Card Data

	Default Forecast ($)		
Month	Synthesis	Analysis	Actuals
Jan-99	2,759,044	3,004,593	2,822,502
Feb-99	2,962,785	3,115,287	2,930,195
Mar-99	3,053,413	3,225,982	2,986,238
Apr-99	3,040,696	3,336,676	3,101,812
May-99	3,274,993	3,447,371	3,307,743
Jun-99	3,465,747	3,558,065	3,514,267
Goodness-of-fit statistics			
R^2 (analysis)		95.08%	
Error % (synthesis)		1.70%	
Error % (analysis)		15.95%	
Ratio of errors		9.4	

Under analysis, we need to forecast six months of data starting from the trend line obtained by the first twelve months of actuals. In general, this is a riskier proposition. Table 11.3 is a summary comparison of results obtained using regression on the one hand and equation (11.3) on the other. For purposes of error computation, the actuals are shown in the last column of Table 11.3. The results are graphically displayed in Figure 11.1.

Analysis versus Synthesis: A Sober Assessment

Based on the results, a credit analyst would be completely justified in using regression as a forecasting tool. Indeed, an R-squared of more than 95% for the first twelve months of default data could have been a great source of comfort. Nevertheless, the regression was unable to capture the physics of the problem. The invariant-based method that produced equation (11.3) did significantly better. Relative to the average realized default balances in those six months, the root mean square error for the latter was 1.7%, compared to around 16% for the regression line. That is because five out of six forecast data points were already implicitly contained in the given data, whereas regression "went out on a limb" for all the data points. Although both methods forecast roughly the same level of defaults after 180 days, regression overshot all intermediary points.

What also helped the result under the invariance method is that a synthetic process often reflects a "pipeline" effect, whereby future defaults are often implicit in current and past data well ahead of their explicit recognition. Even though the absolute dollar values were quite small compared to most credit card trusts, an improvement of approximately one order of magnitude

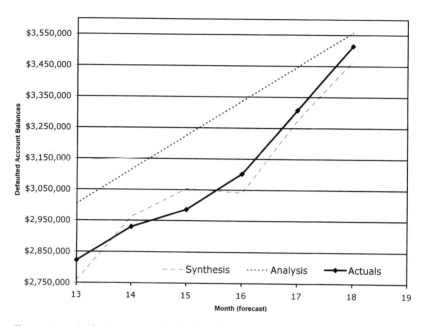

Figure 11.1. Analysis versus Synthesis of the Hypothetical Credit Card Data

was achieved via synthesis. In fact, master trust data have a daily structure denied to us by the convention of month-end reporting. It would be interesting to redo this exercise using the microstructure of the data. In that case, it is virtually guaranteed that synthesis would strongly outperform regression.

To sum up, not only have we achieved superior results, but the insight into the structure of credit card data is now deeper than it would have been from regression analysis alone. Admittedly, the benefits of synthesis came at a cost: it is much easier to talk about invariants after you have found them. Whereas analysis takes a few minutes, synthesis normally takes a few hours or days, at the risk of leading nowhere. However, time spent understanding data is by no means wasted. Apart from error reduction, perhaps the greatest benefit derived from synthetic methods is the store of knowledge accumulated along the way, something that cannot be valued. The use of synthesis is wrapped in the spirit of discovery . . . the kind that usually culminates in success, and the difference between a mere amateur playing with numbers and a highly skilled analyst.

Readers might object that regression is actually better since it is conservative in assessing defaults. Even so, the goal of prediction is not to be conservative or liberal but to be correct. Correctness is impossible when there is bias. Hence the superiority of synthesis is the fact that the forecasting errors were evenly distributed above and below the actual results. On that score, regression did a poor job.

12

Statistical Probability Density Functions

Most structured finance analytical work will involve the selection of random numbers from given probability distributions. Consequently, the following is a brief overview of the distributions most likely to be encountered in a typical structured credit analysis. This section should be read in conjunction with the section on sampling random deviates at the end of the chapter, which deals with sampling from such distributions using the inverse distribution function method (IDFM), the most commonly used of all random sampling methods. We deal exclusively with one-dimensional distributions, as they are by far the most commonly encountered. For multiple dimensions, other straightforward sampling methods exist, notably the *copula function approach,*[1] which is readily applicable to multidimensional normal distributions.

Probability distributions are usually defined via their associated probability density function $f(x)$, a non-negative function of its argument, x. For discrete distributions, $f(k)$ is the probability that the process will take on the value k, where k is an integer. For continuous distributions, $f(x)dx$ is the probability that the process will be found between x and $x + dx$, where x is a real number. Since the entire probability space must be spanned by $f(x)$ over its domain of definition, it follows that in both discrete and continuous distributions, probability density functions must satisfy the following normalization condition:

$$\text{Discrete distributions: } \sum_{k} f(k) = 1$$

$$\text{Continuous distributions: } \int_{x} f(x)\,dx = 1$$

The following distributions satisfy both the non-negativity and normalization conditions.

The Binomial Distribution

The *binomial distribution* is a discrete distribution appropriate in statistical processes where the sample space consists of two possible outcomes, A and B. The probability of event A is p while that of event B is $1 - p$. The probability that in n instances of the process, k of them will result in outcome A and $n - k$ in outcome B is given by

$$f(k) = \frac{n!}{k!(n-k)!}p^k(1-p)^{n-k}, \ k = 0, 1, 2, \ldots, n. \qquad (12.1)$$

The mean $E[k] = \mu$ and the variance $E[(k - \mu)^2]$ of the binomial distribution are given by

$$E(k) = np, \ E(k^2) - \{E[k]\}^2 = np(1-p).$$

The Multinomial Distribution

The binomial distribution can be generalized to more than two outcomes via the *multinomial distribution*. Assume there are m mutually exclusive events A_i, $i = 1, 2, \ldots, m$ with probabilities p_i, $i = 1, 2, 3, \ldots, m$, and that the process is sampled n times, as before. The probability that in k_1 cases A_1 will obtain, in k_2 cases A_2 will obtain, and so on, with the condition $\sum_i k_i = n$ is given by

$$f(k_1, k_2, k_3, \ldots, k_m) = \frac{n!}{k_1! k_2! \ldots k_m!} p_1^{k_1} p_2^{k_2} p_3^{k_3} \cdots p_m^{k_m}.$$

In structured finance, this distribution finds its use in the extension of the standard two-state default paradigm (nondefault and default) to a more accurate multistate delinquency paradigm. For example, we can define A_i as follows:

A_1 = Current loan

A_2 = Thirty-day delinquent loan

A_3 = Sixty-day delinquent loan

This extension allows many more virtual default states than before and will result in a different portfolio loss distribution. For example, the multinomial distribution could be used as an extension of the current binomial theorem method used to assign credit ratings to securities backed by pools of corporate loans or bonds, so-called CBOs, in an effort to provide more realistic estimates of the credit quality of such pools.

The Uniform Distribution Function

The *uniform distribution* is a continuous distribution and is an important distribution in structured finance since it allows, via the IDFM scheme, the sampling of every other probability distribution. It is defined on the interval $[a, b]$ by

$$f(x) = \frac{1}{b-a}. \qquad (12.3)$$

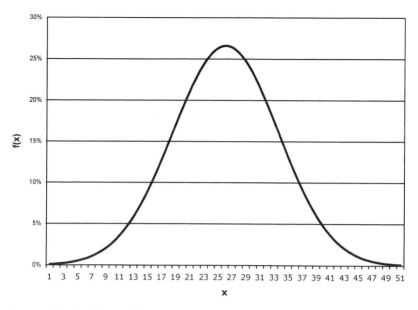

Figure 12.1. The Normal Distribution

The mean and variance are given by

$$E[x] = \frac{a+b}{2}, \; E[x^2] - \{E[x]\}^2 = \frac{(b-a)^2}{12}.$$

The Normal Distribution

The *normal distribution* is the most important continuous distribution and is also known as the *bell-shaped curve* (Figure 12.1). The main interest in it lies in its being involved in the most important theorem of statistics, the *central limit theorem* (CLT), related to the sampling of any scalar probability distribution. We will come back to this theorem in chapter 20 when discussing microeconomic distributions. As a cornerstone of parametric statistics, the CLT is also of central importance to structured finance. Readers to whom the CLT is unfamiliar may wish to consult other statistics texts for additional context.

Defined on the real line $(-\infty, \infty)$, the normal distribution is given by

$$f(x) = \frac{1}{\sqrt{2\pi\sigma^2}} e^{-1/2[(x-\mu)/\sigma]^2} \tag{12.4}$$

Its mean and variance are

$$E[x] = \mu, \; E[x^2] - \{E[x]\}^2 = \sigma^2.$$

The Lognormal Distribution

The *lognormal distribution* has come to prominence in economics in the last twenty years via the common assumption that stock prices are log-normally distributed. The latter boils down to assuming that stock returns are normally distributed. In essence, if the natural log of x is normally distributed with mean μ and variance σ^2, then x itself is referred to as lognormally distributed. Since logarithms are defined for positive values of their argument, the lognormal distribution is similarly defined on the real positive axis $(0, \infty)$ by

$$f(x) = \frac{1}{\sigma x \sqrt{2\pi}} \, e^{-1 \backslash 2 [(\ln(x) - \mu)/\sigma]^2} \tag{12.5}$$

Its mean and variance are given by

$$E[x] = e^{\mu + \sigma^2/2}, \; E[x^2] - \{E[x]\}^2 = (e^{\sigma^2} - 1)e^{2\mu + \sigma^2}$$

Readers should be thoroughly familiar with this distribution as it crops up fairly regularly in statistical analysis of economic processes. We will have the opportunity to use the lognormal distribution when analyzing the CBO of ABS in chapter 21.

The Beta Distribution

This continuous distribution will be used later on when discussing the Cholesky decomposition method of simulating covariance matrices. It is usually defined on the standardized x domain $[0, 1]$ although x can always be mapped to any other interval via linear mapping functions.

$$f(x) = \frac{\Gamma(\alpha + \beta)}{\Gamma(\alpha)\Gamma(\beta)} x^{\alpha - 1}(1 - x)^{\beta - 1}, \tag{12.6}$$

where $\Gamma(\cdot)$ is the standard gamma function and α, β are the parameters of the beta distribution with mean and variance given by

$$E[x] = \frac{\alpha}{\alpha + \beta}, \; E[x^2] - \{E[x]\}^2 = \frac{\alpha\beta}{(\alpha + \beta)^2(\alpha + \beta + 1)}.$$

In passing, in the special case $\alpha = \beta = 1$, the beta distribution reduces to the uniform distribution.

The Gamma Distribution

The *gamma distribution* is used heavily in the insurance industry and is appropriate to high-severity/low-frequency types of exposures such as earth-

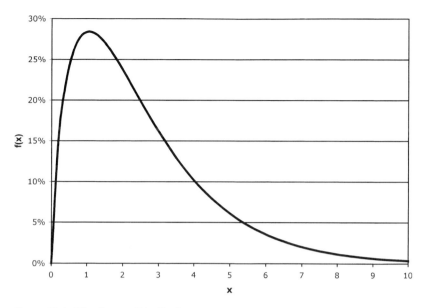

Figure 12.2. The Gamma Distribution

quakes and hurricanes. As shown in Figure 12.2, it has a fat tail, and is defined on the positive real line $[0, \infty)$ via

$$f(x) = \frac{1}{\Gamma(\alpha)\Gamma(\beta)\beta^\alpha} x^{\alpha-1} e^{-(x/\beta)}. \tag{12.7}$$

Its mean and variance are given by

$$E[x] = \alpha\beta, \; E[x^2] - \{E[x]\}^2 = \alpha\beta^2.$$

Sampling Random Deviates from Probability Distribution Functions

Selecting random samples from specified probability distributions is one of the most fundamental operations of statistical analysis and is one of the workhorse techniques of structured finance. Most models used in structured finance, usually in the form of Monte Carlo simulations of likely asset performance, will required the use of random number generators. Consequently, familiarity with this section with respect to both analytical and empirical distributions is a definite requirement of serious credit analysis. Although system-resident functions may make the analyst's task trivial in some cases, in many others there will be a need for building one's own sampling function. We introduce the basic methods of sampling in this section, with further elaboration in Appendix A.

The Inverse Distribution Function Method (IDFM)

The most widely used method to draw a random sample from any statistical distribution is the *inverse distribution function method* (IDFM) described in this section, and to which we will refer in many contexts throughout the rest of this work. In all instances, the goal will be to select a random sample reflecting a given probability density distribution $f(x)$ defined over the interval $[a, b]$. To do this, remember that the associated cumulative distribution function $F(x)$ is defined by

$$F(x) = \int_a^x f(y)\,dy. \tag{12.8}$$

By definition we have $F(a) = 0$ and since $f(x)$ is a probability density function $F(b) = 1$; that is, the cumulative distribution function $F(x)$ spans the entire range of $f(x)$ over its domain of definition $[0, 1]$. This is shown in Figure 12.3.

By definition, the inverse of the distribution function $F(x)$ corresponds to $f(x)$, that is, $dF = f\,dx$. Thus, by repeatedly choosing deviates y from a uniform distribution on the closed interval $[0, 1]$ and setting $F^{-1}(y) = x$, the resulting x will be distributed as $f(x)$. Thus, the random sampling of any distribution function comes down to sampling from a uniform probability density function. Because doing this well is not a trivial exercise, we would like to spend some time discussing alternative methods and giving representative results.

Drawing uniform samples is generally accomplished via random number generators that produce pseudo-random[2] sequences of integers starting from some initial value known as the seed,[3] as shown here:

$$I_{j+1} = aI_j + c \bmod(m) \tag{12.9}$$

In equation (12.9) the parameters m, a, and c are the modulus, multiplier, and increment, respectively. From this equation, the following three facts are clear:

1. The numbers are not truly random;
2. They must repeat themselves with a period $l \leq m$; and
3. With the appropriate choice for the increment and the multiplier, it is possible to make l equal to the modulus, m.

Statistical tests for the randomness of stochastic sequences usually seek to address two main problematic issues: autocorrelation, which relates to how random numbers follow each other in a random sample, and uniformity, which is concerned with the final probability distribution of random deviates across the interval $[0, 1]$, usually the range of interest.

The autocorrelative properties of a random number generator are usually measured by its autocorrelation spectrum, a way of determining whether the

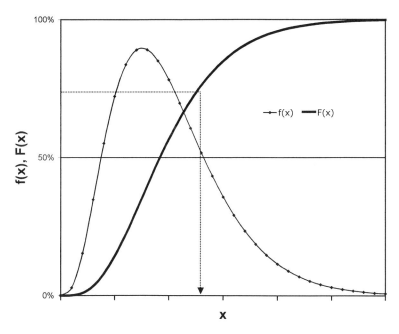

Figure 12.3. Selecting a Random Deviate Using IDFM

sampling gives evidence of a repeatable or specific pattern, which would indicate elements of nonrandomness; however, in structured finance the particular shape of the autocorrelation spectrum rarely plays a critical role in determining the quality and validity of the analysis. This is because of the averaging of credit environments that takes place en route to rating the securities. Therefore, unless the autocorrelation spectrum exhibits sharp peaks at particular locations, most random number generators will be acceptable.

It is with the second requirement—uniformity—that the greatest challenges arise. In order for a Monte Carlo simulation to be credible, reasonable assurance must be given that the entire probability space is sampled, and that low-probability regions, where high-loss scenarios (to which the rating is highly sensitive) may occur, do not receive too much or too little attention. What is required is for equal intervals to contain an equal number of draws, so that if we were to separate the range [0, 1] into ten equal intervals, it would be highly desirable to end up with 10% of the sample in each interval. By ensuring that this condition is met with sufficient accuracy, both tails of the input distribution can be sampled appropriately, and give full rein to our assumptions about pool loss dynamics.

This statistical "uniformity desideratum" can be expressed compactly by saying that each interval should contain equal probability measure. To believe that this uniformity could be achieved simply by choosing equally spaced points within [0, 1], for instance by defining $y_i = i/60$, $i = 1, 2, 3, \ldots, 60$, would be short sighted because doing so would leave gaping holes known as *discrepancies* between the regular lattice points thereby created. What is needed is a truly random arrangement without discrepancies, such that in the limit, the probability measure in each interval dy converges to dy, which is to say a truly uniform distribution.

In large samples, the performance of a generator of the form in equation (12.9) may be acceptable. Once a sufficiently high number of draws are made, the resulting probability distribution might be uniform up to the required level of error. The main caveat at this stage is that, depending on the value of m, the same random numbers might be repeated before the end of the simulation, and this might be acceptable or not. For instance, if one required samples of 50,000 deviates, each using a generator with a period of 10,000, the same number would be repeated five times throughout the simulation. One could then change the seed, the multiplier, the increment, or some combination thereof to alleviate the problem, something relatively easy to arrange. As a rule of thumb, however, picking different sets of random generator parameters to select large samples pertaining to distinct variables will lead to acceptable ensembles of credit environments across the range.

But what if one must select relatively fewer points, say a hundred or even fewer? For example, suppose one has to sample five years of monthly data, amounting to only 60 points. The problem with system-supplied random number generators (as convincingly explained in the book *Numerical Recipes*[4]) is that machine-bound intrinsic functions (e.g., the Excel Rand function) often skew the results considerably and may cause small sequences of random numbers to depart significantly from the required uniformity condition. We now describe two alternative ways of alleviating this problem. In Appendix A, we discuss the performance of all three methods with respect to small samples.

The Antithetic Correction Method

The simplest way to correct for the nonuniformity of system-supplied random number generators like Rand is to use the antithetic correction method, which requires a single line of code to implement. This method boils down to introducing anticorrelation into the sequence by selecting, not individual deviates, but *pairs* of deviates $(y_i, 1 - y_i)$. Every second call to the random number function would simply reference the antithetic deviate. For n deviates, Rand would be invoked only $n/2$ times. The principle underlying the workings of the antithetic method can be understood as follows: suppose there is too much probability mass around some interval, say $[x_1, x_2]$; the antithetic corrective scheme will relocate half of the sample in $[x_1, x_2]$ to the approximate location $1 - ([x_1 + x_2]/2)$, thereby redistributing the excess probability out where there might be a hole—for how else was there too much probability in $[x_1, x_2]$?

In effect, we are leaving untouched only half the sample generated by the system routine and placing the other half symmetrically about the mean value 0.5, eliminating the need to rely on system calls to place the other half where it should be. Because correlation does not play a role at this level, the existence of artificially introduced anticorrelation between the deviates y_i is irrelevant. Although it is easily implemented and improves results tremendously, in general this corrective scheme still leaves holes in our distribution. The next method is more involved but also more effective.

The Low-Discrepancy Sequence Method

Although van der Corput seems to have pioneered low-discrepancy methods in 1931,[5] Hammersley[6] added further confirmation of their effectiveness in 1960.

The basic idea underlying this technique is *prime number decomposition,* a common number theoretic concept. The uniqueness of such decomposition is the key to the uniformity of the resulting sequence. Given a prime number p, it is possible to decompose any integer i into a sum of powers of p as follows:

$$i = \sum_{j=0}^{m} c_j p^j \tag{12.10}$$

Once this is accomplished, the low-discrepancy sequence is defined by

$$x_i = \sum_{j=0}^{m} c_j p^{-(j+1)}. \tag{12.11}$$

It can easily be verified that the deviates x_i satisfy $0 \le x_i \le 1$. First, they are positive by definition, being sums of positive factors. Second, each c_j satisfies $0 \le c_j \le p - 1$, which allows us to write the following:

$$x_i \le (p - 1)\sum_{j=1}^{m+1} p^{-j}$$

$$x_i \le (p - 1)\left[\frac{1 - \left(\frac{1}{p}\right)^{m+2}}{1 - \frac{1}{p}} - 1\right] \le 1 - \left(\frac{1}{p}\right)^{m+1} \le 1$$

The low-discrepancy sequence x_i thus satisfies the basic domain of definition requirement of a uniform probability distribution. To find the x_i we have

$$m = \text{int}\left(\frac{\log n}{\log p}\right)$$

$$c_m = \text{int}\left(\frac{j}{p^m}\right)$$
(12.13)

In equation (12.12) "int(x)" means the integer part of x. The remaining c_j can be found from

$$c_j = \text{int}\left(\frac{i - \sum_{i=1}^{m-j} c_{j+i} p^{j+i}}{p^j}\right), j = m-1, m-2, \ldots, 0.$$
(12.14)

13

Eigenvalues and Eigenvectors

The greatest discovery in linear algebra may well be the existence of eigenvalues and eigenvectors. In addition to underlying much of numerical and statistical analysis, eigenvectors are particularly critical to the study of the long-run properties of the Markov chain, an extremely versatile tool with wide application to cash flow simulation. As a result, eigenvalue and eigenvector concepts are pivotal to the proper understanding of cash flow modeling in structured finance.

A Road Trip through Alabama

Imagine driving on a highway in the state of Alabama, a region with many managed pine forests. From a bird's-eye perspective, your position might look like that of Figure 13.1, where the dots represent rows of trees planted by the forestry department.

If you are driving in the traveling direction but looking off to the left in the direction of arrow a, you see a forest with trees randomly placed. However, if you turn your head in the direction of arrow b or to its perpendicular, arrow c, the randomness dissipates before your eyes as the regular tree lattice suddenly materializes. Directions b and c uniquely present themselves as orderly paths flanked by trees in formation. These are the "eigenvectors" of the forest. They are intrinsic properties of the forest; they are not an accidental coordinate system generated by the observer. If you knew in advance what these eigenvectors were, you would immediately understand the forest as a well-ordered pattern; and in describing the forest to other passengers, it would be much simpler to speak in terms of eigenvectors than in terms of random outcroppings.

All matrices—which we can think of as "numerical forests"—have characteristic directions. A *vector* is a set of coordinates describing some direction;[1] hence, with every characteristic or eigen-direction, there is an associated eigenvector. And since, by definition, N-dimensional space has N mutually independent directions, an N-dimensional matrix has N eigen-directions and hence N eigenvectors. Directions b and c in Figure 13.1 are also special because they are at right angles to each other. Such eigen-directions are interchangeable, or "symmetric." Symmetric eigenvectors are interchangeable because rotating one eigenvector by 90 degrees simply lines it up with another one. If the eigenvectors of a matrix point at right angles to each other, we will refer to them as

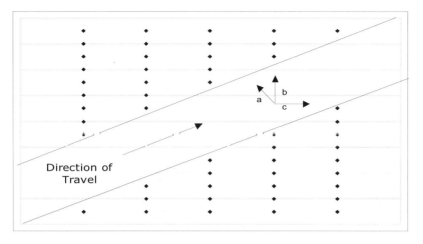

Figure 13.1. A Pine Forest in Alabama

orthogonal, and to the matrix as *symmetric.* The symmetry of a matrix is a telltale sign of the orthogonality of its eigenvectors. But eigenvectors are not always orthogonal: matrices can have eigenvectors pointing in any direction.

Now consider equation (13.1), representing the operation of an arbitrary N-dimensional matrix **A** on an N-dimensional vector **x** to produce another N-dimensional vector **y**:

$$\mathbf{Ax} = \mathbf{y} \tag{13.1}$$

What is the geometry behind a matrix equation like (13.1)? As indicated earlier, any **x** input to equation (13.1) is nothing but an N-dimensional vector whose endpoint in N-space is given by its x-coordinates and whose starting point is the origin, while the result **y** is just another vector in the same N-space.

For example, consider the following two-dimensional matrix **A:**

$$\mathbf{A} = \begin{bmatrix} 1 & -\dfrac{3}{2} \\ -\dfrac{5}{2} & 2 \end{bmatrix} \tag{13.2}$$

Any vector in two or more dimensions can be turned into any other vector in the same space simply by rotating and shrinking or stretching the first one. In two dimensions, the result of the operation of **A** on any **x**, may thus be regarded as a rotation coupled with a stretching or shrinkage of **x**, depending on the entries of **A**. Take the point **x** = [1, 2], for instance. Used as input to **A**, we compute **y** = [−2, (3/2)]. Whereas **x** had a length of $\sqrt{5}$ and was pointing 63° counterclockwise from the x-axis, the new vector **y** is now pointing 143° from the x-axis and has a length 5/2. This means that **x** has been both rotated 80° counterclockwise and stretched by a factor of $\sqrt{5}/2$. Now repeat

Table 13.1
How A Stretches X

Iteration	Input (x)	Output (y)	Length lxl	Angle (θ)°	Δθ
1	(1, 2)	(−2, 1.5)	2.5	143	80
2	(−2, 1.5)	(−4.3, 8)	9.1	118	−25
3	(−4.3, 8)	(−16.3, 26.6)	31.2	121	2
4	(−16.3, 26.6)	(−56.2, 93.9)	109.4	121	0
5	(−56.2, 93.9)	(−197, 328.2)	382.8	121	0

this process iteratively using the output **y** as the new input **x**. Table 13.1 shows what happens during the first few trials. Although the output vector lengthens with every iterate, it winds up pointing in a limiting direction, then keeps its orientation—an orientation that we suspect must be special or preferential. Indeed, if we select a vector pointing right away in that direction, say **x** = (−3, 5), the following remarkable result occurs:

$$
\begin{bmatrix} 1 & -\frac{3}{2} \\ -\frac{5}{2} & 2 \end{bmatrix} \begin{bmatrix} -3 \\ 5 \end{bmatrix} = \begin{bmatrix} -10\frac{1}{2} \\ 17\frac{1}{2} \end{bmatrix} = \frac{7}{2} \begin{bmatrix} -3 \\ 5 \end{bmatrix}
$$

Notice that **A** does not rotate this vector at all but merely stretches it by a factor of 3 1/2, which is the stretching factor, or the eigenvalue associated with this vector. The vector must therefore be an eigenvector. The ratio 382.8/109.4 is indeed precisely 7/2.

In other words, for any vector pointing in one of the eigen-directions, and its corresponding eigenvalue λ, the following condition holds:

$$\mathbf{Ax} = \lambda\mathbf{x} \tag{13.3}$$

However, this amounts to

$$(\mathbf{A} - \lambda\mathbf{I})\mathbf{x} = 0. \tag{13.4}$$

Matrix theory tells us that equation (13.4) does not have a nontrivial solution unless the left-hand-side matrix is singular (i.e., its determinant is zero). Therefore, the defining equation for the eigenvalues is

$$\det(\mathbf{A} - \lambda\mathbf{I}) = 0 \tag{13.5}$$

Now note that since the determinant of $\mathbf{A}^T$, the transpose of **A**, is the same as that of **A**, we could also obtain the eigenvalues by writing down

$$\mathbf{x}^T\mathbf{A} = \lambda\mathbf{x}^T \tag{13.6}$$

Applying equation (13.5) to **A** given by equation (13.2) we find $\lambda^2 - 3\lambda - (7/4) = 0$. This quadratic equation has two roots, $\lambda_1 = 7/2$, $\lambda_2 = -(1/2)$. As expected, 7/2 is one of the roots.

Let us get inside this iterative process more deeply using a simple case. Assume we concoct a matrix with trivial eigenvalues and eigenvectors. For instance, select the original matrix $\mathbf{A}$:

$$\mathbf{A} = \begin{bmatrix} 1 & 0 & 0 \\ 0 & 4 & 0 \\ 0 & 0 & 2 \end{bmatrix}$$

Because $\mathbf{A}$ is diagonal, the eigenvectors of this matrix are [1,0,0], [0,1,0], [0,0,1]. Its eigenvalues are $\lambda_1 = 1$, $\lambda_2 = 4$, $\lambda_3 = 2$. As just shown, if an input vector points in any eigen-direction, it will simply be multiplied by its corresponding eigenvalue. Thus, for any input eigenvector-eigenvalue combination λ_0, $\mathbf{x}_0$ being iterated, we will have $\mathbf{A}\mathbf{x}_0 = \lambda_0\mathbf{x}_0$. Repeated application of this transformation n times would produce $\mathbf{A}^n\mathbf{x}_0 = \lambda_0^n\mathbf{x}_0$, and would cause the initial eigenvector to shrink or expand according to the eigenvalue factor.

Say our initial vector is now

$$\mathbf{x}_0 = \begin{bmatrix} 0.4 \\ 0.5 \\ 0.4 \end{bmatrix}. \tag{13.7}$$

The first iteration yields

$$\mathbf{A}\mathbf{x}_0 = \begin{bmatrix} 0.4 \\ 2.0 \\ 0.8 \end{bmatrix}.$$

This vector is pointing a little closer to the second eigen-direction than its predecessor. To help this analysis a little further, we define a quantity called $R^2(\mathbf{x})$ that equals zero if its vector argument $\mathbf{x}$ is pointing in the second eigen-direction, [0,1,0], and increases as its argument vector points increasingly further away. Now set

$$\mathbf{x}_0 = \begin{bmatrix} a \\ b \\ c \end{bmatrix}.$$

For the eigenvector [0,1,0] we can define $R^2 = (a^2 + c^2)/b^2$. If the argument vector to $R^2(\mathbf{x})$ is pointing in the chosen eigen-direction, $R^2 = 0$; otherwise $R^2 \neq 0$.

Iteration of input vector (equation (13.7)) results in output vectors shown in Table 13.2. Here again, matrix iteration tends to favor the eigen-direction with the largest eigenvalue, and ultimately the iterated vector ends up pointing in that direction, too. This will happen regardless of the direction in which the initial vector was pointing.

For instance, Table 13.3 shows what happens when vector

$$\mathbf{x}_0 = \begin{bmatrix} 0.50 \\ 0.25 \\ 0.50 \end{bmatrix}$$

Table 13.2
Output Vectors after the *n*th Iteration

n	R^2
0	1.280
1	0.2000
2	0.0425
3	0.0101
4	0.0025
5	0.0006
6	0.0001

is iterated with **A**. The iteration also converges to the second eigen-direction, albeit more slowly because the initial vector is pointing farther away from the dominant eigen-direction and thus has farther to travel.

At this point, the dynamic has become clearer: repeated iteration of **A** with some input vector is just a competition between the eigenvalues, with only the largest surviving (in absolute-value terms). The other eigenvalues also try to rotate vectors their way, but they are overwhelmed by the multiplier effect of the largest eigenvalue. It does not matter whether that largest eigenvalue is positive or negative: a minus sign does not change a vector's directional axis but simply rotates it 180° from its original direction. Because the norm of the largest eigenvalue of a matrix is referred to as its *spectral radius*,[2] we conclude that the spectral radius rules long-run behavior in a matrix iteration. This fact is crucial to our analysis of Markov chains.

If equation (13.6) instead of (13.4) is used, the logic is the same but the roles are reversed. Due to the 90° rotation, what was a row is now a column, and vice versa. Not surprisingly, each eigenvalue also switches from one eigenvector to another, becoming associated with an eigenvector that is perpendicular to all eigenvectors corresponding to an eigenvalue other than itself.

Table 13.3
Output Vectors after Iteration with A

n	R^2
0	8.00
1	1.250
2	0.2656
3	0.0635
4	0.0157
5	0.0039
6	0.0010

In other words, any eigenvector $\mathbf{v}_i$ chosen from among the set arising from $\mathbf{A}^T\mathbf{x} = \lambda\mathbf{x}$ and stemming from eigenvalue λ_i is now orthogonal to any eigen-vector arising from $\mathbf{A}\mathbf{x} = \lambda\mathbf{x}$ corresponding to any eigenvalue except λ_i.[3] With a little trial and error, it is not difficult to discover that the other eigenvector of equation (13.4) is just $\mathbf{x} = (1, 1)$. As expected, application of transformation $\mathbf{A}$ to the latter vector simply stretches it by a ratio equal to its eigenvalue:

$$\begin{bmatrix} 1 & -\dfrac{3}{2} \\ -\dfrac{5}{2} & 2 \end{bmatrix}\begin{bmatrix} 1 \\ 1 \end{bmatrix} = \begin{bmatrix} -0.5 \\ -0.5 \end{bmatrix} = -\frac{1}{2}\begin{bmatrix} 1 \\ 1 \end{bmatrix}$$

To find the eigenvectors of $\mathbf{A}^T$, simply rotate the first set of eigenvectors by 90° to yield $\mathbf{x} = (-1, 1)$ and $\mathbf{x} = (5, 3)$. As advertised, eigenvalue $-(1/2)$ is now associated with eigenvector $\mathbf{x} = (5, 3)$ while eigenvalue $7/2$ is associated with eigenvector $\mathbf{x} = (-1, 1)$. To check that these vectors are indeed mutually orthogonal, recall from high school algebra that the scalar product ($\cdot$) of two vectors $\mathbf{a}$ and $\mathbf{b}$ in two dimensions is defined by the algebraic product of their norms and the cosine of the angle θ between them:

$$\mathbf{a} \cdot \mathbf{b} = |\mathbf{a}|\,|\mathbf{b}|\cos(\theta)$$

If the two vectors in questions are perpendicular, their scalar product will be zero because $\cos(\pi/2) = 0$. For the two pairs, we have

$$(1)(-1) + (1)(1) = 0,$$
$$(3)(5) + (-5)(3) = 0.$$

Now, if $\mathbf{A}^T = \mathbf{A}$ (i.e., if $\mathbf{A}$ is symmetric), it follows that its eigenvectors will be orthogonal to each other since each pair is now composed of the same vectors. Defining $\mathbf{V}$ as the matrix of column eigenvectors of a (now) symmetric matrix $\mathbf{A}$, we conclude that since the columns of $\mathbf{V}$ are mutually orthogonal, the product of $\mathbf{V}\mathbf{V}^T$ is a diagonal matrix with diagonal entries equal to the squared length of those eigenvectors.

Remember that eigenvectors are characterized by the fact that they point in a special direction. By equation (13.3), if $\mathbf{v}_i$ is an eigenvector of $\mathbf{A}$, then so is $a\mathbf{v}_i$, where a is any number. So if, in addition, we make each eigenvector of $\mathbf{V}$ a unit vector by dividing each of its elements by the square root of its length, the following remarkable property emerges:

$$\mathbf{V}\mathbf{V}^T = \mathbf{V}^T\mathbf{V} = \mathbf{I} \qquad (13.9)$$

In other words, the transpose of the eigen-matrix of a symmetric matrix is equal to its inverse. A matrix for which this is true is referred to as *unitary*. For reasons that won't trouble us[4] it is always possible to associate $\mathbf{A}$ to an upper triangular matrix using its unitary matrix $\mathbf{V}$. Thus, for some upper triangular matrix $\mathbf{T}$, we can write

$$\mathbf{VAV}^T = \mathbf{T} \tag{13.10}$$

Now the eigenvalues of a real matrix $\mathbf{A}$, generally written λ_i, $i = 1, 2, \ldots, N$, do not have to be all real and distinct, but a real symmetric matrix has real eigenvalues.[5] In addition, when the eigenvalues are all distinct, it turns out that $\mathbf{T}$ is a diagonal matrix with the eigenvalues of $\mathbf{A}$ as its diagonal elements.[6] In that case, we will say that $\mathbf{A}$ is diagonalizable. Defining $[\lambda]_N$ as the diagonal matrix of N eigenvalues of our symmetric matrix $\mathbf{A}$, and combining equations (13.9) and (13.10) we can then write

$$\mathbf{A} = \mathbf{V}[\lambda]_N \mathbf{V}^T \tag{13.11}$$

Even if $\mathbf{A}$ is not quite diagonalizable, it will always be possible to find another matrix essentially equal to $\mathbf{A}$ that is diagonalizable. In practice, we will therefore assume that given real symmetric matrices are diagonalizable.

Admittedly, not every matrix is symmetric, but symmetry appears sufficiently regularly as to make equation (13.11) quite useful. For instance, we will have the opportunity to use it productively in discussing the convergence of the multidimensional Newton-Raphson nonlinear optimization method in Appendix F.

14

Markov Chains

The name *Markov chain* is associated with the celebrated Russian topologist and algebraist Andrei Andreyevich Markov (1856–1922), who, along with Tchebychev, was a leading member of the Recursive School of mathematics. The goal of this section is to introduce the concept of Markov chains to credit analysts and demonstrate how they can be used to build detailed cash flow models simulating the credit dynamics of structured pools. We supplement this discussion with a detailed examination of how the Markov formalism can represent the process of state-equilibrium in obligor accounts.

In a variety of contexts and asset classes, such as mortgage-backed and auto-backed securities, detailed analysis of the underlying pool invariably involves the use of Markovian stochastic processes in either their continuous or their discrete version. Although Markov chains are practically second nature to operations research practitioners, their use in finance in general, and in structured finance in particular, is more recent.

On first encounter, Markov chains should appeal to structured credit analysts. In fact, as we show in Appendix C, the Markov property at the heart of these special stochastic processes is the structured world's credit equivalent of the efficient market hypothesis normally invoked in studies of market risk. Owing to the paramount importance of Markov chains for the proper understanding of structured risk in general, we strongly recommend to all credit analysts that they become at least familiar with their operational mechanics, if not their direct implementation within loan-level credit analysis models. In this section and the next we review the fundamentals of Markov processes. In chapter 20, the fundamentals are used to model the behavior of ABS backed by automobile loans.

The Markov Property

Fundamentally, a *Markov chain* is a stochastic process equipped with certain properties. With respect to a conceptual system consisting of economic agents, a stochastic process is one that can be described by a random variable x depending on some discrete or continuous parameter t often taken to represent time. Structured finance stochastic processes will be characterized by a predefined set of states that the economic agents will be allowed to occupy and x will refer to arbitrary values assigned to these states.

For an n-state stochastic process $x(t)$, $t = 0, 1, 2, \ldots, T, x \in [1, 2, 3, \ldots, n]$, the Markov property is said to hold in the absence of a memory effect. Mathematically, this is equivalent to the statement that the conditional probability of finding the system in a given state during the next time increment depends only on its current location, namely,

$$p[x(t + \Delta t) \mid x(t), x(t - \Delta t), x(t - 2\Delta t), \ldots] = p[x(t + \Delta t) \mid x(t)]. \quad (14.1)$$

Markov Processes in Structured Finance

One of the main benefits of using the Markovian formalism is the elimination of long-term static pool data requirements. Any issuer with sufficient operating history to enable the synthesis of a transition matrix is a candidate for analysis under a Markovian framework. Transition matrices are specific to the asset class and the issuer, and they are derived empirically from portfolio data, as we will demonstrate below.

Henceforth, we will refer to an n-state stochastic process in which the Markov property holds as a *finite-state Markov process*. In structured finance, we will be concerned exclusively with finite-state Markov processes. In general, the states will correspond to recognized delinquency states of an issuer in some asset class and the economic agents will represent the individual obligors or accounts in the pool. In what follows, we use these words interchangeably.

Markov processes may be conveniently specified by arrays of conditional, time-dependent probabilities of the form (14.1). These arrays are referred to as *transition matrices* $\mathbf{P}(t)$ and can generically be written as

$$\mathbf{P}(t) = \begin{bmatrix} p_{11} & p_{12} & p_{13} & \cdots & p_{1N} \\ p_{21} & p_{22} & \cdots & \cdots & p_{2N} \\ \cdots & & & & \\ p_{N1} & p_{N2} & \cdots & & p_{NN} \end{bmatrix}.$$

A series of consecutive states ruled by a statistical process corresponding to a sequence of matrices $\mathbf{P}(t)$ will be referred to as a *Markov chain*. Due to their constant recurrence in statistical analysis, some characteristic Markov chains have been given names. For instance, the following Markov transition matrix characterizes a *random walk*:

$$\mathbf{P} = \begin{bmatrix} \ldots\ldots & .5 & 0 & .5 & 0 & & & \\ 0 & 0 & 0 & .5 & 0 & .5 & 0 & 0 & 0 \\ 0 & 0 & 0 & 0 & .5 & 0 & .5 & 0 & 0 \\ 0 & 0 & 0 & 0 & 0 & .5 & 0 & .5 & 0 \\ \ldots\ldots\ldots\ldots & 0 & .5 & 0 & .5 \\ \ldots\ldots\ldots\ldots & 0 & 0 & .5 & 0 & .. \end{bmatrix}$$

If the entries of the matrices $\mathbf{P}(t)$ do not depend on time, the resulting process will be called *stationary*. Although the vast majority of Markov processes encountered in structured finance are non-stationary, it will be instructive to first understand the long-term behavior of stationary chains, for they provide significant insight into the physics of structured credits.

The credit dynamics of structured securities can be derived using the transition matrices of their associated asset pools. Once these matrices are available, they can be used at each time step to obtain the aggregate state of the pool at the next time step by considering all the allowable transitions of the economic agents in the pool. Practically speaking, the maximum number of time steps is normally very nearly equal to the legal final maturity date of the relevant transaction. The time steps generally correspond to the collection periods found in most structured transactions and during which cash accumulates for later distribution to investors. Most of the time, a time step will be one month.

As the system must be found at all times in one of its n states, it follows that the $p_{ij}(t)$ along each row of a Markov transition matrix must sum to unity. This requirement will be referred to as the *row sum condition* and will turn out to be the main characteristic of Markov transition matrices:

$$\sum_j p_{ij}(t) = 1, \forall i, t \tag{14.2}$$

Ontology of States in Structured Finance Markov Processes

This subsection reviews the two types of Markov states commonly found in structured finance. For ease of understanding, we restrict our attention to stationary chains.

Recurrent State

Consider the following arbitrary three-state stationary Markov process defined by transition matrix equation (14.3):

$$\mathbf{P} = \begin{bmatrix} .2 & .6 & .2 \\ .7 & .1 & .2 \\ 0 & 0 & 1 \end{bmatrix} \tag{14.3}$$

According to our schema, the probability that agent, currently in state 1, will remain in state 1 for the next time step is 20%, while the probability that the account will move to state 2 is 60%. On the other hand, if the account is now in state 2, there is a 70% probability that it will move back to state 1 and a 10% probability it will remain in state 2 during the next time step. An obligor in state 1 can leave and reenter that state according to the transition probabilities given in $\mathbf{P}$. States for which this condition holds are called *recurrent*. With respect to a transition matrix **P**, a recurrent state i of a Markov process is one for which conditions a and b hold:

a. $p_{ii} < 1$

b. $\exists j | p_{ji} \neq 0$

If it is possible for an agent to reach state i from state j, we will we say that states i and j communicate. It is crucial to note that the fact that i and j communicate does not imply $p_{ij} \neq 0$ and $p_{ji} \neq 0$ simultaneously in **P**. This is because there is no requirement for the transition from state i to state j to happen in a single step. In other words, as long as there is a path from i to j, the states will communicate. Although this is a minor point it is an important one since most structured finance Markov processes exhibit such patterns.

Absorbing State

Now, consider state 3, above, and note that $p_{33} = 1$. Once the system enters state 3, it can never leave. For this reason, we refer to such states as *absorbing*. Formally, we define an absorbing state i of a Markov process with transition matrix **P** as one for which the following condition holds:

$$p_{ii} = 1$$

In structured finance, we will normally encounter two absorbing states: *prepayment* and *default.* As soon as an account prepays its loan or defaults, although it is deemed to exit the delinquency process, it is still regarded as part of the global process. The special attention and treatment these two events require is discussed in detail in chapter 20.

Manipulating Transition Matrices

In this subsection, the term *system* will refer either individually or collectively to the economic agents of a structured pool and we will not distinguish between systems consisting of discrete units or continua.

Recall that a Markov process is specified via its n-dimensional transition matrix $\mathbf{P}(t)$ whose entries $p_{ij}(t)$ represent the conditional probability with which an agent of the system, being in state i at time t, will find itself in state j at time $t + 1$. As mentioned earlier, we assume that the process is unable to escape from the predefined set of Markov states. If, in addition, all the states communicate, we refer to the set as *ergodic.* The set of delinquency states of structured finance Markov processes is not ergodic since it is possible, by default or prepayment, to escape into a nondelinquent state.

In many applications, it will be necessary to compute the unconditional probability vector $\mathbf{d}(t + 1)$ of the Markov process, where $\mathbf{d}(t + 1)$ is an n-dimensional vector. Its elements $\mathbf{d}_i(t + 1)$ are the probabilities of finding the system in state i at time $t + 1$ regardless of its state at time t:

$$\mathbf{d}^T(t+1) = [d_1(t+1), d_2(t+1), \ldots\ldots, d_n(t+1)] \qquad (14.5)$$

These values can be computed by summing the probabilities of moving to state i from any other state at time t. For instance, consider a four-state Markov process. To find the unconditional probability of the system's being in state 1 at time $t+1$ given that it is in state 1 at time t we need to compute

$$d_1(t+1) = d_1(t)p_{11}(t) + d_2(t)p_{21}(t) + d_3(t)p_{31}(t) + d_4(t)p_{41}(t). \qquad (14.6)$$

Equation (14.6) for all states can be written compactly using matrix notation:

$$\mathbf{d}^T(t+1) = \mathbf{d}^T(t)\mathbf{P}(t) \qquad (14.7)$$

This process can also be carried out recursively. For example, starting from time $t = 0$ we have

$$\mathbf{d}^T(1) = \mathbf{d}^T(0)\mathbf{P}(0)$$
$$\mathbf{d}^T(2) = \mathbf{d}^T(1)\mathbf{P}(1) = \mathbf{d}^T(0)\mathbf{P}(1)\mathbf{P}(0). \qquad (14.8)$$

In general, for n time steps, we will have

$$\mathbf{d}^T(n) = \mathbf{d}^T(n-1)\mathbf{P}(n-1) = \mathbf{d}^T(0)\mathbf{P}(n-1)\ldots\mathbf{P}(2)\mathbf{P}(1)\mathbf{P}(0). \qquad (14.9)$$

Once the initial vector $\mathbf{d}^T(0)$ and the sequence of transition matrices $\mathbf{P}(t)$ are made available, equation (14.9) can be used to derive how the cash flow environment evolves from closing to maturity and to specify the state occupied by each economic agent in the system. The derivation of these matrices is the heart of the analysis of structured securities.

Asymptotic Properties of Stationary Markov Chains

Interesting analytical results can be derived if we assume that the $p_{ij}(t)$ does not, in fact, depend on time. In this case, defining $\mathbf{P}$ as the now-invariant transition matrix, equation (14.9) reduces to

$$\mathbf{d}^T(n) = \mathbf{d}^T(0)\mathbf{P}^n. \qquad (14.10)$$

Matrix $\mathbf{P}^n$ is referred to as the *n-step transition matrix* of the process. Physically, p_{ij}^n represent the conditional probability with which the system, being in state i at time 0, will be found in state j at time n. For the sake of simplicity, let us further assume that our Markov process does not contain absorbing states and that all states communicate. A typical example of this type of chain is given by equation (14.11):

$$\mathbf{P} = \begin{bmatrix} .2 & .6 & .2 \\ .7 & .1 & .2 \\ .5 & .3 & .2 \end{bmatrix} \qquad (14.11)$$

As we have seen, a three-dimensional matrix implicitly contains three stretching factors known as its eigenvalues. Let us find these values in the case of matrix (14.11) via the defining equation:

$$\det(\mathbf{P} - \lambda\mathbf{I}_3) = 0 \qquad (14.12)$$

Expansion of this third-order determinant leads to the cubic equation

$$\lambda^3 - .5\lambda^2 - .5\lambda = \lambda(\lambda^2 - .5\lambda - .5) = 0 \qquad (14.13)$$

from which we may easily write down the roots as follows:

$$\lambda_1 = 1 \qquad \lambda_2 = -\frac{1}{2} \qquad \lambda_3 = 0$$

Note the following facts:

- One root is equal to 1.
- The norm of the other two roots is less than 1.

This is not a coincidence and, for reasons that do not concern the analysis but that the enterprising reader may wish to pursue independently,[1] Markov transition matrices will always have unit spectral radius. (Recall that the spectral radius is the norm of the largest eigenvalue of a matrix.) In fact, this important property is the key to understanding the long-term properties of stationary Markov processes.

The fact that *at least* one of the eigenvalues of a transition matrix has a norm of unity does not imply that the matrix has *only* one such eigenvalue. If a transition matrix has two or more unit-eigenvalues, we call the associated process *degenerate*. Nondegenerate processes contain the seeds of generality; for the moment, we focus our attention on them and postpone degenerate processes. Like matrix (14.11) non-degenerate Markov matrices have distinct eigenvalues, and one of the eigenvalues will have unit norm.

To begin with, note the first few outcomes of iterating matrix (14.11) with itself, as follows:

$$\mathbf{P}^2 = \begin{bmatrix} 0.560 & 0.240 & 0.200 \\ 0.310 & 0.490 & 0.200 \\ 0.410 & 0.390 & 0.200 \end{bmatrix}$$

$$\mathbf{P}^4 = \begin{bmatrix} 0.470 & 0.330 & 0.200 \\ 0.408 & 0.393 & 0.200 \\ 0.433 & 0.368 & 0.200 \end{bmatrix}$$

$$\mathbf{P}^6 = \begin{bmatrix} 0.448 & 0.353 & 0.200 \\ 0.432 & 0.368 & 0.200 \\ 0.438 & 0.362 & 0.200 \end{bmatrix}$$

$$\mathbf{P}^{10} = \begin{bmatrix} 0.440 & 0.359 & 0.200 \\ 0.439 & 0.360 & 0.200 \\ 0.439 & 0.360 & 0.200 \end{bmatrix}$$

As $n \to \infty$, the sequence seems to converge to a limit when all rows of $\mathbf{P}^n$ become virtually identical.

Let us call this limiting matrix $\mathbf{P}^\infty$ and label the condition of its attainment equilibrium. In other words, when a nondegenerate Markov process has been iterated a sufficient number of times, it reaches equilibrium as we have defined it. According to equation (14.10) we also have

$$\mathbf{d}^T(n) = \mathbf{d}^T(0)\mathbf{P}^n. \tag{14.14}$$

In the limit $n \to \infty$, we can now write $\mathbf{d}^T(\infty) = \mathbf{d}^T(0)\mathbf{P}^\infty$. Since the row elements of limiting matrix $\mathbf{P}^\infty$ are identical, we conclude from the rules of ma trix multiplication that regardless of the initial distribution $\mathbf{d}(0)$, $\mathbf{d}^T(\infty)$ will converge in distribution to the repeated row of matrix $\mathbf{P}^\infty$. In other words, for any vector $\mathbf{d}(0)$, we always end up with the same limiting probability distribution of states: the one given by the repeated row of $\mathbf{P}^\infty$.

If we began the iterative process by selecting $\mathbf{d}(0) = \mathbf{d}(\infty)$ we would already be, in some sense, at the limiting equilibrium point. We might expect the Markov process to have no influence whatsoever on future distributions. Put differently, we might expect that iterating this special Markov process would simply leave the vector $\mathbf{d}(t + 1)$ invariant for all time steps and not merely in the limit $n \to \infty$ and would expect $\mathbf{d}^T(\infty) = \mathbf{d}^T(\infty)\mathbf{P}$ to hold as a special case. This is, in fact, what happens, as we will see shortly.

What is the source of this limiting behavior? From the discussion of matrices Markov chains we know the spectral radius of a matrix rules its long-run behavior. By this we mean that repeated iteration of a matrix with some starting input vector favors the eigen-direction associated with its spectral radius and causes the limiting vector to ultimately point in that direction. The limiting vector is thus an eigenvector of the original matrix. Now, as we just saw, the spectral radius of Markov transition matrices is always unity. As a result, repeated application of equation (14.7) produces a sequence of vectors $\mathbf{d}(t + 1)$ that ultimately point in the direction of the unit-eigenvector, and this vector must then be $\mathbf{d}^T(\infty)$. The unit-eigenvector of $\mathbf{P}$ eventually overwhelms the other eigenvectors. By equation (14.10), and assuming $\lambda_1 = 1$, the upshot is that the limiting row $\mathbf{v}_\infty$ of $\mathbf{P}^\infty$ must be pointing in the direction associated with $\lambda_1 = 1$. Mathematically this is expressed by the equation

$$\mathbf{P}^T\mathbf{v}_\infty = \mathbf{v}_\infty. \tag{14.15}$$

The required eigenvector must then be $\mathbf{V}_\infty = [0.44 \; 0.360 \; 0.200]$. Indeed, we find that

$$\begin{bmatrix} 0.2 & 0.7 & 0.5 \\ 0.6 & 0.1 & 0.3 \\ 0.2 & 0.2 & 0.2 \end{bmatrix} \begin{bmatrix} 0.44 \\ 0.36 \\ 0.20 \end{bmatrix} = \begin{bmatrix} 0.44 \\ 0.36 \\ 0.20 \end{bmatrix}.$$

As expected, $\mathbf{v}_\infty$ is the unit-eigenvector of $\mathbf{P}$, as we have also verified that

$$\mathbf{d}^T(\infty) = \mathbf{d}^T(\infty)\mathbf{P} \tag{14.16}$$

$$\mathbf{d}^T(\infty) = \mathbf{v}_\infty. \tag{14.17}$$

To find $\mathbf{d}^{T}(\infty)$ in practice, it would seem that we can eliminate the iteration by using equation (14.17) to derive $\mathbf{v}_{\infty}$. However, we cannot simply use equation (14.15) because, by equation (14.6), we know that the determinant of $\mathbf{P} - \mathbf{I}$ is zero by definition. Thus, to arrive at a nontrivial solution, we must supplement equation (14.15) with an additional normalizing equation. Since the system must account for the entire probability space, the obvious choice is the following row-sum condition:

$$\sum_{j=1}^{n} d_j = 1 \tag{14.18}$$

With $\mathbf{P}$ given by equation (14.11) choose the first $n - 1$ rows of equations (14.15) and (14.18) to derive the following non-singular linear system:

$$\begin{bmatrix} (0.2 - 1)d_1(\infty) + & 0.7d_2(\infty) + & 0.5d_3(\infty) \\ 0.6d_1(\infty) + & (0.1 - 1)d_2(\infty) + & 0.3d_3(\infty) \\ d_1(\infty) + & d_2(\infty) + & d_3(\infty) \end{bmatrix} = \begin{bmatrix} 0 \\ 0 \\ 1 \end{bmatrix} \tag{14.19}$$

Readers can verify by Cramer's rule[2] that the solution of equations (14.19) is

$$d_1(\infty) = 0.44$$
$$d_2(\infty) = 0.36$$
$$d_3(\infty) = 0.20$$

Strictly speaking, such results apply only to stationary nondegenerate Markov chains. However, the latter form an important subset of practical situations. For instance, they can be used to derive the limiting credit rating distribution of a pool of debt securities from the corresponding rating transition matrix. Unfortunately, although this information could be quite useful in analyzing a CBO, the discretionary elements—when the change in credit quality is recognized and how great a change is acknowledged—in rating agency transitions calls into question the extent to which they represent the real probabilities of state transitions. Readers interested in relating these essentially mathematical concepts to more intuitive notions are invited to read Appendix B, which discusses Markov chains using common-sense notions of a more physical character.

Conservation Laws

We can think of a Markov chain as representing the dynamics of a population wandering through a multistate system, subject to a basic conservation constraint. The conservative nature of these processes is their main feature, which we now review.

Many of the mathematical properties of Markov transition matrices stem from the conservation law or regularity condition, known as the *row-sum condition*:

$$\sum_{j} p_{ij}(t) = 1, \forall i, t$$

This identity expresses the fact that the probability measure is conserved, and that we must account for the system's location somewhere among the states defined by its transition matrix. Systems within which conservation laws hold are called *conservative*. As a result, the use of Markov processes in structured finance makes sense only when an associated conservative physical field can be identified. As explained, the states of a structured finance Markov process are delinquency states of the obligor; so the constraint is to locate a conservative field in delinquency space. It should by now be obvious that the only reasonable candidate for this condition is the number of obligors. By this we mean that at all times, and contrary to dollar balances, the total number of obligors in the system is conserved. Total dollar balances (not just principal balances) are not subject to a conservation law in delinquency space due to such phenomena as interest rates and fees. For this reason, it will be impossible to accurately measure pool cash flows by looking at dollar transitions. Because interest is equivalent to a source of cash, a Markovian dollar transition between two states fails to account for it. By contrast, regardless of whether an obligor's status is current, delinquent, prepaid, or defaulted, the total number of obligors is invariant throughout the life of a structured transaction.

As a canny reader will have surmised, the problem is that a cash flow model clearly cannot be created around mere transitions where the obligor account is the unit. Dollar balances and cash flows will need to be computed from corresponding account transitions. We briefly outline the argument here, saving the details of implementation for chapter 20. The central idea is to "invert" the issuer's credit policy by starting from obligor transitions, and generate the associated cash flow. Whereas, in reality, obligor delinquency states are derived from obligor cash flows, simulated structured finance processes need to invert the usual information flow and first determine obligor delinquency states from transition matrices. Thereafter, the corresponding cash flows can be computed from microstructure transfer functions linking obligor transitions to cash flows, which functions are derived from issuers' credit policy manuals. The invertibility of this process turns out to be one of the greatest strengths of the delinquency-based approach.

Synthesizing Markov Chains

Thus far our analysis assumed that, at the outset, Markov transition data were somehow "given" to the credit analyst. In practice, however, issuers with varying degrees of ABS expertise will have to provide them. In this section, we discuss the three most common situations and present a solution to each one. All credit analysts will, at one time or another, face these problems. As a result, knowledge of the trade-offs involved in various solutions is unavoidable. As we shall see, the world of structured finance is far from perfect, but many of its allegedly insurmountable problems are in fact solvable.

Case A: No Data Are Available At All

In this case, a proxy can normally be found. Usually, the best proxy will be the relevant issuer's closest competitor or another closely related issuer in the same sector or market as that of the relevant issuer. On the other hand, it is tempting to say that an issuer unable to provide a single data point on its obligor delinquency transitions is probably not a likely candidate for securitization. The reason is that, should a transaction ever be consummated, this issuer would have to present such data as part of investor remittance reports. In practice, we can safely assume that these cases will be rare and if they should arise, they can be handled ad hoc.

Case B: A Full Data Set Is Available

Here the credit analyst would be in possession of at least twelve consecutive months of accountwise delinquency transition data. For instance, Table 14.1 displays a typical auto issuer's output in connection with a single collection period. Similar outputs would be received for at least eleven additional monthly collection periods. With these data in hand, and referring to Table 14.1, we would compute the transition probabilities p_{ij} as

$$p_{ij} = \frac{N_{ij}}{\sum_j N_{ij}}. \tag{14.20}$$

As explained earlier, the rows associated with the default and prepayment states would simply have a 1 on the main diagonal and zeros elsewhere. Note that twelve different p_{ij} values would be computed from these twelve monthly transition databases. At this point, two possible paths can be taken:

1. Use twelve, monthly matrices under a nonstationary Markov process with a period of twelve months. This is appropriate for seasoned issuers with large portfolios of pronounced, stable seasonality. It is the

Table 14.1
Snapshot of a Hypothetical Auto Issuer's Account Transitions

Old Status	New Status						
	Current	5–30	31–60	61–90	91–120	Prepaid	Default
Current	N_{11}	N_{12}	N_{13}	N_{14}	N_{15}	N_{16}	N_{17}
5–30	N_{21}	•	•	•	•	•	•
31–60	•						
60–90	•						
91–120	•						

Notes: ABC Auto Finance, Inc., account transitions: Days delinquent, January 2002 collection period.

wrong choice for first-time issuers with relatively unseasoned port-folios, where the first twelve to eighteen months are unrepresentative of the future and are likely to understate delinquency transitions.

2. Average the twelve monthly matrices to synthesize a single matrix representing the mean delinquency transition process and super-impose seasonality factors. This method usually leads to smoother results, something most analysts prize.

In many cases, both methods will be theoretically defensible, and analysts will have to rely on their judgment. In connection with the second method, analysts should also bear in mind that the appropriate central measure for ra-tios is the geometric, not the arithmetic, mean. For a series of twelve numbers, each representing a single p_{ij}, we would compute the geometric mean p_{ig}^{avg} as

$$p_{ij}^{avg} = \sqrt[12]{\prod_{i=1}^{12} p_{ij}}. \tag{14.21}$$

In equation (14.21), probabilities p_{ij} are calculated from the matrices above, with zero-entries ignored. In general, the geometric mean will tend to equal the arithmetic mean when the values are relatively large, but differences could be substantial in later delinquency stages.

When using the first method, zero-entries will often appear due to data ar-tifacts, relatively small portfolios and other factors. These factors will tend to in-crease variance and lead to wider dispersion in the resulting monthly transition matrices. In turn, this increased variance will result in higher required credit sup-port than for an otherwise similar portfolio because it will cause more obligors to enter delinquency and default states. We will come back to this point later.

For instance, Table 14.2 displays two samples of twelve individual monthly transitions calculated from issuer data. The first column refers to an early-stage delinquency transition, while the second addresses a later-stage transition. The geometric mean in the high-delinquency state case was computed by ex-cluding the zero-entry. Actual data will usually display high volatility in default and prepayment transitions—precisely where it matters that they should not be volatile. As a result, analysts will want to be careful when computing default transition probabilities. The difference of 0.0183 between the geometric and arithmetic means of p_{45} may seem insignificant, but even a 5% difference on a late-stage transition probability can have a demonstrably significant impact in-side a Markov process with monthly iterates.

Case C: State Inventories Alone Are Available

This case, by far the most difficult to handle, is a middle ground between cases A and B. Instead of a full transition data set, only account inventories of delin-quency states are made available in the form of prospectus data on previous transactions. Prospectus data generally will look like Table 14.3. This is not ideal, but it is not uncommon, either. It is difficult because, from a single data

Table 14.2
Two Sets of Twelve Monthly Transitions

N	Account Transition Data	
	p_{11}	p_{45}
1	0.952	0.33
2	0.948	0.523
3	0.935	0.413
4	0.945	0.225
5	0.893	0.432
6	0.923	0.623
7	0.978	0.487
8	0.912	0.417
9	0.934	0
10	0.956	0.634
11	0.965	0.289
12	0.987	0.439
Arithmetic mean	0.9440	0.4010
Geometric mean	0.9436	0.4193

set, there is an infinite variety of feasible solutions, only some of which will actually make sense. When the number of transition probability equations exceeds the number of available data points, the equation system is overdetermined. Achieving a unique solution involves a procedure, known as *regularization*, which proceeds as follows:

1. From the transition probabilities, determine an appropriate functional to be minimized (the objective functional).
2. Derive the minimizing Markov transition matrix.

For example, the values of transition probabilities p_{ij} of a transition matrix **P** may be determined by computing account balances around all the delinquency states of the Markov process and finding the set of matrix entries minimizing least-square sums of account sinks and sources. We refer to this procedure as the *method of continuity*.

To demonstrate, we assume that the obligor portfolio is static: there are no account additions and no non-default or non-prepayment deletions over the contemplated time horizon (usually one year). If the portfolio is non-static, a minor change in notation can be made to incorporate account additions. The account inventory mass balance for state i can be written as follows:

$$S_t^i = S_{t-1}^i + \int_{t-1}^{t} dS^i \tag{14.22}$$

We rewrite equation (14.22) as

Table 14.3
Account Inventory by Delinquency Status

Month	Current	5–30	31–60	61–90	91–120	Prepay	Default
January	S_1^1	S_1^2	S_1^3	S_1^4	S_1^5	S_1^6	S_1^7
February	S_2^1	S_2^2	S_2^3	—	—	—	—
March	—	—	—	—	—	—	—
April	—	—	—	—	—	—	—
May	—	—	—	—	—	—	—
June	—	—	—	—	—	—	—
July	—	—	—	—	—	—	—
August	—	—	—	—	—	—	—
September	—	—	—	—	—	—	—
October	—	—	—	—	—	—	—
November	—	—	—	—	—	—	—
December	S_{12}^1	S_{12}^2	—	—	—	—	—

$$S_t^i = S_{t-1}^i + \int_{t-1}^t \left(\frac{dS_{t-1}^i}{dt} \right) dt. \tag{14.23}$$

We may define the sums $\int_{t-1}^t (dS_{t-1}^i/dt)$ using the unknown transition probabilities, and derive equations for the mass balance around every Markov state. These equations are then solved using the least-squares linear regression method.[3] By definition, with S_t^i accounts in state i at time t, the number of accounts that leave state i to enter state j is $p_{ij}S_t^i$. Conversely, the number of accounts that leave state j to enter state i is $p_{ji}S_t^j$. Applying these formulas to the complete set of states yields the net change in inventory for state i, that is $\int_{t-1}^t (dS_{t-1}^i/dt)$.

Consider the situation $i = 1$, $t = 1$. From our previous argument, the mass balance equation for this case can be written as follows:

$$S_1^1 = S_0^1 + p_{21}S_0^2 + \ldots + p_{n1}S_0^n \\ - p_{12}S_0^1 - \ldots - p_{1n}S_0^1 \tag{14.24}$$

Combined with the row-sum condition $\sum_j p_{ij} = 1$, $\forall i$, equation (14.24) yields

$$S_1^1 = (1 - p_{12} - p_3 - \ldots - p_{1n})S_0^1 + p_{21}S_0^2 + p_{31}S_0^3 + \ldots + p_{n1}S_0^n$$
$$S_1^1 = p_{11}S_0^1 + p_{21}S_0^2 + p_{31}S_0^3 + \ldots + p_{n1}S_0^n. \tag{14.25}$$

If the same procedure is applied to every state in the process, the linear equation system (14.26) results:

$$\begin{bmatrix} S_1^1 \\ S_1^2 \\ S_1^3 \\ \cdot \\ \cdot \\ S_1^n \end{bmatrix} = \begin{bmatrix} p_{11} & p_{21} & p_{31} & \cdot & p_{n1} \\ p_{12} & p_{22} & p_{32} & \cdot & p_{n2} \\ p_{13} & p_{23} & p_{33} & \cdot & p_{n3} \\ & & \cdot & & \\ & & \cdot & & \\ p_{1n} & p_{2n} & p_{3n} & \cdot & p_{nn} \end{bmatrix} \begin{bmatrix} S_0^1 \\ S_0^2 \\ S_0^3 \\ \cdot \\ \cdot \\ S_0^n \end{bmatrix} \tag{14.26}$$

In matrix notation, this is equivalent to

$$\mathbf{K}\mathbf{s}_0 = \mathbf{s}_1. \tag{14.27}$$

Note also that, by inspection $\mathbf{K} = \mathbf{P}^T$, where $\mathbf{P}$ is the required transition matrix. Our task is to solve equation (14.27) for the entries p_{ij} of matrix $\mathbf{K}$.

In practice, many entries of $\mathbf{K}$ might be set to zero or to some arbitrary value due to the physics of the problem. We may decide that there is zero probability that an obligor in the fourth delinquency state will pay off the entire delinquent and current amounts outstanding to become current (e.g., moving from state 4 back to state 1). Then, entry p_{41} in $\mathbf{K}$ would be zero, and the solution would be made smoother thereby, with more degrees of freedom remaining to resolve the other unknown parameters. To solve equation (14.27), we apply linear regression as follows.

Define the vector-valued Lagrangian functional L as the sum of mass sources or sinks from l to m, where $m + 1$ is the number of data points available:

$$L = \sum_1^m (\mathbf{s}_i - \mathbf{K}\mathbf{s}_{i-1})^2 \tag{14.28}$$

In equation (14.28) we have defined

$$\mathbf{s}_i^T = S_i^1 \, S_i^2 \, S_i^3 \ldots . \, S_i^n. \tag{14.29}$$

The solution to equation (14.29) is given by the first-order conditions

$$\frac{\partial L}{\partial \mathbf{K}} = 0. \tag{14.30}$$

We proceed by rows, defining the row-wise Lagrangian as follows:

$$L^j = (\mathbf{q}^j - \mathbf{R}\mathbf{u}^j)^T (\mathbf{q}^j - \mathbf{R}\mathbf{u}^j) \tag{14.31}$$

In equation (14.31) we have defined

$$\mathbf{q}^j = [S_1^j \, S_2^j \, S_3^j \ldots . \, S_n^j]$$

$$\mathbf{u}^j = [k_{j1} \, k_{j2} \, k_{j3} \ldots . \, k_{jn}]$$

$$\mathbf{R} = \begin{bmatrix} S_0^1 & S_0^2 & \ldots . & S_0^n \\ S_1^1 & S_1^2 & \ldots . & S_1^n \\ \cdot & \cdot & & \\ \cdot & & & \\ S_{m-1}^1 & S_{m-1}^2 & \ldots . & S_{m-1}^0 \end{bmatrix}.$$

Our regression results from chapter 15 will allow us to write down n solutions for the n rows of $\mathbf{K}$ as follows:

$$\mathbf{u}^j = (\mathbf{R}^T \mathbf{R})^{-1} \mathbf{R}^T \mathbf{q}^j \tag{14.32}$$

Implementation Issues

Although there is nothing mathematically wrong with the foregoing solution procedure, analysts trying to use it on real delinquency data often discover that it does not work. The problem is one of changing scale: later delinquency states have relatively low average populations compared to earlier stages. This causes nonphysical solutions to occur because the algorithm usually fails to impose the two regularity conditions applicable to probabilities, namely, $u_i^j \geq 0$, $\forall i, j$, and $u_i^j \leq 1$, $\forall i, j$.

To help impose the second condition, introduce a diagonal-weight matrix $\mathbf{W}$ to effectively equalize the scales of inventories as they appear in real data. We do this easily by redefining equation (14.31):

$$L^j = (\mathbf{q}^j - \mathbf{R}\mathbf{W}\mathbf{u}^j)^T(\mathbf{q}^j - \mathbf{R}\mathbf{W}\mathbf{u}^j) \tag{14.33}$$

Remembering that a diagonal matrix is equal to its transpose, we obtain

$$\mathbf{u}^j = (\mathbf{W}\mathbf{R}^T\mathbf{R}\mathbf{W})^{-1}\,\mathbf{W}\mathbf{R}^T\mathbf{q}^j. \tag{14.34}$$

To find the diagonal entries w_{ii} of matrix $\mathbf{W}$, pick the state with the largest average population in the data set ($S_{\text{avg}}^{\text{max}}$) and define

$$r_{ii} = \frac{S_{\text{avg}}^{\text{max}}}{\left[\dfrac{1}{m+1}\displaystyle\sum_{j=0}^{m} S_j^i\right]} \tag{14.35}$$

$$w_{ii} = \frac{r_{ii}}{\displaystyle\sum_{1}^{n} r_{ii}}. \tag{14.36}$$

This will work in most cases but will still leave entire the issue of nonnegativity of the u_j. Formally, imposing the inequality constraints $u_j \geq 0$ as part of the global solution involves more work in writing complex optimization subroutines, despite this being quite peripheral to the substance of the problem. Implementing such routines can always be done when time permits, but a detailed discussion is outside the scope of this book. (Commercial packages are available to do this quickly.) In most cases, equation (14.34) will lead to outputs with the correct relative ratios despite occasional negativity. When that happens, choosing the norm of the transition probability and normalizing the elements of $\mathbf{K}$ as shown in equation (14.37) will overcome the problem and produce fairly credible transition matrices.

$$k_{ij} = \frac{|u_j^i|}{\displaystyle\sum_{j=1}^{n}|u_j^i|} \tag{14.37}$$

By now, it should be fairly obvious that the use of the continuity method is to be avoided as much as possible. Not only are the available techniques far from perfect, but the work involved is abnormally large compared to cases A or B. An acceptable compromise could be to use transition matrices from reasonable proxy-issuers in the same market. But there will be situations where doing this will leave the credit analyst open to the question of relevance to the particular situation. In such cases, credit analysts will have little choice but to go through the gyrations described here.

15

Regression Analysis

As discussed in chapter 6, the nonlinear nature of structured finance significantly complicates the credit analysis of structured securities and requires the use of iterative solution procedures that fully articulate the codependence between the shape of the yield curve and the target credit ratings. The complexity of the task usually requires access to high-speed computers. In fact, the greatest contribution of numerical analysis over the past twenty years has probably been the ability to solve nonlinear problems without undue recourse to simplifying assumptions. Before proceeding to the techniques of linear and nonlinear regression, however, we must ask ourselves why nonlinearity makes problem solving so complicated.

The answer is that, although linearity has a formal definition, nonlinearity does not. Linear operators abound in all branches of mathematics, physics, and economics. They tend to be treated uniformly and generically because they all share the same formal properties. By contrast, each nonlinear operator has idiosyncratic characteristics. In some cases, these characteristics contribute to a closed-form solution, but in others, the problem is virtually unsolvable without the aid of numerical analysis. The heterogeneous character of nonlinear problems makes nonlinearity easiest to apprehend as the opposite of linearity.

For instance, an operator $L(y)$ can be said to be linear if it is homogeneous under a linear transformation $f(y)$ of its dependent variable y. To see what this means, first define a linear transformation $f(y) = ay + b$, in which a and b are constants and assume that the operator is

$$L(y) = \frac{d^2y}{dx^2} + \alpha\frac{dy}{dx} + y = 0. \tag{15.1}$$

Now, substitute $f(y)$ inside $L(y)$ to yield

$$L(ay + b) = \frac{d^2(ay + b)}{dx^2} + \alpha\frac{d(ay + b)}{dx} + (ay + b),$$

and simplify:

$$L(ay + b) = a\frac{d^2y}{dx^2} + \alpha\frac{dy}{dx} + ay + b$$

$$L(ay + b) = aL(y) + b \tag{15.2}$$

If substitution of linear transformations $f(y)$ into a given operator $L(y)$ results in the form of equation (15.2), the latter may said to be linear. It can be seen by inspection that when the exponent of y is the same in all terms of a differential operator $L(y)$, the operator will be linear. In this case, the exponent is 1.

Now, set $\alpha = y$ in equation (15.1) to yield

$$L(y) = \frac{d^2y}{dx^2} + y\frac{dy}{dx} + y = 0. \tag{15.3}$$

It is easily verified by the same substitution that equation (15.2) no longer holds. Further, note that this new $L(y)$ is nonlinear, more because equation (15.2) is unverifiable than due to any positive attribute, and that it is only one of many operators that could be derived. The alternative choice $\alpha = y^2$ yields yet another operator; and so on. Note, also, that its nonlinearity stems exclusively from α's dependence on the solution variable y.

For the linear operator (15.1), the solution would have been some functional relationship $g(x; \alpha)$, i.e., $y = g(x; \alpha)$. However, in equation (15.3), α itself would now be some function $f(y)$ and we would have

$$y = g(x; f(y)). \tag{15.4}$$

Since a function cannot be defined self-referentially, we would be left with the unpleasant task of solving equation (15.4) by first guessing y on the right-hand side of the equation; then proceeding iteratively by substituting our current best guess for y and computing the left-hand side of the equation in the hope of recovering the y value we had just used to calculate $f(y)$; and hoping that both sides would become sufficiently close, based on some preestablished criterion of closeness. However, the process might never end, in which case the solution would not be found. This could be because no solution did in fact exist, but more likely because our successive guesses simply moved farther and farther away from the solution.

Many linear operators can be solved by analytical methods; equation (15.1) is an example. By contrast, equation (15.3) may not have a straightforward analytical solution and numerical methods may be needed to find it. However, if one were asked to indicate a promising solution path to equation (15.3), the analogy to equation (15.1) would immediately come to mind. Knowing how to solve linear problems, the easiest technique to solve nonlinear problems is to reduce them to a linear problem via some ad hoc assumption. For example, if some information were available on y's probable functional form, we might begin by guessing a solution to satisfy equation (15.3), in effect guessing the value of α in equation (15.1) above. If we guessed right, the resulting solution would reproduce our guess, and we would have a consistent solution. On the other hand, failure to satisfy equation (15.3) might not be total failure, since it might suggest what the next guess ought to be. In this way, we might proceed iteratively by choosing increasingly successful functional forms for y. In practice, systematization of this iterative procedure is how most nonlinear problems are solved.

The True Meaning of "Linear Regression"

Regression is a familiar topic to most finance professionals and an important tool of structured analysis. We combine herein some illustrations of linear and non-linear examples to present a brief, but unified, treatment of the field. We cover linear regressions first and indicate via chapter 16 how to solve the resulting equations without matrix inversion. In the case of nonlinear regression, we postpone the solution of the resulting equations (using the Newton-Raphson method) to chapter 18.

Contrary to popular belief, the linearity of regression does not stem from the linearity of its defining equation $y = \sum_i a_i z_i$. It arises rather from the relationship between the objective functional to be minimized, which is usually referred to as the *Lagrangian* of the problem, and the unknown parameters a_i. If the Lagrangian is quadratic and the a_i appear linearly in the regression equation, then the result of the minimization procedure will be a set of linear equations (hence the "linear" of linear regression) and will be solved via matrix analysis. All the Lagrangians we will study will be quadratic. (If, on the other hand, the a_i appear nonlinearly, the outcome will be a set of nonlinear equations and will require special handling.) The following are three examples of linear regressions where a, b, and c are unknown parameters, y is the dependent variable, and x is the independent variable:

$$y = ax^2 + bx$$

$$y = a\cos(x^2) + b\tan(x^3)$$

$$y = ae^x + b$$

By contrast, the next two equations are examples of nonlinear regressions:

$$y = ae^{bx}$$

$$y = a\cos(bx) + \log cx^2$$

In other words, the nonlinearity of the assumed functional relationship between the dependent and the independent variable or variables is irrelevant to the linearity of regression.

The Formalism of Multiple Linear Regression

Assume you are given a set of m data points consisting of a column vector of n dependent variates, $\mathbf{y}$, the residual vector, $\boldsymbol{\varepsilon}$, and a known $n \times m$ matrix of independent variates $\mathbf{X}$.

$$\mathbf{y} = \begin{bmatrix} y_1 \\ y_2 \\ y_3 \\ \cdot \\ \cdot \\ y_n \end{bmatrix}, \ \mathbf{a} = \begin{bmatrix} a_1 \\ a_2 \\ a_3 \\ \cdot \\ a_m \end{bmatrix}, \ \mathbf{X} = \begin{bmatrix} x_{11} & x_{12} & x_{13} & \cdots & x_{1m} \\ x_{21} & x_{22} & x_{23} & \cdots & x_{2m} \\ x_{31} & x_{32} & x_{33} & \cdots & x_{3m} \\ \cdot \\ \cdot \\ x_{n1} & x_{n2} & x_{n3} & \cdots & x_{nm} \end{bmatrix}, \ \boldsymbol{\varepsilon} = \begin{bmatrix} \varepsilon_1 \\ \varepsilon_2 \\ \varepsilon_3 \\ \cdot \\ \cdot \\ \varepsilon_n \end{bmatrix} \quad (15.5)$$

The goal is to derive the values of the column vector $\mathbf{a}$ of m unknown parameters shown in (15.5). We also assume that the analyst has modeled the phenomenon properly so that the independent variates have largely uncorrelated residuals with a mean of zero and a variance of σ^2. Mathematically, these assumptions are expressed as

$$E(\boldsymbol{\varepsilon}) = 0 \text{ and}$$

$$E(\boldsymbol{\varepsilon}\boldsymbol{\varepsilon}^T) = \sigma^2\mathbf{I}, \quad (15.6)$$

where $(1/m)\sum_{k=1}^{m} x_k$ is the mathematical expectation and $\mathbf{I}$ is the identity matrix of order n.[1]

Verifying after each regression exercise that equations (15.6) hold is highly recommended, although in practice it is seldom done.

Define the Lagrangian, $L = \sum_i (y_i - \sum_j a_j x_{ij})^2$, and solve for the m unknowns using the first-order conditions:

$$\frac{\partial L}{\partial a_i} = 0, \ i = 1, 2, 3, \ldots, m \quad (15.7)$$

To do this, rewrite L in matrix notation as follows:

$$L = (\mathbf{y} - \mathbf{Xa})^T(\mathbf{y} - \mathbf{Xa}) = \mathbf{y}^T\mathbf{y} - 2\mathbf{a}^T\mathbf{X}^T\mathbf{y} + \mathbf{a}^T\mathbf{X}^T\mathbf{Xa} \quad (15.8)$$

To motivate acceptance of the results, please note the following rules of matrix differentiation. If $\mathbf{a}$ and $\mathbf{b}$ are column vectors and $\mathbf{X}$ is a square matrix, then

$$\frac{\partial \mathbf{a}^T\mathbf{b}}{\partial \mathbf{a}} = \mathbf{b}, \ \frac{\partial(\mathbf{b}^T\mathbf{Xb})}{\partial \mathbf{b}} = \mathbf{Xb} + \mathbf{X}^T\mathbf{b}. \quad (15.9)$$

The derivative of a scalar with respect to a vector is a vector, the elements of which are the derivatives of the scalar with respect to each element of the vector. Then, equation (15.7) reduces to

$$\frac{\partial L}{\partial \mathbf{a}} \equiv -2\mathbf{Xy} + 2\mathbf{X}^T\mathbf{Xa} = 0. \quad (15.10)$$

The solution to equations (15.10) yields our minimizing vector:

$$\mathbf{a} = (\mathbf{X}^T\mathbf{X})^{-1}\mathbf{X}^T\mathbf{y} \quad (15.11)$$

Matrix $(\mathbf{X}^T\mathbf{X})$ will be referred to as the regression matrix. In Appendix D, we will discuss its properties, some of which enable us to solve for $\mathbf{a}$ without matrix inversion.

The Formalism of Nonlinear Regression

By contrast, in the nonlinear case we may no longer write the independent-variable part of the regression equations as $\mathbf{Xa}$, but must be content with a system of the general form

$$L = \sum_i [y_i - f_i(\mathbf{x}; \mathbf{a})]^2 \tag{15.12}$$

The method goes through unaltered and results in the following set of m nonlinear equations:

$$\frac{\partial L}{\partial a_i} = -2\sum_i [y_i - f_i(\mathbf{x}; \mathbf{a})]\frac{\partial f_i(\mathbf{x}; \mathbf{a})}{\partial a_i} = 0 \tag{15.13}$$

Unfortunately, the regression equations (15.13) usually will not lend themselves to a one-step matrix solution of the form (15.11). To help readers visualize the nonlinear situation, a simple example of nonlinear regression is presented in Appendix D. We return to an important application of nonlinear regression with the Newton-Raphson optimization method in chapter 18.

16

Lower-Upper Decomposition

Centuries ago in Europe, aspiring young mathematicians were subjected to the following two-part test to determine their real aptitude for the subject. First, a kettle was placed on a chair and the student was asked to put it on a nearby desk. That usually went well: students took the kettle and proceeded to put it on the desk. Then the kettle was placed on the floor, and the student was asked to "do the same thing." Those who placed it on the desk were never heard of again. The right answer was to place it on the chair and thereby reduce a difficult problem to one already solved.

This anecdote highlights a fundamental principle of mathematics. Try, as much as possible, to reduce a difficult problem to one you have already solved, usually a simpler one. This is the principle underlying the lower-upper (LU) decomposition method for solving linear systems of the form

$$\mathbf{M}\mathbf{x} = \mathbf{y}. \tag{16.1}$$

LU decomposition is a fundamental technique of numerical analysis, one with an indirect application to structured finance by the special case of Cholesky decomposition. The latter, described later in a separate section, is an essential part of covariance simulation and a must for all credit analysts interested in the influence of correlation on credit enhancement requirements.

The Use of LU Decomposition

Suppose that a given square matrix $\mathbf{M}$ of rank n can also be expressed as the product of two matrices, one of which, $\mathbf{L}$, is lower triangular while the other, $\mathbf{U}$, is upper triangular. Therefore, $\mathbf{L}$ and $\mathbf{U}$ will have the following forms:

$$\mathbf{L} = \begin{bmatrix} l_{11} & 0 & 0 & \cdots & \cdots \\ l_{21} & l_{22} & 0 & \cdots & \cdots \\ l_{31} & l_{32} & l_{33} & \cdots & \cdots \\ & \cdot & & & \\ & \cdot & & & \\ l_{n1} & l_{n2} & l_{n3} & \cdots & l_{nn} \end{bmatrix} \quad \text{and} \quad \mathbf{U} = \begin{bmatrix} u_{11} & u_{12} & u_{13} & \cdots & \cdots \\ 0 & u_{22} & u_{23} & u_{24} & \cdots \\ 0 & 0 & u_{33} & u_{34} & \cdot \\ & \cdot & & & \\ & \cdot & & & \\ 0 & 0 & 0 & & u_{nn} \end{bmatrix} \tag{16.2}$$

System (16.1) can now be written as

$$\mathbf{L}\mathbf{U}\mathbf{x} = \mathbf{y}. \tag{16.3}$$

We can solve this system in two steps. First, define

$$\mathbf{Ux = z,} \tag{16.4}$$

$$\mathbf{Lz = y.} \tag{16.5}$$

Now, solving equations (16.4) and (16.5) in succession is easy because of the respective forms of $\mathbf{U}$ and $\mathbf{L}$. The solution of a lower-triangular system of equations is trivial if one starts with the first equation and sweeps forward in a recursive manner, solving each z_i using the calculations from the previous step. This works as follows:

$$l_{11}z_1 = y_1 \rightarrow z_1 = \frac{y_1}{l_{11}}$$

Then,

$$l_{21}z_1 + l_{22}z_2 = y_2 \rightarrow z_2 = \frac{y_2 - l_{21}z_1}{l_{22}},$$

and so on down the line for the forward sweep. A backward sweep occurs when we solve equation (16.5) for the original vector $\mathbf{x}$ as follows:

$$u_{nn}x_n = z_n \rightarrow x_n = \frac{z_n}{u_{nn}},$$

$$u_{(n-1)(n-1)}x_{n-1} + u_{(n-1)n}x_n = z_{n-1} \rightarrow x_{n-1} = \frac{z_{n-1} - u_{(n-1)n}x_n}{u_{(n-1)(n-1)}},$$

and so on up the line for the backward sweep. As a result, system (16.1) may now be solved without the requirement to invert $\mathbf{M}$.

The Cholesky Decomposition

For reasons that need not trouble nonmathematicians, it turns out that the LU decomposition of a matrix that is both *symmetric* and *nonnegative definite* is particularly simple. The LU decomposition of such a matrix is referred to as its *Cholesky decomposition*. Appendix E discusses these two properties in some detail. Here we offer a more focused discussion in the context of structured finance.

The symmetry of matrix $\mathbf{M}$ leads to the condition $\mathbf{U} = \mathbf{L}^T$ so that in general we have

$$\mathbf{LL}^T = \mathbf{M}. \tag{16.6}$$

$$l_{ii} = \left[m_{ii} - \sum_{k=1}^{j-1} l_{ik}^2 \right]^{1/2}, i = 1, 2, \dots n \tag{16.7}$$

$$l_{ji} = \frac{1}{l_{ii}} \left[m_{ij} - \sum_{k=1}^{i-1} l_{ik}l_{jk} \right], j = i+1, i+1, \dots n \tag{16.8}$$

Note that if one proceeds columnwise for $i = 1, 2, \ldots, n$, whenever an element is needed on the right-hand side of equation (16.7) it has already been computed in previous steps.[1]

How does this relate to structured credit analysis? The usefulness of Cholesky decomposition in structured finance stems from the fact that the regression and the covariance matrices fulfill the two requirements that guarantee the existence of their Cholesky decomposition. That they do so is demonstrated in Appendix E. Since in most asset analysis, there will be generally be a need to use linear regression or to simulate covariance matrices, and most likely to do both, the judicious use of the Cholesky decomposition can play a pivotal role in the analysis of structured securities. In chapter 21 ("The CBO of ABS"), we take up the practical aspects of this decomposition and look at its performance and implementation challenges within a realistic setting.

17

Covariance Matrix Simulation

This chapter develops further the idea of LU decomposition and applies it to the simulation of covariance matrices. The vast majority of cash flow models used to analyze the creditworthiness of structured securities or to investigate foreign exchange risk will include an implementation. Credit professionals need to understand these mechanics to make headway in structured finance in general and CBO analysis in particular.

Suppose that you are given a covariance matrix $\mathbf{V}$ for some hypothetical n-dimensional vector whereby each group of elements of the vector would be an instance of the n variables. Suppose further that you are told to produce a set of vectors with just such a covariance matrix $\mathbf{V}$.

For any vector $\mathbf{x}$ with $E[\mathbf{x}] = \mu$, we can write from the definition of the covariance matrix $\mathbf{V} = E[(\mathbf{x} - \mu)(\mathbf{x} - \mu)^T]$.

In addition, from the fact that the covariance matrix satisfies both the symmetric and positive-definite conditions, we know that matrix $\mathbf{V}$ has a Cholesky decomposition and that we can therefore write

$$\mathbf{V} = \mathbf{LL}^T \qquad (17.1)$$

Now suppose you have chosen $\mathbf{x}$ to be a set of independently drawn standard normal deviates. This means that $E[\mathbf{x}] = 0$, and that covariance matrix $\mathbf{V}$ is identical to the associated correlation matrix and that both are equal to $\mathbf{I}$, the identity matrix of order n. In other words, we have $E[\mathbf{x}\mathbf{x}^T] = \mathbf{I}$. Remember, however, that in practice an array of standard normal deviates will not have precisely the identity matrix as their correlation matrix due to statistical errors.

Now, define $\mathbf{y}$ as

$$\mathbf{y} = \mathbf{Lx}. \qquad (17.2)$$

It is clear from equation (17.2) that the components of $\mathbf{y}$ are a linear combination of the $\mathbf{x}$ variables and that, since $\mathbf{x}$ is a set of standard normal deviates with mean zero, the elements of $\mathbf{y}$ will also be normal, since sums of normal variables are also normal. Their mean and variances will be given by the following:

$$E[\mathbf{y}_i] = 0 \qquad (17.3)$$

$$E[y_i^2] = \sum_{j=1}^{i} l_{ij}^2 = v_{ii}, \, i = 1, 2, 3, \ldots n \qquad (17.3')$$

Let's compute the covariance matrix of $\mathbf{y}$ via direct calculation:

$$E[\mathbf{y}\mathbf{y}^T] = E[\mathbf{L}\mathbf{x}\mathbf{x}^T\mathbf{L}^T] = \mathbf{L}E[\mathbf{x}\mathbf{x}^T]\mathbf{L}^\mathbf{T} = \mathbf{L}\mathbf{I}\mathbf{L}^T = \mathbf{L}\mathbf{L}^T = \mathbf{V} \quad (17.4)$$

Thus, to the extent of the statistical errors causing $E[\mathbf{x}\mathbf{x}^T] \neq \mathbf{I}$, the covariance matrix of the vector $\mathbf{y}$ will be the desired matrix $\mathbf{V}$. If the original matrix $\mathbf{V}$ is itself a correlation matrix, the resulting components of $\mathbf{y}$, like the $\mathbf{x}$, will be standard normal variables since their variances will be equal to the diagonal elements of $\mathbf{V}$.

Via Cholesky decomposition, we can thus synthesize a correlated set of standard normal vectors $\mathbf{y}$ as weighted sums of normal variables. If correlated, normal vectors are required, we can stop here; but in general, we will need to simulate variables from a variety of distribution functions, only one of which may be the normal distribution. In other words, analysts will be told to choose variables drawn from normal, Bernoulli, binomial, Beta, Poisson, or other distributions and to correlate them in the manner indicated. This will turn out to be difficult, if not impossible, using the scheme indicated here. Is there any remedy? Yes, there is. We tackle the problem of sampling from any distribution with a two-step process:

1. Linearly map the y_i obtained above onto the range [0, 1]
2. Use IDFM to select the deviates used inside the Monte Carlo simulation engine.

Since correlation matrices are invariant under linear transformations, the mappings in the first step will not change the correlation between y_i, but the second step unfortunately will undo the Cholesky-based correlative transformations to the extent the required inverse distribution functions are nonlinear. Virtually all of them are.

However, the resulting deviates will still capture the relative magnitudes of the variables. This happens for two reasons:

*   A linear map leaves the relative ordering of the variables intact, and
*   All cumulative distribution functions are monotonic.[1]

This means that the relative variability of the y_i inherent in the original correlation matrix will be preserved, although not to the full extent originally intended. As a result, we will be able to simulate correlated variables drawn from any probability distribution with the caveat that the resulting deviates will preserve only the rank ordering implied by $\mathbf{V}$ and not its absolute ordering. In most cases of interest, this will not affect the robustness of the analysis in the least since credit enhancement levels will be much more sensitive to relative than absolute values.

Note in passing that the Box-Muller transformation[2] is a simple, multidimensional method to transform uniformly distributed deviates into normally distributed ones. Thus, the inverse Box-Muller transformation could be used to map the normally distributed $\mathbf{y}$ to a uniform distribution. However, since the transformation involves nonlinear terms, it would also undo the correlative work done up to then. For this reason, we have found it is better to stick to the two-step method above, which assures more control over the outcome, and to take our chances with the inverse distribution function method.

In structured finance, credit analysts will rarely be given a covariance matrix. Rather, they will be given a correlation matrix and, more often than not, the latter will be a compromise position between opposing and subjective assessments of credit dynamics. In practice, the realistic extent of credit knowledge will rarely be so precise as to make actual correspondence with the given matrix a conditio sine qua non of the analysis. In most cases, faithfulness to the relative motions of the variables is sufficient to reflect the true state of credit knowledge of the asset class. Thus, imprecise adherence to the given correlation matrix usually turns out not to be a problem at all.

There is, however, a genuine concern that needs addressing. The IDFM method used in step 2 requires the use of a uniform distribution over [0, 1]. Because our output vectors are generally nonuniform, the resulting deviates will fail to account for the probability measure of the intended distributions at both ends of the range [0, 1]. In this lies the most troubling aspect of the Cholesky method.

To see how this comes about, note first that the normality of the **x** variables was not necessary to show that the decomposition would lead to the required matrix. What was required was merely the condition that the covariance matrix of **x** was the identity matrix. In this context, standard normal vectors were a convenient way to do this while preserving normality in the output vectors. After going through the two-step process just described, we were left with y_i that were also normal and hence nonuniform.

How then do we generate input deviates to IDFM that have the required uniformity? We know of no quick fix to this problem. For now, let us simply state that we can find a makeshift solution, but it is regrettably suboptimal and forces a further departure from the given correlation matrix while preserving the relative ordering of each variable. We will come back to this problem in chapter 21.

The Impact of Correlations in Structured Finance

Does distributional uniformity in the random samples used to simulate covariance matrices matter for credit analysis? Unfortunately, the answer is yes. Without starting from a uniformly distributed sample as input to our IDFM technique or to any other method,[3] both ends of the variable range will be inadequately sampled. In each particular case, one of these ends will represent favorable cash flow environments while the other will correspond to stressed scenarios. As far as the "favorable" end is concerned, we could ignore the problem since such scenarios do not affect credit ratings, but the "stressed" end cannot be so ignored with impunity.

Structured finance lives or dies at the tails of probability distributions. We cannot afford to subsample the meaningful end of a distribution if the earning potential of the collateral in a structure is to be fairly represented. As a result, it becomes necessary to at least partially correct the nonuniformity of the input distributions while to some extent safeguarding their correlative properties. Only then will we be paying due respect to the probability measure at both ends of the credit spectrum to better reflect the expected range of cash flow events contemplated by the chosen distributions. Thus, credit analysts will be forced to carefully navigate between wandering too far away from correlation constraints imposed a priori, and fully exploring the extremities of input variable ranges to a degree that accurately reflects the distributional assumptions. We believe the accuracy of correlation matrix simulation as it is performed today is still an open topic.

If the number of dimensions is low (two or three) there are other ways to synthesize variables with known covariance or correlation matrices, but in general, the problem cannot be entirely solved. We must "pick our poison" and try to steer a middle ground. To do this is far more powerful than to assume that the variables are uncorrelated, as is often done. We can still perform sensitivity studies, observing how carefully one must account for correlations and how sensitive credit enhancement levels are to the relative magnitudes of correlations. This situation truly captures the essence of credit analysis where the art is as important as the science. For example, the solution presented in chapter 21 is admittedly far from perfect but at least captures the essential dynamics of correlations while giving the analyst flexibility to implement various correlation matrix regimes.

18

The Newton-Raphson Nonlinear Optimization Method

Serious cash flow models used in structured finance are generally required to solve systems of nonlinear equations that stem either from nonlinear regression analysis or from an ad hoc asset-behavior model. Commercial packages exist to solve most nonlinear systems, but integrating them smoothly into a structured analysis code can be difficult; the result is often a hybrid construct no one wants to maintain or use. Our main goal in this section is to guide analysts in building nonlinear solution packages that can be maintained and reused for any given asset class. A subsidiary benefit is the ability to write fast routines that reduce the CPU requirements of Monte Carlo simulations by an order of magnitude. In chapter 20, we discuss Newton-Raphson (NR) implementation in detail in the case of auto-loan-backed securities.

Nonlinear solutions require a different set of techniques than the matrix inversion method that can be used in all linear solutions. We discuss here only the most basic non-linear scheme: the NR method, in its scalar and vector forms. For structured finance, one-dimensional (i.e., scalar) solutions are virtually nonexistent because most useful nonlinear models have multiple parameters. However, from a didactic standpoint the vector-valued NR iterative technique is easier to grasp if one first understands the scalar case.

Chief among implementation issues with respect to nonlinear optimization, and one that may cause the scheme to fail locally, is the requirement for a suitable initial guess. We address this problem in Appendix F by investigating sufficient conditions under which the NR scalar and vector iterative solutions will converge uniformly. The vector-valued NR iteration is similar in principle to the scalar case, except for the use of matrix notation. Unfortunately, unlike with linear regression, solving vector-valued NR problems will involve inverting matrices that will usually turn out to be neither symmetric nor nonnegative definite. In that case, the use of standard methods like Gauss-Seidel iteration[1] or Gaussian elimination[2] will be required. Most desktop spreadsheet packages usually contain a matrix inversion routine. Therefore, in practice credit analysts will not be forced to write their own matrix inversion codes. In the worst case, codes can often be lifted wholesale from textbooks—for instance, *Numerical Recipes*[3] is a treasure trove of such techniques. Since matrix inversion is the starting point of much of numerical analysis, we cannot overemphasize the value of writing an inversion routine from scratch at least once in one's lifetime!

The Scalar Newton-Raphson Iteration Scheme

In the scalar case, the goal is to find a solution of $f(x) = 0$ known to exist in some interval $[a, b]$. The general idea is to expand $f(x)$ into its Taylor series, truncate it after the first-order term, and solve for the value of the increment Δx that makes $f(x)$ vanish—in essence, jumping to the root in one step. If that does not happen, simply use the new value of x to which the algorithm does in fact move to advance to the next location and repeat the Taylor series approximation recursively using successive updates to advance the solution until convergence occurs, that is, until $f(x) = 0$ holds to a desired level of accuracy. As the iteration number n increases, Δx should become progressively smaller until, in the limit of $n \to \infty$, $f(x) \to 0$ and $\Delta x \to 0$ simultaneously.

First, the Taylor series expansion of a scalar function $f(x)$ about a point x_0 is given by the following:

$$f(x_0 + \Delta x) = f(x_0) + \Delta x \frac{\partial f(x)}{\partial x}\bigg|_{x_0} + \ldots \ldots \tag{18.1}$$

Setting the left-hand side of equation (18.1) to zero and solving for $x_1 = x_0 + \Delta x$, we then have

$$x_1 = x_0 - \frac{f(x_0)}{f'(x_0)}. \tag{18.2}$$

In equation (18.2), we have defined

$$f'(x_0) = \frac{\partial f(x)}{\partial x}\bigg|_{x_0},$$

and, in general, we have

$$x_n = x_{n-1} - \frac{f(x_{n-1})}{f'(x_{n-1})}. \tag{18.3}$$

Equation (18.3) is then applied recursively until convergence.

As intimated previously, the main problem of the NR solution is the starting guess: if improperly selected, the iteration may diverge. For the NR method to be successful, the mapping $x_{n-1} \to x_n$ must continuously reduce the distance between the root and the current x value. The condition that the mapping be contractive (leading to convergence) is guaranteed nowhere. In general, one needs to be "close enough." However, knowledge that one is close enough to a root implies knowledge of where the root is; and if its location is already known, what is the point of the search?

In practice, a nontrivial way of specifying regions of x space where the iteration is guaranteed to converge is required. Such specification is the subject matter of the convergence analysis presented in Appendix F. It should be noted that, in practice, much of the mathematical and numerical effort involved in analyzing the convergence of the NR iteration is academic because it is fairly obvious that a numerical scheme is not converging. In such cases, the practitioner will seek to start "closer" to the root and hope to converge. However, we recommend that before embarking upon a lengthy derivation of the convergence properties of the scheme under study, a quick fix should always be attempted. In most cases, one will exist.

The Vector Newton-Raphson Iteration Scheme

In the vector case, instead of a single equation we have a system of n nonlinear equations to be solved. Generically speaking, a system of this type may be represented compactly by the column vector $\mathbf{f}(\mathbf{x})$ where both $\mathbf{f}$ and $\mathbf{x}$ are n-dimensional column vectors.

As a first step, define the Jacobian matrix of first derivatives as follows:

$$\mathbf{J} = \begin{bmatrix} \dfrac{\partial f_1(\mathbf{x})}{\partial x_1} & \dfrac{\partial f_1(\mathbf{x})}{\partial x_2} & \cdots & \dfrac{\partial f_1(\mathbf{x})}{\partial x_n} \\ \dfrac{\partial f_2(\mathbf{x})}{\partial x_1} & \dfrac{\partial f_2(\mathbf{x})}{\partial x_2} & \cdots & \dfrac{\partial f_2(\mathbf{x})}{\partial x_n} \\ \cdot & & & \\ \cdot & & & \\ \dfrac{\partial f_n(\mathbf{x})}{\partial x_1} & \dfrac{\partial f_n(\mathbf{x})}{\partial x_2} & \cdots & \dfrac{\partial f_2(\mathbf{x})}{\partial x_n} \end{bmatrix} \tag{18.4}$$

Following the scalar example, the Taylor series expansion of a vector-valued function $\mathbf{f}$ about a point $\mathbf{x}_0$ can be written in matrix notation as follows:

$$\mathbf{f}(\mathbf{x}_0 + \Delta\mathbf{x}) = \mathbf{f}(\mathbf{x}_0) + \mathbf{J}(\mathbf{x}_0)\Delta\mathbf{x} + \ldots \tag{18.5}$$

Setting the left-hand side to zero and solving matrix equation (18.5) for the increment $\Delta\mathbf{x}$ yields

$$\Delta\mathbf{x} = -\mathbf{J}^{-1}(\mathbf{x}_0)\mathbf{f}(\mathbf{x}_0). \tag{18.6}$$

Insertion of the definition $\Delta\mathbf{x} = \mathbf{x}_n - \mathbf{x}_{n-1}$ into equation (18.6) leads to the general iterative scheme

$$\mathbf{x}_n = \mathbf{x}_{n-1} - \mathbf{J}^{-1}(\mathbf{x}_{n-1})\mathbf{f}(\mathbf{x}_{n-1}). \tag{18.7}$$

Again, this NR iteration is not necessarily stable for all choices of the initial vector $\mathbf{x}_0$. The convergence analysis of the vector-valued NR iterative scheme is also presented in Appendix F. Not surprisingly, the convergence analysis of the vector NR iteration will involve the use of eigenvalues and eigenvectors.

19

Tchebychev Polynomials

Tchebychev polynomials, the work of Markov's contemporary Pafnuti Lvovich Tchebychev (1821–1894), are less essential to structured analysis than Markov chains but are nonetheless a workhorse numerical technique. In structured finance, we use the versatility of Tchebychev polynomials, as reflected in the unusual distribution of their roots, to support the simulation of covariance matrices using Cholesky decomposition. Our treatment of CBOs of ABS in chapter 21 demonstrates this method. In modeling other economic phenomena, we can use them to telescope power-series approximations to analytic functions. The approximations can then be put to work describing asset behavior. In the following, we provide (without proof) a background on this class of polynomials and discuss the property that makes them so useful in approximation theory.

Definition of Tchebychev Polynomials

The nth-degree Tchebychev polynomial $T_n(x)$ is defined by

$$T_n(x) = \cos(n \cos^{-1}(x)), \, n \in [0, \infty]. \tag{19.1}$$

It can be shown that Tchebychev polynomials also satisfy the recurrence relation

$$T_{n+1}(x) = 2xT_n(x) - T_{n-1}(x). \tag{19.2}$$

The n roots of the nth-degree Tchebychev polynomial are located in $[-1, 1]$ and are given by

$$x_k = \cos\left(\frac{2k-1}{n}\left(\frac{\pi}{2}\right)\right), \, k = 1, 2, \ldots, n. \tag{19.3}$$

In concert with the special cases, $T_0(x) = 1$, $T_1(x) = x$, equation (19.2) allows us to compute Tchebychev polynomials of all orders.

The Minimax Property

The minimax property is the central concept underlying the usefulness of Tchebychev polynomials. In formal terms, it states that of all nth-degree polynomials $P_n(x)$ defined on the interval $[-1, 1]$ and equipped with the norm

$|P_n(x)|$, the Tchebychev polynomial $T_n(x)$ has the minimum maximum norm, hence the epithet *minimax*. The proof will not be given, but the basic insight hinges on the uniqueness of the nth-degree Tchebychev polynomial in having all its roots in $[-1, 1]$. Any other nth-degree polynomial would have to have more roots in that interval for its norm (the height above or below the x-axis) to be less than $T_n(x)$ everywhere in $[-1, 1]$, and we conclude that this is impossible since an nth-degree polynomial has only n roots.

Use of the Minimax Property

We demonstrate the usefulness of the minimax property via a simple example. Suppose a credit analyst is asked to approximate a function between given data points (x_i, y_i), $i = 0, 1, 2, 3, \ldots n$ in the interval $[-1, 1]$. Assume further that the choice of the given points is arbitrary and up to the credit analyst. In other words, the analyst can ask for any set of $n + 1$ points within $[-1, 1]$ that he or she wishes.

No matter which interpolating function is chosen, it should at least match the given data points and should be as smooth as possible between them. But that leaves a wide array of choices for the data points. To ensure the interpolating function will indeed match the $n + 1$ data points, let's assume the analyst has decided to use the Lagrange interpolation formula and that, for lack of a better idea, the data points are chosen at equally spaced intervals along the x-axis. The Lagrange formula for $n + 1$ points is given by[1]

$$P_n(x) = \sum y_i L_i(x) \tag{19.4}$$

$$L_i(x) = \prod_{\substack{j=0 \\ j \neq i}}^{n} \frac{(x - x_j)}{(x_i - x_j)}. \tag{19.5}$$

Note that

$$L_i(x_j) = \delta_{ij} \equiv \begin{Bmatrix} 1, i = j \\ 0, \text{otherwise} \end{Bmatrix}.$$

By construction, polynomial $P_n(x)$ in equation (19.4) is of degree n, matches the $n + 1$ data points exactly, and interpolates smoothly between them. Unfortunately, as the analyst soon finds out, the problem with using the Lagrange formula with equally spaced points is that $P_n(x)$ is volatile in strange ways. This is shown inside the circles (curve labeled "Lagrange") of Figure 19.1 for the approximation of the relatively straightforward function $y = 1/(1 + 5x^2)$ with eleven equally spaced points in the interval $[-1, 1]$ as inputs.

Now, instead of sampling the function at equally spaced points, imagine the analyst elected instead to sample the function at the roots of the $n + 1$st-degree Tchebychev polynomial given by equation (19.3). To demonstrate how they break out, Table 19.1 shows the roots of the first twelve Tchebychev polynomials. Note that these roots are not equally spaced but are concentrated at

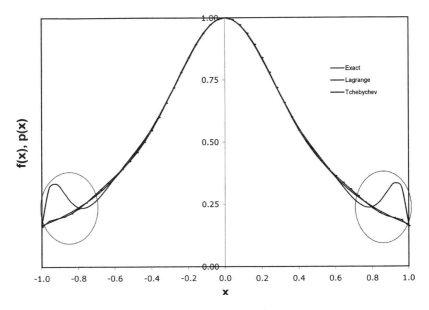

Figure 19.1. The Erratic Behavior of Lagrange Interpolations

both ends of $[-1, 1]$ as n increases. This property is illustrated in Figure 19.2 for selected polynomials.

Table 19.2 and Figure 19.3 contrast the 12th-degree Taylor series approximation $p(x)$ with the actual function $f(x)$, which you will recall is $f(x) = 1/(1 + 5x^2)$. Note how dramatically the error increases for x in the range above 0.35.

The fact of the matter is that much better resolution is needed at both ends of the interval than in the neighborhood of $x = 0$, where the 10th-degree Lagrange polynomial is quite accurate. Tchebychev root loci are clearly a better choice for the x_i. Despite its relative coarseness, the approximation samples data more frequently where higher resolution is required (i.e., at both ends of the target interval).

Figure 19.1 shows how selecting the roots of Tchebychev polynomials as input data points inside the Lagrange formula improves the situation quite dramatically. The Lagrange formula still matches the y_i precisely at the data points, but the maximum error $|P_n(x_i) - y_i|$ is now much smaller. Whereas the naive, equally spaced points Lagrange formula produced a maximum absolute error of 0.14, the Tchebychev technique reduced the error to 0.0083 (a seventeenfold improvement for the same basic effort) by redistributing it almost uniformly throughout the interval. The improvement is shown in Figure 19.4.

To see the role of the minimax property in this improvement, remember that the approximation is now exact at the roots of the $n + $ 1st-order Tchebychev polynomial. If the function $f(x)$ we are approximating (given only at the points y_i) has a Taylor-series expansion that terminates before or at the

Table 19.1

Root Locus of the First Twelve Tchebychev Polynomials

N	Position of the Root x_k											
1	0											
2	−.707	.707										
3	−.866	0	.866									
4	−.924	−.383	.383	.924								
5	−.951	−.588	0	.588	.951							
6	−.966	−.707	−.259	.259	.707	.966						
7	−.975	−.782	−.434	0	.434	.782	.975					
8	−.981	−.831	−.556	−.195	.195	.556	.831	.981				
9	−.985	−.866	−.643	−.342	0	.342	.643	.866	.985			
10	−.988	−.891	−.707	−.454	−.156	.156	.454	.707	.891	.988		
11	−.990	−.910	−.756	−.541	−.281	0	.281	.541	.756	.910	.990	
12	−.991	−.924	−.793	−.609	−.383	−.131	.131	.383	.609	.793	.924	.991

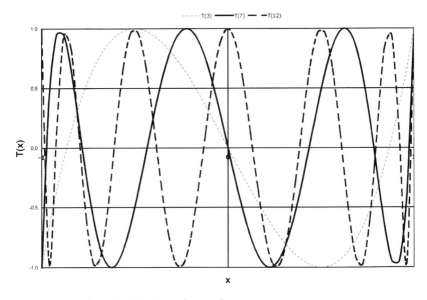

Figure 19.2. Selected Tchebychev Polynomials

Table 19.2
12th Degree Taylor Series Approximation $p(x)$

x	$f(x)$	$p(x)$	Error(x)
0.000	1.000	1.000	0.00%
0.025	0.997	0.997	0.00%
0.050	0.988	0.988	0.00%
0.075	0.973	0.973	0.00%
0.100	0.952	0.952	0.00%
0.125	0.928	0.928	0.00%
0.150	0.899	0.899	0.00%
0.175	0.867	0.867	0.00%
0.200	0.833	0.833	0.00%
0.225	0.798	0.798	0.01%
0.250	0.762	0.762	0.03%
0.275	0.726	0.726	0.11%
0.300	0.690	0.692	0.37%
0.325	0.654	0.662	1.15%
0.350	0.620	0.640	3.23%
0.375	0.587	0.637	8.50%
0.400	0.556	0.672	20.97%
0.425	0.525	0.783	49.00%
0.450	0.497	1.039	109.09%
0.475	0.470	1.563	232.54%
0.500	0.444	2.564	476.84%

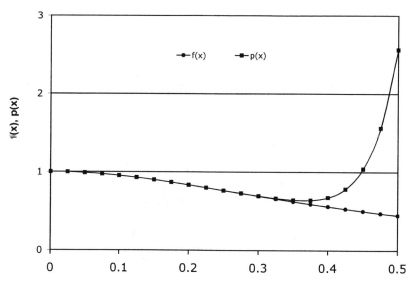

Figure 19.3. 12th Degree Taylor Series Approximation $p(x)$

n + 1st-order term, the error between the actual function and its approximation will itself be a polynomial of degree n + 1, and will, by construction, have
the same roots as the Tchebychev polynomial of that order. The uniqueness of
that polynomial will make it precisely the Tchebychev polynomial of degree
n + 1, which means, therefore, that the error function will have the mini-
mum-maximum norm over the interval $[-1, 1]$.

The test function above does not satisfy this condition: its Taylor series,
given by equation (19.6) does not terminate at the n + 1st term:

$$f(x) = \sum_{n=0}^{\infty}(-1)^n(5x^2)^n \qquad (19.6)$$

As a rule of thumb, though, choosing the roots of the appropriate Tchebychev polynomial as data points is probably the best one can do. Note in passing that if the interval in question is not $[-1, 1]$, it can always be mapped to
$[-1, 1]$ via a linear transformation of the type $x' = ax + b$.

The Use of Tchebychev Polynomials in Data Requests

How do we use the special features of Tchebychev polynomials in structured
finance? We shall show in chapter 21 how to use the root-locus distribution to
improve the accuracy of correlation matrix simulations. Also worthy of mention is how the minimax property can be used directly by credit analysts when
making transaction-related data requests. Generally, the requested master trust
or portfolio data are month-end results, which are more or less equally spaced

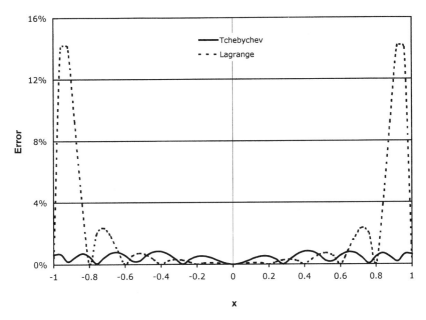

Figure 19.4. Tchebychev versus Lagrange: Distributions of the Approximation Error

points. By the foregoing arguments, it should be possible to dramatically improve the resolution of the approximation (hence the quality of the associated knowledge) without any additional effort on the part of the analyst or the issuer, by asking for data sampled at the roots of the appropriate Tchebychev polynomial. In physical terms, this means sampling the function more frequently at its points of suspected highest volatility. Such a request would be rather unorthodox (!) but would generally produce a better estimate of the dynamics of the actual process than the choice of equally spaced points. With respect to credit card–backed securities, for instance, data are available every business day, or about 230 times per year. However, seasonality is a factor in some asset classes, like this one. The period surrounding December and January is the most volatile in terms of delinquencies and defaults. Accordingly, a Tchebychev request would be skewed toward the beginning and the end of the target year, producing a pattern of target dates like those in Table 19.3. If any of these target dates turned out not to be a business day, the closest business day would be requested.

Obviously, the same argument applies to many other types of data.

Final Remarks on Mathematics and Modeling

Readers might have finished reading the more esoteric parts of part III wondering how they relate to the practice of structured finance. Some may retort

Table 19.3
Target Tchebychev Sampling Dates

Data ID	Business Day
1	January 12
2	January 15
3	February 7
4	March 11
5	April 22
6	June 7
7	July 25
8	September 9
9	October 19
10	November 22
11	December 15
12	December 31

that perhaps we have wandered too far away from the subject matter and lost ourselves in eigenvalues and matrix algebra. Unfortunately, the nuts and bolts of structured credit analysis are often found in this type of work.

In all asset classes, cash flow models containing the appropriate physics are required. Credit analysts must be able to maneuver with complete freedom with respect to the functional form these models may take. In many cases, reasonable models will contain nonlinear terms, leading to the unavoidable requirement for the NR or other types of nonlinear optimization techniques. While available, canned packages for solving nonlinear equations are unwieldy and cumbersome, and will rarely be integrated with the rest of the analysis. Liability models, at least those commonly bought at significant expense to serve as front-end packages to structured analysis, are normally inadequate because they assume cash flows are known a priori or can be derived from simplistic (and therefore unrealistic) processes.

Asset classes have idiosyncratic requirements that commercial software packages fail to incorporate in any meaningful sense. These packages rarely, if ever, have sufficient functionality to include triggers and other asset- or liability-based structural features. Each securitization involves individual characteristics that preclude the use of general models valid for all issuers, let alone all asset classes. Unfortunately, such issues are the heart and soul of structured finance. Similar problems will befall the analyst on the asset side of the balance sheet, where (for instance) revolving periods will require specialized and ad hoc treatments. Without the freedom to innovate, analysts will tend to make convenient assumptions allowing them to use the same formalism in all cases, whether it applies or not. In the process, the first casualty will be the truth. As a result, good analysts have no choice but to write their own special-purpose models and to solve implementation problems as they arise.

Rest assured that the hours spent reading and understanding the theoretical apparatus presented in this and other sections have been well spent. When model solutions start to diverge (and they will), the search for answers will make up but a small part of the analyst's total assignment. In most cases, convergence analysis will not be performed, for the simple reason that it is obvious that an iterative scheme is not converging. However, the intuitive understanding of the mechanics of numerical analysis gained from writing and debugging cash flow and nonlinear optimization models is invaluable to achieve and interpret the results within a reasonable time frame. Hands-on training is the best way to acquire this understanding. A credit analyst who has developed the comfort level required to handle these and similar situations will simultaneously have achieved the freedom necessary to build realistic models for the analysis of structured securities.

Part IV
Case Studies

20

Automobile Receivable Securitizations

Of the three asset classes discussed here, auto-loan-backed securities are by far the most liquid and intuitive. Although they are one of the least "exotic" structured securities available in the capital markets, automobile securitizations nevertheless present interesting challenges.

Most vehicles sold in the United States are not paid for in cash. They are financed by banks, finance subsidiaries of large automobile manufacturers, or specialty finance companies at interest rates that vary with the quality of the underlying borrower, not the automobile. Although the public has had a love affair with automobiles for decades, most drivers do not realize that a significant percentage of their loans are packaged into pools and transferred to SPEs, out of which securities are created and sold to investors. The economic agents of our structured universe are the individual obligors holding loans in the securitized pools; however, the creditworthiness of automobile loan- or lease-backed securities depends on both the driver as obligor and the vehicle as collateral to be liquidated if the obligor defaults.

In what follows, we lay out in greater detail some of the analytical techniques briefly reviewed in part III and attempt to give them shape by applying them to auto ABS. Throughout, we restrict our remarks to the asset side of the SPE balance sheet—by far the most challenging—having discussed the general approach to liability structures in chapter 8. There is no loss of generality in doing this since, as the Modigliani-Miller proposition plainly states, the value of an asset is independent of its financing mechanism.

Statistical Weight and Stratification

The first step in performing structured analysis in the auto sector is to obtain a database of the entire population of loans to be securitized, or at least a representative sample of the pool. Depending on the originator's scale of operations, auto pools may contain hundreds of thousands of obligors while others will consist of a few hundred. Nevertheless, the method we present here is identical regardless of the number of obligors in the pool; the only difference is the percentage of the pool chosen for credit analysis. Statistical averages of consumer data used in multivariate work tend to stabilize once the number of obligors reaches approximately 2,000. Thus, for pools below this critical mass, the target sample will normally consist of the entire pool. Above this number, a random sampling technique can be used to keep sample sizes to around

2,000 (e.g., a pool containing 4,000 obligors would be sampled at a 50% rate, and so on).

The chief advantage of selecting large samples of loans is that loan-level diversification is automatically included and given full credit. Conversely, a pool of a few hundred loans is implicitly viewed as less diverse and, as a result, will exhibit higher credit-loss variance without the need for arbitrary and ambiguous diversity scores. As discussed in chapter 6, the formal separation of the *micro-* and *macro*economic levels of structured finance is one of the main features inherent in our Markovian approach.

The discussion of sample size brings up the issue of stratification, or *stratified sampling*. This problem will arise in cases where the available population is not exactly coincident with the securitized pool, thus forcing credit analysts to synthesize as best they can a representative sample. In this context, stratified sampling refers to a sampling program that selects predefined samples from predefined segments of the entire population in order to ensure that statistical credit judgments are based on a total sample that accurately reflects the target population. In general, the latter will tend to be at least similar to the given population. In that case, stratified sampling will be largely equivalent to random sampling and will return a sample statistically equivalent to the putative target population. By contrast, two examples where this would not be the case are the following:

1. If the securitization were to include loans subject to different underwriting standards from those of the issuer (e.g., if a portion of the securitized portfolio were purchased from a third party). In this case, it would be appropriate to skew the selected sample toward the anticipated pool distribution.
2. If an issuer is targeting a different distribution of credit scores than the one found in its current portfolio. In that case, the approach (rather than making ad hoc adjustments, which are usually subjective and tend to overstate expected losses) would be to bias the chosen sample's credit score distribution to reflect the prospective, not the actual, distribution. The resulting sample would naturally exhibit higher average losses than in the issuer's managed portfolio and would lead to higher credit enhancement levels.

By and large, however, the pool cut submitted by the issuer will closely reflect the servicer portfolio, and the stratification problem will not arise.

Data

Once the target population has been assembled, usually in the form of a flat file listing each loan in the pool along with its key characteristics such as coupon, associated collateral, and so on, the real work of credit analysis can start.

Table 20.1
Minimum Loan-Level Data Requirements

Data Requirement	Unit
Initial balance	$
Current balance	$
New or used vehicle	N/U
Remaining term	Months
Delinquency status	Integer (see below)
Annual loan percentage rate (APR)	%
Origination date	M/D/Y
Origination state	State name
Year of vehicle	YYYY
Model of vehicle	Model name (e.g., Ford Bronco)
Wholesale value (Blue or Red Book)	$
Obligor credit score	FICO, MDS, etc.

Note: Obligor-level data (prime and sub-prime auto ABS).

Rather than work with aggregate values of coupon or maturity, credit analysts will be well advised to use loan-level data within a comprehensive framework. Besides reflecting the innate diversification of the pool, loan-level analysis also automatically incorporates the complete set of statistical moments, thereby allowing the bulk properties of the pools to emerge naturally from their granular decomposition within the Monte Carlo simulation process.

Pool Data

The minimal loan-level data set that we suggest is given in Table 20.1.

Issuer Portfolio Data

In addition to loan-level data, credit analysts will request, and normally receive, the set of data required to define issuer-bound delinquency transition matrices (for questions related to setting up and using delinquency transition matrices, please consult chapter 14 and Appendix B). These data will stem from the issuer's managed loan portfolio, or in the worst case, from a valid proxy issuer. Credit analysts should request portfolio and other data directly from the issuer's information technology (IT) department, not from the underwriters or the issuer's chief credit officer.

As discussed in our review of Markov chains, the delinquency history of any account can be partitioned into individual nonoverlapping regions, or buckets, each one equivalent to one collection period, usually one month. Each bucket is designated by an integer: zero for current accounts, 1 for thirty-day delinquent accounts, and so on, until the last delinquency stage prior to

Table 20.2
Monthly Transition Matrix

Old Delinquency Status	New Delinquency Status						
	0	1	2	3	4	Prepay	Default
0	0.93	0.05	•	•		0.01	0.01
1	0.06	0.89	•	•			
2	•						
3	•						
4							
Prepay	0	0	0	0	0	1	
Default	0	0	0	0	0	0	1

default. In auto-ABS, the last delinquency stage will vary by issuer but will generally be three to four months. Along with these standard delinquency stages, we will normally recognize two additional and absorbing Markov states equivalent to prepayment and default. As previously explained, in the case of absorbing states, the appropriate row of the transition matrix consists of zeros everywhere except for a 1 on the main diagonal. In the unlikely event that reverse defaults are admissible within the issuer's credit policy manual, the diagonal element of the default row could be less than 1. (The authors have not witnessed any real-life example of this.)

The result of summarizing issuer data in this manner is a monthly transition matrix like the one in Table 20.2. Chapter 14 showed how to build this matrix from raw issuer data or synthesize it from account inventories when such data alone, perhaps from an issuer's prospectus, are available. We also pointed out that issuers with more than eighteen months of operating history that are unable to supply Markov transition matrices (or *roll-rate delinquencies*) from their own data are to be viewed with suspicion.

Table 20.2 should be read as follows. Entry (0, 0) means that 93% of the accounts that are current in any given month will remain current during the next month. The other entries of the first row indicate that in a given month, 5% of current accounts will become thirty days delinquent, 1% will prepay, and 1% will default, presumably from bankruptcy. Entry (1, 0) means that 6% of the accounts that are one month delinquent during this collection period will become current again (i.e., will *cure*) during the next period. By definition, there is no way to know in advance which of the obligors in the pool will undergo any given transition.

Issuer Credit Policy

As discussed in chapter 14 under the rubric of conservation laws, the transition matrices discussed here relate to *account* transitions rather than *dollar*

Table 20.3
Actuarial versus Recency Accounting Methods Contrasted

	Cash In ($)	
Delinquency Transition	Actuarial	Recency
0-0	200	200
0-1	0	0
1-0	400	200
2-0	600	200

transitions. As a result, a translation from account transitions to dollar transitions and balances is required. This becomes crucially important when transaction triggers and other features based on pool delinquency balances are to be incorporated into the analysis. For any account transition, the dollar equivalent may be derived from the issuer's credit policy. Thus, the last set of required data consists of the rules making up the issuer's credit policy manual, or failing that, an interview with its chief credit officer.

Many issuers have comparable credit policy features, but none should be taken for granted. Exceptions (payment holidays, overrides, etc.), no matter how seemingly insignificant, require special attention, as they point to areas of issuer discretion—a key reason that loss performance ultimately deviates from expectation. When the allowable range of exceptions is included in the analysis, credit enhancement levels can be set to cover both losses tolerated under the credit policy and losses associated with permissible deviations from credit policy.

In general, U.S. auto-loan issuers use either the *actuarial* or the *recency* delinquency accounting method, with most issuers falling into the first category. These two methods are contrasted in Table 20.3, assuming a hypothetical obligor making contractual $200 monthly payments on an auto loan. The difference between the two methods becomes apparent where it counts: in delinquent accounts. Using issuer-provided portfolio delinquency figures, credit analysts basing cash flow predictions on the actuarial method for an issuer that, in fact, uses the recency method would severely overestimate cash flows to the trust.

Formalism

Given the characteristic multimodal shapes of pool credit and underwriting statistical distributions, a cash flow analysis under the single-loan framework is a poor approximation of reality. Under the latter model, all pool quantities are averaged to construct a fictitious single loan displaying the pool's WAC, WAM, and other key financial variables. This process severely misrepresents the credit dynamics of loan pools at someone's expense, often the issuer's.

Instead, a proper analysis of automobile-backed structured securities formalizes the aggregate credit dynamics of the individual obligors in the pool. This means that each and every obligor must be followed throughout the economic life of the loan using a transition matrix like the one in Table 20.2, and that cash flows arising from this dynamic process must be aggregated and then fed to the liabilities structure of the transaction. Although this procedure is tedious, it is straightforward. What follows is a step-by-step demonstration.

Nonstationarity

In chapter 14, we focused on stationary Markov chains for the sake of simplicity, and obtained fairly intuitive results that allowed us to get at the underlying physics. We assumed that all the obligors in the pool were identical up to their delinquency status, and that no further information could be ascertained about them. On that basis, iterating the chain through time led to a good approximation of account transition dynamics. But in the case of automobile-backed securities, we can do better. This is because the data show that the credit dynamics of auto-loan pools are subject to a characteristic temporal variation of obligor delinquency and, eventually, default probabilities. In layman's terms, this means that the variation $F(t)$ of normalized, cumulative, gross pool defaults as a function of time, known as a *static pool loss curve*, can be fairly accurately represented by a graph like that shown in Figure 20.1. The curve is always normalized to 100% by dividing each loss data point by the last known point, producing a curve asymptotic to unity. Actual losses are computed by multiplying functional values by the total cumulative gross losses on the pool. That number is, of course, unknown a priori.

As we saw in chapter 3, this method associates an issuer's static pools with one such characteristic curve, as opposed to what can be inferred about a managed portfolio, wherein both the number and the identity of account holders change monthly. The difference between the method of chapter 3 and the present method is that the former rating-agency method relies on averaging historical loss curves, whereas the method of the next section synthesizes the loss curve based on the delinquency behavior evidenced by the issuer's managed portfolio.

Depending on the credit characteristics of the obligors in the pool, the curve may exhibit different contours; for instance, the loss curve for sub-prime pools tends to rise faster than for prime pools. By and large, however, static pool loss curves exhibit functional form invariance (similar shapes) across issuers and obligor types. In turn, this invariance enables the use of a generic trial function with adjustable parameters to model credit losses on specific pools. Further more, the use of individual loan characteristics allows us to make fine distinctions between otherwise identical pools.

Automobile-loan pools are not amenable to analysis via a stationary Markov process, because the latter can reproduce only a constant marginal loss pattern, rather than the characteristic **S** shape of an actual loss curve. To model the characteristic loss process, a sequence of nonstationary or time-dependent

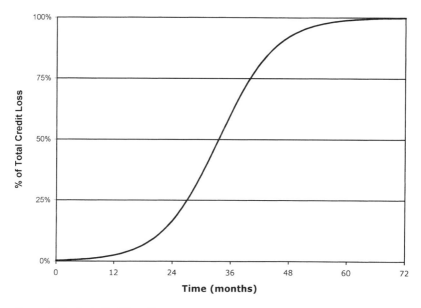

Figure 20.1. Static Pool Loss Curve

Markov transition matrices needs to be synthesized. Taken together, these matrices describe the credit dynamics of static pools. However, the monthly matrices must be derived in a manner that is consistent with the functional form implied by the static pool loss curve of the issuer. In this way, both the macro- and the microeconomic levels are easily included in the analysis.

We now discuss a suitable analytical model for the loss curve and show how to derive and then use nonstationary Markov transition matrices to analyze auto-loan-backed structured securities.

Loss Curve Modeling

For all practical purposes, the following functional form can be used to construct reasonable loss curves for auto-loan static pools:

$$F(t) = M\frac{m}{1 + be^{-a(t-t_0)}} \tag{20.1}$$

In equation (5.1) we have defined the following parameters:

M = Macroeconomic influence factor

m = Microeconomic influence factor

b = Offset factor

a = Spreading factor

t_0 = Measure of maximum marginal loss period

Physically speaking, these parameters are to be understood as follows.

- *Macroeconomic influence factor.* The value of M represents the influence of macroeconomic forces acting on all obligors uniformly. We will show in a future section how to derive this value. Parameter M is the most important because, via its probability distribution, it will determine the proportion of Monte Carlo scenarios likely to cause reductions of yield on the ABS securities. It should always be remembered that the vast majority of such scenarios do not cause any yield reduction at all due to the availability of sufficient credit enhancement. Security-level losses thus arise strictly from tail events of the M distribution.
- *Microeconomic influence factor.* Parameter m is a calibration factor meant to ensure that the expected credit loss computed by our algorithm is equal to the value calculated, inferred, or assumed from issuer data. Details of the method are discussed later.
- *Offset factor.* Parameter b is an adjustment factor used to match equation (20.1) as closely as possible to the issuer's own loss curve as submitted to the analyst. The smaller the b, the sooner the curve steepens. As mentioned earlier, sub-prime loan default curves will rise earlier than prime curves. In practice, b is obtained via curve fitting. Analysts should also keep in mind that b also plays a role in the time at which the maximum marginal loss occurs. If b is unity, the maximum marginal loss occurs at t_0 (see below).
- *Spreading factor.* The parameter a is another empirically derived quantity related to the "breadth" of the curve (i.e., the time span over which it is significantly different from zero). It can be regarded as the "standard deviation" of the loss curve. Large values of a cause sharp peaks whereas smaller values lead to smoother curves.
- *Measure of maximum marginal loss period.* The time period in which maximum marginal losses occur (indicating the deceleration of losses) is an important measure in credit analysis. The parameter t_0 largely dictates the position of maximum marginal loss, and is adjusted based on empirical evidence.

Next, we show how to derive loss curve parameters from issuer data, including the micro- and macroeconomic influence factors. The last two are the lifeblood of the entire analysis and determine whether deals live or die. They are intended to transform what is now essentially circular reasoning into a causally motivated methodology, leading to a common-sense solution that can be appraised by all concerned.

Loss Curve Parameters (a, b, t$_0$)

These three parameters are normally derived from an empirical loss curve shape by curve fitting using the Newton-Raphson or any other optimization technique. Alternatively, a, b, and t_0 can be derived by trial and error. Analysts will find that the time and effort in doing so will generally be minimal since, given equation 20.1, fairly good starting guesses can be made. Remember that only the shape of the loss curve matters at this time; hence, M and m can each be set equal to unity throughout the trial-and-error effort. In the absence of static pool data, loss curves can be obtained from reasonable proxies.

Microstructure Analysis (m)

The microeconomic influence factor is to be determined by calibration to the expected loss $E(L)$ for the pool, a known quantity in most cases because the expected loss is usually an objective estimate stemming from issuer data. In cases where insufficient evidence is on hand to obtain a statistically valid estimate (e.g., small or first-time issuers), reasonable proxies are always available. Moreover, underwriting criteria and credit scores are excellent sources of qualitative data to supplement relatively thin issuer-loss databases. Expected loss estimates should be used without modification, and should never be exaggerated or increased in the name of conservatism. The place to be conservative, if the term can be used at all, is in the macrostructure analysis, treated in the next subsection.

Assume now that $E(L)$ has somehow been determined, and set $M = 1$ for now, all other parameters having been estimated as indicated previously. By Monte Carlo simulation, set the microeconomic influence factor m such that

$$\frac{1}{N}\sum_{i=1}^{N}L_i = E(L). \tag{20.2}$$

Equation (20.2) assumes that N Monte Carlo scenarios have been performed, and that L_i is the cumulative-pool gross credit loss in scenario i.

As we shall see shortly, increasing or decreasing the value of m leads to correspondingly higher or lower cumulative loss values by raising or lowering the probability of an account's becoming delinquent. In practice, a feedback loop is usually introduced inside the cash flow model to let the process converge to the calibrated value of m. As a subsidiary benefit, the realistic microstructure probability distribution of cumulative aggregate credit losses naturally emerges from this calibration process.

However, besides peaking around $E(L)$, this probability distribution normally exhibits a relatively small standard deviation—too small, in fact, to cause credit losses on the related ABS securities. To understand why this is so, remember that the main attraction of ABS is their stability relative to small disturbances. At the micro-level, credit losses vary based only on the "luck of the draw," whereby different individual obligors will be defaulting while still adhering to the macro-level expected loss process. Absent a uniform external causal agency, the resulting microvariance will be unable to cause losses on the security since credit enhancement levels will far exceed even the most pessimistic microstructure scenario. Mathematically, this last statement can be expressed formally by the central limit theorem (CLT). This theorem, which underlies much of statistics, can be stated as in the following section for the case at hand.

The Central Limit Theorem

Take a sample of n independent random variables X_i, each with mean μ and variance σ^2. The CLT states that Z_n, defined by equation (20.3), is a standard normal variable in the limit $n \to \infty$:

$$Z_n = (E(X) - \mu)\frac{\sqrt{n}}{\sigma} \qquad (20.3)$$

A slightly modified version of the theorem can be derived if the X_i variables are not identically distributed.

What does this mean in real-world terms? It means that, viewed as a random variable, the average of n such random variables (i.e., the sampling distribution) will be normal if the samples are large enough. Thus, according to equation (20.3), this normal sampling distribution will have a mean of μ and a standard deviation of $\sigma/\sqrt{n}$.

In a nutshell, the CLT tells us that the credit loss rate variance we can expect from pools with large values of n is relatively small, assuming each pool is chosen from the same underlying population—too small in fact to cause security-level losses. In other words, at the microeconomic level, credit risk has been diversified away and security losses can rarely (if ever) be attributed to microeconomic fluctuations. As a result, security-level losses must stem mainly from macro-level effects.

To illustrate this point, the CLT will now be used to compute credit enhancement levels in the absence of macroeconomic forces (i.e., those represented in our analysis by the parameter M).

Recall that, in simple terms, the equation of obligor-level credit loss is given by.

$$\text{Credit Loss} \equiv L = \text{LEE} \cdot X \cdot \text{LGD}. \qquad (20.4)$$

In equation (20.4), LEE is the loan equivalent exposure, in this case the initial principal balance of the auto loan; X is a Boolean variable equal to 1 if the loan has defaulted and zero otherwise; and LGD is the loss given default as a percentage of LEE. The loss given default is commonly defined as 100% less the recovery percentage.

Assume the following loss data are available:

$$E(X) \equiv \overline{X} = 0.1 \qquad (20.5)$$

$$E(\text{LGD}) \equiv \overline{\text{LGD}} = 0.5 \qquad (20.6)$$

$$\rho = 0.7 \qquad (20.7)$$

$$\sigma_X = 0.3 \qquad (20.8)$$

$$\sigma_{\text{LGD}} = 0.20 \qquad (20.9)$$

Here, ρ is the correlation coefficient between losses given default and default events. It is taken as positive since we expect recoveries to be less than originally expected on vehicles associated with defaulted loans. This assumption is based on the theory that distressed obligors run out of maintenance funds and so fail to care properly for their vehicles, thereby causing higher than originally expected losses.

Furthermore, assume the following data are obtained from issuer disclosures, rating-agency bond default studies, and interest rate markets:

Weighted average loan coupon:	14%
Average life of the pool:	2.0 years
Two-year treasury yield:	4.5%
Aaa ABS credit spread:	50 bps
Servicing fees:	1.5%
Two-year Aaa cumulative default rates:	0.1%

Next, it can be shown by Taylor-series formalism[1] that, to a first-order approximation and as a fraction of LEE, the expected value and the standard deviation of obligor credit losses under constant LEE are given by the following formulas:

$$E(L) \equiv \mu = \overline{X}\,\overline{\mathrm{LGD}} \tag{20.10}$$

$$\sigma_I = \sqrt{\overline{\mathrm{LGD}}^2\sigma_X^2 + \overline{X}^2\sigma_{\mathrm{LGD}}^2 + 2\overline{X}\,\overline{\mathrm{LGD}}\rho\sigma_X\sigma_{\mathrm{LGD}}} \tag{20.11}$$

The problem is now to determine the micro-level credit loss distribution for a portfolio of 500 independent and identical exposures, each with the previously mentioned risk profile. In most cases, this assumption is not too far off, as issuers tend to underwrite according to a profile. In practice, the loan APR distribution is a good proxy for the default probability distribution. We therefore assume that the latter is fairly tight around its mean value. If this is granted for illustration purposes, the CLT allows us to conclude that our portfolio's loss distribution is approximately normal with the following mean μ_p and standard deviation σ_p:

$$\mu_p = \mu \tag{20.12}$$

$$\sigma_p = \frac{\sigma_I}{\sqrt{500}} \tag{20.13}$$

Assume now that we wish to assign Aaa ratings to securities backed by this portfolio; what is the required Aaa credit enhancement? To answer this question, define α as the Aaa-equivalent cumulative default rate for an average life of two years, consistent with the loans in the pools, and make the following three simplifying assumptions:

1. The time value of money is ignored.
2. Defaults all take place at the end of the transaction.
3. Credit ratings are based on a liquidation scenario.

According to the CLT, the required credit enhancement (CE) is then given by the formula

$$CE = F^{-1}(1 - \alpha; \mu_p, \sigma_p). \qquad (20.14)$$

In equation (20.14), F is the normal cumulative distribution function with parameters μ_p and σ_p. Substitution of equations (20.4) through (20.11) into equations (20.12) and (20.13) yields the following:

$$\mu_p = 5.00\% \qquad (20.15)$$

$$\sigma_p = 0.736\% \qquad (20.16)$$

Substitution of equations (20.15) and (20.16) into equation (20.14) gives

$$CE = 7.27\%. \qquad (20.17)$$

This situation is shown graphically in Figure 20.2. Using the pool's aggregate data, shown above, available enhancement in the form of excess spread alone is given by the following:

Available XS $= $ (WAC $-$ Security Coupon $-$ Servicing) $\cdot$ Average Life^2

Available XS $= $ (14% $-$ 4.5% $-$ 0.50% $-$ 1.50%) $\cdot$ 2 $= $ 15%

However, this amount of excess spread is not necessarily available when required. Spread often escapes from real transactions when it is not needed to cover losses, and returns to the issuer through a residual distribution to the equity certificateholder. Assume, for the moment, that 50% of the gross spread is available when losses occur. The effective XS is now 7.5%, and we can therefore issue 100% $-$ (7.27% $-$ 7.5%) $=$ 100.23% of the pool's face value in the form of Aaa-rated securities. In fact, if we granted this issuer more XS through a spread account or better structuring, overissuance of Aaa-rated securities is conceivably justified. Even under somewhat more conservative assumptions, the resulting Aaa issuance would still hover around the 95% mark.

The insanity of these results will have dawned on anyone remotely acquainted with structured finance, and yet everything we have done has been clean, consistent, and above board. What, then, is wrong with the analysis?

The answer is that credit enhancement does not exist to protect investors against the microdynamics of structured pools; diversification alone does that. Rather, enhancement is there to counter undiversifiable changes in default rates that systematically affect all obligors. This is precisely the risk that equity investors are supposed to be rewarded for taking, since it is assumed that they

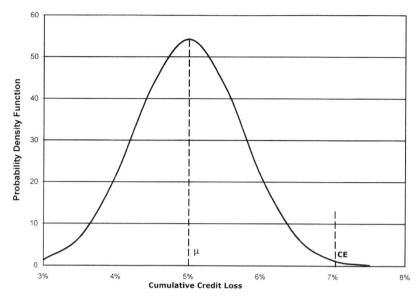

Figure 20.2. Microstructure Loss Distribution for Autos

always have the option of diversifying away the unsystematic risk. In fixed income markets, investors are not even interested in bearing systematic risk. Hence, they require more protection than equity investors and must therefore remain content with much smaller risk premia. Therefore, in order to assess the macrodynamic risks of these pools, we need to estimate separately how macroeconomic forces will influence their behavior.

Macrostructure Analysis (M)

Before describing a feasible algorithm to produce a suitable probability distribution for the macro-influence factor *M*, we wish to point out the subjective factor in debates over macroeconomic risk.

To begin with, *forecasts* are statistical estimates based on uncertain empirical evidence. Hence, the goal of credit analysis is not to eradicate uncertainty but reduce it to an extent compatible with decision making. Any debate over the future status of the macroeconomy should preferably take place within a transparent, common-sense framework that allows credit enhancement calculations to remain indirect, rather than leading to the summary dictation of credit enhancement levels. By *indirect* we mean establishing model parameters that, in turn, determine the amount of credit enhancement needed for protection against macroeconomic risk. In this way, any inconsistent or off-base assumptions in the analysis can be readily identified.

The crux of macroeconomic modeling is the selection of macroeconomic parameter(s) that best reflect(s) the dynamics of the particular asset class. For example, in the case of sub-prime auto loans, unemployment appears to be a suitable target variable, although the choice of a specific index is normally left to the analyst. In many cases an industry consensus already exists, so that the abuse of discretion in index selection is limited. As a case in point, the following example is taken from the United Kingdom with respect to a potential U.K.-based automobile-backed transaction.

The U.K. government publishes monthly time series data on two macroeconomic indicators, the average earnings index (AEI) and the retail price index (RPI). Monthly data are supplied from March 1964 through the present with a few months' lag. Being freely available, plentiful, and authoritative, such time series data are good candidates for index construction. Statisticians from the government's Statistical Research Department have this to say on their website about the macroeconomic significance of these indicators. Boldface text indicates that U.K. statisticians believe that the ratio of AEI to RPI is a measure of purchasing power:

> Income from employment is the most important component of household income. The average earnings index (AEI), a monthly measure of the pay of a representative sample of all employees across all sectors of the economy, is one of the indicators used to judge the state of the UK economy. If the index rises rapidly, this may indicate that the labor market is under-supplied with employees in the right numbers and with the right skills to meet the level of demand within the economy. In addition, a rapid rise may indicate that wage settlements are higher than the rate of economic growth, and this can sustain and thus create inflationary pressures. A fall in the index may be a reflection of reduced demand within the economy and may presage a fall in GDP and an increase in unemployment. **The relationship between the AEI and the retail prices index (RPI) is also of importance. If the AEI rises faster than the RPI, this means that employees' pay is increasing faster than the prices they have to pay for goods and services and that therefore, all things being equal, their purchasing power will rise and they will feel "better off."**[3]

Suppose now that our credit committee has decided that purchasing power (PP = AEI/RPI) is the best proxy for the macrobehavior of auto pools, the rationale being that when PP is increasing, unemployment is generally decreasing and the average worker's economic situation is rising, and hence loan defaults are likely to decrease. A graph of the statistical distribution of U.K. purchasing power for the period March 1964 through September 2000 is shown in Figure 20.3, along with a normal distribution fit to the data. The accuracy of the normal fit is itself remarkable, but the fact that the average of all data points is exactly 1.00 is even more impressive. However, even without this property it will always be possible to normalize the data to create a time series with an average index of unity. In what follows, we assume that this has been done.

In general, macroeconomic data x will be bounded from above and below. Assume the minimum value is a, the maximum value b, and map the full x interval $[a, b]$ to $[0, 1]$ by a linear transformation of the type

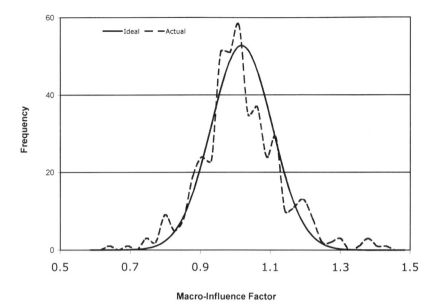

Figure 20.3. Macroeconomic Modeling (autos)

$$x' = cx + d. \tag{20.18}$$

Recalling our discussion of the Beta distribution in chapter 12, fit a Beta distribution to the mapped data. This is done by computing the mean and variance of the mapped time series data, defined as μ and σ^2, respectively, and setting

$$\mu = \frac{\alpha}{\alpha + \beta} \tag{20.19}$$

$$\sigma^2 = \frac{\alpha\beta}{(\alpha + \beta)^2(\alpha + \beta + 1)}. \tag{20.20}$$

Inversion of these two equations gives

$$\alpha = \frac{\mu^2(1 - \mu)}{\sigma^2} - \mu \tag{20.21}$$

$$\beta = \alpha\left(\frac{1}{\mu} - 1\right). \tag{20.22}$$

At this juncture, the interpretive part of the analysis begins. Starting from the complete, unconditional distribution shown in Figure 20.3, the goal is to synthesize a conditional distribution using the general consensus over current economic conditions reached by a committee of credit professionals knowledgeable about the given asset class. To do this, proceed as follows.

1. First, decide whether the relevant country or region is currently in a recession, an expansion, or a normal macroeconomic environment; and second, determine the starting date of the recession or expansion. These decisions are usually straightforward.

2. From the time series underlying the target macroeconomic index distribution, select periods equal to the maturity of the transaction under review, each one beginning at the same relative position with respect to recognized U.K. (in this case) recessions over the last thirty-eight years, since March 1964. This can always be done, since economists have carefully tabulated economic cycles.

3. Fit the resulting data series to a new Beta distribution as shown previously and use the IDFM method presented in chapter 12 to select values of M for each Monte Carlo scenario according to the equation $M = I_p F^{-1}(r; \alpha, \beta)$, in which F is the cumulative Beta distribution function with parameters α and β computed as shown before, r is a random number selected using the van der Corput sequence technique previously described, and I_p is the impact parameter (discussed shortly).

We recommend the use of the van der Corput method in this case because, since a Monte Carlo simulation requires a only a few thousand values of M, an exactly uniform distribution of random numbers must be guaranteed to properly reflect the assumed macrodynamics. As shown in Appendix A, a system-generated random number sequence is unlikely to have the required uniformity. For example, if the committee decides that the economic environment is recession- or expansion-like rather than neutral, this three-step process will give rise to a skewed distribution, either left or right, whereby proportionally fewer data points on one side of the mean than the other will be selected. In turn, the corresponding values of M will cause higher or lower than average credit losses to occur through the mechanism implemented as equation (20.1). This will represent systematic risk.

The range of resulting distributional outcomes can be visualized in Figure 20.4. The distribution labeled "High Risk" refers to conditionally recessionary environments while that labeled "Low Risk" refers to conditionally expansionary environments. It can be readily seen that in recessionary environments, proportionally more high-credit-loss scenarios will be selected than under normal conditions, and vice versa for conditionally expansionary scenarios. Thus, the credit committee should have no direct control over the outcome but should remain able to opine on the current economic environment and thereby indirectly influence it. In this way, no single analyst would have been able to dictate credit enhancement levels by fiat.

The impact parameter I_p is intended to reflect the relative economic position of the obligor base in the pool and relate the ordinal ranking of the chosen M values to their cardinal impact. This is because different obligor bases will respond differently to the same distribution of macroeconomic environ-

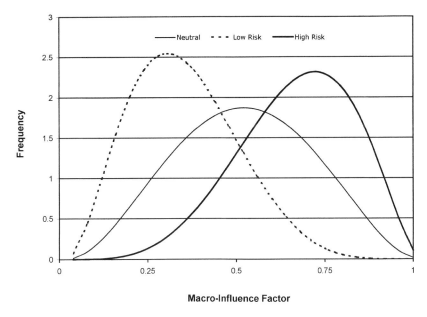

Figure 20.4. Macroeconomic Modeling of Auto ABS

ments. For instance, a sub-prime obligor pool will be more susceptible to deteriorating macroeconomic conditions than a prime base and will recover more rapidly from an improving picture. The impact parameter is thus an objective assessment of the obligor base's vulnerability to changing macroenvironments. It can be determined one of two ways:

1. *Calibration to current market practice.* Simply use the value that leaves credit enhancement levels intact from currently acceptable values. In other words, the I_p matching the average value of senior credit enhancement for this market segment is selected and used thereafter. This process is numerically intensive but trivially implemented.
2. *Industrial distribution calibration.* This second method proceeds by calibrating I_p such that the maximum cumulative loss computed by Monte Carlo simulation is equal to the value observed in the industry over all issuers in the same space (i.e., sub-prime or prime).

In practice, the first method is to be preferred, since the investor marketplace usually will not accept a sharp increase or decrease in credit enhancement values for any issuer or market sector. However, the optimal approach is probably to use method 1 while slowly reducing I_p over time using method 2, as market data accumulate. This is more or less what happened in the mortgage-backed markets where credit enhancement levels eventually stabilized at more efficient (i.e., lower) levels as empirical data on a variety of transactions accumulated over time.

It should be noted that M is an asset class parameter, I_p is a market segment parameter, and m an issuer parameter. Maintaining these distinctions becomes important in practical implementations.

Before leaving this topic, we would like to reiterate the critical importance of carrying out these preliminary steps. The manner in which the credit analysis of auto-loan-backed securities is currently implemented will inevitably lead to massive capital inefficiency, for which no amount of clever structuring can compensate, unless the micro- and macrodynamics of credit losses have been objectively determined.

The Derivation of Time-Dependent Markov Transition Matrices

Assume now that we are to model an auto-ABS transaction with respect to a pool wherein the maximum maturity of the loans in the pool is T months. Thus, each Monte Carlo scenario will require the creation of a sequence of slightly more than T Markov transition matrices (see why, below) $\mathbf{P}(t)$, $t = 1$, $2, 3, \ldots T$, one for each time step in the pool's amortization period. Once $F(t)$ has been synthesized as shown previously, we take its first derivative, yielding the marginal default curve $f(t)$:

$$f(t) \equiv \frac{\partial F(t)}{\partial t} = Mm \frac{abe^{-a(t-t_0)}}{[1 + be^{-a(t-t_0)}]^2} \tag{20.23}$$

The first derivative of $F(t)$ represents the implied periodic (quarterly or monthly) default rate for the accounts in the pool. For instance, the marginal default curve introduced in Figure 5.1 is shown in Figure 20.5.

The maximum marginal default period is given by the solution t_{max} of $\partial^2 F(t)/\partial t^2 = 0$.

After some algebra, we have

$$2abe^{-2a(t-t_0)} - a[1 + be^{-a(t-t_0)}]e^{-a(t-t_0)} = 0,$$

from which we derive

$$t_{max} = \frac{\ln b}{a} + t_0. \tag{20.24}$$

As mentioned before, if the offset parameter b equals unity, maximum marginal defaults occur at t_0.

As partial motivation for the next steps, consider the physics of *obligor default*. By definition, all obligors are either current at closing or at most thirty days delinquent, by virtue of the transaction's eligibility covenants. For argument's sake, assume all obligors are current at closing. The vast majority of them will remain current until the loan's stated maturity, at which point their

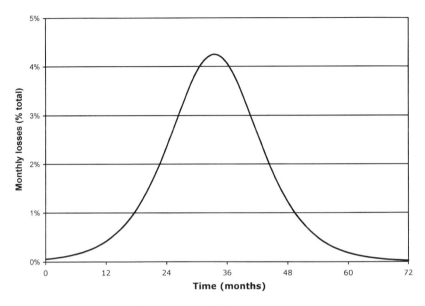

Figure 20.5. Marginal Credit Loss Curve $[f(t)]$

outstanding principal balance will fall to zero. However, a sizable fraction will undergo "life events." The difference between the various types of obligors (e.g., prime and sub-prime) lies in their ability to withstand such fundamentally unpredictable events.

The unfolding of such events over the life of a static pool determines the shape of the loss curve. Most life events, such as an unexpected medical bill or a job change, have only a minor impact on obligor payment performance but may nevertheless create interim shortfalls in obligor monthly cash flows. Prolonged difficulties may become difficult to make up in real time from savings. These occurrences will therefore show up as long-term delinquencies of all orders, including default. For instance, a current account that has become one month delinquent may remain so until maturity and pay off in $N + 1$ months, where N was its original maturity, and incur delinquency fees along the way. These fees provide unexpected windfalls to the trust that should somehow be estimated. Other life events from which the obligor may be unable to recover, such as unemployment or the death of an earning spouse, will be major and may precipitate ultimate default.

To simulate the delinquency process, focus on the top leftmost element p_{11}^0 of a basic N-state Markov transition matrix. Recall that this quantity is the probability that an account now current will remain so during the next time step or collection period. By modulating this entry according to equation (20.23), conditions analogous to the physical delinquency process just described can be approximated. We now show how to do this.

First, define the modulation function $\Delta p_{11}(t)$ as follows:

$$\Delta p_{11}(t) = f(t), \; t = 1, 2, 3, \ldots, T \quad (20.25)$$

Starting from the basic Markov transition matrix $\mathbf{P}^0$, reduce entry p_{11}^0 by the amount $\Delta p_{11}(t)$ and increase the entry immediately to its right by the same amount, thus maintaining the row-sum condition intact. In other words, assuming p_{11}^0 and p_{12}^0 are entries from the issuer's basic Markov transition matrix,

$$p_{11}(t) = p_{11}^0 - \Delta p_{11}(t) \quad (20.26)$$

$$p_{12}(t) = p_{12}^0 + \Delta p_{11}(t). \quad (20.27)$$

All other entries of $\mathbf{P}^0$ remain unchanged for the simulation since they capture life-event dynamics that affect already delinquent accounts. Properly executed, this modulation scheme will give rise to a loss curve in agreement with equation (20.1) because marginal defaults will now be in agreement with its first derivative, equation (20.23).

Implementation is somewhat tricky. First, recall that the time scale equal to the issuer's default point (usually three or four months) offsets the recognition of actual losses. Thus, in order to cause peak marginal losses to occur at step 24, the value of t_{max} would have to be set to approximately 20 in a case where the issuer recognized defaults at 120 days past due.

In practice, we have found that the formula $t_{max} = t_{max}^* - \sum_{i=2}^{n-2}(1/p_{ii})$ works fairly well, where p_{ii} are diagonal entries of the base transition matrix. Here, t_{max}^* is the empirically observed maximum marginal loss point. The summation terminates at $n - 2$ because, as the last two status codes are default and prepayment, respectively, they do not contribute to the delinquency process.

The Use of Nonstationary Markov Transition Matrices

Assume that we now have at our disposal a set of T transition matrices $\mathbf{P}(t)$ of order N, where N is the number of discrete delinquency states recognized by the issuer's credit policy manual.

It is important to point out why T will normally exceed the highest maturity of any loan in the pool. Recall that, owing to delinquencies and the recovery process, cash flows from the last remaining loan in the pool or its liquidation proceeds can be collected after its original maturity. If the loan happens to be one with a fairly high initial maturity, it is quite likely (and realistic) that trust cash flows will be coming in four to five months after the last loan theoretically should have paid off. Thus, in each Monte Carlo scenario the last cash flow will be collected during a different collection period and will require the generation of a sufficient number of transition matrices. For this reason, T will always exceed the highest loan maturity in the pool by a number approximately equal to the rank of the matrix $\mathbf{P}^0$.

At each monthly time step t_k, $k = 1, 2, \ldots, T$, the delinquency status of account A_i at time t_k, defined as $D_i(t_k)$, is determined from its delinquency status at time t_{k-1} using the following stepwise procedure.

1. For each A_i, generate $x_i \in [0, 1]$ using a random number generator. In this case, system-supplied generators with antithetic modifications are more than satisfactory.

To see why the use of the van der Corput method may be overkill, consider the following facts. One random number is needed for each account at every time step of every scenario. Assuming around 2,000 accounts in a target pool with a loanwise maximum maturity of approximately 72, and that the Monte Carlo simulation involves perhaps 5,000 scenarios, roughly 720 million random numbers will be generated for any serious analytical effort. Given this order of magnitude, it is fairly benign to assume that the use of a system-supplied random number generator with antithetic correction is acceptable.

2. Assume that, at time t_{k-1}, account A_i is in delinquency status $j \in [1, n]$ and that the jth row of matrix $\mathbf{P}(t_k)$ is defined as $p_j^k = [p_1^k \, p_2^k \, p_3^k \ldots p_n^k]$ with the usual row-sum condition $\sum_j p_j^k = 1$.

Now, define the row-wise cumulative distribution function $C_j^k = \sum_{l=1}^{j} p_l^k$, $j = 1, 2, \ldots, N$ with the boundary condition $C_0^k = 0$ and let the new account status j be defined by the condition $D_i(t_k) \equiv j | C_{j-1}^k \leq x_i < C_j^k$. In other words, if x_i lies between C_0^k and C_1^k, then account A_i is deemed to move to delinquency state 1 or to stay there if it was in state 1 at time step t_{k-1}. In a similar fashion, when x_i is chosen between C_1^k and C_2^k, the account is deemed to move or stay in delinquency state 2, and so on. In most circumstances, state 1 will be equivalent to a current account.

This method is applied to all the accounts in the pool. For accounts that have already defaulted or prepaid, the foregoing process is moot since the corresponding row simply has unity on the main diagonal and zeros elsewhere. As a result, they will remain either prepaid or defaulted, as the case may be.

3. To determine the cash flow to the trust corresponding to any transition, use a simple look-up function based on the issuer's credit policy manual.

The following are three examples of how obligor cash flows [Pmt(ij)] would be computed from specific credit policies under the contractual delinquency method for the transition of account A_i from state i to state j at time step t_k, assuming a total monthly payment due c_i and a periodic interest rate r_i:

- The delinquency fee is equal to past due interest.

$$\text{Pmt}(ij) = \sum_{n=0}^{i-j} c_i (1 + r_i)^{i-n}$$

- The delinquency fee is equal to d dollars per month of delinquency.

$$\text{Pmt}(ij) = \sum_{n=0}^{0,i-j}(c_l + (i-1)H(i-j)d)$$

Here, we have defined the Heaviside step function $H(x)$ as usual:

$$H(x) = \begin{cases} 0, & x \le 0 \\ 1, & x > 0 \end{cases}$$

- There is no delinquency fee.

$$\text{Pmt}(ij) = \sum_{n=0}^{\max(0,i-j)} c_l$$

Other formulas can easily be derived once issuer credit policy is available. In general, the first two bulleted items are most common among U.S. issuers.

 Provided the *initial* delinquency status of each account is known a priori, the previous cash flow generation process is easily implemented for each time step until the loan amortises completely, prepays, or defaults, according to the relevant transition matrix $\mathbf{P}(t)$. The initial delinquency distribution is usually supplied in transaction documents. The resulting aggregate cash flows are then available to determine security ratings.

Credit Loss Distributions

The upshot of our modeling effort is that after M (the macroeconomic influence factor) has been determined according to the committee process outlined here, the pool's credit loss distribution becomes entirely deterministic and objective via equation (20.1) when the latter is inserted into our Markov chain formalism. This comes about specifically as shown previously (i.e., by the incorporation of the loss curve and the delinquency structure of the pool inside the cash flow generation process). Once a particular liability structure is overlaid onto the cash flow process, credit ratings can be derived. But unlike current approaches, under the Markov formalism credit ratings are computed separately and do not presuppose detailed prior knowledge of the credit loss distribution. In other words, under this framework, the credit loss distribution is an output, not an input. However, it is an important concept in auto-ABS analysis and deserves a special mention.

 We find that once the micro- and macrostructural levels of analysis are addressed and analyzed in the manner indicated within a Monte Carlo simulation framework, the result is a usually non-normal, fat-tailed cumulative credit loss distribution similar to Figure 20.6, shown for a representative non-prime issuer. It displays the expected positive skewness stemming from the assumed macroeconomic distribution, causing the probability mass to extend far beyond the microstructural mean. This distribution, which arises naturally and objectively from our modeling efforts, can be considered the theoretical loss distribution for this issuer.

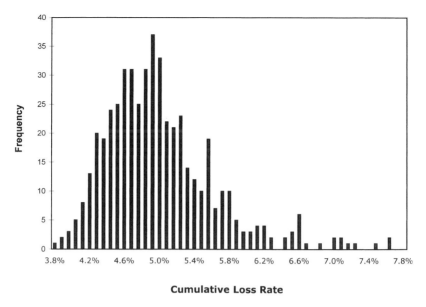

Figure 20.6. Combined Loss Distribution (autos)

It should be mentioned that, in this discussion, the micro- and macro-dynamic aspects of asset pools have been treated within a framework that allows sufficient analyst discretion under special circumstances, but without directly leaving credit enhancement levels to the whims of the moment.

When credit analysts are thus faced with the implications of their decisions with respect to default rates, they begin to realize the precise meaning and import of additional credit enhancement requests. A genuine and intuitive understanding of the logarithmic nature of the credit scale can begin only when credit analysts are no longer able to directly influence credit enhancement values. This is also the beginning of better capital allocation decisions in complex transactions.

Depreciation Modeling

This section is devoted to the important topic of *vehicle depreciation*. Responsible depreciation modeling is crucial for assessing the adequacy of credit enhancement levels in auto-loan-backed structured securities. Each time a loan defaults, the associated collateral is normally liquidated either at auction or privately, and the proceeds contributed to the trust as recoveries. Because recoveries are a significant source of credit enhancement to these structures, their proper modeling is a crucial responsibility of the credit analyst.

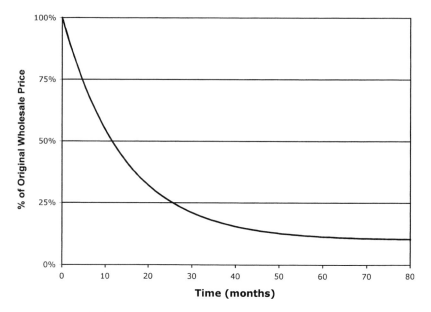

Figure 20.7. Vehicle Depreciation Curve

Automobile market data are plentiful in the United States. The National Automobile Dealers Association (NADA) and other organizations provide adequate secondary market prices on automobiles of all makes and models. In what follows, we show how to make use of such data.

Assume that, for some vehicle type found in the pool, a credit research analyst has assembled the depreciation data shown in Figure 20.7.

Note first that the depreciation curve reflects the known fact that the price of a new vehicle falls dramatically immediately after it is built and sold. Note also that these data are to be interpreted as wholesale and not retail prices since we assume that the trust will be able to recover only the wholesale value of any defaulted vehicle. Although this might be slightly inaccurate and conservative, as an assumption it is quite unlikely to make or break any transaction.

A generic depreciation curve such as the one in Figure 20.7 can be represented reasonably well by the functional form

$$y(t) = W_0[a + be^{-ct}]. \tag{20.28}$$

In equation (20.28), W_0 is the initial wholesale value of the vehicle and is known from issuer disclosure or from market data at closing. If the vehicle is new, W_0 can be taken as the dealer price. The goal is to find the values of parameters a, b, and c that best fit the given set of discrete points $y_i \equiv y(t_i)$, $i = 1$, $2, \ldots, n$. These parameters are not independent since, by definition, we need to enforce the constraint $y(0) = W_0$ as a boundary condition of our solution procedure (since the functional form is solely relevant, we may assume W_0 throughout in what follows without loss of generality). In turn, this implies

$$a + b = 1. \tag{20.29}$$

This problem belongs to a well-known general class of constrained optimization problems and can be solved using a modified version of the Lagrangian method we already applied to regression in chapter 14. First, define the modified Lagrangian $\Im$ as

$$\Im = \sum_{i=1}^{n} [y_i - a - be^{-ct_i}]^2 + \lambda(a + b - 1). \tag{20.30}$$

As before, the four-dimensional solution vector $[a, b, c, \lambda]$ is found by solving the following nonlinear system, also known as the first-order conditions:

$$\frac{\partial \Im}{\partial a} = 0 \tag{20.31}$$

$$\frac{\partial \Im}{\partial b} = 0 \tag{20.32}$$

$$\frac{\partial \Im}{\partial c} = 0 \tag{20.33}$$

$$\frac{\partial \Im}{\partial \lambda} = 0 \tag{20.34}$$

After some rearrangement, insertion of equation (20.30) into equations (20.31) through (20.34) yields the following:

$$f_1 = \sum_{i=1}^{n} [y_i - a - be^{-ct_i}] - \frac{\lambda}{2} = 0 \tag{20.35}$$

$$f_2 = \sum_{i=1}^{n} e^{-ct_i}[y_i - a - be^{-ct_i}] - \frac{\lambda}{2} = 0 \tag{20.36}$$

$$f_3 = \sum_{i=1}^{n} t_i e^{-ct_i}[y_i - a - be^{-ct_i}] - \frac{\lambda}{2} = 0 \tag{20.37}$$

$$f_4 = a + b - 1 = 0 \tag{20.38}$$

These are the four equations we must solve for the solution vector $[a, b, c, \lambda]$. We use the NR formalism from chapter 18 to solve for $f_i = 0$, $i = 1, 2, 3, 4$.

To do this, recall from chapter 18 that we will need the elements of the Jacobian matrix $\mathbf{J}$ defined by $J_{ij} = \partial f_i/\partial x_j$. For convenience, we have defined the simplified notation $x_1 = a$; $x_2 = b$; $x_3 = c$; $x_4 = \lambda$. For the sake of completeness, we present the full Jacobian as follows.

First row:

$$J_{11} = -n$$

$$J_{12} = -\sum_{i=1}^{n} e^{-ct_i}$$

$$J_{13} = b\sum_{i=1}^{n} t_i e^{-ct_i}$$

$$J_{14} = -\frac{1}{2}$$

Second row:

$$J_{21} = -\sum_{i=1}^{n} e^{-ct_i}$$

$$J_{22} = -\sum_{i=1}^{n} e^{-2ct_i}$$

$$J_{23} = \sum_{i=1}^{n} t_i e^{-ct_i}(2be^{-ct_i} - y_i + a)$$

$$J_{24} = -\frac{1}{2}$$

Third row:

$$J_{31} = -\sum_{i=1}^{n} t_i e^{-ct_i}$$

$$J_{32} = -\sum_{i=1}^{n} t_i e^{-2ct_i}$$

$$J_{33} = \sum_{i=1}^{n} t_i^2 e^{-ct_i}(2be^{-ct_i} - y_i + a)$$

$$J_{34} = 0$$

Fourth row:

$$J_{41} = 1$$
$$J_{42} = 1$$
$$J_{43} = 0$$
$$J_{44} = 0$$

The values of a, b, c, and λ found in this Jacobian matrix and of the f_i are to be updated each iteration. Additionally, the repeated inversion of the Jacobian can be accomplished using a system-supplied matrix inversion routine or

Table 20.4
Newton-Raphson Convergence History

n	a	b	c
0	0.1000	0.1000	0.1000
1	0.147	0.852	0.0909
2	0.096	0.903	0.0599
3	0.091	0.908	0.0661
4	0.095	0.0900	0.0696
5	0.099	0.900	0.0699
6	0.100	0.900	0.0700

using one of the techniques described more fully in *Numerical Recipes.*[4] In the worst case, four-dimensional matrix inversion can be implemented easily using Cramer's rule.

As we mentioned before when discussing the properties of the NR iteration, the value of the initial-guess vector is an important factor in determining its convergence properties. Since most vehicle depreciation curves tend to look fairly similar, we have found that the starting vector [$a = 1$, $b = 1$, $c = 0.1$, $\lambda = 1$] works well for most vehicle types. The NR iterative procedure is then efficient and yields a solution within a few iterations.

For instance, Table 20.4 gives a typical NR convergence history for the depreciation data in Figure 20.7. As expected, $a + b$ sums to unity. In general, we find that assumed functional forms of the type in equation (20.28) are adequate and always result in R-squared statistics in the neighborhood of 95%. On a desktop computer, 100 depreciation curves can be processed in less than a minute with the NR method. The resulting improvement in recovery estimates is well worth the effort.

Additional Measures of Credit Losses

This section addresses two additional measures of credit losses that can be used by credit analysts to guide expected loss estimates on pools of auto loans. As you may recall, since the expected loss is instrumental in setting the value of the micro-influence factor m, obtaining the most reliable value is of paramount importance. Sometimes, two seemingly indistinguishable pools can be seen a priori to be different in certain objective risk measures that lurk behind obvious financial parameters like WAC and WAM. These measures enable the analyst to dig deeper into aggregate pool data and ferret out credit risk signals that otherwise would remain undetected.

In general, the dynamics of loan amortization versus collateral depreciation can be represented by the two curves shown in Figure 20.8. A cursory look at the trade-offs between amortization and depreciation as depicted in this

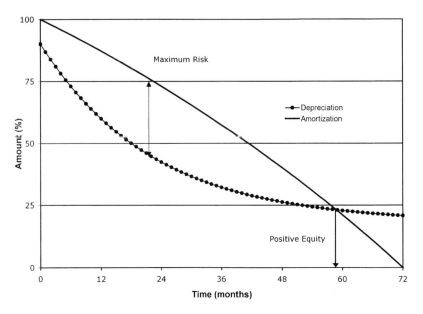

Figure 20.8. Differential Rates of Loan Amortization and Collateral Depreciation

figure suggests two additional measures of credit risk. When the measures are calculated for each obligor in the pool, their average value becomes an aggregate measure of credit risk:

1. The time at which the obligor is expected to begin showing positive equity in the vehicle (positive equity time). The rationale for this is that, ceteris paribus, obligors will be less likely to default in positive than negative equity.
2. The time at which the difference between amortization and depreciation is maximum—that is, when the recovery shortfall is likely to be greatest (maximum risk time).

Define $B_i(t)$ as obligor i's outstanding principal balance at time t, and $W_i(t)$ as the resale value of the associated collateral. Assuming obligor i has a loan periodic rate of r_i, a loan maturity of T_i months, and a monthly payment due P_i, we then have

$$B_i(t) = \frac{P}{r_i} \frac{[(1 + r_i)^{(T_i - t)} - 1]}{(1 + r_i)^{(T_i - t)}}. \qquad (20.39)$$

From equation (20.28), with a minor modification, we also have

$$W_i(t) = (1 - \alpha) W_i(0)[a + be^{-c(t + t_r)}]. \qquad (20.40)$$

In equation (20.40), α is an expense parameter that accounts for items such as repossession and auction costs. In general, we find that revenues to the trust from recoveries on auctioned collateral rarely reach the level that would theoretically result from reliance on published sources. Although market forces and other factors do play an important role in actual recoveries, NADA or Blue Book data are nevertheless solid benchmarks for them.

In this framework, we assume that recoveries on defaulted assets will always equal $W_i(t)$. It should be noted that recoveries should be lagged by an amount equal to the average delay with which the auction process normally takes place. This means that, if loan i defaults at time t_d, dollar recoveries should be computed as $W_i(t_d + t_a)$ where t_a is the liquidation or auctioning delay. In practice, t_a can be set to two or three months.

Parameter t_r is a correction factor to compensate for the fact that the vehicle may be used. This is how the model adjusts recoveries for the percentage of old and new vehicles in the pool. The vehicle's date of manufacture is thus an important variable in assessing recoveries from defaulted assets. If the data are not available, the asset can be conservatively assumed to have been sold in January of its model year. Note that $W_i(0)$ is the wholesale value at the time the ABS transaction is executed, not at the time the vehicle is built. The three parameters a, b, c are collateral specific and, in general, will be different for every loan in the pool. For any issuer, there is a finite number of model types in auto-loan pools, so that the number of depreciation curves to be modeled with respect to a securitized pool is usually small. In general, we find that 100 model makes and types is a reasonable order of magnitude.

Our two measures of credit risk can now be defined as in the following sections.

Weighted Average Positive Equity Time (PE$_W$)

Define $m_e(i)$ as the first time at which the loan to obligor i enters the positive equity zone. This is the region to the right of the arrow in Figure 20.8.

$$m_e(i) = \max[0, \tau | B_i(\tau) - W_i(\tau) = 0]$$

To compute each individual $m_e(i)$, we use the one-dimensional NR formalism with the following definitions:

$$f(t) = P_i \frac{[(1 + r_i)^{(T_i - t)} - 1]}{(1 + r_i)^{(T_i - t)}} - (1 - \alpha)W_i(0)[a + be^{-c(t + t_r)}]$$

$$\frac{\partial f(t)}{\partial t} = \frac{P_i}{r_i} \frac{\ln(1 + r_i)}{(1 + r_i)^{(T_i - t)}} - cW_i(0)b(1 - \alpha)e^{-c(t + t_r)} \qquad (20.41)$$

We then have, assuming a pool of n obligors,

$$PE_W = \frac{\sum_{i=1}^{n} B_i(0) m_e(i)}{\sum_{i=1}^{n} B_i(0)}. \qquad (20.42)$$

Weighted Average Maximum Risk Time (MR$_w$)

Define $m_r(i)$ as the time at which the difference between obligor i's outstanding principal balance and the corresponding depreciated vehicle value is maximal. This is the time value beneath the double-sided arrow in Figure 20.8.

$$m_r(i) = \max\left[0, \tau \mid \frac{\partial}{\partial t}(B_i(t) - W_i(t))\mid_\tau = 0\right] \tag{20.43}$$

Substituting equation (20.41) inside equation (20.43) and solving for t yields

$$m_r(i) = \frac{\ln \delta + T_i \ln(1 + r_i) - ct_r}{c + \ln(1 + r_i)}. \tag{20.44}$$

In equation (20.43) we have defined

$$\delta = \left[\frac{cW_i(0)(1 - \alpha)br_i}{P_i \ln(1 + r_i)}\right]$$

We then have, assuming a pool of n obligors,

$$MR_W = \frac{\sum_{i=1}^{n} B_i(0)m_r(i)}{\sum_{i=1}^{n} B_i(0)}. \tag{20.45}$$

However, the mechanics of securitization are such that the usable version of equation (20.40) is different from equation (20.43) due to the following differences:

1. The time lag between the time when the vehicle was built and the time when the loan was made, which is the time at which the wholesale value is usually available, and
2. The time lag between loan origination and the closing date of the transaction. If wholesale values are known at the closing date of the ABS deal, then set $t_d = 0$.

As a result, we must use the following version:

$$W_i(t) = (1 - \alpha) W_0 \frac{(a + be^{-c(t + t_{\text{off}} + t_d)})}{(a + be^{-ct_{\text{off}}})} \tag{20.46}$$

In equation (20.46) we have defined the following:

$$t_{\text{off}} = \text{Origination Date} - \text{Manufacture Date}$$

$$t_d = \text{Closing Date} - \text{Origination Date}$$

Note that at $t = 0$ (the closing date), the vehicle has already lost some value with respect to the wholesale value computed at the loan's origination date. For new vehicles, this loss may be significant in percentage terms and should never be neglected. In general, timing effects can significantly affect estimated recoveries and should always be included in cash flow models.

It is instructive to calculate the quantities $m_e(i)$ and $m_r(i)$ for a typical subprime obligor. The data were as follows:

Current balance:	$21,689.56
APR:	18.47%
Payment due:	$530.31
Remaining term:	65 months
Origination date:	June 6, 2001
Origination state:	Florida
Model:	Chevrolet Impala
Year:	1999
Wholesale value:	$17,242

Substitution of these data into equations (20.41), (20.46), and (20.43) yields the following:

$$m_e(i) = 46.8 \text{ months}$$

$$m_r(i) = 9.8 \text{ months}$$

Note first that $m_r(i)$ is rather small for this obligor. This is because, as this is a used vehicle, the negative slope of the depreciation curve is relatively small for the remainder of the exposure compared to that of a new vehicle. At first glance, this would indicate that, from an ABS standpoint, used cars are safer than new ones. However, the useful life of a used car is relatively limited compared to that of a new automobile, not to mention that additional maintenance is often required—two factors outside the scope of our current cash flow modeling capabilities. However, such factors are usually secondary when compared to the basic obligor default behavior and the impact of macroeconomic forces.

Judging from $m_e(i)$, this obligor would enter the positive equity region four years after the transaction started. Normally, our cash flow model should assume that default could not occur after approximately forty-seven payments have been made, since the obligor could simply sell the vehicle to a dealer at the wholesale price to retire the debt. In practice, however, obligors are rarely sufficiently knowledgeable to do this, so a default after $m_e(i)$ months should simply be treated as a full recovery, or perhaps a *credit profit*, depending on state laws.

In order to book any credit profit, credit analysts need to know the credit-granting laws in the state where the loan was originated because our Markov formalism has no way of preventing an obligor who has made forty-eight consecutive payments from defaulting just the same. This fact is, however, completely consistent with the previous analysis, since the ability to make forty-eight consecutive payments in no way implies that an obligor is somehow immune from life events. There is thus no reason we should modify our algorithm to prevent a default of any obligor until the last payment has been made; to do so would imply knowledge that is frankly impossible. This is a minor point, but one that can have a non-negligible influence on how auto-loan-backed ABS cash flow models are built.

The measures PE_W and MR_W should remain more or less stable across pools from the same issuer if its underwriting criteria are consistent. In fact, a 5% move is significant for a pool of 1,000 obligors or more. If either PE_W or MR_W has moved by 10% between two consecutive pools, further investigation may be warranted. Issuers have been known to find creative ways of modifying underwriting characteristics, ways that may go unnoticed at first glance. For example, obligors with poor repayment capacity may artificially qualify for a loan even though they would normally be rejected. In these cases, loans with longer maturities or collateral with inflated prices may suddenly appear. Despite the subtlety of the effects, if a sufficient number of such loans are made, the credit risk measures defined earlier will react accordingly. Of course, PE_W or MR_W may have changed for legitimate reasons. In general, however, too much variance at this level should be a red flag.

Other measures can be derived from other obligor characteristics, such as the rate at which weighted average equity increases, and so on. However, the intuitive content of a measure should be a factor in designing it. Simply accumulating new risk measures does not necessarily add information to the original analysis. Nevertheless, starting with objective measures like PE_W and MR_W is a good way to begin the process of reaching beyond the obvious in auto-loan structured analysis.

Defaults and Prepayments

This section briefly discusses how to handle the two absorbing states in transition matrices: default and prepayment. The only difference between a default and a prepayment is the associated cash flow. In both cases, the pool's outstanding principal balance is decreased by the same amount and the account is effectively removed from the Markov process for the remainder of the particular Monte Carlo scenario. In the case of prepayment, the outstanding principal balance of the loan is received, while in the case of a default, the only cash flow is a recovery collected some time later.

For these reasons, and because they have a similar impact on the average life of securities backed by these loans, prepayments and defaults are treated identically by many lenders who publish combined default and prepayment statistics without separating them. But since they are separate elements of transition matrices, credit analysts should ensure they are accounting for prepayments and defaults separately before implementation within the Markov chain.

Handling Prepayments

The single-month mortality (SMM) is a concept used extensively in MBS markets to define prepayment speeds, and we will maintain the practice here. Originally a life insurance concept (hence "mortality"), the SMM is usually defined by reference to annualized prepayment levels expressed as the conditional prepayment rate (CPR):

$$SMM = \{1 - (1 - CPR)^{1/12}\} \qquad (20.47)$$

As shown in equation (20.47), SMM is simply the monthly equivalent of CPR. CPR values are usually readily available and can be calculated by anyone given the data. If required, *Mortgage and Mortgage-Backed Securities Markets*[5] is a good source book for help in computing CPR. In practice, the issuer will be asked to deliver CPR data to the credit analyst who will then convert them to SMM via equation (20.47). Otherwise, SMM values can be calculated from time series data disclosed by issuers on static pools of auto loans.

Although historical prepayment rates are easily computed, prepayment forecasting is a thorny topic about which much has already been written. We do not intend to add to this literature, and merely assume that a forecast of SMM values is available to the credit analyst. Nevertheless, the accurate prediction of prepayment speeds is clearly an important matter, about which we would like to make a few remarks.

In mortgage markets, it is an accepted fact that interest rates play a crucial role in the speed with which a particular pool prepays via the mechanism of refinancing. Thus, prepayment forecasting amounts to interest rate forecasting, a topic in itself. In auto-backed ABS, however, common sense dictates that prepayment speeds should, ceteris paribus, be much less sensitive to interest rates than in MBS. The amount of money an obligor may save by refinancing a five-year auto loan is relatively small. Also, in some markets the majority of obligors simply do not have the wherewithal to refinance. In addition, relative prepayment speeds are probably related to ad hoc factors such as the condition of the automobile industry and the geographical composition of the pool. It follows that using historical auto-ABS prepayment rates is generally more accurate than in mortgage markets. Prepayment research is ongoing but is unlikely to deliver a deterministic model of prepayment behavior based on observable obligor characteristics in the near future. Such a model would clearly be a major contribution to ABS analysis. Until then, we recommend the use of historical speeds for modeling purposes.

The implementation of prepayment speeds is particularly simple within a Markovian framework. Once a time series of single mortality values SMM_i is available for every month until the highest maturity date of any loan in the pool, simply substitute it in the appropriate cell of the nonstationary Markov chain. To illustrate: assume we are operating with a six-state Markov transition

Table 20.5
Prepayment Speed Implementation in a Transition Matrix

Old Delinquency State	New Delinquency State					
	0	1	2	3	Prepay	Default
1	0.95	0.03	0	0	SMM_1	0
2	—	—	0	0	0	—
3	—	—	—	—	0	—
4	—	—	—	—	—	—
Prepay	0	0	0	0	1	—
Default	0	0	0	0	0	1

matrix. For the first month of the transaction, the transition matrix is as shown in Table 20.5.

Because of the row-sum condition, we have implicitly set $SMM_1 = 0.02$. The same procedure applies to all other months until maturity, except that the appropriate value of SMM is substituted each time. Other row entries are adjusted if necessary to maintain the row-sum condition. Since the overwhelming majority of prepayments will arise from current accounts, it is that entry (0.95) that should be adjusted to maintain the row-sum condition under variable prepayment rates and before the economic modulation of equation (20.25) is applied.

It should also be noted that we have lumped all prepayments in state 1, implying that only current accounts may prepay. This is a simplifying assumption based on the rationale that delinquent accounts will be unable to refinance for credit reasons. For instance, this will happen if lenders run a credit check on the obligor prior to making a new loan. In any event, it is fairly reasonable to assume that most auto-loan prepayments will originate from current accounts.

Finally, note that our cash flow model uses account transition probabilities while CPR speeds are normally given in dollar terms. This issue can be addressed by either requesting account prepayment speeds from the issuer or simply by computing the numerical correspondence between dollar- and account-space prepayment data using the pool's amortization dynamics under a single-loan model (for instance). In practice, either method yields sufficient statistical accuracy.

One reason auto-ABS analysts can rest relatively easier about prepayment versus default modeling is the fact that prepayments are generally a second-order effect in credit analysis. On the one hand, if prepayments are high, there is clearly less excess spread available to cover defaults, assumed to remain unaffected. Even if prepayments are within the expected range but preferentially impact high APR accounts, as one would expect, a reduction in effective excess spread will also take place.

On the other hand, high prepayments do reduce extension, and hence default risk, on a security that would otherwise have remained outstanding and exposed to a potentially more harmful macroenvironment. In practice, these effects tend to compensate one another, making prepayment forecasting less critical than default modeling in terms of credit risk. This does not mean that prepayment modeling can be ignored—quite the contrary—but it does mean that credit risk is more forgiving of errors in prepayment forecasting than is market risk.

Handling Defaults

Although defaults were treated in depth earlier in the chapter we did leave out how to deal with defaulted accounts postdefault within the Markov process.

In general, the issuer will indicate to the analyst how many months will commonly elapse before the collateral will be sold at auction or otherwise liquidated. Suppose obligor i defaults at time $t = t_w$ and assume further that the auction delay is t_a. The recovery is simply $W_i(t_w + t_a)$ and this cash flow is deposited into the collection account for further processing. Thereafter, the account is usually dormant save for *deficiency judgments*. Such judgments are court-ordered settlements compensating lenders who have recovered less than the full loan balance outstanding following a default. They do occur but are a minor factor in auto-ABS analysis. However, if data on deficiency judgments are available, they may be used as justification for the recognition of additional cash into the collection account.

Markov chains lead to fairly realistic patterns. For instance, when a model such as the one described here is implemented consistently, aggregate prepayment, default, and recovery profiles like those shown in Figure 20.9 result for each Monte Carlo scenario.

Delinquencies

Delinquencies are an important issue in ABS analysis for two main reasons. First, a delinquency is the first step toward default. As a result, many ABS transactions include delinquency triggers that change future cash flow allocation following a breach. Second, average lives and other important pricing variables are significantly influenced by cash flow delays stemming from delinquency dynamics. Thus, to properly assess the credit quality of an auto-loan ABS security, delinquencies need to be accurately modeled. As was the case for prepayments, Markovian transition matrices are ideally suited to do this.

Delinquencies are easy to calculate because each account is automatically positioned in delinquency space at each time step. To do this, define $d_i(t)$ as the delinquency status of loan i at time t. For instance, a current account has $d_i(t) = s_0$, while a thirty-day delinquent account has $d_i(t) = s_1$, and so on.

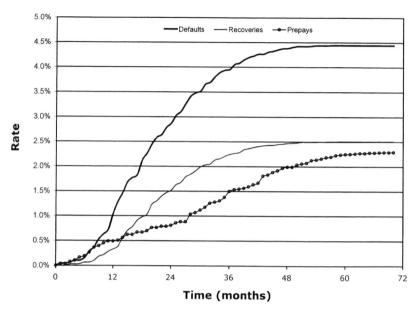

Figure 20.9. Cumulative Defaults, Prepayments, and Recoveries

Define $B_i(t)$ as the outstanding principal balance of loan i at time t and $D_i(t)$ as the aggregate pool principal balance in delinquency status i at time t. Then, by definition, we have for a pool of n obligors:

$$D_j(t) = \sum_{i=1}^{n} \delta(d_i(t) - s_j)B_i(t) \qquad (20.48)$$

In equation (20.48), we have defined the Dirac delta function:

$$\delta(x) \equiv \begin{cases} 1, x = 0 \\ 0, \text{otherwise} \end{cases} \qquad (20.49)$$

In general, we find that the aggregate delinquent balance of the pool goes through a maximum as the default behavior of the pool unfolds according to equation (20.1). A typical temporal pattern is shown in Figure 20.10 for the thirty-day and sixty-or-more-day delinquency buckets. It would be extremely difficult, if not impossible, to reproduce such a realistic delinquency pattern except through a Markovian framework. In general, the cash flow dynamics associated with changing delinquency patterns are too intricate to be replicated to any level of accuracy using single-loan models, or for that matter any other static approach. Next, the handling of delinquency triggers is simply not possible using ordinary methods since delinquencies are not handled in any meaningful way. Yet, it is through features like delinquency triggers that some of the most significant aspects of the analysis of structured securities can be investigated. Without incorporating delinquency transition dynamics directly

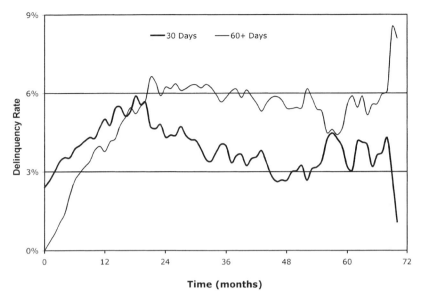

Figure 20.10. Pool Dollar Delinquencies (autos)

into a formal cash flow apparatus via Markov chains, the analysis of auto-loan-backed structured securities usually lacks realism and credibility.

Principal Balances

Thus far, we have not discussed specifically how principal balances are to be computed on each loan in the pool. We have shown how different credit policies led to different cash flows into the trust for an equivalent delinquency pattern. Regardless of how aggregate cash flows are handled, principal balances are always required, and need to be computed from the underlying Markov process.

Readers will recall that our integer-based approximation to delinquency dynamics forced us to consider only whole payments made by obligors, and that we used the issuer's credit policy manual to determine how many such payments were made given any monthly transition by an obligor. The crux of the approach lies in the need to follow each account separately throughout its delinquency history to determine its outstanding principal balance. No longer can we afford to consider accounts in the aggregate, since each account will theoretically follow a different path on its way to maturity. As before, most accounts will remain current, and their principal balance will follow the scheduled amortization pattern. However, the key to the analysis of auto-ABS securities is the proper valuation of cash from delinquent, not current, accounts.

Computing principal balances within a Markov chain is straightforward and consists of the following three steps:

1. Compute the transition made by the account for the current monthly time period.
2. Determine the associated payment made to the trust.
3. Partition the payment made into principal and interest portions.

This can become confusing rather quickly since the number of possible account histories with even a small pool is astronomical. For instance, suppose an account makes twelve consecutive monthly payments. Given the maturity, interest rate, and term of the loan, we can calculate the amount of each monthly payment and the portion thereof consisting of principal. Suppose now that the account becomes thirty days delinquent at month 13, the payment made is zero by definition, and the principal balance remains unchanged, assuming no capitalization of the interest (which is usually the case). At month 14, a payment that includes a late or delinquency fee is made, leaving the account thirty days delinquent and lowering its principal balance by the amount of principal associated with the thirteenth, not the fourteenth, month. At month 15, the same account makes a large payment amounting to two monthly scheduled payments, again including late fees, leaving the account current and reducing its principal balance by the principal amounts associated with months 14 and 15. The portion of any payment made that is not principal is considered interest.

At that point, the account has caught up with the original schedule but has paid late fees along the way in such a way that cash flows are not what they would have been had we simply noted that the account was current at month 15 under both scenarios. Moreover, actual cash flows deviated from their original schedule, and this could have affected the average life of the associated securities. These are the complex dynamics that may be captured through the Markov process. For example, Figure 20.11 shows principal balance histories for two accounts with four-year maturities that pay off simultaneously but have different yield characteristics. The first account amortizes according to the expected actuarial schedule, evidenced by the smooth curve from one to forty-eight months, while the second begins a long delinquency period at month 12.

These curves reflect the fact that, although the total nominal cash supplied is identical in both cases (assuming no late fees) the yield difference between them depends on the area between the two curves. A model that fails to account for these yield effects will also fail to properly distinguish issuers and markets, such as emerging markets, where delinquencies are a way of life. By giving full rein to the delinquency dynamics of auto-loan pools, the yield properties of asset pools can be more accurately represented. The sensitivity of delinquency variance on cash flows and average lives can thus be more precisely investigated. These parametric studies are important when pricing considerations matter. Since ABS credit analysis is concerned mainly with yield and not merely default, ignoring cash flow timings (as is done under static

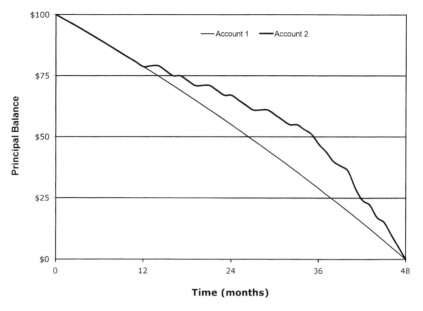

Figure 20.11. Account Delinquency Histories

models of delinquencies) can quite often severely impact the credit rating of the ABS securities.

The Credit Scoring of Automobile Borrowers

The analysis of auto-backed structured securities is enhanced significantly by the addition of credit-scoring data. This section gives a layman's overview of this topic including a discussion of what to look for and avoid when using them. The next section describes the use of the data inside the Markov process.

Automobile financing is heavily influenced by an estimate of borrower credit quality. A *credit score,* computed from credit data amassed on the obligor, normally measures that quality. Many banks and specialty finance companies have developed proprietary scoring algorithms using their customer base as development samples, while other lenders rely on generic scores from commercial credit bureaus. In turn, these latter organizations develop credit scores from performance data submitted to them over the years by various creditors.

The range of theoretically achievable scores is normally divided into nonoverlapping regions into which obligors are classified using letter-grade designations. There are usually four such regions: A, B, C, and D. It is customary to further delineate these into two broad categories: prime and sub-prime. *Prime borrowers* are those falling within the A and B regions, while *sub-prime* obligors make up the rest. A third transitional region, the near-prime segment, has recently come into fashion in an effort to avoid the pejorative label "sub-prime." However, as a rule, the world of automobile-backed structured finance can be assumed to consist of two subpopulations.

Unfortunately, credit scores are often misinterpreted as cardinal measures of credit risk when they are, in fact, merely ordinal rankings of obligors. In practice, this means that they only rank obligors on a continuous scale and do not attempt to measure the average credit loss to be expected from a pool with a given score distribution. In fact, two pools with the same average obligor score can give rise to widely disparate credit risk without in any way impeaching the validity of the scoring algorithm.

To relate an ordinal measure of loss to a cardinal measure, issuers must conduct lengthy and ambiguous default studies—studies complicated by the problem of *censored data*, which refers to the fact that, due to time constraints, selected data samples do not include all outcomes. In this case, the development sample will clearly not reflect defaults that occurred after the sampling period ended. The difficulty arises because businesses need to adjust to changing supply and demand conditions on a shorter time scale than the speed at which a pool will normally amortize. As a result, data samples used in default studies usually contain incomplete (or censored) information on the set of obligors likely to default in the future.

In practice, credit analysts should avoid comparing pools by simplistic metrics like means and standard deviations. Rather than using distributional moments, they should use the entire score distribution in comparing two credit populations (the topic of the next section) as well as use that distribution inside cash flow models.

For instance, Figure 20.12 displays two score distributions with the same average score. In terms of credit risk, the pool with the unimodal distribution is relatively safe while the bimodally distributed population is relatively risky. By this we mean that the latter contains a relatively high number of poor borrowers masked by an equally high number of extremely good borrowers. The problem is that good borrowers usually will not compensate for poor borrowers because debt returns are capped at the coupon. It is in this manner that using mean credit scores to compare pools of obligors can and will result in erroneous conclusions.

Credit Score Modulation

Recall that the epistemological equivalence of all obligors is a fundamental assumption of Markov processes applied to ABS, and that no knowledge of credit dynamics may be relied upon save the delinquency structure of loan pools, where any obligor is considered an equally likely candidate for inclusion in the latter. The default propensity of any obligor is thus considered invari-

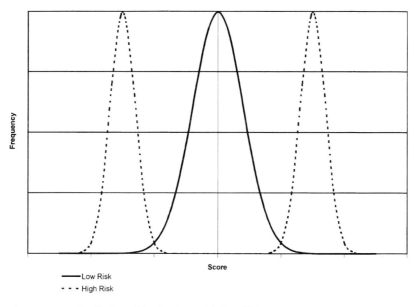

Figure 20.12. Credit Score Distributions with Equal Means

ant; hence the ability to talk about an *issuer's* Markov transition matrix and not an obligor's.

But if new, objective data came to light to change this view, then jettisoning it to replace it with a more realistic default model would certainly be justified. A credit score is just such a datum because it is a synthetic variable that purports to summarize known obligor risk factors into an ordinal ranking and allows us to modify the obligor-specific default drift from the constant value assumed under the first model by a functional form relating score values to default probabilities.

A commonly used scoring function is the logistic curve relating default probability p_d to score value y using

$$p_d = \frac{e^{-y}}{1 + e^{-y}}. \tag{20.50}$$

A typical graph of this functional form is presented in Figure 20.13. As expected, default probability decreases when score value increases. In general, we have $y = \sum_{i=1}^{n} a_i x_i$, where x_i are empirically determined variables related to credit behavior and a_i are regression coefficients determined from default data. It can be readily verified that $y \in [0, 1]$, thus satisfying the basic requirement of a probability measure. Fortunately, the ABS analyst will not be asked to derive the coefficients a_i, but will instead be given a set of score values S_i, $i = 1$, 2, 3, . . . , n, one for each of the n obligors in the pool.

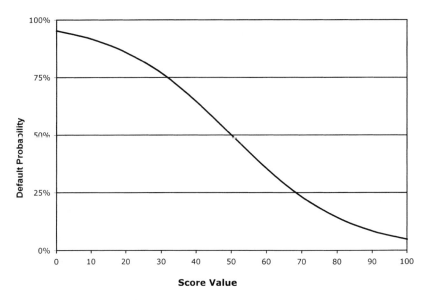

Figure 20.13. Logistic Default Curve

Implementing a score distribution is accomplished via the modulation of each obligor's default probability, in response to equation (20.50) or a similar functional form, so that the relative default propensity of low-scoring accounts will increase, causing them to become delinquent and default with greater frequency than higher-scoring accounts, and vice versa. This is now illustrated using the functional form (20.50) but can be replicated with any given trial function.

First, assume equation (20.50) is a valid representation of the way default probability varies with score value. In practice, the logistic curve is a fairly robust representation and should be preferred to any linear form.

Next, apply a linear transformation to the given score range $[a, b]$ where $a = \min(S_i), \forall i$ and $b = \max(S_i), \forall i$ to a new range $[-d, c]$ such that the transformed values have zero mean and equal aspect ratio, namely

$$S_i' = \alpha S_i + \beta \tag{20.51}$$

with boundary conditions

$$\beta + \frac{\alpha}{n}\sum_{i=1}^{n}S_i = 0 \tag{20.52}$$

$$\sqrt{\frac{1}{N}\sum_{i=1}^{n}(\alpha S_i + \beta)^2} = \frac{\sigma}{\mu}. \tag{20.53}$$

In equation (20.53), the usual definitions $\mu = (1/n)\sum_{i=1}^{n}S_i$ and $\sigma^2 = (1/n)\sum_{i=1}^{n}(S_i - \mu)^2$ are used.

Now, solve for α and β using the NR formalism, or some other nonlinear solution procedure. These two parameters are the issuer's credit-scoring adjustment factors and remain constant for as long as the score is valid. In general, without realignment, a credit score remains valid for about two and a half years after it is developed, which means approximately four years after the corresponding development sample was collected.

Now, set $y = S_i'$ in equation (20.50) and define the modulation factors

$$g_i \equiv 2p_d = 2\frac{e^{-S_i'}}{1 + e^{-S_i'}}. \tag{20.54}$$

This way, score values are related to delinquency propensity in a way that ensures that average accounts (i.e., those with score values close to the mean μ) will satisfy $g_i \approx 1$. Modulation factors g_i are then inserted into our monthly Markov transition matrix as described in the following paragraphs.

From chapter 12, recall that the IDFM method is used at each time step to determine obligor delinquency transitions. Specifically, this is accomplished by partitioning the uniform deviate range [0, 1] as follows with respect to the first row of any monthly transition matrix $\mathbf{P}(t)$:

$[0, p_{11}(t)] =$ The account remains current.

$[p_{11}(t), p_{11}(t) + p_{12}(t)] =$ The account becomes thirty days delinquent.

$[p_{11}(t) + p_{12}(t), p_{11}(t) + p_{12}(t) + p_{1(n-1)}(t)] =$ The account prepays.

$[p_{11}(t) + p_{12}(t) + p_{1(n-1)}(t), 1] =$ The account is bankrupt.

Element $p_{12}(t)$ is the delinquency propensity of the account, which up to now was considered constant for all accounts. Now, define the obligor delinquency propensity $p_{12}'(t)$:

$$p_{12}'(t) = g_i p_{12}(t) \tag{20.55}$$

To maintain the row-sum condition, we also need to set

$$p_{11}'(t) = p_{11}(t) + p_{12}(t) - p_{12}'(t). \tag{20.56}$$

The modulation is effected by using $p_{11}'(t)$ and $p_{12}'(t)$ instead of $p_{11}(t)$ and $p_{12}(t)$, respectively, as inputs to the accountwise IDFM method regardless of the account's prior delinquency history. Accounts with $S_i' < 0$ will have $g_i > 1$, thereby increasing their tendency to become delinquent, and hence to default in accordance with equation (20.50). Exactly the opposite will be the case for accounts with $S_i' > 0$.

This modulation technique increases the delinquency propensity of an account in the ratio given by equation (20.50) and, in doing so, consistently adjusts the relative default tendencies of accounts with different credit scores. Although there is no theoretical equality between default probability and delinquency propensity, the way credit scores are developed is in fact quite consistent with the delinquency-based approach. Samples of accounts for score-development purposes are usually chosen from an issuer's managed portfolio an average of eighteen months after they were placed on the company's balance sheet, at which point they are classified as "good" or "bad." In many cases, however, accounts will be classified as bad prior to default since issuers will want to have advance warning of default. In such cases, score values will refer to delinquency and not default.

Second, even in cases where the definition of a bad account is default, an obligor may have been in default months before the classification period. Thus credit scores may refer instead to cumulative default rates censored at eighteen months, which are much closer in spirit to delinquency than to default propensity.

Implementation

In order to use the previous modulation in realistic settings, a calibration is needed. In general, proceed as follows:

1. For a given score distribution, insert the previous modulating formalism into the basic Markov transition cash flow model.
2. Repeat the microcalibration process and recompute the value of the micro-influence factor m with a pool of known $E(L)$.
3. Once the new calibrating value of m is determined, different pool credit score distributions can be analyzed by keeping the adjustment factors α and β constant during subsequent Monte Carlo simulations.

This method guarantees that credit enhancement levels for pools with score distributions different from the calibrating distribution in lower as well as higher moments will be correctly sized without ad hoc intervention or subjective adjustment.

As mentioned before, credit scores do not remain eternally valid. Analysts should avoid pool comparisons involving a substantial time lag unless the vendor has redeveloped the score and its value has been adjusted to maintain probabilistic equivalence between the two scores.

While robust scores deteriorate rather slowly, many analysts may mistake deterioration in the score's associated *loss rate* for a reduction in its *discriminating power*. Readers should keep in mind that credit scores are ordinal, not cardinal, rankings: the same average score can theoretically lead to quite a different cumulative loss rate without any change in its ability to discriminate creditworthiness. Although in general, errors made from excessive reliance on outdated scores are likely to be manageable, using the same set of α and β adjustment factors more than two and a half years after their initial computation is not recommended.

Benefits

The benefits of using credit score modulation techniques become apparent when an opinion is requested on two pools that are statistically indistinguishable save for the second one's lower average credit score. It should first be noted that the intuitive character of differences in credit enhancement levels associated with changes in pool-averaged scores is remarkably lacking. Consequently, we highly recommend the use of this or a similar method over the mere "eyeballing" of two pools to adjust their credit enhancement levels. Without such techniques, analysts are essentially powerless to accurately value the potential effect of the lower credit score. The current policy at rating agencies to deal with variable credit score distributions is apparently one of appeasement—usually equal to 50 bps—regardless of the actual impact of the new distribution.

It cannot be overemphasized that, because two score distributions with the same average value can have wildly different risk profiles depending on the respective moments of each distribution, proper credit assessment needs to include all distributional moments, not merely the mean value. If the new distribution is indeed associated with a lower aggregate risk profile, use of the previously discussed modulation technique will cause ratings to improve or, alternatively, will allow credit enhancement to decrease at the same rating levels. In any event, a parametric study should always be conducted ab initio to determine the impact of various score distributions on credit enhancement levels.

Liability Structures

As we have said, there is a significant difference between the effort required to analyze the asset side of the SPE balance sheet and the corresponding effort for the liabilities. So far, we have chosen to ignore liability modeling because, in large measure, the analysis boils down to coding the priority of payments disclosed in the offering memorandum. Unlike asset valuation, liability modeling is not asset specific and is better handled as a separate topic. This we have done to a great extent already in chapter 8. In this section, we merely indicate the generic structural type encountered in auto-ABS and then briefly discuss related issues.

Broadly speaking (and assuming a hypothetical two-tranche structure), auto-loan-backed structured securities will allocate cash from the collection account as follows:

1. Servicing fees
2. A interest
3. B interest
4. A principal

5. B principal
6. Reserve account contribution (as required)
7. Equity certificate holder

Servicing fees usually amount to an annualized 1–2% of the current pool balance and are payable monthly. Back-up servicers are usually required for smaller issuers and may entail additional servicing fees in addition to those paid to the primary servicer.

Reserve accounts are generally negotiable but normally hover in the range of 1.5–4.0% of the current pool balance, with a floor between 0.5–1.0% of the initial pool balance. In rare cases, structures have nondeclining reserve accounts.

The two most common *principal allocation schemes* are pro rata and sequential; readers should refer to chapter 8 for further details.

Structural features such as delinquency or default triggers, or both, are often added to legal documents. These essentially modify the waterfall by trapping excess spread that would normally escape from the structure, and use it for various purposes. A trigger can be asset based or liability based. Readers should refer to chapter 23 for further details on triggers.

The challenges of auto-ABS analysis usually derive, not from the complexity of the liability structures, but rather from the interaction between the assets and the liabilities. For instance, breached triggers may cause the reserve account's target percentage to increase, trapping excess spread until all debt classes are retired. Alternatively, a trigger breach may allocate excess spread to "turbo" the bonds—to accelerate their repayment schedule beyond the normal parity condition. These structural features, and others, can only be investigated via sophisticated cash flow models. As already mentioned, because ABS are focused on yield instead of default, the proper timing of cash flows is even more critical.

In this respect, the advantage of using Markovian methods to study auto-loan structures is that, by allowing precise modeling of delinquencies and other transaction variables, the relative merits of various structural features can be properly investigated and their impact on the credit quality of the associated securities accurately assessed. It now becomes feasible to measure the relative credit enhancement requirements of two different delinquency trigger levels to an accuracy of one basis point, or to investigate different triggering mechanisms in search of capital optimality. By enhancing valuation, these methods also enable more creative structuring in a way that can be objectively demonstrated to investors.

Nonlinear Topics

As discussed earlier, a chief characteristic of structured finance is its extreme nonlinearity: transaction inputs and outputs are interdependent, forcing recourse to iterative solutions. To compute ABS security ratings, one needs to know their coupon rates, and vice versa. This "chicken-and-egg" situation usually indicates the need for an iterative solution unless a linear approximation is made at the outset.

Significant improvements in pricing efficiency may be obtained by solving this nonlinear problem exactly. In general, the solution space will be multidimensional, consisting of one dimension for each potential area of flexibility in the transaction. For demonstration purposes only, we wish to illustrate a nonlinear solution procedure in one dimension: the interest rate. However, readers should bear in mind the highly artificial and unrealistic nature of the one-dimensional problem. In practice, it would normally be the case for other structural details to be determined jointly with interest rates.

One-Dimensional Nonlinear Solution

The strategy is clear: first, guess the interest rates, compute the credit ratings, and use these generally different output ratings to update the input rates until input and output rates are within an acceptable margin of error of each other.

Starting from a known coincident yield curve model, we proceed as follows in the case of a two-tranche transaction:

1. Begin by assuming reasonable ratings for the tranches, perhaps from past transactions, or judgmentally. In the same manner, estimate the expected average life of the classes from assumed prepayment–credit loss environments. If no average life estimate is available a priori, use the Markovian cash flow model for the expected case, using rates corresponding to the estimated credit ratings, and compute the average life of both classes. As a last resort, simply use the analytical formulas derived in chapter 9.
2. Given the input credit ratings and average lives, read off the corresponding interest rates via the known yield curve. Label these rates r_A and r_B, respectively.
3. Perform a complete Monte Carlo simulation of approximately 5,000 scenarios.
4. Read off the resulting credit ratings and the expected average lives of Class A and Class B corresponding to the assumed interest rates.
5. Derive new interest rates for Class A and Class B by inserting the output ratings and expected average lives into the yield curve model.
6. Compare the updated to the original rates and choose new rates equal to the geometric mean of the original and output rates. For example, if r_A^u and r_B^u are the updated rates derived from the Monte Carlo simulation, the new provisional rates r_A^p and r_B^p will be $r_A^p = \sqrt{r_A r_A^u}$ and $r_B^p = \sqrt{r_B r_B^u}$.
7. Substitute r_A^p and r_B^p for r_A and r_B and perform a new Monte Carlo simulation.

8. Perform the sequence of steps 3 through 7 until the weighted average difference between input and output rate on both classes is less than a prearranged tolerance, usually 1%. In practice, the algorithm converges in fewer than twenty iterations for a two-class structure.

This solution procedure is fairly straightforward once the basic Markovian cash flow model is written, and can be implemented in less than an hour. Readers should note that a dedicated computer is usually required since CPU times may be fairly high for reasonable pools (i.e., those in excess of 2,500 obligors with loan maturities in the six-year range).

Ill-Posed Problems in Structured Finance

For illustrative and didactic purposes only, the foregoing one-dimensional, nonlinear solution has been boiled down to a series of eight discrete steps. In the process, the important issue of "ill-posedness" has been left out. *Ill-posedness* refers to a situation in which no physical solution exists because of an attempt to impose inconsistent or impossible boundary conditions on a problem statement.

For instance, assume you are trying to solve the steady-state heat equation inside a one-dimensional metal plate with an internal heat source and insulated walls. Such boundary conditions imply that temperature gradients at both ends of the plate vanish identically at all times. Due to the heat source, the temperature inside the plate will start to rise at time zero. However, heat will be unable to escape since the temperature gradient at both ends has been set to zero. The only physical solution consistent with the mathematical situation will be that of a rising plate temperature up to the metal's melting point. This "meltdown" scenario, however, is something entirely outside the scope of the mathematical model. The physical inconsistency will be reflected mathematically by the fact that the solution will never reach steady state. Eventually, computational errors will cause it to diverge and the solution will "blow up," so to speak. This is what we mean by ill-posedness in physics. The remedy, in this case, is obviously to change the boundary conditions and allow heat to escape from the plate at one end or the other.

The concept of ill-posedness is also relevant to structured finance. It may occur when variables assumed to be known a priori in fact turn out to be inconsistent with the rest of the solution. In the same manner, our financial nonlinear system will fail to reach a steady state and the solution will begin to diverge, eventually causing run-time errors to pop up in the form of overflow.

For instance, assume you are a credit analyst trying to analyze a one-tranche auto transaction with a total issuance of 95% of the pool's asset value, and that you estimate this bond to be ratable Aaa. Owing to the independently determined default characteristics of the pool, something outside your immediate control, say the first Monte Carlo simulation yields an output rating of Ba1 instead of the estimated Aaa. According to the stepwise solution just presented, we would adjust the provisional tranche interest rate to a value corresponding to a rating somewhere between Aaa and Ba1, and proceed with the second Monte Carlo simulation (step 7). Unfortunately, this new rate could only increase the trust's liability burden and would make the situation worse, resulting in a rating of perhaps Ba3 instead of Ba1. The third Monte Carlo simulation would begin with yet a higher rate, and the same phenomenon would happen again. Clearly, this process would never converge, because each output rate would simply get away from the previous one in a never-ending search.

Although this logjam can obviously be broken by reducing total issuance, doing so ad hoc (e.g., by reducing it arbitrarily to 90%) might lead to yet another ill-posed problem. Clearly, the problem could be solved in one step by setting total issuance to 60%, thereby ensuring the Aaa rating of the associated tranche. However, issuer nirvana usually lies elsewhere (i.e., in the maximization of proceeds at the lowest average cost of funds). Therefore, their goal cannot be achieved via such a simplistic Gordian knot solution to this problem. As a result, a feasible algorithm free of endless trial and error normally incorporates tranche sizing along with interest rate setting.

Note that ill-posedness is specific to structured finance. It does not exist in corporate finance, where credit ratings are determined independently of interest rates. As a result, capital-efficient auto-ABS transactions will normally involve multidimensional nonlinear solutions. The number of variables involved will be large, being both commensurate with the universe contemplated by the issuer and acceptable to the marketplace. The corresponding computational effort will be significant, but the associated savings well worth it.

Final Remarks on Structural Optimality

Under current market conditions, given an issuer's cash flow dynamics and liquidity position, the question of whether a proposed transaction structure is capital efficient is neither asked nor answered. With respect to most transactions, after a few haphazard trials and iterations of the human sort, and during which the rating agencies have their say, the loop eventually closes based more on the urgent need for funding than on capital optimality. Ecstatic at the mere prospect of closure, issuers are usually neither interested in nor equipped to judge the merits or demerits of their structures, despite having to live with the consequences, good or bad. A comprehensive solution to the problem of suboptimality would surely be a welcome contribution to structured finance in particular and to the capital markets in general.

Throughout this work, we have and will continue to focus on asset valuation because it is both the starting point and the central analytical focus of structural optimization. However, even the best valuation method on earth leaves essentially unanswered the paramount question of how to systematically design capital-efficient ABS structures.

21

CDOs of ABS

A comparatively young asset class, the CDO of ABS is widely misunderstood by the market and the rating agencies. Its credit character is different from other types of CDOs and should be handled within a framework attentive to its special properties.

The Special Nature of ABS as an Asset Class

Compared to the significant modeling effort required for a relatively intuitive asset class such as autos, in chapter 20, the work involved in analyzing these structures is primarily conceptual. Much of the underlying dynamics lie hidden in the asset pools underlying the asset tranches of the CDO. This additional level of abstraction allows us to treat these assets uniformly without reference to the asset class whence they came. For this reason, the fine-grained cash flow dynamics that formed the crux of the original ABS analysis are largely irrelevant to this asset class.

As discussed in chapter 4, the standard rating agency CDO analysis is simple and easily grasped by investors but leaves out most of the payment physics of the particular pool. It also ignores the average yield-reduction calculation. Assets in the pool are defaulted like corporate loans within a recovery framework. In the case of ABS, this is impossible, since ABS securities are specifically constructed to avoid the default-and-recovery process. In CDOs of ABS, the underlying assets are not corporate loans or bonds but rather tranches of previously issued ABS transactions. It is true that these tranches have letter-grade ratings like corporate bonds; however, as has been painstakingly established in the early chapters, the similarity between the two stops there. ABS bonds do not "default" in the sense of corporate defaults. Instead, they deliver the promised yield or less according to their own loss characteristics. As a result, a CDO of ABS cannot be rated like another CDO, but must be handled in a manner that respects the special nature of its underlying assets.

If CDOs of ABS cannot be rated based on default probabilities, how should they be rated? The answer is clear: they should be rated based on the average yield reduction that corresponds to the rating. Note further that each tranche of an ABS transaction is itself backed by a pool of receivables or other assets. Some readers may wonder whether the analysis requires revisiting and reanalyzing each individual pool. That would be unnecessary: regardless of the assets underlying the ABS pool, the credit profile of the tranche is adequately described by the reduction of yield implied by the rating. The analysis of CDOs of ABS must, therefore, begin by regarding and modeling the underlying ABS bonds as cash flow streams with distributions leading to a specified average reduction of yield given by the credit rating. As is true of all ABS asset classes, the underlying default model has two aspects: microeconomic and macroeconomic, and each needs to be incorporated into the analysis to achieve reasonable results. When correlations are included, the CDO of ABS, properly understood, is a powerful arbitrage vehicle from which significant value can be extracted. Achieving this understanding is the goal of analysis.

The Cash Flow Formalism of CDOs of ABS

The analysis of CDOs of ABS consists of two separate steps:

- Calibration
- Transaction analysis

We will discuss briefly the techniques behind each one and then describe actual implementation issues in some detail.

Calibration

The first task is to ensure that each tranche of the CDO is consistent with its average reduction of yield. This is done by calibration.

The idea is to create a stripped-down version of a cash flow model which is then applied to each ABS tranche in the target pool. By design, the cash flow model will include micro- and macroeconomic parameters that effect the calibration and become the workhorse of the analysis step. Because we are interested in liability returns and yield reductions, the fine-grained nature of cash flow dynamics stemming from the behavior of underlying asset pools can be largely ignored. Here, the analyst can afford to be crude at the individual asset level and get away with considering a single macroeconomic distribution for all asset classes.

The microeconomic-level analysis consists of an individual binomial process with a temporal dimension. The underlying pools are partitioned into default cells according to the time at which they default. Current rating agency methods also use a binomial process, but it is at the bond (not the asset) level and does not replicate intertemporal dynamics. Each cell is considered subject to a unique default process. The calibration is carried out by adjusting the parameters of this binomial process to produce the correct reduction of yield.

To do this, the following basic input variables are needed for each asset tranche:

1. Outstanding principal balance (B)
2. Interest rate + servicing fees (APR)
3. WAC of the asset pool − annualized expected loss (WAC)
4. Weighted average remaining maturity of the asset pool (WAM)
5. Normalized asset count in the asset pool (n)
6. Weighted average seasoning of the asset pool (WAS)

Note that knowledge of the seasoning of the underlying pool (WAS) is used to properly reflect the dynamics of expected asset-tranche cash flows. It is not a precondition of the analysis; however, a price is paid for not using that information when it is available, since in the credit sense seasoning shows up as implicit diversification and has a beneficial impact on credit enhancement. Additionally, some measure of cash flow variability—for example, by an industrial-sector index (such as GDP) associated with an ABS sector (like credit cards)—will be required to incorporate correlations. These variables constitute the minimal data set. If less than this information is available, the analyst should query whether such a pool is a candidate for securitization.

Without loss of generality, the following additional tranche-wise simplifying assumptions are made:

- Asset recoveries[1] and over-collateralization are both zero.
- A normalized asset count related to the resolution of cash flows is used. If the actual number of individual assets is unknown, it should be adjusted to approximately 100 assets per cell on average. Although no theory dictates what it should be, in practice $n \approx 10,000$ provides more than sufficient resolution.
- The WAC and the WAM can theoretically be set equal to actual values without affecting the solution procedure in any way. However, in practice small adjustments may help to smooth out the calibration algorithm and allow more resolution in cases where it might be desirable.

The loss curve for each ABS pool is assumed to be of the form

$$F(t) = \frac{a}{1 + be^{-c(t+s-t_0)}}. \qquad (21.1)$$

In equation (21.1) we have defined the following parameters:

a = Asymptote to be found from the calibration procedure

b = Curve adjustment factor found from market data

C = Time constant found from market data

t_0 = Point of maximum marginal credit loss found from market data

s = Seasoning adjustment for the asset pool underlying the ABS tranche

This assumed form for $F(t)$ is sufficiently versatile to accommodate a wide range of behaviors by simply adjusting its input parameters. As stated previously, this microdefault model deals with individual assets in a dynamic con-

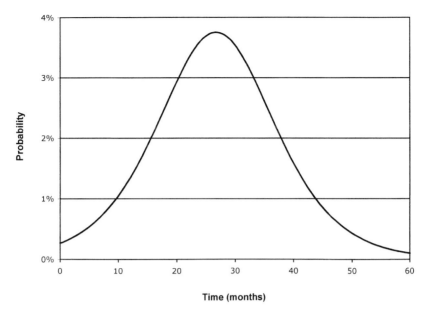

Figure 21.1. Asset Default Probability (p)

text, rather than abstracting at the tranche level in a static environment. In this manner, the cash flow dynamics of the ABS assets are automatically included at very little cost and contribute substantially to demonstrating the strength of the resulting structure, just as ignoring them is the main source of suboptimality in the analysis.

We begin the calibration by uniformly partitioning the assets among an asset count versus time matrix consisting of WAM cells, each containing n/WAM potentially defaulting assets. Within each cell, the following time-dependent binomial distribution $p(t)$ is assumed to rule the default process underlying of the n/WAM individual assets:

$$p(t) = f(t) \equiv \frac{\partial F(t)}{\partial t} \qquad (21.2)$$

For instance, Figure 21.1 is an example of $f(t)$ for the choices $a = 1$, $b = 1.5$, $c = 0.15$, and $t_0 = 24$.

Most reasonable pool credit loss behaviors can be replicated fairly accurately in this manner. Each month, assets are randomly defaulted according to this binomial process, and the corresponding cash flows are removed from the underlying trust without recoveries. The remaining loans are assumed to earn WAC% per year with maturities each equal to WAM months.

At the macro-level, we proceed as in chapter 20, that is, with a suitably chosen and unique macroeconomic influence factor [M] distribution to generate extreme cash flow environments capable of causing the ABS securities to

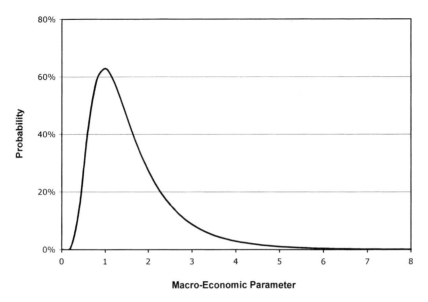

Figure 21.2. Lognormal Process

default. Here a lognormal or gamma distribution may be preferred to the beta distribution profiled in chapter 5, because either distribution can more easily generate the required extreme results. The chosen distribution is also presumably similar to the one a credit analyst would have used to arrive at the initial rating on any ABS tranche in the pool. Its parameters are kept constant during the calibration and merely adjusted once at the outset so as to correctly reproduce the expected reduction of yield (ΔIRR) distributional dynamics of ABS securities.

The results presented in this section were generated with the lognormal distribution displayed in Figure 21.2. This distribution has the following mean and standard deviation:

$$\begin{aligned} \mu &= 1.5 \\ \sigma &= 1.0 \end{aligned} \tag{21.3}$$

The mean m and the standard deviation s of the associated normal distribution are given by

$$m = \ln\left[\frac{\mu}{\sqrt{1 + \left[\frac{\sigma}{\mu}\right]^2}}\right] \tag{21.4}$$

$$s = \sqrt{\ln\left(1 + \left[\frac{\sigma}{\mu}\right]^2\right)}. \tag{21.5}$$

Equations (21.4) and (21.5) are usually required to implement the IDFM method with the lognormal distribution. To reflect the compounding of enhancement on the assets, the lognormal is the best practical choice, although the validity of the algorithm in no way hinges on that choice.

To incorporate the macro-level influence, we simply combine the binomial default process from equation (21.2) with the macroeconomic influence factor into a single process whereby the tranchewise cell default probability at time t for Monte Carlo scenario i, $P_d(i, t)$, is given by

$$P_d(i, t) = M(i)p(t). \tag{21.6}$$

This algorithm is used repeatedly as part of a Monte Carlo simulation whereby the corresponding ΔIRR is calculated. If the Monte Carlo simulation results in an average ΔIRR smaller than the target value corresponding to the asset tranche's ABS credit rating, a is increased appropriately, and vice versa if ΔIRR is greater than the target yield reduction. This iterative loop is continued until convergence, the latter being guaranteed by the fact that the pool's tranches have finite ΔIRR. Once derived in this manner, the parameters a, b, and c remain fixed for the next step (the transaction analysis) where they form implicit cash flow models for the ABS tranches.

Once calibration curves of the form (21.2) are computed, they are used to derive cash flows to the transaction's liability structure. We postpone the discussion of correlations to the next section.

Transaction Analysis

When correlations are ignored, the calibration-modeling effort is sufficient to move into the analysis. The transactional analysis consists in the overlay of a precise description of its liability structure and in the computation of the associated liability-side credit ratings.

As previously discussed, ABS transactions are nonlinear in character and require an iterative solution similar to that presented in chapter 18. The case presented here is the simplest possible, as we have assumed that all transaction parameters are known a priori except for interest rates. Thus, a one-dimensional interest rate nonlinear loop is required to compute the ratings. This proceeds as follows:

1. Credit ratings on the liabilities are first assumed, and initial interest rates derived from these.
2. A Monte Carlo simulation is performed to recomputed interest rates given the output credit ratings. The new rates are compared to the initial rates and the difference used to update the input rates.
3. This process is followed until convergence.

As long as the problem is *well posed* (see chapter 20), the iteration is guaranteed to converge to the correct ratings and interest rates.

The implementation of correlations is straightforward and natural. For each macroeconomic index, use a single macroeconomic influence factor for each Monte Carlo scenario and choose them in accordance with correlated random deviates. Since there are n macroeconomic indices involved, one vector of n macroeconomic influence factors is selected for each Monte Carlo scenario.

To properly incorporate correlations, a special numerical algorithm is devised. Described in detail in the next sections, the algorithm modifies basic Cholesky decomposition outputs so as to partially correct for their lack of distributional uniformity. As explained in chapter 16, the lack of distributional uniformity is the major practical disadvantage of the Cholesky method in generating IDFM inputs. The output values of this algorithm are then used to select correlated macro-influence factors.

A Simple Example of CDO of ABS Analysis

The target structure is a plain-vanilla, two-tranche transaction. Results are presented with and without correlations. Although the structure of CDOs of ABS in the market is normally more involved, the analytical method to deal with them is the same. The results are compared to putative agency ratings for the target pool in the uncorrelated case. It should be noted that rating agencies do not have a formal method to address correlations in ABS securities to date, and that the committee process allows for rating results that deviate materially from what a straightforward implementation of the published methodology would say. However, such discrepancies are often reduced when tranche-level data are given. This discussion assumes that the ratings would be exactly those implied by the numbers.

Transaction Terms

Basic terms of the target transaction are summarized in Table 21.1.

Collateral Pool

The target collateral pool of forty ABS tranches is given in Table 21.2. For the sake of simplicity, we have chosen n such that each matrix cell contains exactly 100 individual assets. A realistic CDO clearly would rarely fill this requirement, but reducing the number of variables usually helps focus on the credit dynamics of the pool rather than incidental data issues. The tranchewise calibrated parameters a, b, c, t_0, and s are given in Table 21.3. For demonstration purposes, seasoning has been randomly selected from a reasonable distribution.

It should be mentioned in passing that credit card receivables are different in character from other widely held asset classes found in most CDO pools in

Table 21.1
Terms of the Hypothetical Transaction

Item	Value
Class A issued amount	TBD
Class B issued amount	TBD
Class A desired credit rating	Aaa
Class B desired credit rating	TBD
Initial pool balance	$973,362,616
Class A interest rate	TBD
Class B interest rate	TBD
Principal allocation	Pro Rata
Spread account (% of pool)	1.5%
Servicing fee (paid monthly)	1.0%
Trustee fee (paid monthly)	0.20%
Legal final maturity	December 2030

that these receivables are inherently short-duration assets. To transform them into the required long-duration ABS liability structures, they are continuously sold to monolithic revolving legal entities (see the "Revolving Periods" section, later in this chapter) known as *master trusts*. The latter eventually terminate over amortization periods commensurate with asset behavior. As a result, the cash flow dynamics of credit card receivables structures are different from those of other asset classes and require special handling outside the scope of this book.

The objective of this chapter is not to give a comprehensive treatment of each asset class in a CDO pool, but merely to address the crux of asset valuation within a unified context. Digressing on the additional complexities of realistic transactions would only take us away from the core issues. However, readers should be reminded that each new layer of realism in the cash flow analysis is normally amply rewarded by reduced credit enhancement requirements. As pointed out many other places in this book, structured finance is unique in its ability to give credence to capital efficiency via statistical analysis.

Before moving onto final results, we take some time to discuss the ad hoc numerical method used in the analysis of correlations. Intermediate results are provided as an inside look into the workings of the method. For the sake of completeness, the Tchebychev root-locus scattering method is implemented in the Visual Basic code supplied in the appendix.

Treatment of Correlations

Recall from the discussion of covariance matrix simulation in chapter 17 that the general problem of correlating arbitrary random variables is not solvable

Table 21.2
Hypothetical Collateral Pool

Asset ID: Tranche No.	Sector	Rating	B ($)	APR	WAC (%)	WAM	n
1	Credit cards	Baa3	25,112,576	7.60	10.98	40	4,000
2	Autos	Baa1	23,284,005	8.57	11.25	55	5,500
3	Credit cards	Baa1	30,077,709	6.80	10.35	45	4,500
4	Autos	Baa1	23,111,842	7.89	12.08	62	6,200
5	Home equities	Baa2	27,057,725	9.61	10.72	276	27,600
6	Autos	Baa1	25,778,633	8.28	12.16	62	6,200
7	Aircraft leases	Baa1	25,566,092	8.50	9.39	247	24,700
8	Credit cards	Baa3	20,214,989	9.11	16.07	40	4,000
9	Credit cards	Baa2	26,134,593	9.38	13.20	40	4,000
10	Mortgages	Ba1	26,325,455	10.13	11.54	267	26,700
11	Autos	Baa2	23,351,117	7..27	11.62	66	6,600
12	Settlements	Baa1	18,819,745	8.03	9.04	287	28,700
13	Home equities	A2	29,640,529	6.00	7.26	204	20,400
14	Settlements	Baa1	27,776,923	8.68	9.56	256	25,600
15	Credit cards	Baa2	25,912,273	7.65	10.90	45	4,500
16	Autos	Baa2	21,016,234	9.65	12.92	53	5,300
17	Settlements	Baa1	25,126,090	9.43	10.15	238	23,800
18	Credit cards	Ba1	24,315,312	10.22	13.61	55	5,500
19	Settlements	A2	22,451,681	8.14	9.07	260	26,000
20	Autos	A3	25,634,083	9.00	12.73	69	6,900
21	Credit cards	Baa2	27,267,635	6.83	9.22	48	4,800
22	Mortgages	Baa3	19,873,383	6.50	7.86	321	32,100
23	Credit cards	Baa1	22,360,362	8.28	11.50	44	4,400
24	12b-1 fees	Baa2	26,740,858	8.38	12.27	41	4,100
25	Autos	Ba2	21,959,411	9.85	13.60	54	5,400
26	Home equities	Ba1	23,649,848	9.97	11.24	276	27,600
27	Autos	Ba1	23,926,214	9.30	12.69	69	6,900
28	Aircraft leases	Ba3	22,468,785	9.45	9.75	255	25,500
29	Autos	Ba1	24,860,873	8.42	12.57	59	5,900
30	Credit cards	Baa1	23,652,389	7.59	10.20	55	5,500
31	Mortgages	Baa2	24,141,427	6.50	7.45	223	22,300
32	Credit cards	A3	31,055,666	7.84	10.89	53	5,300
33	Autos	Ba3	26,034,356	9.38	13.30	68	6,800
34	Mortgages	Baa1	23,079,407	6.50	8.05	242	25,500
35	Settlements	Ba2	22,262,043	10.48	10.89	225	22,500
36	Credit cards	Ba2	19,352,822	9.04	12.20	54	5,400
37	12b-1 fees	Baa1	19,662,932	8.81	12.08	58	5,800
38	Autos	Ba2	23,822,557	8.29	12.94	47	6,900
39	Credit cards	Baa2	25,314,083	7.27	8.54	51	5,100
40	Credit cards	Baa3	25,169,959	7.52	8.95	41	4,100

Table 21.3
Parameters of the Hypothetical Collateral Pool

Asset ID: Tranche No.	Sector	a	b	c	t_0	s
1	Credit cards	6.6	1.0	0.04	40	6
2	Autos	2.1	1.5	0.15	22	8
3	Credit cards	5.7	1.0	0.04	45	10
4	Autos	3.3	1.5	0.15	25	6
5	Home equities	31.4	2.0	0.03	79	19
6	Autos	3.2	1.5	0.15	25	8
7	Aircraft leases	20.8	1.0	0.03	99	12
8	Credit cards	14.3	1.0	0.04	40	1
9	Credit cards	5.9	1.0	0.04	40	3
10	Mortgages	47.5	2.0	0.03	77	23
11	Autos	4.2	1.5	0.15	26	8
12	Settlements	140.7	1.0	0.004	287	14
13	Home equities	14.8	2.0	0.03	58	11
14	Settlements	119.2	1.0	0.004	256	21
15	Credit cards	6.7	1.0	0.04	45	1
16	Autos	2.6	1.5	0.15	21	6
17	Settlements	97.6	1.0	0.004	238	10
18	Credit cards	12.2	1.0	0.04	55	5
19	Settlements	94.5	1.0	0.004	260	13
20	Autos	3.3	1.5	0.15	28	5
21	Credit cards	6.0	1.0	0.04	48	3
22	Mortgages	53.1	2.0	0.03	92	22
23	Credit cards	5.5	1.0	0.04	44	5
24	12b-1 fees	7.4	1.5	0.03	17	7
25	Autos	4.4	1.5	0.15	22	9
26	Home equities	47.5	2.0	0.03	79	15
27	Autos	5.2	1.5	0.15	28	10
28	Aircraft leases	42.6	1.0	0.05	102	14
29	Autos	4.5	1.5	0.15	23	5
30	Credit cards	6.5	1.0	0.04	55	5
31	Mortgages	20.7	2.0	0.03	64	18
32	Credit cards	5.9	1.0	0.04	53	10
33	Autos	7.5	1.5	0.15	27	7
34	Mortgages	26.2	2.0	0.03	69	26
35	Settlements	158.5	1.0	0.004	225	12
36	Credit cards	13.0	1.0	0.04	54	4
37	12b-1 fees	8.2	1.5	0.03	23	2
38	Autos	3.8	1.5	0.15	19	6
39	Credit cards	4.0	1.0	0.04	51	9
40	Credit cards	4.3	1.0	0.04	41	3

exactly—at least not for dimensions higher than three or four. It could be cleanly solved only in the very special case of a set of normal deviates. However, normality should never be an operational constraint. The key analytic challenge is to strike a balance between reflecting the correlation structure in the macroeconomy and preserving the properties of the loss distributions underlying individual asset pools. What follows is a description of a method that strives for a workable, reasonable compromise between the requirements of correlations and distributional rigor

Before embarking on this journey, readers should remember that there are many mathematically valid ways to handle correlations. The simplest is to assume that they don't matter! This assumption is not necessarily simpleminded; many divergent views currently exist on the topic. In many instances, assuming the independence of cash flow behavior at the asset level (in other words, an absence of correlation structure) is a politically useful compromise. The authors do not recommend this approach on analytical grounds. On the other hand, correlation structures are rarely chosen so that the resulting matrix is more favorable to the issuer as would be the case under the independence model. In practice, correlations seem to be granted the artificial character of always being "net positive" as opposed to "net negative," in order to confirm preconceived notions. Consistency is to be preferred to false conservatism. It is better never to use correlations than to abuse them. Best is always to use them, but only under a transparent regime. If correlations are to be included inside numerical methods, the data should be used objectively and the results accepted regardless of whether the results "make the transaction look better." Credit analysts should view the arbitrary selection of correlation matrices with suspicion. The next section does not purport fully to address the selection method but suggests a rational scheme that is not subject to circularity.

One Method of Correlation Treatment

Once the basic model of this chapter has been written, incorporating correlations within this asset class is a straightforward task that can be accomplished in the following stepwise manner:

1. Acquire the desired correlation matrix $\mathbf{V}$. The matrix $\mathbf{V}$ will have as many dimensions as the number of independent asset classes in the given pool. In the case of a pool like the one in this section, it will have seven dimensions.
2. Perform the n-dimensional Cholesky decomposition algorithm outlined in chapter 16.
3. Using an initial set of independently drawn, standard normal deviates $\mathbf{x}$, derive the corresponding set of correlated deviates $\mathbf{y}$ by equation (21.7).
4. Map each of the $\mathbf{y}$ deviate vectors, initially defined on some range $[a, b]$, to a new set of deviates $\mathbf{y}'$ defined on the new range $[0, 1]$ using a linear transformation of the form $\mathbf{y}' = \alpha\mathbf{y} + \beta$.

5. Perform the Tchebychev root-locus scattering algorithm (discussed shortly) on the mapped variables using a reasonable choice for the scattering parameter. The value 0.5 is not a requirement but achieves a midpoint balance between the two conflicting requirements of distributional accuracy and correlative fidelity. This will lead to a set of shifted variables $\mathbf{y}''$ derived from $\mathbf{y}'$ but still defined on the interval [0, 1].

6. Use the shifted set $\mathbf{y}''$ to correlate each ABS tranche inside the pool appropriately. This is accomplished by using the $\mathbf{y}''$ vectors to select (via IDFM) macroeconomic influence factors inside a Monte Carlo simulation during which the microeconomic parameters of equation (21.2) are left unchanged. Given the asset class represented by each individual tranche, the appropriate value of $\mathbf{y}''$ is selected. Under the basic correlation framework, it is thus assumed implicitly that all tranches within a single asset class are perfectly correlated to each other and to the index causing the correlation effect.

7. Steps 3 through 6 are repeated for each Monte Carlo scenario. Two to three thousand scenarios are usually needed to achieve statistical convergence.

Readers familiar with chapter 16 will remember that, according to the Cholesky decomposition method, a set of standard normal deviates $\mathbf{y}$ with this correlation matrix can be synthesized given a cash flow correlation matrix $\mathbf{V}$ for pool assets and starting from a vector of independently drawn, standard normal deviates $\mathbf{x}$. As we saw, these new correlated vectors $\mathbf{y}$ are defined by

$$\mathbf{y} = \mathbf{Lx}. \tag{21.7}$$

In equation (21.7), $\mathbf{L}$ is the lower-triangular Cholesky matrix given by the familiar condition

$$\mathbf{LL}^T = \mathbf{V}. \tag{21.8}$$

Alternative Method of Correlation Treatment

The assumption that all ABS tranches within an asset class are perfectly correlated to each other is the most expensive position in terms of credit enhancement, something we are by no means advocating. It is to be expected, however, that an analyst at a rating agency, when faced with this issue, would probably embrace this option. A different, more liberal approach could assume that each tranche can have its own idiosyncratic credit behavior while remaining 100% correlated to its macro-index.

To show how to do this cleanly, suppose that for some asset class, the pool contains five ABS tranches whose cash flows must be estimated. Under the conservative approach discussed before, we would have simply taken the relevant element of the appropriate vector $\mathbf{y}''$ and used it as our sole IDFM argument for all five tranches. In fact, this is how the results discussed in this section were derived.

By contrast, to simulate intra-asset class independence we must select five independent random deviates from some probability distribution. The easiest way to do this is to choose a distribution with a mean equal to the appropriate element of $\mathbf{y}''$ and a standard deviation equal to that of the corresponding vector. A readily available distribution that also fulfills the requirements of IDFM is the beta distribution. For instance, if "Autos" were the asset class associated with the time series y_1'', then at each time t we would select five independent random deviates from a beta distribution with a mean $\mu = y_1''(t)$ and a standard deviation $\sigma = \sqrt{E[(y_1'' - \mu)^2]}$. This way, the resulting deviates still belong to the interval $[0, 1]$, a conditio sine qua non of IDFM.

From a credit enhancement perspective, this second approach is less conservative but equally valid analytically. Any combination of the two is possible and should be investigated if only in the spirit of parametric sensitivity.

The Derivation of Matrix V

The derivation of a suitable correlation matrix for use in numerical simulation is by no means obvious. The correlations we are trying to capture are not *default* but rather *cash flow shortfall* correlations. As mentioned before, in contrast to corporate loans or bonds, ABS securities do not default in the corporate sense but instead are subject to potential cash shortfalls over their lifetimes. Although it may be obvious a long time before maturity that a particular security will not deliver its promised yield, such realization is wholly different in character from a corporate default.

The Corporate Default Case

Within the corporate paradigm, it is possible to define default correlations in a way suggested by Stephen Kealhofer of the KMV Corporation.[2] KMV derives the default *covariance* between two individual exposures in a portfolio by using equity correlations within an option-theoretic framework.

KMV first computes the actual probability that both exposures would default together and subtracts from this the probability of their joint default under an independence assumption. The default *correlation* is computed by dividing that difference by the individual standard deviations of default for each individual exposure. In other words, if ρ_{XY} is the correlation between two default events X and Y associated with two portfolio exposures, and $P(A)$ is the default probability of exposure A, then we have

$$\rho_{XY} = \frac{P(X, Y) - P(X)P(Y)}{\sigma_X \sigma_Y} \qquad (21.9)$$

Although equation (21.9) suffers from confusing the common-sense notions of linear correlation and independence, it is still a consistent measure of association between default events that can be used profitably in the context of corporate default analysis.

The ABS Cash Flow Case

The previous formulation is not applicable in structured finance because, theoretically speaking, there is no singular and identifiable event we can call default. What happens instead is that more or less cash than expected comes into the structure as time unfolds. What is needed, therefore, is a good proxy for the ebb and flow of cash streams associated with selected asset classes. The following suggestion is not a bulletproof analytical solution but an alternative method: that of using broad-based market indices as proxies for the required cash flow correlations. It is true that such indices are backward looking, whereas forward-looking indices are preferable. While this is a shortcoming that affects all methods, the transparency it affords greatly mitigates this weakness. In the final analysis, contingent events are by definition unpredictable.

Once this method is accepted, the remaining problem is to find empirical data to compute the correlations. The Dow Jones Titan Indexes published daily in the *Wall Street Journal* would be an example of indices that are credible, independently generated, transparent, and extensive in their coverage of industrial sectors.[3] Indices such as those contain more than enough data to compute a robust estimate of **V**. As required, they can be supplemented by major macroeconomic time series (unemployment, gross national product growth, etc.) published by most governments or central banks.

Nevertheless, no single method or algorithm can be said to be right or wrong. This aspect of the credit analysis must remain in large measure subjective but by no means arbitrary. By choosing externally produced and validated data to derive correlation matrices, we are able both to avoid circular thinking and to produce consistent results.

The Tchebychev Root-Locus Scattering Method

This section describes in some detail the implementation of the Tchebychev root-locus scattering algorithm, a method that attempts to strike a balance between the competing requirements of correlation and distributional assumptions. To do this, we use the roots of Tchebychev polynomials of various orders. Recall from chapter 19 that the n roots of T_n, the Tchebychev polynomial of degree n, are given by the formula

$$x_k = \cos\left(\frac{2k-1}{n}\left(\frac{\pi}{2}\right)\right), \, k = 1, 2, \ldots, n. \tag{21.10}$$

Recall also that the roots of T_n are not equally spaced, but rather are concentrated at both ends of their range of definition $[-1, 1]$—for example, see Figure 19.7. In fact, we have already used that property to significantly reduce the maximum error made when using the Lagrange interpolation formula to approximate functions given as discrete point-pairs. Recall also that, when discussing the beta distribution with parameters α and β, we mentioned that this distribution reduces to the uniform distribution under the special case $\alpha = \beta = 1$. For most choices of the parameters, the distribution will have the expected bell-shaped curvature, and will be truncated to fit into the range $[0, 1]$.

By construction, the $\mathbf{y}''$ have been arranged in a certain temporal sequence by the Cholesky decomposition method. However, we can also view them in a pure statistical context, ignoring the timewise correlations that exist between them. In other words, they can simply be fitted to a statistical distribution given the domain of the independent variable they occupy. Suppose we do this and fit the appropriate beta distribution to the $\mathbf{y}''$; since they are standard normal variables, the map will be such that mapped deviates will have a mean of approximately 0.5, and will correspond to a beta distribution with nearly equal values of α and β, albeit different from and higher than unity. This is because the beta distribution has $\mu = \alpha/(\alpha + \beta)$, yielding a mean of 0.5 for the case of equal α and β, regardless of their value.

Now, if α and β were set equal to 1, they would yield a perfectly uniform distribution and would reproduce exactly the intended distribution once used inside the IDFM.[4] Hence, the fundamental idea behind the root-locus method is to modify the location of $\mathbf{y}''$ such that the common value of α or β is decreased to some intermediate value between its original value and unity, thus achieving the required balance. In most cases, this intermediate value will be set exactly halfway between these two points.

For instance, say the value of α (or β) that result from the above mapping process is 5. The idea would then be to modify $\mathbf{y}''$ such that $\alpha = 5 - (5 - 1)/2 = 3$. This is demonstrated generically in Figure 21.3. Credit analysts may select any value of α between 5 and 1 as a target, but a choice other than the midpoint value will favor one or the other of our conflicting requirements—a position difficult to defend given the importance of remaining faithful to both intents.

Once it has been admitted that the values of the $\mathbf{y}''$ must be changed, the best way to do this remains unclear. A major stumbling block is that such changes must be effected while respecting the ordinal relationships between the $\mathbf{y}''$. Figure 21.3 shows the y''_i without regard to their temporal ordering. If we cannot remain faithful to the cardinality of the $\mathbf{y}''$, we must at least retain their ordinal ranking, thereby maintaining the directionality of the relationships between the cash flows of the assets in the pool. If the alteration process must retain the original relative ordering of the $\mathbf{y}''$, one cannot simply displace the individual y''_i at will in an effort to reduce α to its target value.

Second, the disturbances introduced must deliver maximal efficiency at the lowest cost in terms of lost correlation. Since the motivation behind the entire exercise is to sample both ends of the range $[0, 1]$ at the appropriate rate, it would seem to make sense to preferentially move the elements farthest from the mean of 0.5. This would have the favorable twofold impact of modifying the associated beta parameters more quickly than a move at the center of the range and, more importantly, of simultaneously increasing the sampling rate

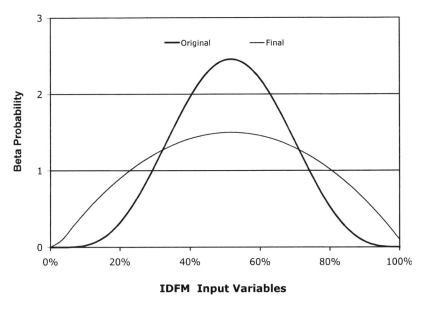

Figure 21.3. Tchebychev Root Locus Scattering

of the ends of the corresponding statistical distribution where it matters most. Putting these requirements together forces us to conclude that our modification algorithm must be skewed toward the ends of the range [0, 1].

The easiest way to implement this manipulation systematically would be to take advantage of the spatial distribution of the roots of Tchebychev polynomials. Since these roots are arranged to form a skewed pattern with concentrations at locations where they are needed, a shifting process that uses their positions will accomplish our two goals simultaneously. For an N-element vector, Tchebychev scattering is therefore based on a selective shifting of the $\mathbf{y}''$ in the following twofold manner:

1. Using successively lower-order polynomials, starting from degree $n = N/\varepsilon$ down to $n = a$, shift the elements of $\mathbf{y}''$ closest to the roots of each polynomial in the sequence while retaining their relative positioning. The parameters ε and a are chosen by trial and error such that the sequence converges smoothly.
2. Using successively higher-order polynomials, starting from degree $n = a$ up to $n = N/\varepsilon$, shift the elements of $\mathbf{y}''$ in the same manner.

This is an iterative solution in which the vector elements approach their final resting positions successively as each complete cycle unfolds, and with relatively little disturbance to their original positions.

Assuming $\alpha = \alpha_i$ and $\alpha = \alpha_f$ are initial and final values of the associated beta distributions, this cyclic procedure will traverse all intermediary α positions along the way such that the number of cycles required to achieve any value of α is a measure of distance to the original location. This way, the extent to which the original correlated distributions have been disturbed can be placed within a numerical context.

For N data points x_i, $i = 1, 2, \ldots, N$, where index i refers to time, the Tchebychev root-locus scattering algorithm can be formalized as follows:

1. Starting with $n = \text{int}(N/\varepsilon)$, map the roots r_i, $i = 1, 2, \ldots, n$ of the Tchebychev polynomial or order n from the range $[-1, 1]$ to $[0, 1]$ using a linear transformation of the form $r_i' = ar_i + b$.
2. Rank the time series x_i in ascending order from 0 to 1 and label the resulting ascending series y_i, $i = 1, 2, \ldots, N$.
3. Locate the y_i closest to the root r_i' from step 1 and shift it according to the following rules. If $r_i' \leq 0.5$, then $y_i = y_i - \delta(y_i - y_{i-1})$; if $r_i' \geq 0.5$, then $y_i = y_i + \delta(y_{i+1} - y_i)$. The net impact of these rules will be to shift elements while preserving their rank order. The parameter δ is a scaling factor controlling the process. Its value is usually found by trial and error, but we recommend $\delta = 0.5$ as a first guess.
4. Repeat step 3 with a sequence of Tchebychev polynomials of descending orders $n = \text{int}(N/[\varepsilon + 1])$ to approximately $n \approx N/10$.

The order of the last Tchebychev polynomial in the sequence is usually found by trial and error—that is, no hard-and-fast rule may be given. In practice, an order of magnitude difference between the first and the last polynomial seems to work well without leading to serious curvature distortions in the resulting beta distribution.

5. Repeat steps 3 and 4 in ascending order starting with $n \approx N/10$ to $n = \text{int}(N/\varepsilon)$.
6. Steps 3, 4, and 5 constitute one full cycle. They should be repeated as many times as required to achieve the target value α_T. That number is the midpoint between the original value $\alpha = \alpha_i$ and unity, that is, $\alpha_T = \alpha_i - ([1 - \alpha_i]/2)$. The expression $(\alpha_i - \alpha_T)/(\alpha_i - 1)$ is the scattering parameter s_p. We recommend $s_p = 0.5$, but any other value in $[0, 1]$ may be used when warranted.
7. Once $\alpha = \alpha_T$, invert the original ranking transformation from step 2 to recover the shifted and correlated deviates in time-domain; that is, perform $y_i \rightarrow x_i$ using the original time sequence to do the re-ordering.
8. Use the new, shifted values of x_i inside the IDFM algorithm for Monte Carlo simulation.

Repeat steps 2 through 8 for each Monte Carlo scenario.

For instance, for a vector consisting of thirty years of monthly data, the choice $\varepsilon = 2$ would lead to the Tchebychev half-sequence 180, 120, 90, 72, 60, 51, 45, 40, 36. The other half-sequence would simply proceed in the reverse direction. By choosing other values for ε, we could make the iteration finer and lengthen the sequence at will. This could be useful for smoothing out of the distribution of the shifted y_i.

Intermediate Results

Cholesky Decomposition

Our objectives in this subsection are threefold:

1. Show how close to the original correlation matrix the Cholesky decomposition allows us to come.
2. Map the resulting correlated deviates to the range [0, 1] and verify the neutral impact on the correlation matrix.
3. Obtain the value of the corresponding beta distribution parameters α and β as an input to the Tchebychev scattering algorithm (see next subsection). Compare those values to our working assumption $\alpha = \beta$.

First, assume the analyst is given the sectorwise seven-dimensional correlation matrix $\mathbf{V}$ displayed in Table 21.4 in connection with the analysis of the previous target pool. Note that $\mathbf{V}$ satisfies the required symmetry condition $\mathbf{V} = \mathbf{V}^T$; that is also satisfies the positive-definite condition will be assumed.

If the matrix is derived from actual data, positive-definiteness will always obtain, and the Cholesky decomposition will always work. Otherwise, the program will eventually attempt to take the square root of a negative number, which will result in an error. If this occurs, the analyst may have to make ad hoc changes to $\mathbf{V}$ entries in order to satisfy the second condition. This would have to be done in the least disruptive manner, probably by going to the source and amending the data appropriately. This problem sometimes occurs when analysts try to create a correlation matrix ex nihilo and "stress" the correlations at will, which cannot be done in a vacuum. An empirically valid correlation matrix can come only from data, and the attempt to forgo this requirement may backfire. Hence the need for a formal procedure.

Table 21.4
Correlation Matrix for the Hypothetical Pool

CBO of ABS	Credit Cards	Autos	Home Equity	Mortgages	Settlements	12b-1 Fees	Aircraft Leases
Credit cards	1.00	0.78	0.55	−0.96	0.60	−0.68	0.50
Autos	0.78	1.00	0.30	−0.75	0.37	−0.94	0.29
Home equity	0.55	0.30	1.00	−0.56	1.00	−0.18	0.96
Mortgages	−0.96	−0.75	−0.56	1.00	−0.61	0.66	−0.53
Settlement	0.60	0.37	1.00	−0.61	1.00	−0.25	0.95
12b-1 fees	−0.68	−0.94	−0.18	0.66	−0.25	1.00	−0.17
Aircraft leases	0.50	0.29	0.96	−0.53	0.95	−0.17	1.00

Table 21.5
Results of Applying the Cholesky Decomposition to the Hypothetical Pool

Cholesky Matrix	Credit Cards	Autos	Home Equity	Mortgages	Settlements	12b-1 Fees	Aircraft Leases
Credit cards	1.000						
Autos	0.782	0.623					
Home equity	0.548	−0.205	0.811				
Mortgages	−0.965	0.003	−0.041	0.260			
Settlement	0.601	−0.155	0.783	0.003	0.040		
12b-1 fees	−0.684	−0.658	0.078	0.023	0.038	0.303	
Aircraft leases	0.505	−0.168	0.797	−0.023	0.028	0.011	0.283

The Cholesky decomposition algorithm, reproduced in *Numerical Recipes*,[5] yields the values shown in Table 21.5 for the lower-triangular seven-dimensional matrix **L**.

To get a feel for the range of errors that can generally be expected of this method, assume we spawned a set of seven independently distributed, standard normal vectors of 360 elements each, corresponding (for instance) to a CDO transaction with a 360-month legal final maturity date. The correlated vectors are computed using

$$\mathbf{Lx} = \mathbf{y}. \tag{21.11}$$

With the usual definitions $\bar{y}_i = E(y_i)$ and $\sigma_i = \sqrt{E[(y_i - \bar{y}_i)^2]}$, their empirical correlation matrix is then calculated using the defining equation

$$v_{ij} = \frac{E[(y_i - \bar{y}_i)(y_j - \bar{y}_j)]}{\sigma_i \sigma_j}. \tag{21.12}$$

This process yields the typical result displayed in Table 21.6. Coming within two decimal places, the fit is quite good. However, the repeatability of these re-

Table 21.6
Results of Applying the Empirical Correlation Matrix to the Hypothetical Pool

Empirical V-Matrix	Credit Cards	Autos	Home Equity	Mortgages	Settlements	12b-1 Fees	Aircraft Leases
Credit cards	1.00	0.79	0.56	−0.96	0.61	−0.67	0.52
Autos	0.79	1.00	0.30	−0.75	0.37	−0.94	0.30
Home equity	0.56	0.30	1.00	−0.57	1.00	−0.16	0.96
Mortgages	−0.96	−0.75	−0.57	1.00	−0.62	0.65	−0.53
Settlement	0.61	0.37	1.00	−0.62	1.00	−0.23	0.96
12b-1 fees	−0.67	−0.94	−0.16	0.65	−0.23	1.00	−0.15
Aircraft leases	0.52	0.30	0.96	−0.53	0.96	−0.15	1.00

Table 21.7
Tabulated Results of Thirty Scenarios Using Cholesky Decomposition

Scenario ID	χ	Scenario ID	χ	Scenario ID	χ
1	1.85%	11	11.54%	21	8.35%
2	8.55%	12	7.53%	22	5.13%
3	1.52%	13	1.92%	23	6.54%
4	16.34%	14	8.73%	24	1.90%
5	5.97%	15	2.64%	25	6.75%
6	1.52%	16	3.30%	26	3.46%
7	3.22%	17	9.25%	27	3.99%
8	11.00%	18	11.95%	28	3.46%
9	8.54%	19	10.10%	29	5.08%
10	8.68%	20	7.23%	30	2.68%

sults depends on the degree to which the set of standard normal vectors generated as inputs approximate the seven-dimensional identity matrix (see "Covariance Matrix Simulation," chapter 17). There is no guarantee that a set of (computer-generated, independent) standard normal vectors will have zero entries off their correlation matrix's main diagonal.

The range of such errors can be investigated by performing numerical experiments in which Cholesky-correlated deviates are repeatedly generated, their correlation matrix computed as in Table 21.6 and the distance to the target matrix measured.

First, define the figure of merit

$$\chi = \frac{1}{49} \sum_{i,j=1}^{7} \left| \frac{(v_{ij}^{\text{actual}} - v_{ij}^{\text{target}})}{v_{ij}^{\text{target}}} \right|$$

that will be used to measure the quality of the statistical approximation $\mathbf{V}^{\text{actual}}$ to the desired result $\mathbf{V}^{\text{target}}$. If all matrix entries of $\mathbf{V}^{\text{target}}$ have been matched exactly, χ will be zero; otherwise it will measure the mean relative departure from the target value. Table 21.7 gives tabulated values of χ for a series of thirty Cholesky decompositions using vectors of 360 elements in seven dimensions.

Mean value of χ: 6.29%

Standard deviation of χ: 3.75%

Note that, for a thirty-year transaction, the decomposition is fairly accurate. Except for the iteration with an average error of about 17%, the mean error is more or less below 10%, and a 10% mean error in correlation estimation is better than one could hope for. Further, in practice other sources of errors (e.g., those caused by inaccuracies in the definition of $\mathbf{V}$ itself) will usually swamp these errors and make the Cholesky method quite acceptable. Approximation performance can be expected to decrease or increase with the square root of N. In other words, longer legal final maturities are preferable to shorter ones when it comes to simulating correlations, in accordance with common sense.

Also, note in passing that simulation errors can always be reduced by ensuring that the set of independent standard normal vectors used as inputs to the decomposition are more precisely independent—for instance, by using low-discrepancy sequences (see chapter 12 and Appendix A). However, given the usual crudeness of empirical data, this is probably not worth the effort.

Mapping and Beta Distribution Parameters

The next step in our treatment of correlations is to linearly map the correlated vectors to the interval [0, 1] and compute the associated beta parameters. Recall that simple inversion of the defining equations for the mean and variance of a beta distribution yields

$$\alpha = \frac{\mu^2(1-\mu)}{\sigma^2} - \mu \tag{21.13}$$

$$\beta = \alpha\left(\frac{1}{\mu} - 1\right). \tag{21.14}$$

We will use equations (21.13) and (21.14) to derive values for α and β.

Now, defining y_{min} and y_{max} as the original minimum and maximum values, respectively, of the correlated deviates obtained from our Cholesky decomposition, and x_i as the deviates to be shifted, the mapping equation is $x_i = (y_i - y_{min})/(y_{max} - y_{min})$. Note that it is both linear and satisfies the boundary conditions $x(y_{min}) = 0$, $x(y_{max}) = 1$.

Figure 20.4 shows a comparison between the implied initial beta distribution given by equations (21.13) and (21.14) and the empirical distribution of deviates. Note that, due to the usual statistical variations, it will rarely be the case that the best least-squares fit will correspond to the values of α and β computed directly from the empirical distribution using equations (21.13) and (21.14). This fit, which would be unacceptable in many other instances, is acceptable here given the fairly crude statistics on which it is based and the use we intend to make of it. The situation is not as bad as it may appear at first blush given that we will perform thousands of Tchebychev transformations within a single Monte Carlo simulation. When repeated distributions are superimposed, the hills and valleys seen in the figure are usually smoothed out.

As indicated earlier, before using these deviates inside our correlation method, we must shift them to create a more uniform empirical distribution for IDFM input—for example, to change the common value of parameters α and β, from about 3 (as in Figure 21.4) to about 2.

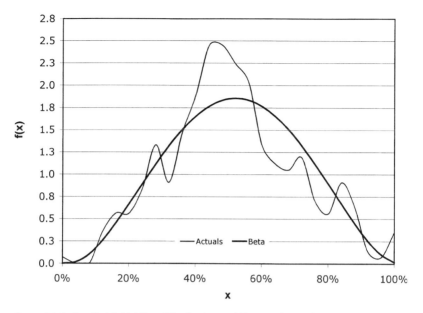

Figure 21.4. Implied Initial Beta Distribution and Empirical Distribution Deviates Compared

Tchebychev Root-Locus Scattering

Table 21.8 shows convergence results obtained with a mapped Cholesky-correlated vector x_i of length $350 \in [0, 1]$ to which the Tchebychev root-locus scattering method has been applied using $s_p = 0.8$. The common value of the beta parameters α and β is shown for each complete hemicycle, starting with α_i.

Figure 21.5 shows the complete uniform convergence history for an actual Tchebychev scattering in the case of a vector of 350 elements using the values $\varepsilon = 3$, $a = 10$. In the figure, the ordinate is the common value of the beta-distribution parameters α and β at each stage. The chosen final value was 1.37, and the starting value was 2.83. Despite the usual recommendation that s_p should be around 50%, we opt for 80% here merely to illustrate the method and test its convergence properties. This should not be interpreted to mean that we endorse this choice in practice.

The empirical distributions associated with these beta-distribution equivalents are shown in Figure 21.6. Note that the final distribution shows how the scattering algorithm takes probability mass away from areas closer to the middle of the x range (the inside circles) and pushes it toward either end (the outside circles) while leaving the bulk of the correlation structure intact. This is to be expected, given the root distributions of the associated Tchebychev polynomials along the hemicyclical sequences. Bear in mind that this case was

Table 21.8
Beta Distribution Parameters under the Root-Locus Scattering Method

Cycle ID	α, β
0	2.833
1	2.567
2	2.336
3	2.125
4	1.943
5	1.779
6	1.635
7	1.510
8	1.395

done for illustration purposes only. Ideally, the final distribution should be much less lopsided than Figure 21.6. For this reason, $s_p = 0.5$ is usually satisfactory.

Figure 21.7 shows the beta-equivalent distributions corresponding to the starting and ending situations depicted before. Although the actual ideal beta-curvatures are not replicated in the empirical distributions of Figure 21.6, the main goal of the method is to shift points away from the center toward the ends where they may properly influence the level of credit losses within the structure. As thousands of IDFM-based Monte Carlo scenarios are performed,

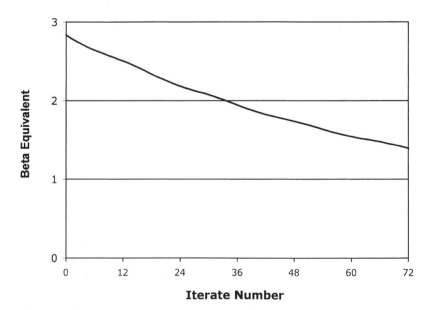

Figure 21.5. Tchebychev Scattering Convergence History

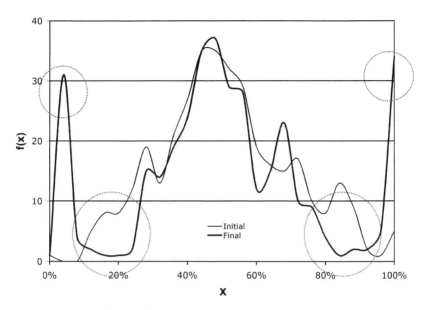

Figure 21.6. Distributions of IDFM Inputs

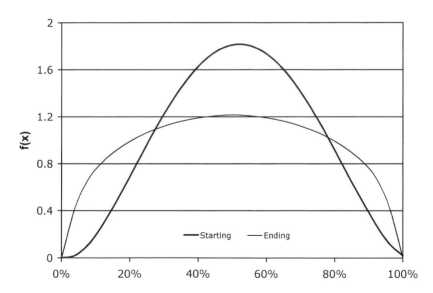

Figure 21.7. Beta-Equivalent Distributions

the net distribution smoothes itself out and comes fairly close to the ideal case of Figure 21.7.

The final distribution is nonstandard, to say the least! As discussed, it attempts to strike a balance between conflicting requirements. We have increased the sampling rate at the ends of the corresponding binomials used inside our Monte Carlo simulation, causing higher sampling in areas of severely reduced cash flows. The result is more conservative and more heavily stressed than under the straight correlation case. As pointed out before, using $s_p < 0.5$ would reduce the sampling rate at the ends of the range, producing a more faithful rendition of the intended correlation structure while reducing the probability of an extreme cash flow scenario.

Some will argue that we have simultaneously, and perhaps unintentionally, increased sampling rates in areas of increased cash flows as well, but such scenarios are no more important to the ultimate rating of the securities than are those found in the middle of the range. The key is to increase sampling rates where they count without causing the probability mass to fall asymmetrically in areas unfavorable to the issuer, with punitive consequences. Since statistical distributions have two ends, increasing the proportion of unfavorable cases ad hoc without a corresponding increase in that of favorable cases is incorrect and unfair to the issuer and the investor. Investors need to be aware of the realistic risk profile of their investments, and issuers need a balanced view of their portfolios to be taken.

The impact of this spreading technique depends on the asset correlation structure itself. For net-positive correlation structures, a de-emphasis on the correlation structure could be expected to offset (to some extent) the effects of increased distributional rigor, making the ratings on the securities relatively insensitive to the scattering parameter over a wide range of s_p values. This is an ideal credit situation, for it relieves the analyst of the burden of picking the right s_p value. Unfortunately, the exact opposite would tend to occur in net-negative correlation structures. Increasing s_p would both reduce the beneficial credit impact of correlations and increase the end sampling rates. In this case, the analyst would have to make a pure judgment call. As a result, securities issued under such circumstances would inevitably be riskier, since "model risk" would be added to all the other risks already considered. How to enhance for this increase in risk is an open question.

Yield Curve Modeling

All the models in this book assume prior knowledge of the term structure of interest rates. Given the size of the task, the low predictive power of most analytical models is not surprising. In the main, interest rates remain fundamentally unpredictable for this reason. However, for purposes of this book we may assume that the current term structure of interest rates is known and available to credit analysts. In practice, market rates for ABS securities can be regarded as forming an implicit term and credit spread structure, obviating the need for yield curve modeling. For now, a BOTE model supplying ABS credit spreads suffices. The following is a simple diffusion model of the form

$$r(t, \Delta_{IRR}) = \alpha\sqrt{t\Delta_{IRR}} + f(t). \qquad (21.15)$$

In equation (21.15), $r(t, \Delta_{IRR})$ is the rate of interest for a given term and rating level (expressed as a reduction of yield), α is a calibration multiplier, and $f(t)$ is the basic risk-free curve that must generally satisfy conditions of asymptotic behavior and negative curvature. With Δ_{IRR} expressed in percentage terms (e.g., 15 bps = 0.15%) and time in years, our choices for α and $f(t)$ are as follows:

$$\alpha = 2 \qquad (21.16)$$

$$f(t) = \frac{r_\infty}{1 + \beta e^{-\delta t}}; \; r_\infty = 8.00\%, \beta = 0.9, \delta = 0.21 \qquad (21.17)$$

These choices lead to the curves depicted in Figure 21.8 for selected rating levels. For instance, the credit spread above treasuries on a two-year average life Baa2 security with an average reduction of yield of 20 bps would be

$$\text{Spread}(2 \text{ yrs, Baa2}) = 2\sqrt{2(0.20)} = 126 \text{ bps.}$$

By contrast, the spread on a three-year Ba2 security with an average reduction of yield of 75 bps would be

$$\text{Spread}(3 \text{ yrs, Ba2}) = 2\sqrt{3(0.75)} = 300 \text{ bps.}$$

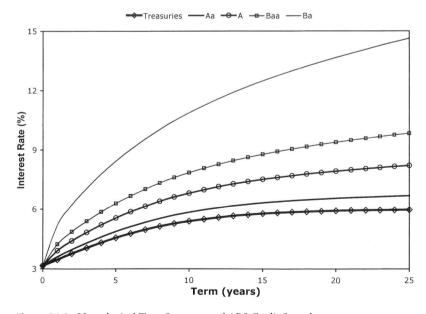

Figure 21.8. Hypothetical Term Structure and ABS Credit Spreads

This credit-spread structure was used in deriving the output ratings shown in the next section. Readers should remember that the quality of conclusions stemming from the analysis of CDOs of ABS is in no way affected by the accuracy of yield curve models, since any model can be used. What matters is the relationship between the tranches of a given CDO, not whether interest rates can be predicted.

Revolving Periods

The results and conclusions presented herein are intended for amortizing structures. Revolving structures add another layer of implementation complexity to structured financings without, however, adding to the CDO conceptualization framework. To address the analytical issues related to revolving pools would jeopardize fundamental understanding and obscure the real issues. In this section, we merely outline those difficulties and point the way toward a solution.

If, during some length of time from inception, principal collections deposited in trust accounts are not returned to investors as partial repayments but instead are used to buy new receivables, the trust is said to be in a *revolving period*, so called because the amount invested in the structure remains constant. For the transaction to come to an end, principal collections must be returned to investors during an amortization period that normally begins at the end of the revolving period until trust liabilities have been repaid in full (or not).

The main advantage of a revolving structure is that it makes possible the extension of the life of a trust consisting of short-dated assets, enabling it thereby to issue long-dated liabilities. Recently, the revolving-period concept has been applied to cases where the assets are of sufficient duration, like CDOs, with mixed results from a credit standpoint. Revolving periods are riskier for the obvious reason that they lengthen the time until investors receive their return of principal. They are also riskier because the quality of the receivables in the pool tends to decrease over time, as new receivables are unknown a priori. Asset-based covenants are usually in place to guard somewhat against this potential deterioration, but it is difficult to draft covenants that are effective limits without simultaneously constraining collateral managers unnaturally. As a result, the "implicit preapproval" of new receivables during the revolving period usually causes average credit quality to decrease over time. The extent of quality decline must be ascertained at closing in order to properly assess credit enhancement requirements.

To prevent the credit situation from deteriorating in this manner, revolving structures are usually equipped with triggers that end the revolving period prematurely and cause principal collections to be retuned to investors immediately. From that point on, whether investors are repaid in full depends on the rate of collateral deterioration versus that of principal repayment, including defaulted receivables that are then regarded as principal payments. The main value provided by credit enhancement stems from the safeguards it provides against excessive collateral deterioration.

The analysis of revolving structures becomes much more complicated by the revolving-period requirement to abide by asset-based covenants. The analysis of revolving CDO structures thus requires these tests to be properly analyzed to reflect the rejection of ineligible collateral. Failing that, the rate of potential collateral deterioration imputed to trust assets would be exaggerated by unrestricted asset inclusion.

Meeting eligibility tests is nontrivial, and is compounded by the possibility that eligible assets may not be available. It is quite possible that the intersection of all covenants with market supply is "empty," which would force collateral managers into a corner. As a result, proper analysis requires that the selection process itself be modeled, by synthesizing statistical distributions for new candidate assets to be included in the pool. This may be mathematically impossible to execute, just as it would be physically impossible for collateral managers to execute in the same situation. Knowledge of the unfeasibility of the eligibility constraints emerge out naturally from the analysis, and would force the relaxation of covenants at the expense of credit enhancement. Such intricate dynamics make revolving structures quite complex and increase the level of required analytical expertise by an order of magnitude.

Final Results

As indicated previously, our rating algorithm does not address optimization per se (i.e., the problem of maximizing issuance at given rating levels). The goal is rather to present the first level of analysis of the CDO structure with ABS collateral, and not to question whether more efficient use of the available asset pool could be made via increased sophistication in liability structuring.

The Convergence Process

Recall that our demonstration structure is a plain-vanilla, two-tranche pro rata structure with a starting pool balance of $973 million and a spread account of 1.5% on a current basis with no initial deposit. The goal here is to derive credit ratings for given issuance amounts.

As explained earlier, the nonlinear solution proceeds by first assuming credit ratings and estimated average lives using a BOTE solution or from a previous transaction. The results are fed to the Monte Carlo engine to compute mean average lives and average yield reductions, from which output interest rates are derived. These output rates are compared to the input rates and the difference is used to compute new estimated rates for the next Monte Carlo iteration. This procedure is continued until the output rates are, to a sufficient approximation, equal to the input rates. Upon convergence, this method produces final credit ratings and compatible interest rates.

Table 21.9
The Optimal Structure: Case 1-A

CBO of ABS	Class A	Class B
Size	$827,357,700	$146,004,300
Average life (years)	5.93	5.93
ΔIRR (bps)	0.00	0.00
Credit rating	Aaa	Aaa
Interest rate	5.96%	5.96%

Case 1-A: Independent Asset Behavior

Our first case is based on the assumption that all asset tranches behave independently—that is, that no correlation structure exists between the assets. The amount issued in this case was $973,362,000. The converged solution is presented in Table 21.9.

Discussion. The results are as expected. Owing to the highly diversified pool in which every tranche is deemed to behave independently, we can issue at par and have both classes rated Aaa despite the average pool rating of approximately Baa2. Readers may be wondering how it is possible that both classes can be Aaa. Remember that ABS securities lose cash flows over time and that significant excess spread is available to make up for that deterioration as it occurs. The principal allocation mechanism is pro rata, which is the most advantageous to the junior class. Finally, diversification is such that every time one tranche experiences a severe loss, the other tranches tend to perform, since we have assumed no correlation whatsoever. Despite the low absolute number of assets, a pool of forty ABS tranches is extremely well diversified because each tranche is itself backed by a well-diversified pool of assets, a process also reflected in our algorithm.

Thus, this case is quite issuer-friendly and indicates that we can actually overissue (ignoring the legalities associated with doing so).

Case 1-B: Overissuance under Independent Asset Behavior

This subcase simply attempts to find the amount by which we can overissue while still retaining the Aaa rating on the A class. The results in Table 21.10 show what happened when total issuance was raised to $986,000,000.

Discussion. The overissuance is mild, although significant. Note that because of the pro rata capital-allocation structure, the reduction of yield ratio between the classes is very favorable to the B-class holders. We can expect this ratio to be maintained throughout if we leave the structure invariant. Table 21.10 shows that the reduction of yield on the A class ended up in the middle of the Moody's Aaa range. Most likely, we could issue another $10 million

Table 21.10
The Optimal Structure: Case 1-B

CBO of ABS	Class A	Class B
Size	$838,100,000	$147,900,000
Average life (years)	5.98	5.98
ΔIRR (bps)	0.028	0.104
Credit rating	Aaa	Aa1
Interest rate	6.04%	6.12%

while still maintaining the Aaa rating on the A class, which merely requires a ΔIRR below about 0.05 bps.

Is this a realistic case? Absolutely not!

First of all, the assumption of total lack of correlation between the assets flies in the face of common sense. ABS tranches in a single asset class are bound to show some correlated behavior. Second, some asset classes could be viewed as related to the general economic climate, and could be considered correlated. Thus, depending on the prevailing macroeconomic mood, correlation structures anywhere from complete independence to complete dependence could be viewed as defensible.

In this context, determining an objective method of computing correlation structures takes on enhanced significance. We have outlined one such method above, but there are others. Being "right" is not the point in economic modeling because it cannot be proved at the outset; being consistent matters much more, since that is easily checked. Once a calculation method is adopted, it must remain the same across transactions and analysts. Data selection does not have to be the same in all cases, but the treatment of data does.

Case 2-A: Correlation Structure

To gauge the impact of asset correlations on this transaction, assume that matrix **V** from before is a fair representation of the correlation structure of the asset classes represented in the pool. In other words, each ABS asset belonging to a specific asset class is deemed perfectly correlated to its index. Table 21.4 is the converged solution for a total issuance of $885,000,000.

Discussion.   Total issuance at the Aaa senior rate is reduced significantly, from $986,000,000 to $885,000,000. In fact, the average yield reductions shown in Table 21.11 indicate that this would even be an upper limit if the Class A were to maintain its Aaa rating. What is perhaps unexpected is the magnitude (10.4%) of the reduction in issuance with respect to the pool's initial principal balance.

The relative invariance of the relationship between tranche credit ratings could have been forecast as well. Given the pro rata structure in both the in-

Table 21.11
The Optimal Structure: Case 2-A

CBO of ABS	Class A	Class B
Size	$752,250,000	$132,750,000
Average life (years)	4.61	4.61
ΔIRR (bps)	0.060	0.324
Credit rating	Aaa	Aa1
Interest rate	5.68%	5.82%

dependent and the correlated case, the junior tranche rating of Aa1 remains one notch below the senior rating. The increase in the ratio of average yield reduction between the notes from 3.7 to 5.4 can be attributed to nonlinear effects. A different structure—for instance, sequential principal allocation—would enable higher Aaa issuance at the expense of a lower Class B rating. Intermediate structures can evidently be devised, and serious credit analysts in search of arbitrage opportunities would certainly want to investigate most of them.

The CDO of ABS is unique in obviating the need to compute the impact parameter discussed in chapter 20. This is because the underlying assets, being ABS securities themselves, enable us to ignore the underlying pool dynamics and calibrate credit losses based on a unique macroeconomic distribution. Assuming the credit ratings of the ABS assets in this analysis were derived consistently and updated monthly with changing credit quality, our results have a level of certainty not usually achievable in other asset classes and which should increase investor interest in this asset class.

Unfortunately, current rating agency methods among asset classes are highly inconsistent, resulting in correspondingly inconsistent levels of protection associated with seemingly equivalent credit ratings. Although such discrepancies are often reflected in pricing, one must realize that secondary market pricing is an output derived from credit quality as an input—not the other way around.

Case 2-B: Correlation Structure Sensitivity

Ratings sensitivity to the cardinality of correlation matrices is a critical issue for analysts: the worst possible situation is for a small change in the value of correlation matrix entries to lead to a large change in the credit rating of the associated securities.

To formally but briefly investigate this issue, assume Table 21.12 represents a new correlation matrix $\mathbf{V}$. The elements of this new matrix have been significantly modified compared to those of our first correlation matrix. In fact, our figure of merit for them is $\chi = 0.68$. This means that the new matrix entries are 68% different, on average, from the old ones. If, as is generally believed, the accuracy of correlation matrices matters, the large difference should

Table 21.12
New Correlation Matrix for Hypothetical Pool

CBO of ABS	Credit Cards	Autos	Home Equity	Mortgages	Settlements	12b-1 Fees	Aircraft Leases
Credit cards	1.00	0.81	0.71	−0.89	0.72	−0.12	0.67
Autos	0.81	1.00	0.58	−0.68	0.61	−0.46	0.55
Home equity	0.71	0.58	1.00	−0.64	1.00	0.43	0.93
Mortgages	−0.89	−0.68	−0.64	1.00	−0.65	0.04	−0.58
Settlement	0.72	0.61	1.00	−0.65	1.00	0.40	0.93
12b-1 fees	−0.12	−0.46	0.43	0.04	0.40	1.00	0.38
Aircraft leases	0.67	0.55	0.93	−0.58	0.93	0.38	1.00

lead to a noticeable change in the ratings. Such a change need not happen at all since, for a broad range of independent **V** selections, assetwise compensation may take place leaving the ratings essentially invariant. In other words, a randomly distributed error pattern should not unduly impact ratings. An example of this phenomenon is when low-loss scenarios from one asset class compensate high-loss scenarios from another.

By contrast, problems develop when loss correlations are selectively increased in one or two formerly uncorrelated asset classes with the remaining entries remaining unchanged. The new correlations add to the loss variance of the pool without compensation and cause lower security ratings. Either small or large changes in correlation matrices should leave ratings largely untouched, while targeted changes would be more problematic. The practical problem is clearly how to set correlations without arbitrariness or wishful thinking.

Table 21.13 shows the widely disperse discrepancy pattern associated with the change from the first to the second correlation matrix. Unless we made exactly the wrong type of changes everywhere, we would expect rating outcomes to be roughly similar.

Table 21.13
Results of Applying the Cholesky Decomposition to the New Hypothetical Pool (%)

CBO of ABS	Credit Cards	Autos	Home Equity	Mortgages	Settlements	12b-1 Fees	Aircraft Leases
Credit cards	0						
Autos	−4	0					
Home equity	−29	−94	0				
Mortgages	7	10	−14	0			
Settlement	−21	−64	0	−7	0		
12b-1 fees	83	51	343	94	262	0	
Aircraft leases	−35	−91	3	−11	2	328	0

Table 21.14
New Optimal Structure

CBO of ABS	Class A	Class B
Size	$752,250,000	$132,750,000
Average life (years)	4.56	4.56
ΔIRR (bps)	0.141	0.485
Credit rating	Aa1	Aa1
Interest rate	5.73%	5.88%

Our new correlation matrix leads to the results shown in Table 21.14 for an identical total issuance of $885,000,000.

Discussion.   Luckily, the new correlation matrix causes a small, one-notch downgrade on the senior tranche and leaves the junior tranche rating unaffected. However, these changes are better analyzed in terms of yield reductions than generic letter-grade ratings. Although the A tranche suffers a mild downgrade, its fundamental credit quality is essentially unchanged. What is most comforting is that, given the relatively large differences in corresponding entries of **V**, the results are identical. A full sensitivity analysis certainly yields more pertinent information and should be standard operating procedure with all structured analysts.

There is no point haggling over whether a particular class is Aaa, Aa1, or even Aa2. In all cases, investors are taking essentially zero risk. This is not true of barely investment-grade securities made Aaa by a monoline. In that case, investors are merely being shielded from the specific risk of the assets whose real credit quality is still opaque. There is much greater flexibility, and hence variability, in deciding whether wrapped assets are investment-grade, since their actual credit quality is unlikely to surface. This type of analysis would go a long way toward ferreting out solid from marginal investment-grade assets.

Case 3: Complete Correlation

One may reasonably ask what would happen if, rather than obeying some correlation matrix, the assets in the pool were subject to a single index—in other words, if they were completely correlated to each other. This situation can be simulated by a trivial modification to our algorithm. However, although it is equally trivial to state confidently that this is the worst case from the standpoint of the issuer, it is more difficult to say how much worse.

For ease of comparison, we ran case 2-A once again, assuming that the first macro-index (credit cards) governed all asset classes. We chose credit cards because they are probably the most globally diversified mainstream asset class—one that may also be the best proxy for the consumer economy underlying most asset-backed securities. Table 21.15 is the converged solution for a total issuance of $885,000,000.

Table 21.15
The Optimal Structure: Case 3

CBO of ABS	Class A	Class B
Size	$752,250,000	$132,750,000
Average life (years)	4.63	4.63
ΔIRR (bps)	4.917	19.457
Credit rating	A1	Baa2
Interest rate	6.55%	7.50%

Discussion.   Classes A and B do not fare nearly as well as before. Note also that, although the ratio of yield reductions (3.96) is consistent with previous cases, the associated letter-grade rating impact is markedly different owing to the ΔIRR ranges assigned to the credit scale. These results are clearly at the low end vis-à-vis credit ratings given this total issuance; with structural readjustments, better outcomes are certainly possible.

Case 4: Back-of-the-Envelope BET Analysis

It is useful to contrast the previous range of results with the outcomes obtained under the standard binomial expansion framework. The following BOTE rating analysis was performed using the average life from the preceding section,[6] in accordance with Moody's published default method and most recently published expected loss table.[7]

Assuming that each collateral type represents an "industry concentration," this portfolio of forty securities is equivalent to nineteen independent, identically distributed securities. As always, the debate over advance rates revolves around the determination of excess spread. Tentatively, the coupons on Class A and Class B reflect Aaa and A levels. The stressed BOTE analysis affords approximately 2.45% of excess spread per annum, which, together with the 4.6-year assumed average life produces approximately 9% of excess spread net of losses. (Note that more severe loss assumptions in the cash flow analysis could reduce the credit for spread by 2 or 3 percentage points.)

Table 21.16
Case 4 Structure Using 85-15 "Senior-Sub" Split

CBO of ABS	Class A	Class B
Size	$827,358,224	$146,004,392
Average life (years)	4.6	4.6
Expected loss	0.00	31.30
Credit rating	(strong) Aaa	(weak) A2
Interest rate	5.78%	6.3%

Table 21.17
Case 4 Structure Using 90-10 "Senior-Sub" Split

CBO of ABS	Class A	Class B
Size	$895,493,607	$77,869,009
Average life (years)	4.6	4.6
Expected loss	5.88	68.13
Credit rating	Aa3	Baa1
Interest rate	5.78%	6.8%

Our two-class structure with an 85% advance rate on Class A (see Table 21.16) produces an overenhanced Aaa Class A and a Class B of weak single-A credit quality. In fact, Class A issuance can increase to 90% of the pool balance and remain solidly Aaa. In this analysis, the reduction in Class B issuance means that the Class B credit enhancement is more leveraged, making it riskier, increasing its coupon and further reducing annualized excess spread to 2.32%. The new tranche ratings are Aaa and Baa1, respectively. (See Table 21.17 for an output of the 90-10 structure.)

In the two examples of Tables 21.16 and 21.17, the credit given for excess spread is based on the ABS BOTE method, justified by the fact that CDOs of ABS have the monthly payment characteristics of ABS and are, in fact, a complex form of ABS. In reality, rating agencies exercise considerable discretion is determining the amount of spread protection. In a full-blown BET framework (Table 21.18) much less credit is given for excess spread. For comparison purposes, therefore, we present also the CDO-oriented treatment. The Class A, with advance rate of 85%, now produces a bond of mid-Aaa credit quality, while the Class B is deemed to be of B1 credit quality.

Although direct comparisons are difficult, owing to the differences between rating agency techniques and the method of chapter 21, the results obtained using the latter show consistently higher Class B ratings than those produced by rating agency techniques. Unfortunately, as mentioned in connection with the CDO method (chapter 4), those techniques are too opaque to be subjected to meaningful criticism.

Table 21.18
Case 4 Structure (85-15 split) without Credit for Excess Spread

CBO of ABS	Class A	Class B
Size	$827,358,224	$146,004,392
Average life (years)	4.6	4.6
Expected loss	6.61	892.52
Credit rating	Aa2	Ba1
Interest rate	6.5%	13.0%

Concluding Remarks on CDOs of ABS

To borrow a page from Keynes, a rational analysis of this asset class consists of parametric studies of various aspects of the transaction, with a focus on their interactions and on the corresponding rating sensitivities. Rather than wantonly stressing in every direction until default, the central focus of the analysis should be to witness, from a sufficiently responsive and articulated model, the transaction's realistic behavior under feasible cash flow scenarios. The universe thus constructed would represent the transaction's effective risk environment seen through the eyes of investors—a universe whose visualization could form the basis of mature buying decisions.

On the liability side, endless use of trial and error is not recommended without some guidance as to the optimal parameter set. A wide variety of asset- and liability-based triggers can be devised, as can other structural features aimed at either lowering cost of funds or enhancing proceeds. To have any chance of success under realistic market conditions, however, attempts to introduce these and other features presuppose the availability of an automated system operating in a highly nonlinear space and trying out different combinations in search of arbitrage. Until such a system is created, underwriting and modeling efforts can be expected to continue to focus on the assets.

Appendix
Tchebychev Root-Locus Scattering Subroutine in VB

```
Sub Tchebychev_Root_Locus_Scattering(time As Integer)
Dim Root_Locus As Double, Split_Parm As Integer, n_dist As Integer
Dim k_start As Integer, k_end As Integer, k_step As Integer, k_set As Integer
Dim II As Integer
'
'Place time sequence into sheet for all indices
'
For j = 1 To time
Worksheets("Temporary").Range("Time_Sequence").Cells(j, 1).Value = j
Next j
'
'Do each index in turn
'
For i = 1 To Macro_Indices
'
'Place the data points in the sheet for manipulation
'
For j = 1 To time
```

```
Worksheets("Temporary").Range("Numerical_Sequence").Cells(j,
1).Value = Correlated_Deviates(i, j)
Next j
'

'Sort in numerical order
'

Worksheets("Temporary").Activate
Range("Time_Sequence").Select: Fac(1) = ActiveCell.Row
Fac(2) = ActiveCell.Column: Fac(4) = ActiveCell.Column + 1
Selection.End(xlDown).Select: Fac(3) = ActiveCell.Row
Range(Cells(Fac(1), Fac(2)), Cells(Fac(3), Fac(4))).Select
Selection.Sort Key
1:=Worksheets("Temporary").Range ("Numerical_ Sequence"),
Order1:=xlAscending,
Header:=xlGuess_
,OrderCustom:=1, MatchCase:=False, Orientation:=xlTopToBottom
'

'Prepare vectors for semicycle
'

For j = 1 To time
Correlated_Deviates(i, j) = Range("Numerical_Sequence").Cells(j,
1).Value
Normal_Deviates(i, j) = Correlated_Deviates(i, j)
Next j
'

'Initial Beta distribution parameter
'

Fac(5) = Update_Beta_Parms(time, i)
'

'Pick the target Beta distribution somewhere inside the range [1,Fac(5)].
'The standard value is Beta_Margin = 0.5, although any other value can be
used.
'In fact, this parameter could be randomized to investigate sensitivities.
'

v1 = 1 + Beta_Margin * (Fac(5) − 1)
II = 0
'

'Start
'

Do While Fac(5) >= v1*(1 + Beta_Convergence)
'

'Descending semicycle
'

k_start = 1: k_end = Last_Order: k_step = 1: k_set = 0
```

```
Do While k_set <= 1

For k = k_start To k_end Step k_step

For l = 1 To Tchebychev_Sequence(k)
'
'Root locus mapped from [−1,1] to [0,1]
'
Root_Locus = Affine_Parameter * 0.5 * (Cos((2 * 1 − 1)/Tchebychev_
Sequence(k) * Pi * 0.5) + 1)
'
'Locate the closest data point and shift it according to its
'position with respect to 0.5 * Affine_Parameter
'
j = 1
Do While (Correlated_Deviates(i,j) − Root_Locus) < 0
j = j + 1
Loop

Select Case j
Case 2
Normal_Deviates(i, j) = Normal_Deviates(i, j) − Shift_Parm(j) *
Shift_Ratio * _
(Correlated_Deviates(i, j) − Correlated_Deviates(i, j − 1))
Shift_Parm(j) = 0
Case time
Normal_Deviates(i, time − 1) = Normal_Deviates(i,
time − 1) + Shift_Parm(time − 1) * Shift_Ratio * _
(Correlated_Deviates(i, time) − Correlated_Deviates(i, time − 1))
Shift_Parm(time − 1) = 0

Case Else

First_Number = Root_Locus − Correlated_Deviates(i, j − 1)
Second_Number = Correlated_Deviates(i, j) − Root_Locus
n_dist = Sgn(Second_Number − First_Number)

Select Case n_dist
'
'j−1 is closest
'
Case 1
Split_Parm = Sgn(0.5 * Affine_Parameter − Correlated_Deviates(i, j − 1))
Select Case Split_Parm
Case 1 ' below 1/2
```

```
Normal_Deviates(i, j − 1) = Normal_Deviates(i,
j − 1) − Shift_Parm(j − 1) * Shift_Ratio * _
(Correlated_Deviates(i, j − 1) − Correlated_Deviates(i, j − 2))
Shift_Parm(j − 1) = 0

Case − 1 ' above 1/2
Normal_Deviates(i, j − 1) = Normal_Deviates(i,
j − 1) + Shift_Parm(j − 1) * Shift_Ratio * _
(Correlated_Deviates(i, j) − Correlated_Deviates(i, j − 1))
Shift_Parm (j − 1) = 0
End Select
'
'j is closest
'
Case −1
Split_Parm = Sgn(0.5 * Affine_Parameter − Correlated_Deviates(i, j))
Select Case Split_Parm
Case 1 ' below 1/2
Normal_Deviates(i, j) = Normal_Deviates(i, j) − Shift_Parm(j) *
Shift_Ratio * _
(Correlated_Deviates(i, j) − Correlated_Deviates(i, j − 1))
Shift_Parm(j) = 0

Case −1' above 1/2
Normal_Deviates(i, j) = Normal_Deviates(i, j) + Shift_Parm(j) *
Shift_Ratio * _
(Correlated_Deviates(i, j + 1) − Correlated_Deviates(i, j))
Shift_Parm(j) = 0

End Select
End Select
End Select

Next l

For j = 1 To time
Shift_Parm(j) = 1
Next j

'
'Update Beta parameters and update vector
'
Fac(5) = Update_Beta_Parms(time, i)
ll = ll + 1
Worksheets("Temporary").Cells(1 + ll, 20).Value = Fac(5)
```

```
For j = 1 To time
Correlated_Deviates(i, j) = Normal_Deviates(i, j)
'Worksheets("Temporary").Cells(1 + j, 19).Value = Normal_Deviates(i, j)
Next j

Next k
'
'Ascending semicycle
'
k_start = Last_Order: k_end = 1: k_step = −1: k_set = k_set + 1

Loop
Loop
'
'Converged vector, now resort into proper temporal order
'
For j = 1 To time
Range("Numerical_Sequence").Cells(j, 1).Value = Normal_Deviates(i, j)
Next j
Worksheets("Temporary").Activate
Range("Time_Sequence").Select: Fac(1) = ActiveCell.Row
Fac(2) = ActiveCell.Column: Fac(4) = ActiveCell.Column + 1
Selection.End(xlDown).Select: Fac(3) = ActiveCell.Row
Range(Cells(Fac(1), Fac(2)), Cells(Fac(3), Fac(4))).Select
Selection.Sort Key1:=Worksheets("Temporary").Range("Time_Sequence"),
Order1:=xlAscending,
Header:=xlGuess_
,OrderCustom:=1, MatchCase:=False, Orientation:=xlTopToBottom
'
'Put back for use in Monte Carlo routine
'
For j = 1 To time
Correlated_Deviates(i, j) = Range("Numerical_Sequence").Cells(j, 1).Value
Next j
'
'Process next macro vector
'
Next i
End Sub
```

22

Aircraft Receivable Securitizations

One day, as he was returning from a lecture tour in Asia Minor, a famous Sophist spotted Socrates on the street. It was common for the philosopher to spend hours talking to a cobbler about what a shoe was. Approaching Socrates, the rhetorician remarked sarcastically, "My dear Socrates, are you still saying the same thing about the same thing?" Socrates replied, "Yes, that I am. But you, who are so extremely smart—you never say the same thing about the same thing!"[1]

This chapter is an attempt to introduce a new approach to the credit analysis of structured securities backed by aircraft leases or loans. Some would argue that the current approach seems to work well, judging from the size of the transactions executed so far. In fact, it is rather surprising that so *few* transactions have been done, not so many. From where we stand, the reason is obvious: most aircraft transactions are suboptimal. This inefficiency stems largely from a lack of rigor in the analysis of the associated collateral, which lack then causes large amounts of precious capital to go to waste. The weak epistemological basis of aircraft ABS credit analysis means that inconsistencies are common; the valuation of aircraft is haphazard and unresponsive at best, and the treatment of structure, essentially nonexistent. In aircraft ABS analysis, it is virtually impossible to hear the same thing about the same thing twice. If there is one asset class that deserves a better treatment, this is it.

Aircraft as an Asset Class

Most people take air travel for granted and do not realize that modern long-range passenger and fighter airplanes are one of the crowning achievements of modern technology, being the result of more than three centuries of philosophical and scientific speculation. To build and operate a transatlantic commercial jet aircraft is an exceedingly complex undertaking requiring a manufacturing and maintenance infrastructure that only the richest industrialized nations can afford. It should come as no surprise, then, that this inherent complexity has an impact on the analysis of cash flows from aircraft securitizations.

Although commercial aviation has been around for about fifty years, the financing of aircraft receivables in the capital markets is a relatively young phenomenon. Consequently, many fundamental issues facing credit analysts are still far from settled. Each new deal poses new analytical challenges that must be either overcome or explained away to achieve consistency. This chapter's main objective is to bring about greater consistency for an asset class characterized by an intricate cash flow environment in which the exception is the rule.

From a practical standpoint, the credit analysis of aircraft-backed structured securities is complicated by idiosyncratic factors, of which the following four are but the most obvious:

1. Diversification usually cannot be counted on. Whereas an auto-loan pool may consist of thousands of individual exposures, even the largest aircraft ABS transaction ever executed, the Guinness Peat Aviation securitization of 1996, was based on fewer than 250 units—a small number by ABS standards.

2. In contrast to most other asset classes where the credit environment can best be described as high frequency/low severity, the brave new world of aircraft ABS is characterized by a low-frequency/high-severity credit risk environment. Generally, insurance is useful in such circumstances; but since we may not assume the availability of insurance for aircraft ABS, proper valuation of the aircraft over time becomes even more critical. Systematic analysis of liquidation scenarios and the microanalysis of each asset as nonconforming collateral are integral to the valuation analysis.

3. Although an aircraft on the ground represents a significant amount of idle capital, it is practically impossible to redeploy that capital within the time scale to which the capital markets are generally accustomed. On the other hand, aircraft that are not flying do not require maintenance. Thus there is an implicit, inverse correlation between the availability of cash from leasing or "passenger-mile revenues" and the need for cash for scheduled maintenance. This offsetting relationship forms the basis of designing better structures, but only if our analytical framework is flexible enough to recognize this and a few other related facts.

4. The airline industry is notoriously cyclical, an unavoidable phenomenon stemming largely from the lead time required to design, produce, and deliver any new aircraft model. As a result, once a production line is ready to roll, there is a strong tendency to do just that, regardless of actual demand. The resulting mismatch between supply and demand quickly leads to the well-known "feast or famine" feature of the industry. The combination of cyclicality and long asset duration is one of the most troublesome aspects of this asset class because it requires credit analysts to project cash flow potential far beyond the current macroeconomic cycle, into the next twenty to thirty years, in an attempt to predict the likely amplitudes of future cash flow cycles. The basic challenge is then to estimate the proper phase of each asset within its life cycle so as to measure, as accurately as possible, cash flow peaks and valleys and to give credit to the potentially favorable correlation structure immanent in the pool.

The most redeeming feature of aircraft ABS is probably the availability of massive amounts of data. Since the loss of an aircraft is usually accompanied by loss of human life, the flight and maintenance history of all commercial aircraft is recorded down to the minutest detail. As a result, the economic status of an aircraft, and hence its cash flow potential, is knowable to a much more precise degree than is the case for even the most expensive automobile. This available precision is the cornerstone of the analysis of aircraft-backed structured securities.

As always, the end game of credit analysis is to assess the variance of cash flows around their expected values more accurately, giving full benefit to issuers for whatever amount of diversification can be objectively demonstrated within their pool. Once structural features are overlaid, appropriate credit enhancement levels can be computed for any desired risk level. As is true of all relatively young asset classes, after considering all sources of cash available to the structure, the weight of the evidence normally leads to the conclusion that current enhancement levels are excessive in relation to historical default risk.

The next few pages attest to the difficulty of analyzing aircraft ABS transactions, and of accounting for the various covenants and warranties commonly found in governing documents and for standard practices in collateral management. Such structural and asset-valuation features are currently ignored analytically despite clear evidence of mainly positive credit impact. The net outcome is an overestimation of credit risk that translates directly into higher credit enhancement levels than those consistent with stated rating levels. We believe that, given that passenger jet aircraft cost anywhere between $20 million and $125 million, and that ABS issuance averages $1 billion per portfolio deal, the improvements in capital and structural efficiency attending careful analysis will more than compensate the credit analyst for the incremental work.

Following a brief but necessary historical review, we discuss several topics germane to aircraft securitizations that mainly contribute to their credit-related heterogeneity. Along the way, we indicate how to deal with each one in a consistent manner and how to combine them into an integrated, measurable whole. Our objective is to present a conceptual underpinning robust enough to inspire confidence in the investing public and, hopefully, to enable aircraft ABS to find their rightful place in the pantheon of asset classes.

Aircraft Flight and Its Impact on Aircraft Longevity

Although the principles of flight are mostly irrelevant to the financing of aircraft, a passing acquaintance with them is useful when trying to understand the aging of an airplane, and hence its economic prospects.

The basic governing equation of aircraft flight is Bernoulli's[2] equation for fluid flow. It is valid on any geometric path kept parallel to the fluid velocity vector, a so-called *streamline*:

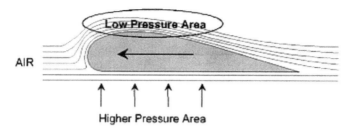

Figure 22.1. Flow over an Airfoil

$$\rho\frac{v^2}{2} + P = \text{Const.} \qquad (22.1)$$

In equation (22.1), ρ is the density of the surrounding fluid, v its velocity, and P the static atmospheric pressure. Now, consider Figure 22.1, which shows an airfoil placed in a moving fluid. The central idea is that in order for the fluid above the airfoil to reach the back of the airfoil (the trailing edge) at the same time as the fluid below it, it has no choice but to accelerate since, in order to do so,[3] it must travel a greater distance in the same time interval. Otherwise, there would exist a relative vacuum at the trailing edge, something that is usually not allowed. Since the left-hand side of equation (22.1) must remain invariant,[4] the equation tells us that the value of the static pressure above the airfoil must be lower than its corresponding value below it. This pressure difference causes an upward vertical force or "lift" to be felt anywhere along the airfoil where this imbalance obtains. When summed over the width and breadth of both wings, this lifting force must, by definition, be sufficient to bear the entire gravitational weight of the craft. In other words, the fuselage and the passengers are essentially suspended on both wings as the plane moves through the air. Suspension causes severe mechanical stresses at various points of the craft's structure owing to the levered action of the wings on the fuselage.

Second, in order to get off the ground, an airplane must acquire sufficient velocity for the pressure difference to build up and create a lift force with an aggregate sum at least equal to the weight of the plane. For a sixty-ton modern passenger jet aircraft, this velocity can be achieved only with powerful engines that consequently undergo severe heat stresses as they ramp up to full power on take-off.

Finally, transoceanic aircraft usually fly at the top of the troposphere, approximately 33,000 to 35,000 feet above sea level. At this cruising altitude, the static pressure around the craft is much lower than on the ground and is usually insufficient for normal breathing. If nothing were done, most people inside the plane would suffocate within minutes after take-off. To prevent this, the entire fuselage is pressurized, allowing a peaceful ride without the need for oxygen masks. This pressurization causes the aircraft's skin to expand ever so slightly each time the craft ascends to cruising altitude, making the total circumference of the fuselage greater at 35,000 feet than at sea level. When the craft returns to sea level, the skin deflates or shrinks back to its former location. This constant expansion and deflation pattern, dubbed a *cycle*, is another physical stress that causes the nacelle, or fuselage structure, to wear out slowly over time. Clearly, the number of cycles is highly dependent on the flight history of the craft. Transpacific voyages that average twenty hours of flight time per cycle are less stressful in this sense than short Boston–New York hops. Thus the age of an aircraft is an elusive quantity, of which chronological age is only one component. An aircraft that has been on the ground for thirty years is not a thirty-year-old aircraft and should not be treated as such. We shall come back to this issue shortly when we discuss the future economic potential of an aircraft and contrast it to its remaining physical life.

A Brief Review of Aircraft Finance

In the Beginning Was the Bank

Like most other asset classes, the world of aircraft finance began as the exclusive purview of commercial banks. A bank would make a loan to an airline that would use the proceeds to buy specific equipment that served as security for the loan. This form of financing originated in the railroad industry and gave birth to the concept of the *Equipment Trust Certificate* evidencing ownership in particular assets placed in a trust.

However, airline bankruptcies in the United States did not always proceed smoothly. Often unrelated creditors could wind up with liquidation proceeds from "segregated" assets. Yet, because of the severe regulatory environment associated with the airline industry, banks had very few losses despite the "high severity" aspect of default mentioned earlier. Once airlines were deregulated, though, the rate of defaults increased sharply, and so did loan losses following bankruptcy. Eventually, the U.S. government came to realize that aircraft finance would fare better if these assets could be extracted from the estates of bankrupt airlines. This gave rise to a special provision in the bankruptcy code, Section 1110, which allowed banks and other financial institutions that had secured positions in aircraft to liquidate them outside the bankruptcy proceedings within sixty days, and thereby hopefully recuperate their outstanding principal. The basic qualification was for the airline to be a U.S.-based operator with a certificate issued by the Department of Transportation. This protection was clearly a form of enhancement to the standard Equipment Trust Certificate and, coupled with additional enhancement in the form of a liquidity facility giving investors eighteen months[5] to liquidate the aircraft, formed the nucleus of a structure known as the Enhanced Equipment Trust Certificate (EETC). This form of financing still exists today.

From a credit standpoint the advantage of the EETC was that, with a reduced risk that the assets would be tied up indefinitely in bankruptcy, the ratings on the associated debt could be higher. Remember that corporate credit ratings are meant to measure default rates, not credit losses. Although it was common for a lender—even without an EETC—to successfully enforce its secured position in court and come out whole, the resulting time delays would cause cash flows to cease for a while. Under the EETC structure, the prospect of a lower default probability via a forced sale without cash flow interruption (thanks to the liquidity facility) was sufficient justification for a higher rating, and allowed EETC structures to achieve significantly higher credit ratings. In the case of the senior tranche, this increase usually amounted to six or seven notches above the underlying corporate rating of the airline. Because EETCs were still tied to a single airline, even the lowest tranche was at least as creditworthy as the airline itself, and so EETC ratings would always match or exceed the airline's corporate rating. At the other end of the credit spectrum, although there was no theoretical impediment to a tranche's being rated Aaa, rating agency sentiment was that the notoriously cyclical airline industry could not support the implications of that rating category. Thus it came to be that the ratings of EETC-borne senior tranches became subject to an Aa[6] ceiling.

Enter Portfolios

Things remained relatively quiet on the innovation front until 1992, the year of the first lease portfolio securitization: the ALPS 92-1 transaction. Rather than a single piece of equipment, this transaction involved a portfolio of aircraft. However, it still required the manager to sell aircraft to repay debt when due. This was unfortunate, because forced sales into the market tended to be correlated with a lower clearing price for the aircraft due in large measure to the usual suspect: industry cyclicality. As a result, the next transaction by the same issuer alleviated this concern by allowing sales to be delayed until market conditions improved. But the waiting period could be long; and if market conditions improved, why sell at all?

The Modern Era

The modern era began in the spring of 1996, when the investment bank Morgan Stanley underwrote the $4.05 billion Airplanes Pass-Through Trust securitization (hereinafter "Airplanes"). This was the largest aircraft ABS transaction ever successfully executed, and it remains the benchmark deal in this asset class. It involved a fleet of roughly 230 aircraft owned by the Ireland-based lessor Guinness Peat Aviation (GPA). The main innovative feature of the transaction was that repayment of debt was to stem exclusively from lease cash flows from lessees of the underlying aircraft. There would be no forced sales of aircraft, delayed or not.

The liability structure of the Airplanes transaction was complex and involved multiple levels of principal repayments interspersed with interest, reserve requirements, and derivative wizardry. The complexity and size of this transaction challenged investors, bankers, and credit rating agencies alike to more creatively utilize the rules they had created with respect to the analysis of aircraft leases. The Moody's model made use of the Cholesky decomposition to investigate the impact of diversification on cash flows, while Morgan Stanley used derivatives to hedge interest rate risk in a highly fluid setting. In short, the GPA transaction was the genesis of the bulk of the structural innovations now commonplace in this asset class. Most aircraft portfolio lease securitizations executed or attempted since then represent, in one form or another, the legacy of GPA.

The Recent Past and the Future

Since GPA, however, the paradigm has yet to shift, although new structures keep emerging, mostly as variations of the same theme. GPA was refinanced in 1998, and the concept of the master trust was introduced during the same year by the Morgan Stanley Aircraft Finance transaction. In contrast to the credit card master trust, the expression *master trust* here simply means that additional aircraft may be "sold" to the trust under a previously agreed upon set of eligibility requirements; no longer is it a requirement that repayment of existing debt be the sole source of cash for these new purchases. Thus the aircraft ABS master trust looks more like a variable funding certificate (VFC) than a credit card master trust despite the inherent cross-collateralization of all aircraft assets in the combined pool.

As a rule, aircraft ABS transactions are expensive and inefficient, and make sense only in isolated cases. If aircraft ABS is to become a mature asset class, it will have to be handled with greater sophistication and deeper fundamental analysis.

The Age of an Aircraft

From a credit standpoint, the main motivation for knowing the chronological age of an aircraft stems from the negative relationship between its age and its market value. Although market value and lease rates both decline with age, the ratio of these two quantities (the *lease rate factor*[7]) tends to be much more stable than either quantity separately. As a result, the lease rate factor has become a convenient characteristic parameter for an airplane: given a reasonable valuation for the craft, a fairly reliable estimate of the corresponding expected lease cash flows can be made by multiplying its lease rate factor[8] by its market value.

As mentioned earlier, the concept of age in aircraft is rather elusive. Although it is generally believed that under equilibrium supply-and-demand conditions, chronological age is the best measure of value for relatively new aircraft, empirical and anecdotal evidence points to a more complex relationship. For instance, in the first ten to fifteen years of its life, a large, well-maintained jet aircraft will lease for about the same dollar price assuming constant supply-and-demand conditions. Airlines provide a service, not a commodity, so as long as safety is not compromised, passengers will pay market rates for that service. The problem with projecting cash flows as the product of the plane's lease rate factor and its declining value as a function of age is that this method inevitably underestimates revenues.

If the lease rate factor and the lease rate are to remain constant, it follows that the value of the aircraft must remain constant as well, which contradicts the common-sense notion that aircraft depreciate over time, albeit at different rates. On the other hand, if its lease rate factor is allowed to change such that the product of the lease rate factor and aircraft value remains invariant, we conclude that, ceteris paribus, an older plane is more expensive to lease per dollar of value than a younger one—another counterintuitive notion. In this section, we hope to restore common sense to this state of affairs and obtain lease rates that actually agree with the facts. We do this by replacing the measure "chronological age" with another measure, "age by useful life," which more accurately reflects the economic life of the craft.

As explained earlier, an aircraft is a very complex animal subject to various types of stresses. As passenger safety has been a major concern of all governments for some time, the maintenance and flight history as well as the record of every take-off and landing of passenger aircraft are recorded daily in excruciating detail and are available to any credit analyst who bothers to ask. The answer to a rational aircraft age computation lies in those records. As a rationale, compare this problem to one of measuring the age of an automobile. It has been known for decades that the right measure of remaining useful life for a road vehicle is not so much its chronological age, although that is still a somewhat relevant parameter in extreme cases, but more the number of miles it has traveled since it was manufactured. When making this statement, we are in effect creating an abstraction and replacing the concept of chronological age with a numerical index equal to the odometer reading. The solution to our problem lies in the creation of the same abstraction for aircraft. But what is the "odometer reading" of an aircraft? The answer is simple: *cycles*. In the remainder of this section we explain how; but first, let us briefly review rating agency methods with respect to this issue.

The Rating Agencies and Aircraft Useful-Life Measures

Although the major rating agencies both state that the useful life of a passenger jet aircraft is twenty-five years based on chronological age, both have also acknowledged that cycles are a factor in the useful-life estimation.[9] To address the factor of cycles, Moody's uses a benchmark straight-line depreciation curve[10] with some minor inflation adjustment and a 10% residual value. However, the problem with Moody's method of recognition is that the agency imputes the number of cycles to an aircraft based on its age. This amounts to imputing the number of miles driven by an automobile given its model year, something no buyer would ever do. Effectively, chronological age is Moody's measure of economic value. By contrast, Standard & Poor's shows a little more sophistication in computing aircraft values from chronological age.[11] The published S&P aircraft depreciation schedule (delivery value versus chronological age without inflation adjustment) is as follows: 3% when the chronological age of the plane is one to fifteen years; 4% in years sixteen to twenty; 5% in years twenty-one to twenty-five; and a residual of 10% at the end of the twenty-fifth year.

Standard & Poor's also makes depreciation adjustments for older planes that take into account the current cost basis of the aircraft versus its delivery basis. Last, judging from the relevant Fitch Ratings publication,[12] the concept of cycle-age seems to have escaped the agency altogether, presumably because they do not use it either. Fitch is, however, more generous on the back end and imputes a 20% residual value.

In the case of cargo planes, Moody's and Standard & Poor's both acknowledge the higher useful lives of these aircraft. Moody's fixes cargo useful life at thirty-five years,[13] while Standard & Poor's[14] uses thirty years and 3% depreciation per year for new cargo planes with the same 10% residual shown in Table 22.1 later in this chapter.

Neither of the two major rating agencies (Moody's nor Standard & Poors) is clear on the valuation method for twenty-five-year-old passenger planes converted to cargo status—at considerable expense, we might add. It is virtually certain that a thirty-year useful life would be inappropriate in the case of Standard & Poor's. Interestingly, in one recent cargo transaction[15] Moody's imputed a useful life of forty-five years to the aircraft assets in the trust. Where these extra ten years came from is not clear, but this bold accommodation by the agency further highlights the inadequacy of chronological age as a measure of useful life (not to mention the agency's own philosophical inconsistencies and confusion).

The general conclusion is that, in one form or another, all rating agencies use chronological age as the basic measure of value and hence of useful life, despite the recognition by Moody's and Standard & Poor's that cycles are a definite factor. We contend that cycles are the appropriate measure and indicate in the next section a rational method of using them.

The Use of Cycles as a Measure of Value

First, aircraft of all types are rigorously tested before the first one is delivered. Part of this testing program consists in repeated simulations of the pressurization/depressurization cycle mentioned earlier. Broadly speaking, these synthetic cycles become an objective measure of the number of actual cycles the craft is expected to withstand throughout its life while still maintaining its integrity, a number that may be as high as 150,000 or 200,000. In all cases, the number of such design cycles is known a priori for each aircraft type.

Second, the rate of change in aircraft technology is much slower than originally predicted. Although there have been improvements in flight and maintenance efficiency, the basic paradigm has never shifted. The one glaring exception is the Concorde, a clear technological success but one that has never displaced much slower planes from market dominance and that is not the economic basis of Airbus's competitive position, although it is the latter's technological basis. Aircraft built in the 1970s are still flying profitably today, perhaps not on the most lucrative routes or with well-capitalized carriers, but nevertheless demonstrating that a useful life of twenty-five years is off the mark.

Third, the engines of a jet aircraft are constantly being rebuilt according to a rigorous schedule established by the manufacturer.[16] As crucial components of the safety program for the plane, the maintenance status of an engine and its overall condition cannot be neglected. It can be argued that engines never really age, although this would be something of an exaggeration. Meanwhile, the airframe is subjected to a variety of checks[17] and inspections that maintain its airworthiness at a fairly constant level over time, albeit with a secular downward trend in value in spite of these. These and other factors contribute to the conclusion that the usefulness of a plane cannot be gauged merely by its chronological age.

Since the lease rate factor is a synthetic concept,[18] it is intended to remain invariant, or very nearly constant, throughout the life of an aircraft. The reason lease rate factors are seen to vary is failure to properly account for the aging phenomenon, not a flaw in the concept. In other words, the effective age of an aircraft is simply out of step with its chronological age. The way to compensate for this is clearly not to use a distribution of lease rate factors, which nullifies their meaning, but simply to adjust the value curve. Once the value-time relationship is given its proper functional form, the desired constancy of average lease rate factors is restored.

We propose the following compromise cycle-based method for any target aircraft:

1. Determine the number of design cycles for planes of the target type and divide that number by a normalization factor such that a life of twenty-five generalized years[19] (chronological age adjusted by the number of cycles) would be assigned to a target plane with a hypothetical marginal cycle utilization equal to the 95% confidence level calculated from the distribution function of cycles for all planes in the fleet of the target type. In essence, we assume that the most utilized planes in the fleet will have useful lives of at least twenty-five chronological years, a very mild assumption by all appearances.
2. Divide the actual number of cycles for the target, known from its tail number, by the cycle rating for that type, yielding the *cycle index* for the target.
3. Multiply the cycle index by 25 to obtain the generalized age of the craft.
4. For the remainder of the transaction, use the actual cycle history of the target to compute generalized age. To do this, simply advance the number of cycles for the target at every time period using its empirical cycle distribution. This results in aging the aircraft according to its expected utilization to better reflect its useful life potential.

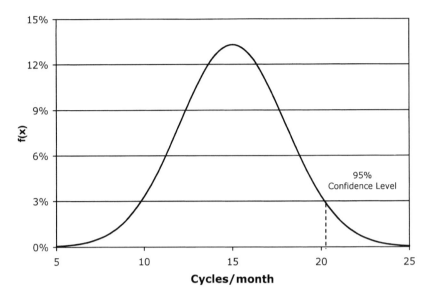

Figure 22.2. Marginal Cycle Distribution

We illustrate this method with an example. Say the target plane was manufactured fourteen years ago and has a design life of 100,000 cycles, a current total utilization of 2,664 cycles, and a mean cumulative monthly utilization of fourteen cycles. Further assume that Figure 22.2 is the actual[20] marginal cycle distribution of all planes in the target fleet. The vertical bar shows the 95% confidence level (CL) falling at twenty cycles per month. The normalization factor, computed as previously indicated, is $100,000/(20 \times 300) = 16.67$ per cycle. The normalized utilization is thus $2,664 \times 16.67 = 44,400$ cycles.

Now, the calculations go as follows:

Chronological age:	14 chronological years
Age (by useful life): $44,400/100,000 \times 25$:	11.1 generalized years

Assuming the same mean monthly utilization for the next five years, the following would be the situation at that time:

Chronological age:	19 chronological years
Age: $(25)(44,400 + 14,003)/100,000$:	14.6 generalized years

In implementation, we would use the target aircraft's statistical distribution of monthly utilizations to determine its aging pattern throughout the life of the transaction. Those records may be obtained from the operator.

Under this method, an aircraft can only be "useful" for twenty-five generalized years, but the relationship between chronological age and position on the useful-life axis is now individualized rather than unique. Depending on utilization, chronological life may extend to fifty years, although in general it will be less. Two sixteen-year-old planes are no longer assumed to have the same earning potential once their individual cycle histories are factored in. Now, lease or passenger-mile revenues can be computed on a normalized basis using a single generic depreciation curve while taking into account supply and demand conditions. In fact, one would expect that prices in the secondary market would tend to follow the cycle-based method more accurately than the chronological-age method. Finally, this method replaces an arbitrary distribution (lease rate factor) with an empirical one (utilization) representing a more consistent measure of value than chronological age. This is by far the most compelling reason for adopting it.

Granted, the cycle-based method is not a panacea for all aircraft types in all market conditions; there is no such measure. As with automobiles, cycle utilization will fail to take into account specific or idiosyncratic factors that will either decrease or increase the value of an airplane with respect to its benchmark value. However, as a conceptual framework, it is far more compelling than current analytical methods and likely to yield lease rates more in line with market forces than will bare chronological age. As mentioned in earlier sections, failure to recognize this and other realities is a major source of financial suboptimality in aircraft ABS analysis.

Next, we show how to combine the cycle-based method with market conditions to arrive at a current estimate of lease rates.

Aircraft Valuation (the Snake Algorithm)

In view of the results of the previous section, we can approach the valuation question more formally by using a generalized age curve to compute lease cash flows. As previously explained, aircraft values are linked to dollar lease rates via lease rate factors. For instance, if the appropriate lease rate factor is 1.5%, the yield on the asset is $12 \times 1.5\% = 18\%$ per annum.

The valuation concept here involves letting aircraft values fluctuate by generalized age and anticipated market forces while holding lease rate factors fixed, implying constant yields on the assets. On the generalized age axis, a ten-year-old aircraft is truly twice as old as a five-year-old aircraft in terms of normal wear and tear, and should rent for about half the monthly cost of the first one. This is surely not how market participants see it, but credit analysts will rarely be privy to these pricing discussions and some reasonable middle ground must be sought. As a result, we believe that a straight line with negative slope is a reasonable compromise for the functional form to describe the relationship between price and generalized age.

Finally, aircraft lease rates are subject to inflation like any other asset. The latter can be estimated from industry data and can be a non-negligible factor in computing current lease rates. Since values in the low single digits are normally used, it will rarely be the case that a transaction will or won't make sense based solely on inflation figures.

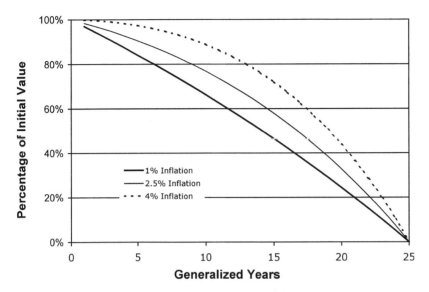

Figure 22.3. Aircraft Valuation Chart

Combining the foregoing observations, our basic aircraft equilibrium valuation model takes the following form for an assumed economic life of T generalized years, after which the plane is deemed to have zero economic value, whether because it is too old or because it is now economically obsolete:

$$V = V_0\left(1 - \frac{t}{T}\right)(1 + r)^t \qquad (22.2)$$

In equation (22.2) we have defined

  t = Current time (generalized years)

  V = Replacement value of an aircraft ($)

  V_0 = Original delivery value at time 0 ($)

  r = Yearly inflation rate (%)

  T = Economic life (generalized years)

If a residual value is required, simply use $T/(1 - R)$ instead of T in equation (22.2) where R is the residual value expressed as a percentage of delivery value.

A graph of equation (22.2) is shown in Figure 22.3 for the assumed economic life of twenty-five generalized years, zero residual, and various inflation factors. Note how the target aircraft of the last section would still lease for about 85% of its initial equilibrium lease rate under the cycle-based method nineteen years after manufacture, compared to the approximately 45% figure that would result from the chronological-age method. The use of the cycle-based method yields outcomes much more in line with empirical evidence of approximately constant lease rates for about the first two decades of operation than the chronological-age method.

The Snake Algorithm

So far, supply-and-demand cyclicality has been entirely neglected despite our knowledge of its centrality to the aircraft leasing business. The value of an aircraft is rarely the "equilibrium" quantity that has been assumed up to now and tends to oscillate with the relative surplus or dearth of that particular type of aircraft.

In essence, a generic aircraft of any type can be thought of as finding itself at a particular moment in its life cycle, weaving around its equilibrium value (or *base value*) as it slowly depreciates over time. In order to properly account for the observed behavior of market prices, the upshot is that a life-cycle oscillation needs to be superimposed onto the aircraft's depreciation curve represented by equation (22.2). This phenomenon was recognized some time ago by the aviation consulting firm Morton Beyer & Agnew and given the name *snake algorithm*. We will continue to use this term hereafter.

Figure 22.4 shows the resulting behavior, combining both the monotonic depreciation of the last section and the life-cycle oscillation that gives rise to the "snake." The curve labeled "FMV" represents the equilibrium fair market value with an inflation factor of 1.5%, while the curve labeled "CMP" repre-

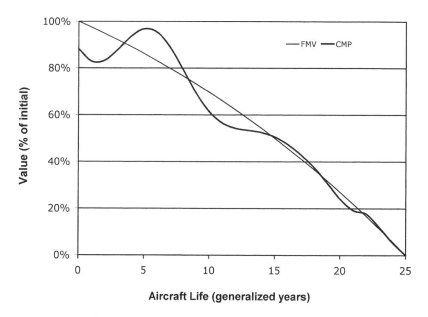

Figure 22.4. Snake Algorithm

sents the current market price of the aircraft given our forecast of future market conditions.

A feasible functional form for the snake algorithm can be given as follows:

$$V = V_0\left(1 - \frac{t}{T}\right)(1 + r)^t(1 + Ae^{-\delta\kappa\tau}\cos(\omega\tau_s + \phi)) \qquad (22.3)$$

In equation (22.3) we have defined the following quantities:

t = Current time (generalized years)

T = Useful life (usually twenty-five generalized years)

V_0 = Initial fair market value of the plane (\$)

A = Maximum amplitude of market price fluctuations (from market data)

κ = Average damping factor (from industry data)

$\tau = t/(1 - [t/T_c])$ = Normalized time (generalized years)

T_c = Chronological useful-life estimate (normally $T_c = 2T$)

$\omega = 2\pi/C$ = Market oscillation frequency

C = Average length of aircraft industry cycle (generalized years)

ϕ = Phase angle (position of the aircraft type in its life cycle)

$\tau_s = \alpha\tau(\beta/\delta)(e^{\delta\tau} - 1)$ = Stretched time (generalized years)

The parameters α, β, and δ are found from fitting equation (22.2) to the following functional form via the NR method or some other nonlinear technique.

$$V = \alpha - \beta e^{\delta t} \qquad (22.4)$$

Although this is easily done by trial and error, a quick estimate may be obtained by matching the first three terms of the Taylor series expansion of equations (22.2) and (22.4), respectively, about the point $t = 0$. We obtain the following three-dimensional nonlinear equation system to be solved for these three parameters:

$$\alpha - \beta = 1 \qquad (22.5)$$

$$\beta\delta = \frac{1}{T} - \ln(1 + r) \qquad (22.6)$$

$$\beta\delta^2 = \frac{2\ln(1 + r)}{T} - [\ln(1 + r)]^2 \qquad (22.7)$$

This system is easily inverted, and we obtain the following:

$$\delta = \frac{\dfrac{2\ln(1 + r)}{T} - [\ln(1 + r)]^2}{\dfrac{1}{T} - \ln(1 + r)} \qquad (22.8)$$

$$\beta = \frac{\dfrac{1}{T} - \ln(1 + r)}{\delta} \tag{22.9}$$

$$\alpha = 1 + \beta \tag{22.10}$$

Figure 22.4 was drawn for illustrative purposes only using the following set of parameters:

$T = 25$

$T_c = 50$

$r = 0.015$

$\alpha = 2$

$\beta = 1$

$\delta = 0.0275$

$\kappa = 0.1$

$C = 10$

$\phi = 2.5$

$A = 0.15$

These are the parameters we need to define the value of an aircraft over time. They can all be estimated from industry and market data or actual operator experience.

Deriving the input parameters to the snake algorithm requires considerable effort in terms of data analysis. Each month, the forecasted current market price (CMP) of the aircraft is computed. If the aircraft is re-leased at that time, the new lease rate is set equal to the product of the CMP forecast and the associated lease rate factor. Unlike current methods that use triangular distributions[21] of lease rate factors to compute cash flows, this method automatically adjusts lease rates via the predicted variation in aircraft valuation and allows us to keep lease rate factors unchanged throughout the simulation. Remember that their invariance is why we use lease rate factors in the first place.

Note that given constant generalized age, equation (22.3) will always impute the same lease rate to a given aircraft type at the same position in its life cycle. In practice, however, different cycle utilization rates and phase angles will cause different lease rates to arise from the same nominal fleet. These variable lease rates will be driven not by differences in lease rate factors, but rather by the quantifiable statistical variations in utilization. In effect, this is the transformation of an arbitrary cash flow estimation procedure into an empirical, data-intensive method.

We recommend that, once the parameters described previously for Figure 22.4 are estimated from market and industry data, they should be kept constant throughout the simulation as this will tend to anchor the calculations and help ensure that the range of cash flow histories that can be expected from the fleet is consistently reflected.

Sources of Variation in Cash Flows

Thus far we have looked at the main source of variation in aircraft-backed securitization: aircraft values and their impact on lease rates. In this section, we briefly review other sources of variation in cash flows. Although the full range of variables that may affect the earning potential of an aircraft is beyond the scope of this book, the following are some of the most important:

- Lessee credit quality
- Lease rates
- Lease terms
- Remarketing time
- Remarketing expenses

Except for lease rates, discussed in the last two sections, we deal with each one in turn and then briefly discuss their correlation structure.

Lessee Credit Quality

The difference between EETC transactions and portfolio transactions is that the former rely on a single credit for repayment while the latter are predicated on the re-leasing of the aircraft to multiple lessees over the repayment period. In portfolio deals, lessee default is somewhat expected since the credit quality of the average lessee is usually much lower than that of the single name normally found within a EETC structure. Mainly for this reason, portfolio securitizations normally contain covenants that limit the concentration of lessees with relatively low credit ratings, usually those below investment grade, although these restrictions are commonly broad enough to give fleet managers sufficient operational flexibility.

A related topic is geographical diversification of the lessee universe. Except under unusual circumstances, investment-grade or near-investment-grade lessees in developed nations are commonly seen as independent of each other, while those based in less developed countries are commonly linked together by government support, where one default is often accompanied by other defaults. This *cross-collateralization effect* results in further portfolio concentration restrictions on fleet managers with respect to the geographical location of lessees. Regardless of whether such covenants are effective at averting bond defaults, diversification is clearly a positive factor of any structured financing. As mentioned earlier, compared with most asset classes aircraft ABS securitized pools are, in the first instance, already plagued by relatively few large assets.

The effective credit quality of a lessee is also an issue. Many non-U.S. carriers rely heavily on U.S. traffic to survive, and their credit quality is more related to what is going on in North America than in their own country. It is quite possible that a lessee from a sub-investment-grade country may, in fact, possess a higher current credit standing than the sovereign ceiling would lead one to suppose. Since leases normally extend for five years or less, the risk return profile of a lower quality lessee in the prevailing environment could be more favorable to the trust than a better-capitalized U.S. lessee able to extract favorable price concessions from fleet managers. Aviation is a global business in which domicile, like value, is an elusive concept. Nevertheless, in the absence of objective facts to the contrary, credit ratings from rating agencies or commercial vendors like KMV are probably the best available proxies for actual credit quality.

Lease Terms

Lease terms are relatively easy to handle with respect to the Monte Carlo simulations involved in the credit analysis of aircraft ABS. The normal case is for the operator or servicer to make available to the analyst fleet data from which a suitable lease-term distribution can be built. Lease terms will tend to be correlated with other factors (discussed shortly) and generally can not be selected independently of lease rates or lessee credit quality. Thus, instead of using an analytic probability distribution (triangular, normal, etc.), it is recommended to derive lease rates from the empirical distribution provided by the servicer. This latter distribution will usually lead to more realistic vectors of lease rates–lessee credit quality combinations than those that would result from selecting lease terms from independent probability distributions. In essence, this is the difference between *random* simulation and *historical* simulation.

Remarketing Time

Remarketing time also includes repossession time with both usually concurrent. They are logically separated to reflect the way leases terminate. In the case of a normal termination, the lessee would normally return the aircraft to an agreed-upon location and repossession time would be zero. Under abnormal termination—for example, default—the lessor could be called upon to repossess the plane itself, which would add to the total length of time the asset would not be generating cash flow. The reality of the situation is, however, that a lessor will usually know of an impending default months before it occurs and will attempt to remarket the craft in advance of repossession. Thus, remarketing and repossession times are concurrent more often than not. In Monte Carlo implementation, these two times are kept separate and used according to whether the lease was normally or abnormally terminated.

Further, it is not uncommon for a lessor to give a lessee some breathing room before declaring a default on technical matters, especially if the lessee can reasonably be thought to have liquidity problems. This grace period could be considered a repossession time if the technical default is not cured.

Data for remarketing and repossession times also come from the servicer. The selection of a remarketing time is not independent, for two reasons:

- Remarketing times will clearly depend heavily on the position of the aircraft type in its lifecycle.
- Lessors may want to hold out for a higher lease rate or a longer lease term rather than remarket the plane on a first-come, first-served basis.

For these reasons, lessors upon lease termination will normally face an array of choices, only one of which will obviously take place. A proper Monte Carlo implementation thus requires that an array of possibilities be considered and that an independent choice be made from among the family of possible choices. In other words, what is independent is not the choice of a remarketing time per se, but rather that of a vector of available choices for various linked parameters. The situation is exactly analogous to lease terms discussed previously.

Remarketing Expenses

As with remarketing times, remarketing expenses also include repossession expenses. In the first instance, it is not uncommon for a plane to require some sprucing-up before it can be delivered to the next lessee. Likewise, it may need to be stored somewhere pending delivery. Depending on the terms of the new lease, the aircraft may also be subject to maintenance (see Maintenance Reserves") ahead of its original maintenance schedule before it can be delivered to the next lessee. In fact, such maintenance requirements may be the source of the default in the first place. Concerning repossession expenses, legal fees could be required to extract the plane from an unfriendly jurisdiction, up to and including the use of a S.W.A.T. repossession team to forcibly remove the plane from that jurisdiction. All these costs would be counted as remarketing or repossession expenses, and the servicer would have to make these data available for a proper credit analysis.

In practice, they may be difficult for analysts to obtain since a servicer may not want to let it be known that relationships with lessees are not always harmonious. In that case, analysts would be forced to be conservative. It is usually the case that conservatism is worse than the truth. However, it is difficult to imagine how remarketing expenses could be zero, save in cases where the same lessees re-lease the same planes. Consequently, a properly constructed Monte Carlo simulation algorithm has to monitor the identity of the new lessee and act accordingly with respect to this parameter. In the case of normal lease termination, the simulation must decide on the identity of the new lessee before assigning remarketing expenses to the trust.

Clearly, the feasibility of the analysis requires that the prior identification of potential lessees be drawn up beforehand by the analyst and the servicer, with only those on the list counted as eligible candidates for re-leasing. In addition to being a requirement of remarketing expense selection, the development of an eligible pool is an implicit diversification mechanism since it accurately and objectively reflects the distribution of expected pool lessees. This method prevents the generation of "nonfeasible" lessees (those with artificial or unrealistic business or credit profiles) such as a South American, A1-rated lessee. Once these and other real-life effects are duly accounted for, the empirical content of the simulation increases markedly.

Correlation Structure

When discussing the foregoing sources of variation, we indicated several ways in which parameters are constrained and cannot simply be randomly selected from probability distributions. For instance, a higher lease rate may be obtainable from a lower rated lessee with a "hot route" for the time being than what an investment-grade U.S. lessee would pay. Even though the default rate of the former would be higher, the plane would simply be re-leased to yet another poor-quality lessee upon default, assuming the environment is still comparable. This process would clearly result in higher yields than would a shorter series of longer leases to solid lessees. The best course of action for bondholders is not clear, and credit analysis cannot base judgments on either one.

What is undeniable is that at any given time, a matrix of choices will be available to fleet managers, each one of which could have positive and negative factors. The strength of a Monte Carlo simulation is its ability not to take any particular view of the prospective cash flow environment, but to provide instead a blended opinion of what lies ahead. As long as the common-sense requirements of correlation are met, it can be said that the simulation will reasonably and objectively reflect the range of possible credit events with their associated probabilities.

The easiest solution to this problem is to impute a correlation structure to the previous set of four parameters.[22] Readers of chapters 16 and 21 are already familiar with the use of the Cholesky decomposition as a means of tackling the correlation problem; it is therefore not our intention to go over this ground again. However, in the case of aircraft ABS, the derivation of the target correlation matrix is far from simple, and owing to the large influence of credit enhancement levels on correlation structures, we cannot simply dismiss the issue as minor. Data are scarce, forcing credit analysts to synthesize matrix entries ad hoc, sometimes imposing large positive correlations between critical default parameters simply to stress the structure without any data-bound knowledge of the impact this may have on enhancement levels, or whether such stresses make any sense at all.

In general, though, results will depend in a complex manner on the combination of correlation values and the associated individual distribution functions. For instance, a large negative correlation between remarketing times and aircraft values may not matter much if it is always compensated by a large positive correlation between lease rates and remarketing times. Given a unique correlation matrix of four to six variables, it is relatively easy to produce wildly different credit enhancement levels simply by manipulating the range of the associated univariate statistics. The problem addressed in chapter 21 through the Tchebychev root-locus scattering algorithm is present here as well, and needs to be solved in the same manner.

Fundamentally, there is no replacement for good data. At this time, leading aircraft servicers like General Electric Capital Aviation Services (GECAS) and International Lease Finance Corporation (ILFC) have in their databases much of the required data. It would be quite easy for a rating agency to commission a correlation study that would, in our opinion, result in a reduction of credit enhancement levels overall, of which they would be the largest beneficiaries. Failing this, common sense is our sole fallback tool for assigning correlations to deal parameters such as remarketing times or lease terms. Making up correlation structures is nontrivial since the credit analyst must ensure that the resulting matrices meet the two basic requirements of symmetry and non-negative definiteness (see chapter 16 and Appendix E). This problem does not occur in the case of real correlation matrices since they already satisfy these conditions, by definition.

Once the purely mechanical issues of positive-definiteness and symmetry have been dealt with, we still have to have the means of arriving at actual numbers. There is no magic formula, but choosing a range of values around some benchmark number while keeping the sign of the entry fixed seems to be a reasonable approach. In other words, if the correlation is known to be negative from physical considerations, then choosing a range of values between -0.5 and -0.8, and likewise for positive correlations, should reveal any sensitivity cliffs. Correlations less than 0.5 in absolute value are usually too small to make a significant positive or negative impact on enhancement levels. If need be, it is important to modify correlations randomly, and not to engage in wishful thinking and impute a secondary structure to the correlative environment that would always make things worse for the issuer. The luck of the draw will usually suffice to cover a wide range of values.

The output of such a parametric study should be carefully analyzed for outliers, and the latter should be related to the input correlation matrix. In general, analysts will find that credit enhancement levels will be fairly invariant in a respectable range about the root mean square value of the matrix. If this occurs, the particular choice of correlation matrix is largely moot and the problem is solved. If it does not, it will usually indicate that a pair of target variables are problematic and have too much influence on the output. To find them, univariate statistics as well as the correlation matrix that resulted in the outliers should be examined. The solution will usually be to restrict the univariate range to a smaller, more realistic value, or to relax the correlation function. Given the normal tenor of portfolio deals, even a portfolio of twenty-five planes should demonstrate remarkable credit enhancement stability, more than might be surmised from the small number of assets. The lack of actual enhancement stability will usually stem from inattention to, or ignorance of, the covenants and credit-related restrictions that have been placed on servicers in the deal. A properly structured aircraft ABS transaction is remarkably resilient.

Security Deposits

Anyone who has ever rented an apartment is familiar with the notion of a security deposit. Every time an aircraft is leased, the lessor demands, and usually receives, an additional one or two months of rent to cushion the impact of unexpected default by the lessee. Investment-grade lessees can sometimes lease a plane without security deposits, but most lessees in large aircraft-lease portfolios will not escape that requirement. The probability that a lessor will not ask for a security deposit is most likely zero. The probability that a lessor will ask for and not receive a security deposit is clearly nonzero but is quantifiable from empirical evidence. Furthermore, this situation can always be corrected structurally by adding a covenant stipulating that lessors will obtain security deposits from all prospective lessees, although lessors would most likely view this operational requirement as too restrictive. To assume, as rating agencies are wont to do, that future lessees will never contribute security deposits is inconsistent, since they are counted when the transaction closes.[23] They should be either always or never counted. The fact of the matter is that rating agency models currently lack security deposit mechanics. This leaves them no choice but to ignore them.

These deposits are not always made in cash. A standby LOC from a credible bank is usually acceptable and is sometimes cheaper than pure cash due to special arrangements by the lessee. But in general, all security deposits are cash or cash-equivalents and, by their very nature, are clearly sources of credit enhancement to the trust. It is also a simple empirical fact that lower-credit-quality lessees are the most likely candidates for contributing security deposits. This positive correlation is real and cannot be conveniently ignored.

Some may view security deposits as liquidity, but to do so is to misunderstand the nature of liquidity. The simple fact that collateral comes in the form of cash, and is therefore liquid, does not automatically qualify it as liquidity for purposes of the transaction. A reserve account comes in that form too but is clearly credit enhancement. The defining characteristic of credit enhancement sources is not whether they are cash, but rather where in the waterfall are draws on them to be reimbursed. If reimbursements on a credit facility are senior to all principal distribution amounts on an ABS security, this facility acts as liquidity for the latter; otherwise it is to be considered credit enhancement because it sits below the credit-loss level, formally defined as loss of principal. The fact that such amounts may never be reimbursed due to misjudged credit quality is irrelevant since the definition is formal, not practical. As security deposits are free and clear of any liens once they are confiscated after default, they are definitely credit enhancement and not liquidity and should be incorporated as such into any serious analysis of aircraft ABS securities.

In fact, it is quite likely that under favorable leasing environments a large aircraft lease portfolio could suffer an average profit, and not a loss, from lessee defaults as a result of both cashing in the security deposit and quickly releasing the plane. It is true that security deposits, being segregated funds of the servicer, are not the property of the ABS trust unless lessees actually default. On the other hand, if no one defaults there is no need for these amounts, either. The substantial risk is not that lessors will fail to anticipate normal terminations, but rather that defaults will be excessive. Since credit enhancement from security deposits is either largely unnecessary or available, the only way to really assess their impact on ABS credit quality is to build their mechanics into analytical models in a way that reflects how they actually work.

Handling security deposits in a credit analysis model is straightforward once their probability distribution is known. It should be noted that, in addition to sampling favorable environments, probability distributions built from empirical data will also sample unfavorable scenarios with the appropriate frequency as long as the distribution has been derived from a representative sample. In practice, a representative sample is one where the sampling interval is at least equal to the length of the transaction, although we recognize that this is clearly impossible in most cases since transactions have maturity dates of twenty years or more. And while deciding on the propriety of a given probability distribution is the province and function of credit analysis, making simplistic and unnecessary assumptions out of expediency is not.

Handling security deposits analytically is done as follows. Upon a lessee default, the associated security deposits are simply placed into the collection account, whereupon they become commingled with available funds from regular collections and lose their separate credit identity. Available funds left over at the end of the waterfall are simply returned to the servicer according to transaction documents.

Readers should also note that once security deposit mechanics are included in credit analysis, their credit impact can easily be determined by turning this feature off and computing the resulting, lower ABS security credit ratings. In general, the lack of analytical recognition of this source of enhancement is one of the main reasons for the suboptimality of aircraft ABS structures. It is not sufficient to allow issuers to count security deposits as sources of "liquidity" at closing as part of a semantic exercise. They must also be part of the fundamental analysis from the beginning. The argument that security deposits are optional is fallacious, since they have become as much a part of the aircraft leasing business as they are of the real estate business. A harsh leasing environment is an additional motivation in favor of, not against, the requirement for a security deposit.

At least one rating agency, Moody's, seems inconsistent on this issue. Large issuers like Morgan and Stanley Aircraft Finance (MSAF) are allowed to count security deposits as part of required liquidity[24] while smaller issuers like AeroFreighter are not.[25] Moody's aircraft ABS analysis also appears to confuse the concepts of liquidity and credit enhancement.[26] Finally, the fact that obvious forms of credit enhancement are wrongly counted as liquidity should be ample motivation for a reevaluation of the original, EETC-borne requirement of an eighteen-month liquidity facility. We take up this subject later.

Legal Requirements

The legal analysis of an aircraft ABS transaction is quite involved but peripheral to the main issues of valuation and cash flow analysis. We only note this complexity and advise the reader to consult legal professionals in the field who can speak more authoritatively on this aspect of aircraft ABS. As a rule, we take for granted that adequate legal protection exists, for without it, the entire transaction is in jeopardy. Although in theory a lack of clear security interest in an asset will clearly impact recovery upon default and its speed, it is virtually certain that the transaction would not proceed without it. In practice, the issue is thus largely moot.

Beyond the standard aspects of true sale and nonconsolidation, it should be mentioned that bondholders with assets located in foreign jurisdictions, and thus not subject to the U.S. bankruptcy code, will usually benefit from the modalities of the June 1948 Geneva "Convention on the International Recognition of Rights in Aircraft," of which the United States and most major European and South American countries are either parties or signatories. This document has essentially the same practical impact as Section 1110 of the U.S. bankruptcy code except that, instead of the sixty-day recovery provision found in the U.S. bankruptcy code, the Geneva Convention allows up to ninety days to effect recovery.

In addition, ensuring the validity of liens on planes located abroad by placing local mortgages on them is commonly impractical since removing them from the local jurisdiction may be onerous and lengthy. In lieu of a mortgage, and in addition to the standard security interest, a pledge of SPE stock is normally the way investor concerns are alleviated. Readers interested in the legal nuances of this asset type may wish to consult additional legal sources. Rating agency publications may be a good place to start, and some are listed as references in the following pages.

The Handling of Covenants

It was mentioned earlier that transaction documents usually place restrictions on the quality and origin of lessees represented in the asset pool. These restrictions represent diversification constraints on the trust and are used (for example) to avoid concentrations of lessees in any one rating category, normally below investment grade, or in sub-investment-grade countries where repossession or remarketing expenses may be high. For example, they will prevent servicers from leasing to a particular lessee when doing so would cause the ag-

Table 22.1
Illustration of a Hypothetical Covenant on Regional Concentration

Region	Max A/C $ Conc.
North America	75%
Europe	50%
Asia-Pacific	40%
South America	35%
Africa/Middle East	15%

gregate appraised value of planes in the pool to exceed certain geographical or lessee quality thresholds.

An example of such a regional concentration covenant is shown in Table 22.1. Similar requirements may exist, for instance, with respect to lessee credit quality, individual lessee concentration, concentrations of the top five lessees, and others. When imposing these constraints, rating agencies clearly assume that the intersection set of all these covenants is nonempty without, in fact, ascertaining that such is the case.

Unfortunately, current credit analysis methods ignore these covenants altogether. Under the current analytical framework, lessees with assumed, usually low credit ratings are chosen at random from a synthetic universe and placed in the pool in a way that may violate many of the legally binding transaction covenants. The credit profiles of the synthesized pools that are used in cash flow simulations are far worse than what is conceivable under the transaction documents.

For instance, assuming that all subsequent lessees in a securitized pool will be rated Caa is clearly wrong. If there are five lessees in the world with this credit rating, it is obviously impossible for the pool to have six Caa-rated lessees unless such new lessees are assumed both to come into existence at just the right rate and to be interested in leasing just the plane that has become available, a ludicrous notion. Yet under current methods, this is what is deemed to happen. Either covenants need to be built into the analysis, or they should be removed wholesale from the requirements of an aircraft ABS transaction.

It is relatively easy to incorporate credit quality covenants within the simulation and thus to reject in real time lessees that violate concentration restrictions. If the lessee turns out to be unacceptable, another lessee is then selected at random from a given credit quality distribution. As long as the intersection of all credit quality covenants with the available universe is nonempty, this loop will terminate and a new lessee will enter the pool in accordance with potential reality.

Although a "no-name basis" works well for credit quality covenants, it is clearly insufficient to handle geographical concentration restrictions such as in Table 22.1. To do so, one must also keep track of the domicile of each new lessee being considered for pool inclusion. If the prospective location violates the requirements of a Table like 22.1, the candidate lessee is rejected interactively and a new candidate lessee is selected. As before, if the intersection of geographical covenants with the potential universe is nonempty, the loop will always terminate. There is no dearth of published data on registered airlines, such that drawing up a list of geographies and their lessees is relatively painless. Note that by using such a list, no assumption is made that the names will not change, only that the distribution will remain invariant, a much more forgiving notion. In fact, the aircraft-leasing universe is such that companies are born and die almost yearly.

As mentioned earlier, a second significant source of suboptimality arises when transaction covenants, which can be quite numerous, are flagrantly ignored. In practice, this flawed analysis may impose a significant burden on a trust that must now be able to support fictitious pools with default rates completely out of line with the logic of the transaction. Nonsense in the name of conservatism is not a virtue.

Readers should also note that implementing covenants is not as trivial as it may seem, and is directly linked to the snake algorithm discussed previously. This linkage stems from the fact that covenants regulate concentrations as percentages of the appraised value of the planes in the pool. As we saw earlier, these values will fluctuate in nonlinear fashion depending on life-cycle phase angles, aircraft types, utilization rates, and other factors. These parameters and others are included in the snake algorithm and contribute to changes in the forecasted market value of each aircraft in the pool. By taking individual life-cycle effects into consideration, we are better able to reflect dynamic market conditions and properly monitor covenants.

For example, if five years after closing, a Ghana-based lessee is interested in leasing a defaulted asset (in other words, it has been selected from a target list as a candidate lessee) forecasted by the snake algorithm to be in a down period, its proportional contribution to the pool may likely be less than it was at closing. Hence leasing this aircraft to such a lower-quality lessee might not, in fact, violate the appropriate regional concentration covenant at the time, contrary to the original situation. In this manner properly accounting for aircraft valuation has a beneficial side effect on our ability to objectively and rationally analyze the transaction's creditworthiness.

Our point here is not to agitate against covenants. We believe they are necessary operational safeguards in a fluid and complex environment where moral hazard may cause initial diversification to dwindle if no constraints are imposed. In aircraft ABS, covenants make up much of the structure in structured finance. However, a "decent respect to the opinions of mankind" compels us to include them in any self-respecting credit analysis. Anything short of that is doing a disservice to one party or the other.

Maintenance Reserves

Given the number of passenger-miles flown every year around the world and the significant technical challenges involved, air travel is a remarkably safe method of transportation. One reason for this impressive record is that aircraft components, such as airframes and engines, are the subject of a rigorous scheduled maintenance program.

In terms of credit analysis, this is both a blessing and a curse: a curse, because it increases the complexity of the valuation task. For instance, an aircraft with a fuselage two months away from a major mandatory overhaul is clearly worth less than another, identical aircraft five years away from the same overhaul. But it is a blessing because the certainty of maintenance work has a favorable impact on the precision and reliability of credit analysis. From an ABS point of view, detailed knowledge of the maintenance program presents the analyst with a golden opportunity to increase both the efficiency of the transaction's capital structure and the investors' knowledge of its realistic risk-return profile.

In general, aircraft lessees are financially responsible for performing engine or airframe maintenance when due. However, to ensure sufficient funds are always on hand to do so, lessees are normally required by lessors to make additional monthly payments in the form of maintenance reserves. The latter, albeit somewhat negotiable, are normally calculated to cover anticipated maintenance costs should the lessee default on the eve of a major airframe overhaul.

As a rule, maintenance reserves are both requested and received but are by no means a conditio sine qua non of the aircraft-leasing business. There is no guarantee that all lessors will or should operate by always requesting such additional reserve payments and it is quite possible for a lessor to forgo maintenance reserves altogether in an attempt to quickly remarket the plane by bundling maintenance contributions with normal lease payments as part of a lower total package. Conversely, others may perhaps be playing a massive shell game whereby maintenance obligations are continuously transferred to subsequent lessees willing to take over the aircraft at rock-bottom prices in exchange for footing the bill on whatever maintenance is needed. The idea of mortgaging tomorrow to pay for today is certainly not new but should be viewed with suspicion by credit analysts. Whereas maintenance reserves may be optional, maintenance itself is not.

The cash flows associated with maintenance reserves are complicated and require formal treatment. In this section, we discuss engines and airframes separately and then briefly discuss the central question of whether maintenance reserves should properly be regarded as either trust liquidity or credit enhancement, or simply be ignored and excluded from the analysis of aircraft-backed structured securities.

Engine Reserves

Engines are by far the most critical component of any aircraft and consequently require the heaviest and most frequent maintenance. The main credit-related analytical feature of engine maintenance programs is that modern jet engines are essentially self-renewing commodities. Two identical engines fresh from an overhaul are deemed essentially interchangeable, having more or less been completely rebuilt. What matters is not so much when the engine was manufactured, but how long ago it was overhauled.

Surprisingly, there is usually no contractual requirement for the engines with the same serial numbers as those that were attached to the wings at lease origination to be on that plane when it is returned to the lessor. Instead, lease contracts will normally mandate that, whichever engines happen to be on the wings at lease end, they should have the same or fewer hours remaining till the next overhaul as they had when the aircraft was first delivered to the lessee. Thus, unless the lessee has perfect foresight, it is highly likely that it will have partially paid for maintenance in advance by returning the plane with engines that are on average farther away from an overhaul than those that were delivered to it. This is because the lessee usually has spare "fresh" engines, allowing those needing overhauls to be taken off the wings while preventing aircraft down-time. In essence, a game of "engine musical chairs" is being played in which the identity of the three or four live engines is moot and the likelihood of a net maintenance gain to the lessor is high.

Readers should note the difference between *scheduled* and *required* maintenance. An engine that may not be due for an overhaul may have flown under adverse conditions, and thus may require unscheduled maintenance. There could be an airworthiness directive issued by the FAA that could force all engines of a given type to undergo special maintenance. In general, however, these events will be rare. The owner of a car also runs this risk, but the probability that something unforeseen will happen to an aircraft flying at an average altitude of 35,000 feet at Mach 0.7 is much smaller. Thus, as a rule we may assume that scheduled and required maintenance coincide.

Cash Flows

Formerly, all scheduled maintenance was performed on an hourly basis. However, maintenance requirements on certain recent models[27] are based instead on cycles flown. Consequently, a portion of engine reserve contributions may be assessed on a cycle basis. As a practical matter, though, cycle-based contributions are still collected on an hourly basis. If necessary, a true-up adjustment mechanism is used to convert the contractual hours-cycle ratio into an additional lease-end engine reserve contribution adjustment.

In the case of hourly contributions, the calculations are straightforward. The lessee simply pays a flat rate per hour flown based on airframe logbooks.

Table 22.2
Actual Lessee in Profile

Item	Value
Contractual rate	2.5 hours/cycle
Engine reserve rate	$50/hour
Lease term	4 years
Flight time	1,760 hours
Cycles flown	800

This hourly rate is obviously different for different engine types but is generally in the $100 range. In principle, engine reserves act as security deposits for future engine overhaul work. If the lessee defaults, they normally become the property of the lessor. In the non-default case, if required or scheduled maintenance is due, the lessee can draw on its own aggregated and cumulative contributions to offset that cost. No refunds are given for unused maintenance contributions and no advances are made on future contributions. As we shall see, this process acts as a source of credit enhancement to the trust, assuming maintenance reserves are legally part of the corpus.

In the case of cycle-based contributions, the collection process is identical save for the asymmetric true-up mechanism just mentioned. To see how that works, assume Table 22.2 represents actual data for a given lessee. Having logged 1,760 hours, the aircraft should have flown $1,760/2.5 = 704$ cycles. However, it took off and landed 800 times, representing a hypothetical $800 \times 2.5 = 2,000$ hours of flight time. The difference $2,000 - 1,760 = 240$ hours would constitute excess wear and tear, and the lessee would owe the lessor an additional $240 \times \$50 = \$12,000$ at lease termination over and above what was already contributed for that engine. Given that a jet aircraft may have four engines, this can be significant when added to normal contributions.

Now, assume instead that Table 22.3 provides the actual data for our hapless lessee. In this case, the lessee has flown fewer sorties than originally estimated and contractually agreed upon. Given the number of cycles flown, it should have logged $600 \times 2.5 = 1,500$ hours. To be fair, the lessor should

Table 22.3
Hypothetical Lessee in Profile (fewer cycles flown)

Datum	Value
Contractual rate	2.5 hours/cycle
Engine reserve rate	$50/hour
Lease term	4 years
Flight time	1,760 hours
Cycles flown	600

owe the lessee $(1,760 - 1,500) \times \$50 = \$13,000$ at lease termination, but life isn't fair and the lessor in fact owes nothing. Needless to say, the probability that this or any other lessee will fly exactly 704 cycles in four years is essentially zero.

Even in the case of normal lease terminations, if the engines returned with the plane are closer to their next overhaul date than those that were delivered, the lease-end true-up assessment will normally be levied to compensate the lessor for prospective maintenance. This asymmetry acts as credit enhancement to the structure since amounts earned by this process become available to the trust to make other payments—for instance, interest payments on the securities. For the reason cited, the fact that an engine may have flown a greater absolute number of hours, or that the engines on the craft are different from those that were delivered with it, is not a factor in the true-up assessment.

This merry-go-round process has another hidden feature that makes it even more lucrative to lessors. The next lessee, unless it is the same as the previous one, is in no position to take advantage of these advance maintenance deposits. It simply starts paying maintenance reserves starting from where the last lessee delivered the engines. If the engine was favorably positioned in its overhaul cycle, the amount of maintenance reserves paid in before the next overhaul will be large, and the lessor will benefit from these extra cash earnings along the way. If the engine was not favorably positioned along the same axis, the lessee will still be financially responsible for maintenance, but the lessor will not fund required maintenance with advance payments made by previous lessees.

Under normal circumstances, this is a game whose odds are skewed in favor of lessors, and as a result, engine reserves are usually a profit center for lessors.

Airframes

Airframes are also subject to a scheduled maintenance program, one usually partitioned into the four alphabetical designations A, B, C, and D. In alphabetical order, these letters refer to increasingly costly maintenance work, or *checks*. Airframe reserves, like engine reserves, are normally flat hourly fees in the $100 range.

Compared to the total cost of operating an aircraft, A, B, and C checks are relatively small-ticket items, but the D check is another matter and can run into the millions. It represents a major airframe overhaul and will cause the aircraft to be unavailable for a period of months. However, D checks are extremely rare, being scheduled approximately every 25,000 hours.

A D-check may impact cash flows two ways: first, by requiring a large draw from accumulated maintenance reserves, and second, by potentially reducing lease cash flows via an accommodation to a lessee unable to generate passenger revenues during the check. Such an accommodation may be part of the total lease package and must be factored in by the credit analyst. Regardless of the amount actually spent, the cost of a D check is borne by lessees and will vary depending on the precise condition of the plane. Although the exact amount will not be known until the precheck examination is conducted, fairly reliable estimates can be made from historical data. In the last resort, it would be fair to assume that the principal balance of all airframe reserves contributed by a lessee would be liquidated to pay for the D check.

Cash Flows

The calculations involved in properly accounting for airframe reserves are straightforward. To compute cash inflows, monthly utilization is multiplied by the contractual airframe reserve rate. Conversely, when a C or D check is due based on forecast utilization rates, the estimated amount due for performing the check is subtracted from cumulative contributions and returned to the lessee, thereby reducing the maintenance reserve balance by the same amount. A further caveat here is that due to the high cost of the D check, a cost borne entirely by the lessee, lessors may accommodate lessees by allowing them to forgo airframe reserve contributions until the number of hours till the next D check is equal to what it was upon delivery. Thus, if the same lessee re-leases the plane after a D check, aggregate fleet contributions will be reduced by the amount of this "reserve holiday." However, in the case where a new lessee leases the same plane, maintenance reserves contributions will begin on day 1 without the potential reimbursement of past contributions. On average, this will lead to a net gain to the trust. Thus, as was the case with engine reserves, airframe reserves are usually a net profit center to lessors.

Maintenance Reserves as Liquidity

The legal status of security deposits was clear. They acted to cushion the impact of default on the lessor and were either available in cases of default or largely unnecessary in the opposite case. Although security deposits were clearly not part of the estate upon normal lease termination, this was precisely what diversification was all about. In that case, lessors would know months in advance that the lease would not be renewed and could act accordingly with very little effective cash flow disruption to the trust. On balance, it was concluded that, despite their contingent legal status, security deposits, considered dynamically and properly accounted for, fulfilled the basic requirements normally associated with credit enhancement.

As discussed previously, the status of maintenance reserves is different but more favorable to the trust. Not only are lessors benefiting upon lessee default by being able to transfer the cost of maintenance onto the next lessee (perhaps subject to accommodation), but they also benefit upon normal lease termination by being able to potentially retain significant unused maintenance reserves while the lessee has no right to offset lease payments against these amounts. Here the balance is definitely tilted in favor of lessors.

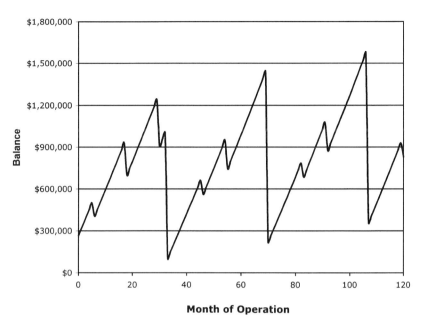

Figure 22.5. Engine Reserve Account History

Owing to such lease modalities, maintenance reserve accounts will normally maintain positive balances that could be available for other purposes, since future lessees would not be able to draw on amounts paid by their predecessors. Therefore, we find that a portion of maintenance reserves is a true source of credit enhancement, and another could represent potential liquidity. As a result, aircraft ABS transactions could be made more efficient by creatively managing these funds.

For instance, Figure 22.5 shows the engine reserve account history of a typical wide-bodied aircraft over a ten-year operating period with the following assumptions:

1. The plane is always re-leased to the same lessee, and
2. The entire cumulative contribution of the lessee on any engine is returned to it as reimbursement for the overhaul.
3. Reserve earnings are included in the account balance.
4. Swapped-out engines are replaced with delivery-equivalent engines.

The large reserve draws correspond to engine overhaul dates where the lessee had contributed a significant portion of the outstanding balance, while the smaller draws correspond to engines where lessee contributions were relatively small prior to overhaul.

Note that these assumptions are rather extreme cases. Under normal operation, lessors would usually fare better than this, either because the lessee would be different or because actual costs would not always equal contribu-

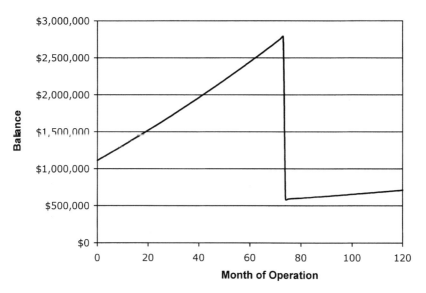

Figure 22.6. Typical Jet Aircraft Reserve History with a D Check

tions. Yet even under these conditions, the engine reserve account balance remains positive and is a source of credit enhancement.

On the airframe side, although a D check is a rather rare event, Table 22.3 shows the airframe reserve balance history of a typical aircraft under identical assumptions as Table 22.2. Here, the initial airframe reserve is approximately $1 million and accumulates steadily until the D check. The D check in Figure 22.6 was valued at about $2.5 million, which may or may not be in line with actual costs. Since reimbursements are capped at the principal amount contributed by the lessee, airframe contributions are seen to be another net source of credit enhancement to the trust.

When both airframe and reserve balances are combined, there result cash flow histories such as the one shown in Figure 22.7 for a typical jet aircraft's ten-year history without a D check, a more likely case. Note that significant positive net cash flow is generated over this ten-year simulation in a stable utilization environment.

When aggregated over an entire fleet, the history of cash inflows and outflows can be quite involved. In a Monte Carlo simulation, this history obviously varies with each scenario according to the utilization vectors chosen for each aircraft throughout the transaction. For instance, Figure 22.8 is an aggregate fleet cash flow history for a fleet of ten prototypical wide-bodied jets.[28]

The few large peaks in Figure 22.8 correspond to D checks on fleet aircraft while the more numerous, smaller peaks correspond to engine draws. Engine draws are much more numerous because each plane was assumed to have four engines. All maintenance draws are accurately positioned at intervals that

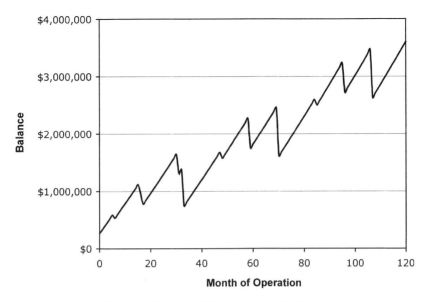

Figure 22.7. Typical Jet Aircraft Reserve History without a D Check

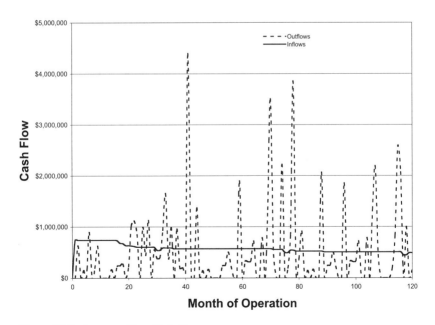

Figure 22.8. Aggregate Fleet Cash Flows

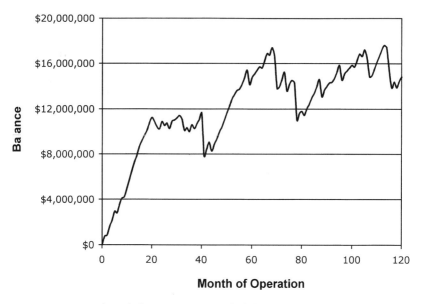

Figure 22.9. Hypothetical Fleet Maintenance Schedule

depend on the detailed hourly utilization history of each aircraft. Since aircraft on the ground are neither generating revenue nor requiring maintenance, the utilization-based method properly accounts for reserve draws in relation to reserve collections and to the re-leasing of the plane.

The cumulative aggregate reserve balance of our putative ten-aircraft fleet is shown in Figure 22.9 for the same Monte Carlo scenario as in Figure 22.8. From a standing start, this hypothetical maintenance-reserving process is seen to generate more than $15 million of net positive cash flows to the trust over a ten-year period. Although it is clearly difficult to evaluate the surplus precisely, maintenance calculations tend to be less prone to error due to the relatively high predictability of engine overhauls and airframe checks dates once utilization is known.

As can be seen, the combination of steady cash inflows and intermittent cash outflows generates significant float yield to the structure. Credit analysts are fortunate in that aircraft maintenance schedules represent one of the least speculative elements in the analysis of aircraft-backed structured securities, and we conclude that the inclusion of these contributions in the corpus would give bondholders another source of liquidity and credit enhancement and would increase the efficiency of the transaction.

Maintenance reserves are a source of credit enhancement in the sense that a portion of them will eventually become the property of the trust, free and clear of any liens and encumbrances by the processes described earlier. On the other hand, they are liquidity in the sense that a portion of idle funds in the maintenance reserve account could eventually be borrowed therefrom to pay interest on the notes and later returned to the account until used by individual lessees to pay for maintenance, or else become trust property and hence transferred to a different trust account. If reimbursements take place above senior interest, then they act as liquidity.

Aircraft will not fly if they are not properly maintained. Therefore, ignoring the existence of maintenance reserves in credit analysis will only help issuers at the expense of bondholders. Conversely, counting them benefits both. Issuers have a right to demand that sources of enhancement legally included in the corpus should impact their credit ratings. To be fair, if they are to be part of the trust for some purposes, they should be counted for all purposes.

The Need for Outside Liquidity

Readers who have stayed with us till now may have come to the mistaken conclusion that we are advocating the complete elimination of outside liquidity in aircraft ABS transactions and its replacement by a combination of security deposits and maintenance reserves. Nothing could be further from the truth. We are, however, calling for a rational and quantitative investigation of the real need for outside liquidity in these complex structures. This section is an attempt to formulate a partial answer to the question of exactly how much excess liquidity an aircraft ABS transaction really needs.

The Legacy of EETC Structures

Readers will recall from our earlier brief survey of aircraft finance that EETC structures are equipped with an eighteen-month liquidity facility to give bondholders breathing room to liquidate trust assets upon a default by the sole airline lessee in the transaction. An EETC default means that cash flows drop essentially to zero. In that context, a year-and-a-half cushion does not seem unreasonable to effect an orderly liquidation at better than fire-sale prices. In an EETC default event, the liquidity facility is the only source of cash able to avert a default on the bonds. For that reason, although one can argue about the exact amount, there is no question that significant external liquidity is needed to the extent that a high rating on the bonds is sought.

However, in the case of a lease portfolio of aircraft, the situation is quite different. In that case, we are generally faced with an array of aircraft types and lessees since we exclude cases where the fleet is leased to only one or two lessees as just another name for an EETC. In the portfolio case, a lessee default in no way implies that cash flows totally cease; and although total cash flow interruption is still possible, its probability is exceedingly remote since the operator is generally adept at generating demand for aircraft rather than running an airline. The main credit feature of these transactions from the investors' standpoint, and the way cash crunches are to be avoided, is precisely via the releasing upon default of a diversified pool of aircraft.

In this environment, it is highly unlikely for many reasons that eighteen months of liquidity will turn out to be the right number, including the following:

1. In the context of a portfolio of aircraft, liquidity needs are proportional to the likelihood that insufficient cash flows will be generated to cover bond interest pending re-leasing of the planes. In most cases, the percentage of the fleet required to be off-lease to miss an interest payment will far exceed historical norms. Whether it is smaller than the probability required for Aa ratings on the senior class is a question that requires detailed analysis of lease cash flows over the life of the transaction. Diversification will enter implicitly into these calculations and will cause liquidity needs stemming from insufficient lease cash flows to be mitigated by the proper application of deal covenants (discussed earlier). In practice, the standard restrictions on lessee concentrations will go a long way toward a more robust structure.

2. As mentioned before, the direct and positive correlation between the availability of security deposits as a source of cash credit enhancement and their need will contribute to reducing average outside cash requirements. In other words, liquidity needs will be higher following lessee defaults, at which time security deposits will also become the property of the trust. The only conceivable scenario in which security deposits would have no impact would be one whereby all lessees had normally ended their leases and not re-leased any of the planes at any price, and the entire air travel industry essentially shut down. Although this may now be conceivable, it is not the basis for a rational allocation of capital. Of course, the absence of security deposits at precisely the moment where they are needed should be considered, but credit analysis is founded not on doomsday scenarios but on a probability distribution of events. Using a worst-case scenario as a basis for credit rating is also disingenuous when used as an excuse to sidestep an intricate analytical issue that has clear credit consequences. In fact, the absence of security deposits should be a red flag to any credit analyst. In any event, the relative frequency with which security deposits are available is a decidable proposition that is well within the purview of ABS analysis.

3. There is obviously a direct correlation between hours flown and maintenance requirements. Aircraft on the ground do not require maintenance but neither do they generate revenues. However, as we saw in the last section, the maintenance-reserving process is tilted in favor of the lessor, especially in the case of lessee default where all maintenance reserves become its irrevocable property. In effect, in precisely the cases where cash is more likely to be needed, the trust will on average benefit from windfall contributions consisting of forfeited reserves. This direct correlation between the need and the availability of cash

from reserves is a neglected aspect of aircraft ABS analysis and indicates that reserves do represent sources of cash credit enhancement to the trust. In addition, they are liquidity in the real sense that reserves from one plane may be used to defray maintenance expenses due on another. Further, even assuming that fleet reserve balances remain at least constant despite repeated draws, a significant portion of initial reserve balances represent additional credit enhancement to the trust, while future reserve contributions are more akin to liquidity.

As a result of these factors, we conclude that the combination of security deposits and maintenance reserves will partially offset outside liquidity needs. The question, then, is by how much?

Answering this question definitively would require a statistical analysis of immediate cash needs, such as the one indicated before, whereby we would systematically vary the percentage of outside liquidity until the probability of missing any portion of a timely interest payment on a given tranche were consistent with its assigned rating. As readers can readily surmise from the earlier reserve account histories in relatively benign cases, this dynamic analysis would be quite complicated, having to link utilization rates, engine overhaul, and airframe check dates with such things as the snake algorithm and deal covenants (to mention just a few things).

An Alternative Proposal

Putting these observations and speculations together, we conclude that it would be difficult for investors to accept a reduction in available cash below the eighteen-month benchmark, even though we have indicated that this numerical requirement is clearly inapplicable in the portfolio context, having arisen solely as a holdover from EETC structures. As is currently done, liquidity requirements can be met artificially by redefining any source of cash as liquidity. Instead, we prefer to call things by what they really are and propose that outside liquidity requirements should be reduced to the amount that is effectively used, which is approximately six months. In addition, security deposits and maintenance reserves should be included within a more sophisticated analysis that would assess their impact, as a source of cash, on bond cash flow performance.

Perhaps an acceptable compromise could proceed along the following lines:

1. Outside net liquidity is set equal to six months of weighted average bond coupon.
2. Deemed available cash sources consist of eligible credit facilities, security deposits, and initial maintenance reserves, whatever they might be. If more of either or both is potentially available, the trust benefits and credit enhancement is seen to increase.
3. As the transaction progresses, external liquidity is slowly replaced with forfeited maintenance reserves or security deposits such that the sum

of all external liquidity sources remains constant and equal to six months of current bond interest. External liquidity remains in place if insufficient additional reserves or security deposits are collected to reduce it to zero.

4. Once external liquidity requirements are met with new cash, additional cash available can be allocated to amortization. In practice, though, external liquidity may be less expensive than cash.

5. Shortfalls caused by draws by one lessee to pay for engine or airframe maintenance are made up from future reserve contributions or confiscated security deposits.

Although specifying a priori the precise liquidity requirements of an aircraft ABS transaction is a difficult task, using a formulaic approach to such an idiosyncratic asset class is inappropriate. Each aircraft is unique and must be described by its own cash-generation mechanics. On a percentage basis, a pool with higher lessee concentrations will require more liquidity than another with comparable asset quality but better lessee diversification. Without careful analysis, the relative trade-offs between two such pools are basically impossible to estimate.

Liability Structures

Although we formally introduced liability structures in chapter 8, no discussion of aircraft ABS can be considered complete without a review of the basic bond structure found in most aircraft lease portfolio transactions.

Being essentially an exercise in logic, the quantitative aspects of SPE liability modeling are far less involved than those of asset modeling. This is not to minimize the creativity required to devise bond structures with certain characteristics, but only to say that the credit analyst's task of implementing a set of rules is relatively simple compared to that of forecasting aircraft market values and their cash flow potential for the next thirty years. The field of structural optimization remains open, and we do not purport to make any contribution to it herein.

In the context of this book, we take liability structures as given and simply derive their logical consequences with respect to the credit quality of issued securities. However, if the process of designing optimal aircraft ABS capital structures is ever to reach convergence, the rational investigation of the credit dynamics of its subject matter will have to be taken up formally.

The Basic Aircraft ABS Structure

Largely as a result of historical circumstances stemming from the first large aircraft lease portfolio transaction,[29] a relatively complex waterfall has been developed to allocate available funds within most large aircraft-ABS structures. Despite the total lack of theoretical justification for following a traditional pattern in a field that prides itself on creativity, most aircraft lease portfolio transactions nevertheless stick to the basic waterfall created by GPA, the main feature of which is the existence of multiple levels of principal reimbursements. In what follows, we review the basic GPA-inspired waterfall for a generic three-tranche capital structure, and then make two remarks related to the former's impact on the credit behavior of the associated securities. Readers should note that actual transactions would most likely evidence some variations on this theme.

1. *Servicing fees and expenses.* These may include basic servicing fees, administrative agency fees, maintenance expenses, certifications, and so on.
2. *Class A Notes interest.* This may include additional amounts, to be paid at this level, owed to derivatives counterparties.
3. *Senior liquidity reimbursements* (see our comments on the meaning of *liquidity* in earlier sections).
4. *Class A Notes Minimum Principal Amount.* These payments are made according to a preestablished schedule drawn up by the underwriters.
5. *Class B Notes interest.*
6. *Class B Notes Minimum Principal Amount* (see item 4).
7. *Class C Notes interest.*
8. *Class C Notes Minimum Principal Amount* (see item 4).
9. *Junior liquidity reimbursements.* This is a hybrid facility that protects junior-tranche interest payments as well as some principal reimbursements.
10. *Class A Notes Scheduled Principal Amount* (see item 4).
11. *Class B Notes Scheduled Principal Amount* (see item 4).
12. *Class C Notes Scheduled Principal Amount* (see item 4).
13. *Minimum equity distribution* (optional).
14. *Class A Notes Supplemental Principal Amount* (see item 4).
15. *Class B Notes Supplemental Principal Amount* (see item 4).
16. *Class C Notes Supplemental Principal Amount* (see item 4).
17. *Special distributions* (such as note redemptions).
18. *Remainder to equity.*

Observations

With respect to item 1, Servicing fees and expenses, the availability of maintenance reserves clearly plays a critical role. As a part of the trust estate, they provide a ready source of cash to pay those expenses. Bondholders usually know little about the amount of maintenance expense that will be incurred, and this represents a risk to them since these payments are senior in priority to their investment. If maintenance reserves are either unavailable or not included in the trust estate, then the risk to bondholders is magnified since required maintenance comes out of lease payments made by other lessees.

Under normal operations, this risk is mitigated by the standard practice of making lessees responsible for all maintenance. However, as discussed before, it may be impossible to re-lease a plane without performing advanced maintenance because a lessee may not be able or willing to contemplate any down-time in the short term. Maintenance work comes in chunks and cannot be predicted with 100% accuracy. It would be inconsistent to count maintenance reserves as a source of available funds, and therefore of security to bondholders, and then to not analyze prospective maintenance payments as a source of risk following lessee defaults, given their privileged position in the waterfall. The difficulty of doing this is real, but is not a defense against capital inefficiency. In the final analysis, investors need to be provided with a rational, consistent, and realistic evaluation of the total risk-reward profile of the transaction, not just its simple or obvious aspects.

Multiple levels of principal distributions introduce a peculiar credit phenomenon that bondholders need to keep in mind. As we have repeatedly said, credit analysis happens at the margins. In the expected case, all transactions are successful. The risk of principal shortfall becomes a reality only at the tail of some cash flow probability distribution. During those stress scenarios, the controlling feature of the waterfall will be the *Minimum Principal Distribution schedules* disclosed in transaction documents. Since Class A Minimum Principal is senior to Class B interest, and Class B Minimum Principal senior to Class C interest, available funds normally allocated to interest payments on relatively junior classes will instead be diverted to fund the minimum principal amounts on relatively senior classes. Left unattended, this type of structure severely and negatively affects the credit rating of subordinated classes. Moreover, given that, outside of credit arbitrage, structured finance is largely a non-linear zero-sum game, this negative impact will be accompanied by an equally strong and positive improvement of the senior-class credit quality. But since the latter's credit rating has been capped at Aa2 or thereabouts, such improvement usually comes to nought.

The situation can clearly be remedied by eliminating minimum principal schedules, but doing this only begs the question of why they were there in the first place. In general, although a missed interest payment on any class of notes is an event of default under the indenture, in practical terms only the senior-most class of bondholders can effectively exercise its rights upon default events because all junior bondholders have waived their legal remedies until the class immediately above them has been fully repaid. In practice, a default notice could cause the structure to switch to a secondary waterfall whereby all *interest* and *principal* on each class of notes become due and payable before any available funds are allocated to the next (i.e., lower) class.

Analytically, a senior-class event of default, while practically unthinkable, would be even worse for the subordinated noteholders since it would preclude a return to the primary waterfall and guarantee the permanence of the secondary waterfall. For instance, during a random stress case, a situation where sufficient cash is available to pay Class A interest, Class A Minimum Principal,

Class B interest, and Class B Minimum Principal but *not* Class C interest is conceivable. This would not cause an effective event of default but would deprive Class C bondholders of any allocation, and the effect on its rating would be disastrous.

An obvious structural fix would be to change the default waterfall to allow current interest allocations on all classes along with the principal turbo-feature already contemplated. The declaration mechanics of default would also have to be modified in order to grant all classes of notes the power to cause a switch to the default waterfall. In that case, junior bondholders could still benefit from favorable asset prices at the transaction's legal final maturity date, helping to reduce their principal loss under a stress case.

The argument that these extreme cases are academic, and can therefore be ignored, is fallacious since credit analysis needs to reflect even cases of diminutive probability. As already explained, the problem arises because the latters' impact on credit ratings is disproportionate to their likelihood of occurrence. Since junior investors tend to rely more heavily on ratings to price their risk than do senior investors, the impact on yield of a structural mishandling of tail events is material. As a result of these and other factors, and assuming they are required, devising sensible minimum principal schedules is probably the greatest challenge to the structural optimization of contemporary aircraft ABS transactions.

Properly analyzed, the credit rating of junior tranches can fall by five or six rating notches via modifications in principal distribution schedules. In turn, these further raise overall interest costs and increase average reductions of yield, and hence decrease credit ratings. This death spiral may have no solution without a drastic change in tranche issuance levels, leading to the conclusion that the deal simply does not work at those levels. Therein lies the value of serious credit analysis.

Putting It All Together

The last few pages have touched briefly upon the many complicated aspects of the analysis of aircraft-backed structured securities, from the snake algorithm and maintenance reserves onto covenant handling. Putting all this together inside a statistical analysis code is not a sinecure. However, the stakes are high and the efforts amply rewarded by a vastly increased knowledge of this difficult asset class.

But it goes beyond rewards. When investors purchase a security with a given rating, they have a right to expect that credit analysts have structured it in a manner consistent with the same overall financial risk profile as all other securities with the same rating. Lawyers and accountants may have spent months fine-tuning the details of legal documents and giving meaning to the "structure" in structured finance. Therefore, attention to those details is not an option or a luxury, it is a duty. Often, it is the only way to bring to light the unexpected, and mostly unintended, consequences of complex structures operating within even more complex environments. To casually eyeball two aircraft pools of equal appraised value, comparable aircraft types, and lessee composition and then expect the same credit enhancement or liquidity needs is to misunderstand the nature of credit analysis.

Part V
Advanced Structural Features

23

Trigger Theory

Chapter 8 provided an extensive review of standard items in liabilities modeling, beginning with a description of the cash cycle and proceeding with the mechanics of allocation and distribution of cash to the liability accounts. The discussion delved fairly deeply into the mechanics of apportioning principal to competing claimholders. What was missing from our earlier review was a systematic discussion of triggers. The reasons for saving triggers until last are twofold. The first is practical: the lack of granularity and precision in cash flow modeling today means that triggers are not quantitatively evaluated. The second is a philosophical point. The analogy between triggers in financial structures and control structures in physics has not penetrated market awareness. Hence we have chosen to delay the discussion of triggers to the end of the book, to intimate the range of what may be accomplished through advanced liability structuring, without giving the false impression that it exists today.

Triggers

Triggers are one of the most intricate aspects of the credit analysis of structured securities. Their benefits and costs can be evaluated, and from this analysis an unambiguous definition of the optimal trigger level may be established. The search for such optimality is the crux of trigger analysis.

Analytically, the most interesting trigger type allows a reallocation of cash aimed at strengthening transactions and at providing relatively inexpensive enhancement at the expense of operational constraints. The mechanics of such triggers can be flexibly keyed to any aspect of performance (delinquency, default, cushion) judged to be a leading indicator of cash flow health. These are known as *cash flow triggers*. Their analogues in non–cash flow credit structures are generally keyed to asset prices, ratings, or other measures of performance by the primary credit reference in the structure (collectively, *credit structure triggers*).

Another type of trigger is that which provides fail-safe protection, rather than cash reallocation. For instance, if the servicer is placed in bankruptcy by a court of competent jurisdiction, legal documents may force the transaction to unwind ahead of schedule. In other cases, the ABS securities backed by the pool may become due and payable upon certain events. As mentioned before, a revolving period may come to an end upon the declaration of an early amortization trigger, causing the deal to start amortizing early and bringing it to a close in as orderly a manner as possible. Although such triggers are interesting as a practical matter, they are legal in character and less amenable to statistical analysis than the first type. Because of their binary nature, macrotriggers are easily implementable within the waterfall and rarely require optimization. In addition, most trigger events contemplated within this type are fairly standardized and leave essentially no room for analytical creativity. In many instances, these events will fall in the category of force majeure about which very little can be done. For these reasons and others, we focus our discussion on cash flow triggers, an area where structuring talent can be put to use. In what follows, unless otherwise specified, the expression *trigger* will refer exclusively to cash flow triggers.

Triggers in Structured Finance

In most cases, cash reallocation is effected through a trigger index defined with respect to a variety of transaction variables, the most common of which are delinquencies, defaults, and tranche principal balances. Although such reallocations are usually permanent, when they are temporary we shall refer to the trigger as *curable*. Note also that, although trigger indices are computable on any determination date, the basis for such computation may include more than one determination date. For instance, a typical trigger index might be the average portfolio sixty-plus days delinquency level over the last three determination dates. Such quarterly average delinquency trigger indices are common and are generally designed to avoid accidental triggering due to seasonality and other transitional, non–credit related factors.

   In its basic operation, a trigger is referred to as *breached* if the associated trigger index exceeds a suitably chosen threshold on any determination date. Upon a breach, cash that would normally return to the seller is instead typically captured inside a spread or reserve account as additional credit enhancement. That cash becomes available on future payment dates to fulfill debt obligations if current collections fall short of the mark. Obviously, the concept of a trigger is predicated on the fact that excess spread would normally escape from the structure. In a pure cash flow environment in which the structured liabilities amortize using all available excess spread, the presence of a trigger does not enhance performance.

   In another format, a two-tranche ABS transaction under a nominal pro rata principal allocation waterfall could switch to a new, sequential scheme upon the breach. Under stressed cash flow scenarios, doing this would transfer some of the risk of losses borne by the senior bondholders to the subordinated bondholders. The ex ante impact of the trigger would be to raise the senior bond's credit rating at the expense of the junior rating. As mentioned earlier, it is theoretically impossible to improve both credit ratings simultaneously from one collateral pool if one excludes hypothetical arbitrage opportunities stemming from market inefficiencies.

In all cases, however, the choice of the index is a crucial component of its effectiveness. For instance, a coincident default trigger may be completely ineffective against a slowly deteriorating pool, allowing too much excess spread to escape before the trigger level (set, e.g., at two times expected losses on a run-rate basis) is finally breached. Rather than a coincident default index, the way around this problem would be to use a cumulative default index as a signal of impending security loss. Thus, in general, trigger indices will be designed with specific asset behaviors in mind. Consequently, knowledge of the asset class is paramount to the art of crafting realistic triggers.

Regardless of the index, the benefits of a trigger may be realized immediately via reduced interest costs, and the trigger costs nothing if the stressed cash flow scenarios never materialize. In that sense, it may appear costless. From the investors' vantage point, however, the existence of a barrier often is perceived as an invitation not to cross it. This moral hazard is unavoidable and highlights the need for proper analysis of a seller's operations to ensure that no "black hole" exists in which nonperforming assets might be parked to avoid a breach. In the prototypical case, a default trigger could be avoided with payment holidays or some other form of account-level debt restructuring that prevented the affected accounts, usually highly delinquent, from rolling into default, thus forestalling the inevitable.

The obvious fix is to supplement the default trigger with a delinquency trigger capturing the resulting increase in delinquencies. Properly defining the index requires detailed knowledge of a seller's credit policy, something already encountered in the chapter 20 discussion of auto-loan-backed securities. Thus, trigger design is yet another instance where familiarity with the seller's credit policy is a crucial aspect of the analysis of structured securities.

Taxonomy of Triggers

As a preamble to trigger optimization, we outline the standard taxonomy of cash flow triggers. Four basic types exist:

- Binary
- Proportional
- Differential
- Integral

We review each type under the following definitions and assumptions:

1. Transactions have maturity T, resulting in $t \in [0, T]$.
2. A suitable trigger index $I(t)$ and its associated trigger level I_s have been defined.
3. Transaction documents include the concept of a spread account with an outstanding principal balance of $R(t)$ at time t.
4. The impact of the trigger is to reallocate available cash beyond what is required for current amortization to the spread account.

5. We define $P(x(t))$ as the proportion of the excess spread to be so real-located, where $x(t)$ is some variable function of the trigger index $I(t)$ and other deal parameters. By definition, $P(x(t)) \in [0, 1]$.

6. Although $R(t)$ is usually capped at a given percentage of the outstand-ing aggregate bond or pool balance, we assume no such cap exists. Amounts remaining in the spread account at time T are simply flushed back to the equity certificateholder.

Binary Triggers

The most interesting aspect of liability structuring in the context of trigger de-sign is the analyst's ability to fashion indirect incentives aimed at behavior modification on the part of sellers without the need to devise all-or-none situ-ations that create explicit reverse moral hazard. A properly designed trigger should be proactive and symmetric, meaning that it provides incentives in both directions ahead of a serious problem.

The easiest form of trigger is the *binary trigger*, whereby all excess cash is reallocated to the spread account upon breach at time t. This trigger is defined thus:

$$P(x(t)) = H(x(t)) + G(x(t)) \tag{23.1}$$

In equation (23.1), we have defined the Heaviside step function $H(x(t))$, the curing function $G(x(t))$ and $x(t)$ by the following:

$$H(x(t)) = \begin{cases} 0, x(t) \leq 0 \\ 1, x(t) > 0 \end{cases} \tag{23.2}$$

$$x(t) = \frac{I(t) - I_S}{I_S} \tag{23.3}$$

$$G(x(t)) = \begin{cases} 0, & \text{Curable Trigger} \\ H[\int_0^t H(x(t'))dt'] - H(x(t)) & \text{Noncurable Trigger} \end{cases} \tag{23.4}$$

Proportional Triggers

Under the proportional, curable trigger mechanism, $P(x(t))$ is proportional to the value of $x(t)$ as follows:

$$P(x(t)) = \min[1, Kx(t)]H(x(t)) \tag{23.5}$$

Parameter K is an arbitrary proportionality constant set at the analyst's will and aimed at handling various rates of collateral deterioration. In essence, a binary trigger is a proportional trigger with $K \to \infty$. In practice, it is sometimes con-venient to replace equation (23.5) with the following alternative form:

$$P(x(t)) = \left[\frac{1 - e^{-ax(t)}}{1 + e^{-ax(t)}}\right]H(x(t)) \tag{23.6}$$

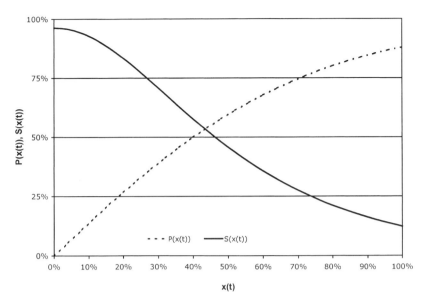

Figure 23.1. Alternative Form of Proportional Triggering

In equation (23.6), parameter *a* plays the implicit role of *K*. To see this, note that the slope $S(x(t))$ of equation (23.6) is given by

$$S(x(t)) = \frac{2ae^{-ax(t)}}{[1 + e^{-ax(t)}]^2}. \tag{23.7}$$

As equation (23.7) indicates, *a* appears linearly in the slope equation and causes nearly proportional increases in $P(x(t))$. Both $P(x(t))$ and $S(x(t))$ are plotted in Figure 23.1. Although not strictly proportional to $x(t)$, $P(x(t))$ is sufficiently linear for most purposes. In addition, the asymptotic behavior of equation (23.6) as $x(t) \to \infty$ makes its especially convenient while allowing greater flexibility in setting trigger levels.

This type of triggering mechanism might be used, for example, with a relatively low trigger level to start trapping excess spread early inside the structure and to slowly ramp up to 100% in case asset performance does not improve. The cash balance remaining in the spread account, should the trigger later cure, would remain there until the maturity date of the transaction, thus providing additional incentive for the seller to cure the trigger as soon as possible but minimizing the moral hazard of full allocation that would have resulted from the use of a binary trigger. Although we generally do not allow for it, we have contemplated the possibility of a reversible trigger whereby excess spread would be removed from the spread account for negative values of $x(t)$. Removals would proceed at the rate given by the value of $x(t)$ until the spread account had a zero balance. Reversible triggers would act as true control mechanisms, adding and removing credit enhancement depending on collateral performance. To our knowledge, no contemplated or else currently outstanding ABS transaction makes use of this type of triggering mechanism.

Differential Triggers

Under differential triggering, $P(x(t))$ is proportional to the first derivative of $x(t)$ rather than its absolute value. In other words,

$$P(x(t)) = K\frac{\partial x(t)}{\partial t}H(x(t)). \tag{23.8}$$

In equation (23.8), parameter K is a proportionality constant used to adjust the rate of cash buildup into the spread account. In practice, the first derivative of $x(t)$ is usually rendered on a monthly basis via

$$\frac{\partial x(t)}{\partial t} = \frac{x(t) - x(t - \Delta t)}{\Delta t}. \tag{23.9}$$

In equation (23.9), Δt is the time interval between two record dates. In general, this is one month.

As mentioned previously, the anticipated performance characteristics of the collateral and the trigger index are major determinants of the latter's effectiveness. In specific asset classes, there might be instances where stellar and steady performance should obtain unless some low-frequency/high-severity macro-event occurred. In that case, a sudden and drastic increase in defaults or delinquencies would result, and we would therefore want to capture excess spread based on monthly changes in index values, no matter how slight, rather than the index values per se—for example, when such changes were clear signals of impending doom that should be heeded. Here again, the trigger value I_S could be set lower (e.g., a mere 5–10% above the expected performance level), ready to be activated at the first sign of trouble. A typical case would be a transaction benefiting from loan-level default or excess of loss insurance and in which the insurer would either default itself or simply balk at fulfilling its contractual obligations. This has been known to happen.

Differential triggering is ineffective when a sudden and isolated jump in delinquencies or defaults is followed by stabilization. In those cases, $\partial x(t)/\partial t$ would quickly fall to zero, and the release of excess spread back to the seller would continue unabated. If such rise did not unduly prejudice bondholders and was seen as an "analytical" adjustment, the new steady-state value of $R(t)$ could be considered as adequate additional protection. The inclusion of reversibility in the definition of the trigger would motivate the seller to improve the delinquency situation by permitting withdrawals from the spread account upon a corresponding decrease in delinquencies back to the original level.

To contrast the effects of proportional and differential triggering under similar scenarios, consider Figures 23.2 and 23.3 showing time histories for $P(x(t))$ and $R(t)$ for the latter and the former, respectively, with respect to

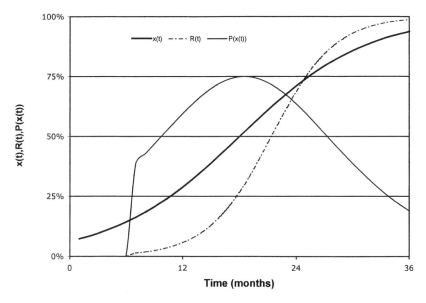

Figure 23.2. Differential Triggering Mechanism

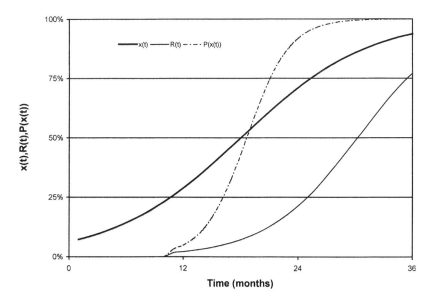

Figure 23.3. Proportional Triggering Mechanism

identical $x(t)$ performance. Assume that the index refers to delinquencies, showing a sudden rise that stabilizes at a new, higher level. A sharp, permanent jump in delinquencies could reflect a seller's tightening credit policies by ceasing to allow obligors to skip monthly payments. Here we place the value I_S of the seller's differential triggers lower than the seller's proportional trigger value.

The main difference between the two schemes is how $R(t)$ behaves over time. Following the change in credit policy, stabilization causes excess spread eventually to return to the seller at a new steady-state $R(t)$ level. Under a reversible triggering system, the same but symmetric $x(t)$ behavior after month 36 would cause withdrawals to be made and $R(t)$ would return to zero over time. This mechanism could perhaps be appropriate in the case of flexible credit policy mentioned earlier.

Under proportional triggering, a trigger breach causes the spread account to rise without bounds. The proportionality constant K should be set so that any breach captures much of the excess spread without the need for referencing the cause of the breach. It provides a mechanism for the seller to address the effects of deterioration without making emergency ad hoc obligor-level debt-restructuring changes and without artificially changing the performance profile of the pool with an artificial debt extension process. It would appear that, for seasoned sellers at least, differential triggering might be a more responsible approach to risk management than the harsher, less malleable method of proportional triggering.

Integral Triggers

With integral triggering, $P(x(t))$ is proportional to the integral of $x(t)$ over a time horizon bounded from below by the time at which the trigger is breached and from above by the current time. A nonreversible integral trigger is thus:

$$P(x(t)) = K\int_{t_b}^{t} H(x(t))x(t)\,dt \qquad (23.10)$$

In equation (23.10), we set the lower bound for the integration via

$$t_b = t\,|\,[I(t) \geq I_S \cap I(t - \Delta t) < I_S]. \qquad (23.11)$$

Once a breach occurs, excess spread begins to accumulate in the spread account for as long as the index remains above the trigger level. If and when $I(t)$ subsequently drops below that threshold, the right-hand side of equation (23.10) remains constant, and so does the rate of accumulation in the spread account. Even if the rate of accumulation never reaches 100%, it nevertheless causes the spread account to grow without bounds over time.

The real benefit of integral triggers lies in their reversibility, obtained by removing $H(x(t))$ from under the integral sign in equation (23.10). With a reversible integral trigger, should $I(t)$ fall below I_S in subsequent time periods, the right-hand side of (23.10) would begin to decrease, causing the rate of accumulation in the spread account to slow down proportionally. Unabated, this would cause accumulation first to stop entirely, then eventually to reverse itself under the condition $P(x(t)) \leq 0$. The associated emptying of funds from the spread account benefits the seller and entices it to keep the index below the trigger level at all times.

The difference between integral and proportional triggers is that, because the cash flow impact of the former is felt mainly when $I(t)$ remains above its trigger level for an extended period of time, they can be set at relatively low levels compared to the latter. Integral triggers act slowly and should be regarded more as preventive corrective measures. As a result, integral triggers are preferable to proportional triggers as risk management tools for relatively unseasoned sellers.

The previous three types of triggers can of course be used in various combinations to achieve complex goals that usually target a variety of seller and asset behaviors. The range of possibilities being almost limitless, we prefer to end the discussion here and postpone such speculation to a different forum. At this point, suffice it to say that much more basic research is needed in this area if structured finance is ever to move beyond binary triggering. In addition, although triggers are not appropriate to all asset classes, in specific instances they provide opportunities for creativity in achieving structural optimization, the endgame of structured finance.

Trigger Optimization

The trade-offs in setting trigger levels are fairly intuitive. On the one hand, because rating agencies sample far into the tail of loss distributions to justify the assignment of high ratings, high trigger levels have little practical impact on seller/servicer operations since the latter neither view such levels as realistic nor seriously contemplate their occurrence; and, when they have occurred, rating agencies have been relatively permissive about permitting thresholds to be raised. Nevertheless, because extreme loss events contribute disproportionately to the creditworthiness of structured securities, high trigger levels confer relatively small but still tangible funding benefits to the seller and the SPE, at essentially no cost.

Conversely, triggers set at lower levels become effective operationally and tend to constrain the working capital of the seller. At such levels, resistance to their inclusion increases, even though the borrowing cost advantage of triggers that are "in the money" can be much more significant, as well as being much more in line with seller expectations. Given the trade-offs, some intermediate level must exist at which an optimal balance between the costs and the benefits of a trigger is reached. The search for this level is the essence of trigger optimization.

Trigger optimization is implemented via a series of Monte Carlo simulations, such as the one presented in chapter 21 for the CBO of ABS. As we have seen, such simulations involve significant computation time, as each is equivalent to an entire rating exercise. Trigger space is often tricky and nonlinear, and may leave no choice but to sample a large number of index values without any expeditious way of systematically narrowing the search for optimality. Notwithstanding, the resulting savings can be well worth the computing effort, given the relatively low cost of a trigger compared to other forms of credit enhancement. The authors have found that trigger optimizations rarely take more than one day of CPU time on a desktop Pentium PC.

The essential analysis consists of formalizing the trade offs (as just outlined) to arrive at a definition of trigger optimality. The process is numerically intensive and usually demands a "fast" transaction cash flow routine, largely because it typically operates at two levels, as follows:

- The optimal trigger level I_S must first be determined for each trigger type through a series of exploratory numerical simulations in I_S-space
- The analysis must be repeated for each trigger type. The optimal trigger is the "best" among all trigger types and I_S index values.

The Benefits of a Trigger

Put simply, the aggregate benefit of a trigger $T_B(I_S)$ may be regarded as the cost-of-funds advantage it confers the seller over the non-triggered structure. This benefit depends on the trigger level I_S. Alternatively, the funding advantage may also be expressed in terms of the reduction in credit enhancement. (These two expressions are equivalent in a rational market, although significant differences may exist between rating agency preferences [the determinant of credit enhancement levels] and investor preferences [the determinant of pricing levels].)

Formally, we have

$$T_B(I_S) = \Delta r\, B_0\, L_{\text{avg}}. \tag{23.12}$$

In equation (23.12), we have defined the following:

$\Delta r = r_n - r_t$

B_0 = Tranche initial principal balance ($)

L_{avg} = Mean average life of the security (years)

r_n = Credit spread without the trigger (%)

r_t = Credit spread with the trigger (%)

Clearly, the benefits of a trigger can be computed only from two separate numerical simulations, with and without the trigger. There is no guarantee that both simulations will yield the same average life; if both average lives are noticeably different, the mean value is used. In fact, we expect average lives to be somewhat, but not significantly, different.

The Costs of a Trigger

If it serves only to cause excess spread capture, the aggregate cost of a trigger $T_C(I_S)$ is related to the difference between earnings on funds invested in the spread account, and earnings on the same funds invested in the seller's operations. Funds withdrawn from the spread account in the form of liability coupon or principal payments are implicitly counted toward the benefit, since these funds contribute to raising the rating and hence lowering the interest rates on liabilities to their post-trigger values. These funds must not be double-counted. Hence, the average outstanding principal balance of the spread account $R(t)$ across all Monte Carlo scenarios is a consistent measure of the trigger's cost to the issuer:

$$T_C(I_S) = \frac{\Delta E}{N} \sum_{j=1}^{N} \int_0^{T_j} R_j(t)\, dt \qquad (23.13)$$

In equation (23.13), we have defined the following:

$\Delta E = \text{ROE} - r_S$

$N = $ Number of Monte Carlo scenarios used in the simulation

$R_j(t) = $ Spread account balance at time t in scenario j (\$)

$T_j = $ Computed maturity of the transaction in scenario j (years)

$\text{ROE} = $ Issuer's return on equity (%)

$r_S = $ Spread account earnings rate (%)

Generally, each scenario gives rise to a separate maturity date, since the defaulted accounts may experience recoveries beyond the last maturity of any loan in the pool. But since most transaction maturities will lie within a fairly tight neighborhood around T (the transaction's nominal maturity), such effects will be second order, at best.

The Value of a Trigger

With respect to a given trigger type, capital structure, and cash flow environment, we can define the *value* of a trigger $V_T(I_S)$ as its benefits less its costs:

$$V_T(I_S) = T_B(I_S) - T_C(I_S) \qquad (23.14)$$

The optimal trigger level I_{opt} will be that for which $V_T(I_S)$ is maximum:

$$I_{\text{opt}} = I_S \left| \frac{\partial V_T(I_S)}{\partial I_S} = 0 \right. \qquad (23.15)$$

Assuming the cash flow environment and the capital structure to be fixed, I_{opt} will have different values for different trigger types within the same structure.

As just indicated, it will then be possible to find an optimal trigger level across all trigger types.

In the end, the asset classes may turn out to have idiosyncratic optimal structures, within which triggers may be called upon to play an essential role. In the future, identification and utilization of such optimal structures through the engineering of triggers will go a long way toward the standardization of credit structures.

An Example of Trigger Optimization

In this example, we demonstrate how a proportional trigger may be optimized in a case where the trigger index is "current defaults." A nonreversible trigger is used, for simplicity's sake. This means that if even performance improves, funds diverted to the spread account are not permitted to leave it. The point of this exercise is simply to demonstrate aspects of trigger dynamics and not to provide a realistic illustration of an actual transaction.

The assets consist of a diversified pool of loans with an aggregate initial principal balance of E_0 and with arbitrary and uniform loan characteristics, onto which variable default behavior without recoveries is superimposed. The pool consists of N_L loans with identical maturities of WAM months and coupon rates of WAC percent. Liabilities are trivially structured as a single, fixed-rate tranche with an initial principal balance of B_0 and a coupon of r_l%, again for simplicity's sake.

The analytical method is fairly simple and consists of varying the pool's asset default propensity to create loss conditions that will breach the trigger. The default process $F(t)$ is familiar from chapter 20:

$$F(t) = \frac{a(t)}{1 + be^{-c(t - t_0)}}, \; t \in [0, \, T] \tag{23.16}$$

In equation (23.16), dynamic asset behavior is partly represented by parameter c, which indicates the rate of deterioration, and partly by the asymptote $a(t)$, which indicates the ultimate loss level. The latter is assumed to follow

$$a(t) = \frac{a_\infty}{1 + \beta e^{-\delta(t - t_m)}}, \; a(0) = a_0. \tag{23.17}$$

In equation (23.17) δ is an empirical measure of anticipated deterioration in the default dynamics of the assets and t_m is an arbitrary adjustment factor. Second, we choose β such that the boundary condition $a(0) = a_0$ is always satisfied. This implies

$$\beta = \left(\frac{a_\infty}{a_0} - 1 \right) e^{-\delta t_m}. \tag{23.18}$$

Starting from equations (23.16) and (23.17), the marginal default propensity $p(t)$ is given by the first derivative of $F(t)$:

$$p(t) \equiv \frac{\partial F(t)}{\partial t} = F(t) \left\{ \frac{bce^{-c(t-t_0)}}{[1 + be^{-c(t-t_0)}]} + \frac{\delta\beta e^{-\delta(t-t_m)}}{[1 + \beta e^{-\delta(t-t_m)}]} \right\} \quad (23.19)$$

Within the model, the default process is explored by repeated sampling of the parametric vectors a_∞, c, and t_0 in the following steps:

1. Parameter a_∞ is assumed to follow a lognormal process with parameters μ and σ.
2. Parameter c is assumed to follow a uniform process with known minimum (c_m) and maximum (c_M) values. As a result, values of c will be sampled via the equation $c = r(c_M - c_m) + c_m$ where r is a uniformly distributed random number satisfying $r \in [0, 1]$.
3. Parameter t_0 is assumed to follow a Beta process centered on the benchmark value t_0^* and bounded by a known interval Δt_0 on either side. Thus, t_0 will be sampled via the equation $t_0 = \Delta t_0(2F_{\text{Beta}}^{-1}(r; \alpha, \beta) - 1) + t_0^*$, where r is a uniformly distributed random number satisfying $r \in [0, 1]$ while the expression $F_{\text{Beta}}^{-1}(r; \alpha, \beta)$ is the inverse cumulative Beta distribution function with parameters $\alpha = 2$ and $\beta = 2$.

In the next step, the parameters of the triggering mechanism are established so that it has the following formal characteristics:

Trigger type:	Proportional (equation [23.6])
Parameter a:	10 (equation [23.6])
Trigger index:	Annualized coincident defaults $d(t)$
$I(t)$:	$12d(t)/B(t-1)$
	$B(t-1) =$ Previous pool balance
I_S:	Variable (see following tables)
$x(t)$:	$(I[t] - I_S)/I_S$ (equation [23.3])

To effect the simulation and calculate costs and benefits, the following quantities were selected:

ROE:	18%
r_S:	2.5%
N:	2000
Yield curve:	See chapter 20 for yield curve definition
E_0:	\$21,000,000

The parameters used to implement equations (23.16) and (23.18) were as follows:

δ:	0.1 (month^{-1})
μ:	20

σ:	50
a_0:	1
b:	1
c_m:	0.01 (month^{-1})
c_M:	0.05 (month^{-1})
t_0^*:	65 months
Δt_0:	10 months
t_m:	35 months
N_L:	5,000 loans
B_0:	$21,000,000
T:	72 months
WAC:	16.00%
WAM:	72 months
Recoveries:	0%

A few implementation comments are in order. First, a calibrating Monte Carlo (MC) simulation excluding the trigger is performed. As was shown in chapter 20, each such MC simulation requires a nonlinear convergence process whereby the tranche interest rate and its rating are simultaneously derived within a simple feedback loop. The output of this calibration run yields the benchmark interest cost of the transaction without the trigger and from which trigger benefits are computed.

For each trigger level, a separate MC simulation is performed. The costs, benefits, and value of the trigger are then computed according to equations (23.13), (23.12), and (23.14), respectively. This process is repeated for a range of I_S values and I_{opt} is determined according to equation (23.15). Thanks to the simplicity of the model, each MC simulation requires ten to twenty minutes on a desktop Pentium PC. Table 23.1 summarizes our results for the values of I_S shown on the left. Using Table 23.1, we can calculate the costs, benefits, and value of the trigger at each level; this is shown in Table 23.2. The optimum trigger level is around 1.5%.

Discussion

Although the value of the optimal level may not require precise determination, relative trade-offs inherent in setting trigger levels and discovered along the way to determining I_{opt} are critical to a proper understanding of trigger dynamics.

An optimum level of 1.5% is surprisingly low, considering the amount of nominal excess spread available in this transaction (about 7%). To understand this behavior, remember that triggers have an impact only under stress loss sce-

Table 23.1
The Credit Consequences of Different Trigger Levels

I_s (%)	ΔIRR (Bps)	Rate (%)	Rating	L_{avg} (months)
No trigger	32.00	7.67	Baa3	41.4
3.0	27.22	7.52	Baa3	41.4
2.5	25.10	7.43	Baa2	41.3
2.0	21.67	7.30	Baa2	41.3
1.5	15.61	7.03	Baa1	41.2
1.0	12.68	6.88	A3	41.2
0.5	5.75	6.45	A2	41.1

narios. On a statistical basis, these scenarios rarely happen, even for low-investment-grade transactions, and the entire game is played at the tail of the loss distribution.

What is the effect of the trigger in such cases? The answer is not cut-and-dried, and is subject to the subjectivity of the analyst's a priori construction of stress loss dynamics. If high-loss cases are characterized as relatively calm seas followed by ten-foot squalls, the trigger will be largely ineffective because too much excess spread will have already escaped. On the other hand, if stress scenarios are constructed as an initial "warning" phase whereby losses first rise to some abnormal level and stay there awhile before leaping into the stratosphere, then that intermediate stage forms the basis of effective triggering.

In the example given, the optimal level is low because we have opted for the first type of stress scenario, where losses are assumed to deteriorate quickly and indefinitely once they start to exceed normal levels. Figure 23.4 shows a typical stress scenario implied by the process just described. The trigger is able to trap cash only in the spread account within the triangular region labeled "A" in Figure 23.4 because, once credit losses reach the level labeled "Excess Spread" in the figure, no cash is left at all at the spread account level in the waterfall after current defaults, principal, servicing fees, and interest expenses.

Table 23.2
Quantifying the Value of (I_s)

I_s (%)	Benefits ($)	Costs ($)	$V_r(I_s)$ ($)
No trigger	0	0	0
3.0	115,360	57,223	58,137
2.5	173,040	104,326	68,714
2.0	266,770	185,441	81,329
1.5	461,440	348,565	112,875
1.0	569,590	623,840	−54,250
0.5	879,620	1,227,480	−347,861

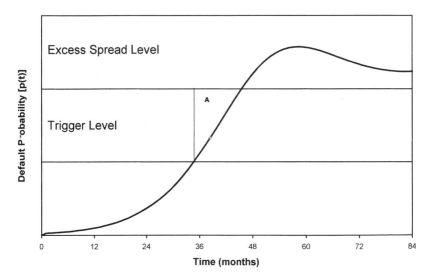

Figure 23.4. Coincident Loss Rate Distribution: Stress Case

Even supposing that the excess spread were funneled into the spread account between months 35 and 47, the effectiveness of the trigger is severely limited by the assumed speed with which losses advance to the zero–excess spread line.

Thus, in cases where the trigger shows its mettle, it is made largely irrelevant and unable to increase the yield on the tranche much above the no-trigger value. Is this behavior a fair representation of asset performance? If anything, the degree of subjectivity underlying scenario analysis in triggers exceeds the subjectivity underlying assumptions about the statistical distribution of cumulative losses.

Had we assumed a different stress loss profile, things might have worked out differently. For instance, Figure 23.5 shows a stress loss scenario more propitious to triggering, giving the trigger more time to react and redirect cash to the spread account (given, of course, an appropriate trigger level). The problem with the second stress loss assumption (in the unstressed case) is that it is difficult to justify in practice. Once a pool begins to show deterioration, the behavior of Figure 23.4 (the stressed case) is more realistic. Observers may object that the "double-plateau" loss distribution of Figure 23.5 stretches the imagination of investors looking for real downside protection, and may find Figure 23.4 to be a more credible basis for trigger evaluation. In any event, the importance of detailed knowledge of asset cash flow dynamics in setting trigger levels, or in giving them proper credit, cannot be overstated.

The relatively low value of I_{opt} also highlights a related aspect of trigger mechanics, namely how trigger definitions affect their usefulness. The simple model used to construct Tables 23.1 and 23.2 did not address the pool's delinquency structure, as more sophisticated models would. Hence, losses come

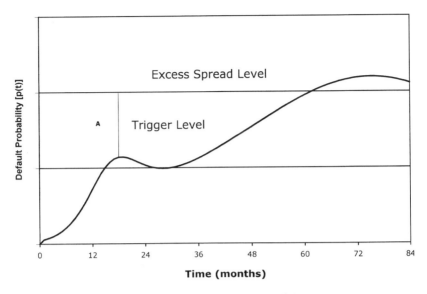

Figure 23.5. Coincident Loss Rate Distribution: Unstressed Case

without warning. In a more realistic and professional model, delinquency dynamics would also be used for trigger analysis purposes. The failure of the previous trigger to be effective stems in large measure from the lack of advance warning, so that excess spread may be trapped inside the structure rather than released to the certificateholder. Use of coincident delinquencies rather than coincident losses in defining the trigger index partially addresses this shortcoming, as delinquencies provide a natural advance warning mechanism. The focus on delinquencies also brings the analysis closer to the essence of triggering: capital optimality. But without a comprehensive delinquency structural framework (e.g., via the Markovian techniques of chapters 14–15), it is difficult to see how suitable triggers may be properly investigated or analyzed.

Table 23.1 also highlights an important, sometimes forgotten aspect of trigger analysis: some triggers are worthless. Too often, the same credit is given to triggers at all thresholds. Often triggers are merely reactive features reluctantly placed inside legal documents to achieve cheaper funding costs. Although they have their place in specific instances, triggers should not be viewed as a general-purpose panacea able to rescue lowly rated pools from their fate, as a way to raise issuance proceeds, or as a magic wand that can lift a pool that is nominally below investment-grade above it. If a deal does not work without a trigger, it probably does not work with a trigger either. Rather, triggers should mainly be aimed at event risks where the scenarios actually make sense. But serious analysis of trigger value is rarely attempted. Rather, once the stress loss scenario has been decided, it is virtually guaranteed that trigger levels will be uniformly rewarded with a rating concession. To award a 50-bp credit enhancement benefit to a trigger at any or all levels is simply wrong.

The Influence of the Credit Scale

Having barely scratched the surface of trigger analytics, we move on to a discussion of their relationship to the nonlinearity of the credit scale. You will recall that the structured finance rating scale is mainly logarithmic at lower rating levels but loses much of that functional form moving toward the lowest end of the credit spectrum because losses are capped at 100% of investment. As it is easier to raise a relatively low-rated security than a relatively high-rated security by a few notches, it is unfortunately also more efficient to use triggers in the range of marginal investment-grade than in the range of higher investment-grade transactions. In other words, even going from Baa1 to A1 requires more drastic measures than going from Baa3 to A3, and with respect to any Aaa transaction, a trigger is clearly useless. One would expect I_{opt} to be more "out of the money" in the Baa3 case, and to result in smaller net benefits to sellers.

This phenomenon is demonstrated with a case similar to the one before, but arbitrarily adjusting the initial rating to Baa1 instead of Baa3. All parameter values remain untouched except these:

WAM: 84 months

σ: 20

Table 23.3 summarizes the results of the simulation process for the same set of I_s values as those in Table 23.1. Table 23.4 is the equivalent of Table 23.2 for this case.

As expected, the optimum trigger level has increased to 2.5% from 1.5%, and the net benefits to the seller at that level are much smaller than in the previous example. In fact, they are negligible on a $20,000,000 transaction. As stated, the reasons for this behavior are to be found largely in the shape of the

Table 23.3
Outputs for Simulation in Table 23.1

I_s (%)	ΔIRR (bps)	Rate (%)	Rating	L_{avg} (months)
No trigger	13.16	7.24	Baa1	48.7
3.0	10.02	7.05	A3	48.7
2.5	8.15	6.93	A2	48.6
2.0	6.40	6.80	A2	48.6
1.5	4.58	6.64	A1	48.6
1.0	2.41	6.40	Aa3	48.5
0.5	1.27	6.23	Aa2	48.5

Table 23.4
Outputs for Simulation in Figure 23.1

I_s (%)	Benefits ($)	Costs ($)	$V_T(I_s)$ ($)
No trigger	0	0	0
3.0	161,595	153,093	8,502
2.5	263,655	254,560	9,095
2.0	374,220	411,635	−37,415
1.5	510,300	723,607	−213,307
1.0	569,590	623,840	−551,068
0.5	859,005	2,213,521	−1,354,516

credit scale. Whereas the yield-reduction ratio between Baa3 and A3 is approximately 3.5, that between Baa1 and A1 is about 4.3. To achieve the same three-notch benefit, the seller ends up paying too much in added costs in the (many) more numerous cases where the transaction is, in fact, not in trouble. Given these results, most sellers would rightly conclude that a trigger is simply not worth the contingent operational cost, and that in any event the net benefits are marginal. Unfortunately, many sellers are unaware of such trade-offs, and a "penny-wise, pound-foolish" attitude normally prevails.

In sum, trigger dynamics are intricate and highly specific. Even if analysts concur on which scenarios describe likely cash flow behavior, individual asset classes exhibit idiosyncratic features when trigger levels are set. To set realistic levels, structured analysts need proper tools. An underwriter recommending that a trigger be placed inside legal documents to save 40 bps of coupon or to raise issuance proceeds by 50 bps may in fact be giving bad advice if excessive amounts of excess spread wind up trapped inside a transaction that performs below expectations but performs nevertheless.

Concluding Remarks

In some sense, an amortizing pass-through security embodies the assumptions vis-à-vis the behavior of firms that were artificially constructed to demonstrate Modigliani-Miller, proposition 1 (MM-1). By definition, amortizing structures are no-growth structures. Constant returns to scale do not need to be assumed because the costs of a structured security are known up front. Legitimate servicing costs are determined ex ante and reserved against; incidental costs are assigned to parties outside the structure. Bankruptcy costs are "known" to be close to zero because the issuer is a bankruptcy-remote entity. The issuer's tax liabilities are also structured away. Leverage is introduced into the structure by the element of subordination, whereby principal cash flows due to the firm's subordinated class are borrowed at the risk-free rate to pay down the riskless class first. As the senior class amortizes, the remaining cash flows gradually de-lever and become available to pay down the subordinate debt. But because the SPE has no tax liability, leverage does not change the value of the portfolio by creating a tax shield. Rather, it permits monetization of uncertain cash flows, which are priced with an appropriate risk premium. The hurdle rate for each of the riskless and risky classes is determined mainly by the rating, which is itself determined by the expected reduction of yield on the riskless and risky streams of cash flows. The value of the asset pool is therefore completely independent of the structure of liabilities.

For the plain-vanilla amortizing structure, which has no possibility of capitalizing its residual cash flow, the fact that the assets and liabilities are independent is as trivial as it is straightforward. For synthetic collateralized debt obligations, which extend the paradigm to permit infinite leverage on the risky class through external borrowing and extend the maturity of the portfolio with revolving debt, the SPE increasingly takes on the character of a firm, and the debates surrounding MM-1 come into focus.

If the capital structure of issuers (broadly defined to include revolving and amortizing portfolios) can be manipulated to create arbitrages that enhance the value of the issue in the eyes of investors or reduce the cost of funding to the SPE, the search for structural optimality is worthy of the quest. The fact that banks tout their corporate finance advisory services to their clients, and that the clients pay for it, suggests that structural optimization may indeed have a point. To reconcile theory and marketplace realities, some academicians have offered the following justifications:[1]

- Leverage alters the value proposition to the investor by marginally increasing bankruptcy costs.

- Leverage alters the value proposition to the seller by raising the cost of additional indenture provisions required by the investors.
- Asymmetries of information and agency conflicts motivate the adoption of a globally suboptimal structure.
- Unanticipated changes in asset performance change the option value of noteholders' claims over the life of the transaction.

Of these justifications, for the structured case, bankruptcy costs have the least explanatory power, for reasons that have been explained but that bear repeating. The SPE is structured to avoid winding up in bankruptcy court. The definitive credit event for structured transactions is thus not default but losses, whose impact on the transaction is supposed to be fully impounded in the expected loss analysis. The "cost-of-indenture provisions" argument is also less meaningful for structured securities, which operate in accordance with the comprehensive rules in the P&S. The one arena where cost-of-indenture provisions may apply concerns eligibility criteria in revolving structures, which do vary from structure to structure in the amount of discretion permitted. Some actively managed CDOs are written with loopholes that allow over-collateralization requirements (which are enforced) to be brought into compliance via the simultaneous violation of some minimum rating requirements (which are not enforced). It is plausible that tightening the covenants could alter investor perceptions of value and reduce the attractiveness of certain CDO structures.

This observation leads us to consider "agency conflict" explanations, which offer more promise. Although structured transactions can achieve superior executions because the level of disclosure about asset performance exceeds the information content from corporate transactions many times over, the lack of granularity in the rating agency model allows a certain level of results to be "managed." Remember that ratings are a judgment about the certainty of receipt of cash flows based on an analysis of underlying risk and cushion. Since investor assessments of relative value are dependent on ratings, it would not be surprising for investors to have somewhat homogeneous expectations for structured securities of the same rating. But, as argued in preceding chapters, sources of inconsistency in the rating analysis introduce variance in rating outcomes. The treatment of volatility and the loss distribution as an input rather than an output under the static loss method, as discussed in chapter 3, are key sources of rating variance, as the use of an alphanumeric credit scale is a key source of ratings arbitrage. If imprecise valuation methods allow the seller to cherry-pick assets and manipulate outcomes, an incentive exists for the seller to adopt a structure that keeps adverse selection below the radar screen of the rating agency, which focuses on the level of aggregates. It then makes sense to issue subordinated pieces in the low-investment-grade or high non-investment-grade ranges, where the tolerance for variation within the rating level is much wider. The seller may also actively manage the expected loss calculation by substituting a small number (less than 10%) of bad assets for good ones, thereby hiding the true profile of credit losses. Conversely, if imprecise valuation methods lead to systematic undervaluation of the seller's assets in ABS and, in some cases, MBS deals (as has been maintained in this book), then—absent offsetting regulatory capital incentives—the seller may be better served by holding some of its own, cheap subordinated debt rather than selling off all of the risk. These are real-life examples of how agency conflicts can motivate structuring preferences.

The richest explanatory vein—and the most legitimate rationale for seeking optimality—is the possibility of controlling the "optionality" among investor claims to maximize the average wealth of claimholders. The proof of MM-1 assumes perpetual cash flows and thereby assumes away the vagaries of cash flow dynamics (to which the rating agency analysis also gives short shrift in part II). But a mastery of cash flow dynamics lies at the heart of structural optimization.

Assuming that spreads in the credit markets are proportional to the risk of credit loss, the optimal solution of a structured transaction will always be to maximize proceeds at the lowest cost of funds. If credit spreads misprice risk, the optimum is a credit arbitrage realized by funding against the mispricing in the richest segment of the spectrum. With perfect tracking of cash flows through time, it is possible to craft a structure that minimizes overall funding costs by controlling the timing and amount of capital required by the AAA tranche through some combination of mechanisms described in the preceding sections. A formal discussion of whole-structure optimization builds on the methods introduced in all 23 chapters of this book but ultimately lies beyond its scope and design.

Appendices

Appendix A

Numerical Experiments in Random Number Generation

To see how each of the three random sampling techniques discussed in chapter 12 fares in practice, we now perform small-sample numerical experiments with m random deviates using

1. The Visual Basic Rand ( ) system call,
2. The antithetic corrective scheme, and
3. The van der Corput low-discrepancy method.

Our index of relative comparison (figure of merit) will be

$$\chi = \frac{1}{10}\sum_{i=1}^{10}\left(n_i - \frac{m}{10}\right)^2.$$

The ith interval, or *bin*, is defined by $[(i - 1)/10, i/10]$, $i = 1, 2, 3, \ldots, 10$. If the selection is perfectly uniform, each interval will contain $m/10$ points and the value of χ will be zero. The idea is to minimize χ. Table A.1 gives results using the three methods with $m = 100$. The resulting figure of merit, χ, is shown at the foot of the table.

As is plainly obvious, the Rand ( ) uniform random-number generator in Visual Basic is weak. The antithetic corrective scheme fares better by an order

Table A.1
Results of the Three Sampling Techniques Compared (sample of 10)

Bin No.	VBE	Antithetic	Low-Disc
1	14	10	11
2	8	8	10
3	18	8	10
4	7	12	10
5	8	12	11
6	15	12	10
7	9	12	9
8	6	8	10
9	5	8	10
10	10	10	9
FOM	16.4	3.2	0.4

Table A.2
Results of the Three Sampling Techniques Compared (sample of 200)

Bin No.	VBE	Antithetic	Low-Disc
1	24	17	21
2	17	18	20
3	27	21	19
4	18	21	22
5	23	23	20
6	27	23	19
7	19	21	20
8	15	21	21
9	11	18	19
10	19	17	19
FOM	12.2	2.4	0.5

of magnitude, while the low-discrepancy sequence is better than the antithetic method by another order of magnitude. Given the extremely low value of m, the performance of the van der Corput method is remarkable. However, we would expect the Visual Basic Rand function to improve as m gets larger since the random sequence should have time to patch some of the "holes" referred to before. The antithetic method should also improve, but it has clearly less upside given its earlier performance.

Table A.2 displays what happened for $m = 200$. As expected, the Visual Basic method has improved by a wide margin. We would expect that for sufficiently large values of m, say for 10^3 or more, it should yield acceptable results.

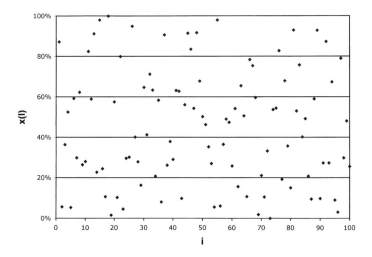

Figure A.1. "Randomness" Using the Visual Basic Random Number Generator

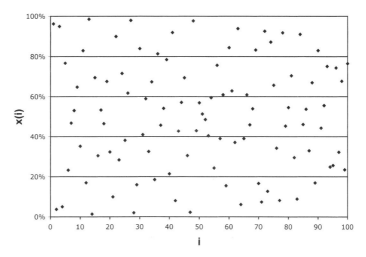

Figure A.2. "Randomness" Using the Antithetic Corrective Method

The antithetic scheme is true to itself and probably overkill in view of the typically poor quality of structured finance credit data. The low-discrepancy technique, which has little room to improve, remains our chief contender.

Pictorially, the contrast among the three is even more stunning, as shown in Figures A.1 through A.3. The level of uniformity shown in Figure A.3 usually exceeds the requirements of Monte Carlo simulation. Space permitting, it would be instructive to perform additional experiments to observe the asymptotic behavior of the first two generators. In practice, though, the data will often dictate the acceptable level of error within a simulation environment.

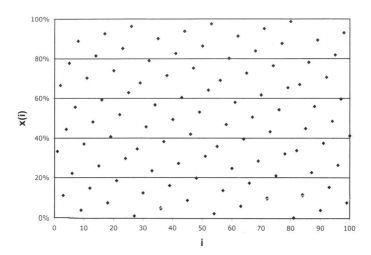

Figure A.3. "Randomness" Using the Low-Discrepancy Random Numbers Method

Appendix B

The Physics of Markov Chains

The dialectic of rotations and eigenvectors, explained in considerable detail in chapter 13, may appeal to geometrically inclined readers, but it will not help analysts develop the required intuition for the physics of Markov processes. In fact, once the physics are understood, the mathematics becomes self-evident. Consequently, we would like to spend some time discussing the path to equilibrium in physical terms, in view of the applications explained in chapters 13 through 15.

Assume that, instead of a singular system wandering in probability space, our stationary Markov process consists of N commodity-like economic agents. Let's assume further that all of the agents are initially located in state 1, and that all states communicate. Given these assumptions, the statewise probability distribution at any time will be equivalent to the population distribution of agents.

Imagine now that there are too many agents in a given state. "Too many" is measured by the difference between the current state population and the equilibrium value discussed earlier. By equation (14.6) relabeled [B.1] here, we have

$$d_1(t+1) = d_1(t)p_{11}(t) + d_2(t)p_{21}(t) + d_3(t)p_{31}(t) + d_4(t)p_{41}(t). \quad \text{(B.1)}$$

By construction, the adjustment mechanism will cause more agents to leave the excess state than to reenter it from other communicating states. If there were too few agents in the same state, the converse would apply, and more would enter than leave that state. To see this, simply note that the number of agents leaving state i for state j at time t is $Nd_i(t)p_{ij}$ and that only $\mathbf{d}(\infty)$ leaves state populations invariant. As the process is marched forward, overpopulated states will thus be net losers while underpopulated states will be net winners. This multilateral exchange will continue indefinitely, but there will come a time when an exact dynamic balance will exist between the agents leaving and those entering any state. It is this dynamic balance that we call *equilibrium*. Therefore, although the system's equilibrium population macrostructure will remain invariant, its microstructure will be constantly changing. In other words, although the net rate of change of any state population is zero at equilibrium, individual agents constantly move in and out of that state.

We can put this physical understanding to the test by predicting what will happen if we relax any of the foregoing assumptions. For instance, what would be the result of letting one of the states be absorbing? According to our definition of a recurrent state, that state will no longer communicate with the others because it would be impossible for the system to leave once it entered it. We can immediately surmise that this Markov chain can reach only a special type of equilibrium in which all economic agents eventually end up in the absorbing state. For example, assume we modify **P** from equation (14.11) in order make state 3 absorbing:

$$\mathbf{P} = \begin{bmatrix} .2 & .6 & .2 \\ .7 & .1 & .2 \\ 0 & 0 & 1 \end{bmatrix} \tag{B.2}$$

Our physical intuition would lead us to expect that the entire probability measure would eventually be allocated to state 3 and that $\mathbf{d}(\infty) = [0\ 0\ 1]$ would ensue. The result of actual iteration is

$$\mathbf{P}^2 = \begin{bmatrix} 0.460 & 0.180 & 0.360 \\ 0.210 & 0.430 & 0.360 \\ 0.000 & 0.000 & 1.000 \end{bmatrix}$$

$$\mathbf{P}^4 = \begin{bmatrix} 0.249 & 0.160 & 0.590 \\ 0.187 & 0.223 & 0.590 \\ 0.000 & 0.000 & 1.000 \end{bmatrix}$$

$$\mathbf{P}^8 = \begin{bmatrix} 0.092 & 0.076 & 0.832 \\ 0.088 & 0.080 & 0.832 \\ 0.000 & 0.000 & 1.000 \end{bmatrix}$$

$$\mathbf{P}^{12} = \begin{bmatrix} 0.037 & 0.032 & 0.931 \\ 0.037 & 0.032 & 0.931 \\ 0.000 & 0.000 & 1.000 \end{bmatrix}$$

Finally,

$$\mathbf{P}^{35} = \begin{bmatrix} 0.000 & 0.000 & 1.000 \\ 0.000 & 0.000 & 1.000 \\ 0.000 & 0.000 & 1.000 \end{bmatrix} \tag{B.3}$$

Note that, to achieve this level of accuracy, it took about thirty-five time steps for matrix (B.2) to reach this pseudo-equilibrium, instead of approximately fifteen time steps for the almost identical chain in equation (14.11) without an absorbing state. Note also that $[0\ 0\ 1]$ is the ruling unit-eigenvector of **P**. In other words, the rate at which Markov processes reach their equilibrium distribution varies according to the entries of **P**. If the entire population is to end up in the absorbing state, the rate at which agents communicate with it from other states and the initial distribution of state populations are obvious factors in the time required for equilibrium.

Now, assume for argument's sake that we have two absorbing states. What happens then? Physically, if not mathematically, the answer is clear. There is a competition between the communication rates of one versus the other absorbing state, a process made slightly more complicated by the initial distribution. If the rate of entry into the first absorbing state is large compared to that into the second, we should expect that, in the limit, most of the probability measure would end up in the former, and vice versa. In that case, there would be two unit-eigenvectors instead of one, and no convergent equilibrium process could take place. To see how this works, say our matrix is now the following:

$$\mathbf{P} = \begin{bmatrix} 1 & 0 & 0 \\ .7 & .1 & .2 \\ 0 & 0 & 1 \end{bmatrix} \tag{B.4}$$

Iterating process (B.4) we obtain

$$\mathbf{P}^2 = \begin{bmatrix} 1 & 0 & 0 \\ .77 & .01 & .22 \\ 0 & 0 & 1 \end{bmatrix}$$

$$\mathbf{P}^\infty = \begin{bmatrix} 1 & 0 & 0 \\ .778 & 0 & .222 \\ 0 & 0 & 1 \end{bmatrix}.$$

Here, depending on the initial vector $\mathbf{d}(0)$, we end up with a different $\mathbf{d}(\infty)$ each time contrary to the previous cases where $\mathbf{d}(\infty)$ did not depend on $\mathbf{d}(0)$.

This last case is important. In addition to the nonstationarity of their transition matrices, real structured-finance Markov processes are further complicated by the presence of two absorbing states: prepayment and default. If the loans had no maturity dates, obligors initially in the pool would ultimately prepay or default, depending on their relative prepayment and default rates. In the case of real structured finance Markov processes, obligors effectively exit the chain in cash flow terms upon full repayment of their principal balance, thus preventing this binary outcome.

Because such complications unleash the full spectrum of Markov chain behavior, it is generally not possible to derive analytical results from realistic situations. To achieve meaningful results, the analyst will have to resort to numerical analysis. Given this requirement, structured credit analysts are unlikely to make significant progress without developing an intuitive understanding of the relevant physics to be modeled. The rudimentary introduction contained here will sometimes suffice, but those interested are urged to complement these basics with further reading.[1]

Appendix C

The Markov Property and the Efficient Market Hypothesis

Perhaps not unexpectedly, market risk practitioners have already encountered the Markov property under another guise: the efficient market hypothesis. The identity of these two assumptions is significant enough to spend some time discussing how these seemingly disparate concepts amount to the same thing.

The *efficient market hypothesis* can be colloquially paraphrased as follows: assume, first, that a free market of rational buyers and sellers exists where goods can be traded without coercion; and assume further that the dissemination of information to market participants is free, symmetric, and uniform throughout. An efficient market is one in which the current price of any traded good is the best available proxy for its future price, and is referred to as its *fair market value*. In essence, the current price is the expected value of the future price.

Mathematically, the efficient market hypothesis states that if x is the unknown future price of the good in question and V its fair market value, then $E(x) = V$ must hold at the time the transaction is consummated, where $E(\cdot)$ is the mathematical expectation operator. In other words, the current price of a good contains all the information known about it that is relevant to price discovery. This is deemed to apply to all traded goods, including such commodities as money, whose price is known as the rate of interest.

Let's see how this might come about in physical terms. We have assumed that both buyers and sellers are rational agents. Thus, a buyer who thought the future price of the good was more likely to fall than rise would either delay the purchase, thereby reducing demand and hence price, or start talking the price down. Conversely, if the seller felt that the price was more likely to rise than fall, the exact opposite result would obtain and the price would naturally start to rise. When a trade takes place, it follows that both the buyer and the seller agree at the time that the exchange price is the best available estimate for the future price of the good.

In statistical terms, this is equivalent to the statement that at the traded price, the probabilities of price increase and decrease must exactly cancel out in the eyes of buyers and sellers, and must therefore be equal to 50% each. In essence, the free market can be likened to a self-adjusting random walk with an expected value equal to the current price. Since, by assumption, the information set is symmetric and uniform, if any information were capable of rationally influencing the price of the good, it would have done so already. Hence we cannot escape the further conclusion that the traded price implic-

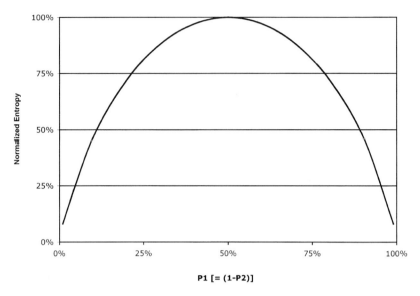

Figure C.1. Two-State Entropy Distribution

itly contains that information. According to this view, there is no point look-ing for answers in the price history of the good when its currently traded price already contains such history.

The conclusion that, under a free market assumption, the probabilities of a price rise or fall are each 50% affords an interesting information-theoretic in-terpretation that further lends credence to the assertion that the traded price contains whatever is known of the good. Within information theory, the average rate of information transferred in a coded message is measured by the entropy of the probability distribution of its coding elements (letters), and the maximum rate of information transfer occurs when that entropy is maxi-mized, which turns out to correspond to a state of maximum uncertainty. Is entropy maximized at the traded price? Yes, it is.

To see this, recall that entropy S of a probability distribution p_i is given by $S = -\sum_i p_i \log p_i$. If the elements of the process are the price movement prob-abilities p_1 and p_2, S attains its maximum value when $p_1 = p_2 = 0.5$. This is shown in Figure C.1. In other words, a free market as defined is efficient be-cause it naturally leads to conditions of maximum information transfer.

To summarize, the efficient market hypothesis is founded on the principle that the traded price of a good is the best estimate of its future price. As a re-sult, the probability distribution of its future price can be derived solely from its current price, assumed to contain all the relevant information. Now, if $x(t + \Delta t)$ is the price of the good at time $t + \Delta t$ as of time t, then the effi-cient market hypothesis is equivalent to the following statement:

$$p(x(t + \Delta t) \mid x(t), x(t - \Delta t), x(t - 2\Delta t), \ldots) = p(x(t + \Delta t)|x(t)) \quad (C.1)$$

As equation (C.1) is a restatement of equation (14.1), the efficient market hypothesis and the Markov property are one and the same. Within structured finance, the fortuitous correspondence of these two fundamental assumptions enables the worlds of credit and market risk to be housed under a single roof.

Appendix D

An Example of Nonlinear Regression

Assume a given set of point-pairs (x_i, y_i), $i = 1, 2, 3, \ldots N$ is to be fitted to the following nonlinear functional form:

$$x^a y^b = c \tag{D.1}$$

In equation (D.1), a, b, and c are unknown parameters to be determined.

As usual, to start the process, we define the Lagrangian L as

$$L = \sum_i (y_i - [cx_i^{-a}]^{1/b})^2. \tag{D.2}$$

And, as usual, the unknown parameters are the solutions to the following three equations:

$$\frac{\partial L}{\partial a} = 0 \tag{D.3}$$

$$\frac{\partial L}{\partial b} = 0 \tag{D.4}$$

$$\frac{\partial L}{\partial c} = 0 \tag{D.5}$$

After some algebra, we arrive at the following relationships:

$$\frac{\partial L}{\partial a} \equiv 2\sum_i (y_i - [cx_i^{-a}]^{1/b}) \frac{c^{1/b}}{b} x_i^{-(a/b)} \ln x_i = 0 \tag{D.6}$$

$$\frac{\partial L}{\partial b} \equiv 2\sum_i (y_i - [cx_i^{-a}]^{1/b}) \frac{1}{b^2} [cx_i^{-a}]^{1/b} \ln[cx_i^{-a}] = 0 \tag{D.7}$$

$$\frac{\partial L}{\partial c} \equiv 2\sum_i (y_i - [cx_i^{-a}]^{1/b}) \frac{1}{cb} [cx_i^{-a}]^{1/b} = 0 \tag{D.8}$$

As can readily be seen, even after simplification, equations (D.6) through (D.8) cannot be expressed as a matrix system in terms of the unknown parametric vector $\mathbf{a}$ that can be solved using equation (15.11) which we repeat here for convenience:

$$\mathbf{a} = (\mathbf{X}^T\mathbf{X})^{-1}\mathbf{X}^T\mathbf{y} \tag{15.11}$$

A specific and, in general, different nonlinear system will result from any postulated nonlinear functional form. In some cases, the nonlinearity will be mild and the system will easily be solved as a quasi-linear system. In others, as is the case here, the nonlinear dependence will be strong and will demand more attention in its solution. There are a few proven ways to approach nonlinear solutions. In this book, we discuss only the simplest of them, the Newton-Raphson method. Interested readers should consult *Numerical Recipes*[2] for a more comprehensive treatment.

Appendix E

The Symmetry and Nonnegative Definiteness
of Two Special Matrices

In chapter 16 we observed that the Cholesky decomposition method, which is useful in analyzing correlations, is made possible by two properties of a matrix: symmetry and nonnegative definiteness. Here, we delve into the physics of two special matrices with these properties: the covariance matrix and the linear regression matrix commonly used in model building.

The Covariance Matrix

Symmetry

Any covariance matrix $\mathbf{M}$ is symmetric by inspection. For a column vector $\mathbf{x}$ with mean $\boldsymbol{\mu}$, we have by definition

$$\mathbf{M} = E[(\mathbf{x} - \boldsymbol{\mu})(\mathbf{x} - \boldsymbol{\mu})^T].$$

Each element of $\mathbf{M}$ is $m_{ij} = E[(x_i - \mu_i)(x_j - \mu_j)]$ and is thus symmetric with respect to an exchange of the indices i and j.

Nonnegative Definiteness

A matrix $\mathbf{M}$ is said to be nonnegative definite, when the following condition holds for any column vector $\mathbf{v}$:

$$\mathbf{v}^T \mathbf{M} \mathbf{v} \geq 0$$

Now for any covariance matrix $\mathbf{M}$, we have

$$\mathbf{v}^T \mathbf{M} \mathbf{v} = \mathbf{v}^T E[(\mathbf{x} - \boldsymbol{\mu})(\mathbf{x} - \boldsymbol{\mu})^T]\mathbf{v} = E[\mathbf{v}^T(\mathbf{x} - \boldsymbol{\mu})(\mathbf{x} - \boldsymbol{\mu})^T\mathbf{v}]$$

$$E[\mathbf{v}^T(\mathbf{x} - \boldsymbol{\mu})(\mathbf{x} - \boldsymbol{\mu})^T\mathbf{v}] = E[\{\mathbf{v}^T(\mathbf{x} - \boldsymbol{\mu})\}^2] \geq 0.$$

The Regression Matrix

Symmetry

Recall that the regression matrix was defined by $\mathbf{M} = \mathbf{X}^T\mathbf{X}$. From matrix algebra we have for any two matrices $\mathbf{A}$ and $\mathbf{B}$, $(\mathbf{AB})^T = \mathbf{B}^T\mathbf{A}^T$. In the case of the regression matrix, we then have

$$\mathbf{M}^T = (\mathbf{X}^T\mathbf{X})^T = \mathbf{X}^T\mathbf{X} = \mathbf{M}.$$

Which proves the symmetry of $\mathbf{M}$.

Nonnegative Definiteness

Recall that the regression Lagrangian L was the functional we sought to minimize and that, in the defining equation for L, $\mathbf{a}$ was a vector of unknown parameters. Consequently, L can be regarded as a functional in parameter space ($\mathbf{a}$ space), and not in $\mathbf{x}$. By construction, L is a quadratic functional with a minimum value at the solution vector $\mathbf{a}_0$. For instance, in one dimension L is just a scalar function of one variable, say x, and the geometry looks like Figure E.1, where we have labeled the solution x_0.

Recall also from geometry that a quadratic function can be defined by the equation $y = ax^2 + bx + c$, and that its constant curvature is equal to $2a$. If $a > 0$, then y is convex and has a minimum. If $a < 0$, y is concave and has a maximum. By construction, $L \geq 0$ and is therefore convex with $\partial L/\partial x = 0$ holding at the solution x_0, since this is where L takes on its minimum value. The solution x_0 sits at the bottom of a one-dimensional bowl and is unique due to L's convexity. In fact, the main reason to use a quadratic functional in regression analysis is not that there is no other choice, but that a convex quadratic functional always has a unique minimum value.

Note further that, as shown in Figure E.1, the tangent vector pointing in the direction $\partial L/\partial x$ makes an angle θ with the x-axis obeying $\theta \in [0, (\pi/2)]$. Further recall from geometry that the scalar product $(\cdot)$ of two vectors is the product of their respective norms and the cosine of the angle between them. Since $\cos(\theta) \geq 0$, $\theta \in [0, (\pi/2)]$, we have

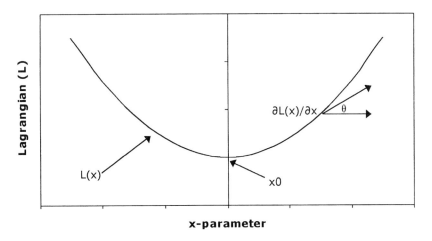

Figure E.1. The Lagrangian Function in One Dimension

$$\frac{\partial L}{\partial x} \cdot x = \left| \frac{\partial L}{\partial x} \right| |x| \cos(\theta) \geq 0. \tag{E.1}$$

Thus, in one dimension, the scalar product of the first derivative of a convex quadratic Lagrangian with any trial solution x is always positive, and this is what we mean by positive semi-definiteness in one dimension. In multiple dimensions, we simply transfer the idea to a vector space and start speaking of hyper-bowls, generalized angles, and hyperplanes. For a trial vector $\mathbf{v}$, equation (E.1) reduces to

$$\frac{\partial L}{\partial \mathbf{v}} \cdot \mathbf{v} \geq 0, \tag{E.2}$$

and this becomes our criterion in multiple dimensions. Now recall from our discussion on regression that for any vector $\mathbf{v}$,

$$\frac{\partial L}{\partial \mathbf{v}} = [-2\mathbf{X}^T\mathbf{y} + 2\mathbf{X}^T\mathbf{X}\mathbf{v}]. \tag{E.3}$$

From equation (E.2) this means that for any trial vector $\mathbf{v}$,

$$\mathbf{v}^T \mathbf{X}^T \mathbf{X} \mathbf{v} - \mathbf{v}^T \mathbf{X}^T \mathbf{y} \geq 0.$$

Since equation (E.4) must hold for all $\mathbf{y}$, the first term on the left must be non-negative for all $\mathbf{v}$, which concludes our proof. Therefore, the positive semi-definiteness of $\mathbf{X}^T\mathbf{X}$ expresses that fact that L is a convex functional; in other words, that this condition is the vector representation of the positive curvature of the Lagrangian. To see this, note that the curvature tensor $\mathbf{T}$ is obtained by differentiating the right-hand side of equation (E.3) with respect to $\mathbf{v}$. We then have

$$\mathbf{T} \equiv \frac{\partial^2 L}{\partial \mathbf{v} \partial \mathbf{v}^T} = 2\mathbf{X}^T\mathbf{X}. \tag{E.4}$$

As claimed, this is the vector analogue of the one-dimensional case where $\partial^2 L / \partial x^2 = 2a$.

Appendix F

Convergence Analysis for the
Newton-Raphson Optimization Method

This appendix addresses specific convergence issues related to the NR nonlinear optimization method of chapter 18. However, the formalism is widely versatile across a range of problems invoking similar properties, making the investment of time in understanding the analytical treatment well spent.

Convergence of the Newton-Raphson Scalar Iteration

We begin our convergence analysis of the NR method through a study of the fixed-point map

$$x = g(x). \tag{F.1}$$

A well-known theorem of analysis[3] states that every contractive mapping into itself and equipped with a metric has a fixed point. The fixed point is attained when the left-hand side of equation (F.1) is equal to the mapped iterate given by the function $g(x)$. Hence, the search for the fixed point is equivalent to the search for a solution to (F.1).

In practice, the sequence of iterates x_n will be generated by the equation $x_n = g(x_{n-1})$, $n = 0, 1, 2, \ldots$ and our goal will be to determine the condition on $g(x)$ such that this sequence converges in the sense that

$$\lim_{n \to \infty} |x_n - x_{n-1}| \to 0. \tag{F.2}$$

As long as equation (F.2) holds, we will say that the map is contractive. In general, we will not be able to prove that such limit yields the root we seek, but with proper specification of $g(x)$, some fixed point will correspond to it. That is, as long as the mapping equation (F.1) is contractive, the sequence x_n will converge to one of the fixed points of $g(x)$. Therefore finding the conditions on $g(x)$ that guarantee the truth of equation (F.2) is the real problem. In what follows, we will use the *mean value theorem*, another one of Lagrange's many contributions to numerical analysis. The proof will not be given here but is found in most calculus textbooks.[4] It states that for every continuous function $f(x)$ on a closed interval $[a, b]$ and everywhere differentiable on the same but open interval, there exists at least one point $c \in (a, b)$ such that $f'(c) = (f[b] - f[a])/(b - a)$, where $f'(x)$ is the first derivative of $f(x)$. In other words, there will always be a point on the curve $f(x)$ that will be tangent to the

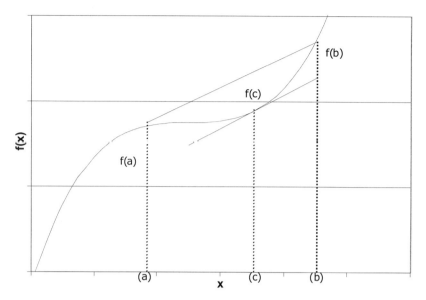

Figure F.1. The Mean Value Theorem

chord drawn between the endpoints a and b. In practice this means that if you drive from New York to Boston and your average speed is 100 kph, you must have gone 100 kph at some point between those two cities. The idea underlying the mean value theorem is shown in Figure F.1.

In what follows, we assume that our chosen functions $g(x)$ can satisfy the conditions of the mean value theorem. Starting from some initial guess x_0, repeated application of the mapping equation (F.1) yields the following set of equations:

$$x_1 = g(x_0)$$
$$x_2 = g(x_1)$$
$$x_3 = g(x_2)$$
$$\cdot$$
$$\cdot$$
$$x_n = g(x_{n-1})$$

After subtracting each equation from the preceding one, we have

$$x_2 - x_1 = g(x_1) - g(x_0) \tag{F.3}$$
$$x_3 - x_2 = g(x_2) - g(x_1)$$
$$\cdot$$
$$\cdot$$
$$x_{n+1} - x_n = g(x_n) - g(x_{n-1})$$

The mean value theorem applied to each interval $[x_i, x_{i+1}]$ tells us that there exists a $\xi_i \in [x_i, x_{i+1}]$ such that

$$g(\xi_i) = \frac{g(x_{i+1}) - g(x_i)}{x_{i+1} - x_i}. \tag{F.4}$$

Substituting into equation (F.3) and taking norms yields the following:

$$|x_2 - x_1| = |g'(\xi_1)| |x_1 - x_0| \tag{F.5}$$
$$|x_3 - x_2| = |g'(\xi_2)| |x_2 - x_1|$$
.
.
.
$$|x_{n+1} - x_n| = |g'(\xi_n)| |x_n - x_{n-1}|$$

Since we assumed $g(x)$ to be finite within each interval $[x_i, x_{i+1}]$, it is possible to find the largest value of any of the norms $g'(\xi_i)$ in the sequence (F.5). Label the resulting maximum value M, such that $M = \max_i g'(\xi_i)$. Now, instead of equation (F.5), we can write the following by definition:

$$|x_2 - x_1| \le M|x_1 - x_0| \tag{F.6}$$
$$|x_3 - x_2| \le M|x_2 - x_1|$$
.
.
.
$$|x_{n+1} - x_n| \le M|x_n - x_{n-1}|$$

Repeated substitution of each equation in (F.6) into the equation below it yields our final result:

$$|x_{n+1} - x_n| < M^n|x_1 - x_0| \tag{F.7}$$

Now, if $M < 1$ for every i in the sequence x_i, $i = 0, 1, 2, .. n + 1$, the map (F.7) will converge because $\lim_{n \to \infty} |x_{n+1} - x_n| \to 0$, as required for convergence.

Therefore, the NR scalar iteration is guaranteed to converge if the norm of the first derivative of $g(x)$ is everywhere less than 1 in the interval $[a, b]$. For this reason, we say that $M < 1$ is a *sufficient* condition for the convergence of the NR scheme. As we shall see shortly, if $M > 1$ somewhere in $[a, b]$ for some n, the scheme may still converge, but if $g'(x)$ is greater than 1 for x_0 already, we have a right to expect trouble along the way.

Let's take a simple example to illustrate our convergence criterion. Say $f(x) = e^x - 5x$ as shown in Figure F.2. The first root is found at around $x = 2.5$ and the second around $x = 0.25$. Now, calculate the quantities needed to monitor convergence. From before, we have the following:

$$g(x) = x - \frac{f(x)}{f'(x)} \tag{F.8}$$

$$f'(x) = e^x - 5$$

$$g'(x) = \frac{f(x)f''(x)}{f'^2(x)}$$

$$f''(x) = e^x$$

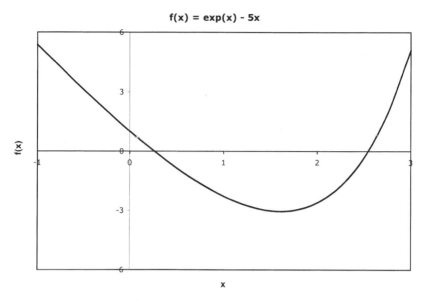

Figure F.2. A Newton-Raphson Trial Function

From our earlier criterion, we conclude that the NR iteration will be stable for the x interval $\mathfrak{R}$ such that $g'(x) < 1$ holds everywhere inside $\mathfrak{R}$. Computation using equations (F.8) yields

$$g'(x) = \frac{e^x(e^x - 5x)}{(e^x - 5)^2}. \tag{F.9}$$

This function is plotted in Figure F.3. From the behavior of $g(x)$ in the areas of the roots, we might expect some trouble around the starting guess $x = 1.6$, which is indeed the approximate location ($\log(5)$) where the slope of $f(x)$ vanishes.

Table F.1 shows a convergence history of the scalar NR iteration for four selected values of the initial guess x_0. Cases C1 and C2 are close enough to the two roots to converge nicely, although not uniformly. Case C3 is interesting because we chose x_0 close enough to our expected trouble spot, but the method still manages to converge to the smaller root. Case C4 is displayed to demonstrate how fast the method converges when $g'(x)$ satisfies our criterion. Here $g'(x)$ was around 0.76 at $x = -4$, compared to -3.38 at $x = 2$. This means that we should expect uniform convergence, and we do. Figure F.4 shows this behavior pictorially. Note the sharp contrast between cases 3 and 4. Case 3 actually overshoots the root at first before recovering.

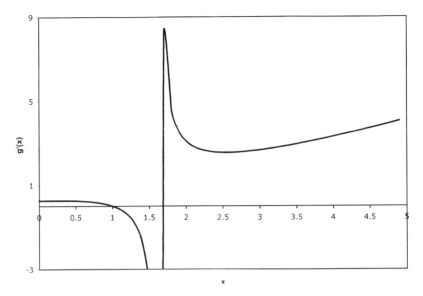

Figure F.3. The Newton-Raphson Convergence Function $g'(x)$

Table F.1
Scalar Newton-Raphson Iteration Convergence

N	Case 1	Case 2	Case 3	Case 4
0	2.0000	1.000	1.609	−4.000
1	3.0929	0.687	−1,390	0.018
2	2.7070	0.506	0.000	0.251
3	2.5618	0.402	0.250	0.259
4	2.5429	0.341	0.259	0.259
5	2.5426	0.306	0.259	0.259
6	2.5426	0.286	0.259	0.259
7	2.5426	0.275	0.259	0.259
8	2.5426	0.268	0.259	0.259
9	2.5426	0.264	0.259	0.259
10	2.5426	0.262	0.259	0.259
11	2.5426	0.261	0.259	0.259
12	2.5426	0.260	0.259	0.259
13	2.5426	0.260	0.259	0.259

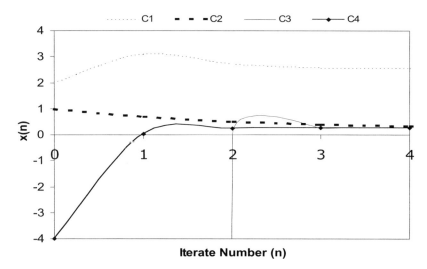

Figure F.4. Newton-Raphson Convergence History

Convergence of the Newton-Raphson Vector Iteration

The vector NR convergence analysis follows the same schema as the scalar case, save for the use of matrix notation. Recall from chapter 18 that the NR vector map is given by

$$\mathbf{x}_n = \mathbf{x}_{n-1} - \mathbf{J}^{-1}(\mathbf{x}_{n-1})\mathbf{f}(\mathbf{x}_{n-1}).$$
(F.10)

The right-hand side of equation (F.10) is the vector $\mathbf{g}(\mathbf{x})$ that becomes our convergence function. The vector-valued convergence derivation, which will not be repeated, is identical to the scalar case and uses the multidimensional version of the mean value theorem. In the end, we end up with a sequence similar to equation (F.5), but now understood in m-dimensional space. The resulting sufficiency condition criterion on matrix $\mathbf{G}'(\mathbf{x}) \equiv (\partial g_i[\mathbf{x}])/(\partial x_j)$ for the NR iterative scheme to converge uniformly is the same as in the scalar case, and we thus require the following to hold everywhere along the vector sequence similar to the sequence (F.5):

$$|\mathbf{G}'(\mathbf{x})| < 1$$
(F.11)

Inequality (F.11) is a sufficiency condition on the iteration, but what does it really mean if $\mathbf{g}(\mathbf{x})$ is now a vector? First note that any matrix, symmetric or not, can be decomposed into the sum of a symmetric and a skew-symmetric[5] matrix. To see this, take any matrix $\mathbf{A}$ and consider the following decomposition:

$$\mathbf{A} = \frac{1}{2}[\mathbf{A} + \mathbf{A}^T] + \frac{1}{2}[\mathbf{A} - \mathbf{A}^T]$$
(F.12)

Table F.2
Results of Iterating A with the Starting Vector [1, 1]

N	Input	Output	θ	Δθ
1	(1, 1)	(−1, 1)	135°	90°
2	(−1, 1)	(−1, −1)	−135°	90°
3	(−1, −1)	(1, −1)	−45°	90°
4	(1, −1)	(1, 1)	45°	90°

Defining $\mathbf{A}_1 = (1/2)[\mathbf{A} + \mathbf{A}^T]$ and $\mathbf{A}_2 = (1/2)[\mathbf{A} - \mathbf{A}^T]$, it can be readily verified that $\mathbf{A}_1 = \mathbf{A}_1^T$ and $\mathbf{A}_2 = -\mathbf{A}_2^T$. What is more relevant for our purposes, though, is that the skew-symmetric term on the right-hand side of equation (F.12) is a matrix with zero diagonal entries. As a result, it can be shown[6] that skew-symmetric matrices have either zero real eigenvalues or complex-conjugate eigenvalues with no real part. This means that the skew-symmetric part of a matrix does not contribute to the stretching or shrinking of its iterated vectors, which stretching is due to the multiplicative effect of the real part of its eigenvalues. Instead, the complex part of the eigenvalues of a matrix contributes to the rotation of its iterated vectors.

For instance, note what happens when a prototypical skew-symmetric two-dimensional matrix $\mathbf{A}$ is iterated with the starting vector [1, 1]. Table F.2 shows the results of the first few iterates:

$$\mathbf{A} = \begin{bmatrix} 0 & -1 \\ 1 & 0 \end{bmatrix}$$

In general, the skew-symmetric part of any matrix $\mathbf{A}$ merely causes rotations of its input vectors while the symmetric part is what causes contractions and expansions in such vectors.

Since we are solely interested in the successive contraction of input vectors from the eigenvalues of $\mathbf{G}'(\mathbf{x})$ along the sequence (F.5), we can ignore its skew-symmetric part and concentrate exclusively on its symmetric part. Without loss of generality, we may therefore assume that $\mathbf{G}'(\mathbf{x})$ is symmetric since, by construction, the real parts of its eigenvalues are identical to those of $\mathbf{A}_1$.

Now recall from chapter 14 that real symmetric matrices have a unitary-equivalent representation. (In all cases, the functional will virtually guarantee that all eigenvalues are distinct as well.)

$$\mathbf{G}'(\mathbf{x}) = \mathbf{V}[\lambda]\mathbf{V}^{-1}. \tag{F.13}$$

In equation (F.13), $\mathbf{V}$ is the matrix of column eigenvectors of $\mathbf{G}'(\mathbf{x})$ and $[\lambda]$ is a diagonal matrix consisting of its eigenvalues. Please note that these eigenvectors are different for every matrix $\mathbf{G}'(\mathbf{x})$ along the sequence equivalent to equation (F.5) in our m-dimensional parametric space. Now, proceed as before and select the matrix with the largest spectral radius, ψ, in the sequence

$$\psi = \max_{i=1}^{n} \max_{j=1}^{m} |\lambda_{ij}|. \tag{F.14}$$

Further, define the condition number $\kappa(\mathbf{V})$ of matrix $\mathbf{V}$ as

$$\kappa(\mathbf{V}) = |\mathbf{V}| \, |\mathbf{V}^{-1}|. \tag{F.15}$$

In equation (F.14), λ_{ij} is the j'th eigenvalue of the i'th matrix $\mathbf{G}'(\mathbf{x})$ along the vector-space sequence similar to equation (F.6) from $i = 0$ to $i = n$.

Then $\psi < 1/\kappa(\mathbf{V})$ is a sufficient condition for the NR vector iteration to converge.

To see this, define $\mathbf{M}$ as the norm of the selected maximal-norm matrix and $\mathbf{V}$ as its eigenvector matrix. Remembering that for matrix norms $|\mathbf{AB}| \leq |\mathbf{A}| \, |\mathbf{B}|$, we have

$$\mathbf{M} \equiv \max_{i} |\mathbf{G}'(\mathbf{x})| \leq |\mathbf{V}| \, \psi \, |\mathbf{V}^{-1}|. \tag{F.16}$$

We can rewrite the vector analogue of sequence (F.5) as follows:

$$|\mathbf{x}_2 - \mathbf{x}_1| \leq \mathbf{M} |\mathbf{x}_1 - \mathbf{x}_0| \tag{F.17}$$
$$|\mathbf{x}_3 - \mathbf{x}_2| \leq \mathbf{M} |\mathbf{x}_2 - \mathbf{x}_1|$$
$$.$$
$$.$$
$$.$$
$$|\mathbf{x}_{n+1} - \mathbf{x}_n| \leq \mathbf{M} |\mathbf{x}_n - \mathbf{x}_{n-1}|$$

Substitution of each inequality in equation (F.17) into the subsequent one yields our final result in multiple dimensions:

$$|\mathbf{x}_{n+1} - \mathbf{x}_n| \leq \mathbf{M}^n |\mathbf{x}_1 - \mathbf{x}_0| \tag{F.18}$$

Equation (F.16) allows us to rewrite equation (F.18) in terms of $\mathbf{V}$ and ψ:

$$|\mathbf{x}_{n+1} - \mathbf{x}_n| < |\mathbf{V}| \psi^n \kappa(\mathbf{V})^{n-1} |\mathbf{V}^{-1}| \, |\mathbf{x}_1 - \mathbf{x}_0|$$
$$|\mathbf{x}_{n+1} - \mathbf{x}_n| < \frac{1}{\kappa(\mathbf{V})} |\mathbf{V}| [\psi \kappa(\mathbf{V})]^n |\mathbf{V}^{-1}| \, |\mathbf{x}_1 - \mathbf{x}_0| \tag{F.19}$$

If the condition $\psi < 1/\kappa(\mathbf{V})$ holds for all n along the sequence (F.17), then equation (F.19) shows that the increment $\Delta\mathbf{x} = |\mathbf{x}_{n+1} - \mathbf{x}_n|$ will be driven toward the vector zero, and the iteration will converge. In practice, the condition number is usually of order 1. Note that, by definition,

$$\kappa(\mathbf{V}) = |\mathbf{V}| \, |\mathbf{V}^{-1}| \geq |\mathbf{V}\mathbf{V}^{-1}| = 1. \tag{F.20}$$

For instance, for the condition number of matrix $\mathbf{A}$ below, we have the following:

$$\mathbf{A} = \begin{bmatrix} 1 & 3 & 7 \\ 6 & 8 & 2 \\ 5 & 2 & 3 \end{bmatrix}$$

$$\mathbf{A}^{-1} = \begin{bmatrix} -0.1 & -0.025 & 0.25 \\ 0.04 & 0.16 & -0.2 \\ 0.14 & -0.065 & 0.05 \end{bmatrix}$$

From this, we readily derive $\kappa(\mathbf{V}) = |\mathbf{A}| \, |\mathbf{A}^{-1}| = (16)(0.4) = 6.4$.

The condition number $\kappa(\mathbf{V})$ tends to remain of order 1 in actual iterations, and so numerical instability usually stems from the behavior of ψ. For this reason, the convergence analysis of the multidimensional NR iterative scheme is usually accomplished by monitoring the value of ψ along sequences of the type (F.17). To bring this to life we review a simple two-dimensional case.

Vector-Valued Newton-Raphson Convergence Analysis Example

Assume that we have decided to use the Gamma distribution function to simulate the behavior of some random process. However, rather than simply computing the values of its two parameters (α and β) from the mean and standard deviation of the given process (μ and σ, respectively), it has been decided to use the two-dimensional NR nonlinear iteration method to solve for their values. This would never occur in practice, as α and β are easily found by inverting the known formulas for μ and σ. However, knowing the actual locations of the roots will allow us to monitor the convergence of the vector NR method. The objectives to solve the equation system $\mathbf{f}(\mathbf{x}) = 0$, $\mathbf{f} = [f_1, f_2]^T$.

We begin with some basic algebra to simplify subsequent calculations. The two-dimensional Jacobian of a function $\mathbf{f}(x_1, x_2)$ of two independent variables x_1 and x_2 is

$$\mathbf{J}(\mathbf{x}) = \begin{vmatrix} \dfrac{\partial f_1}{\partial x_1} & \dfrac{\partial f_1}{\partial x_2} \\ \dfrac{\partial f_2}{\partial x_1} & \dfrac{\partial f_2}{\partial x_2} \end{vmatrix}.$$

The determinant is

$$\det(\mathbf{J}(\mathbf{x})) = D = \frac{\partial f_1}{x_1} \frac{\partial f_2}{\partial x_2} - \frac{\partial f_1}{\partial x_2} \frac{\partial f_2}{\partial x_1}. \qquad (F.21)$$

Inversion of the square, two-dimensional matrix $\mathbf{J}(\mathbf{x})$ yields

$$\mathbf{J}^{-1}(\mathbf{x}) = \frac{1}{D} \begin{bmatrix} \dfrac{\partial f_2}{\partial x_2} & \dfrac{-\partial f_1}{\partial x_2} \\ -\dfrac{\partial f_2}{\partial x_1} & \dfrac{\partial f_1}{\partial x_1} \end{bmatrix}. \qquad (F.22)$$

The fixed-point vector map $\mathbf{g}(\mathbf{x})$, defined by $\mathbf{g}(\mathbf{x}) = \mathbf{x} - \mathbf{J}^{-1}(\mathbf{x})\mathbf{f}(\mathbf{x})$, can be written as follows:

$$g_1(x) = x_1 - \frac{1}{D}\left\{ f_1\frac{\partial f_2}{\partial x_2} - f_2\frac{\partial f_1}{\partial x_2} \right\}$$ (F.23)

$$g_2(x) = x_2 - \frac{1}{D}\left\{ f_2\frac{\partial f_1}{\partial x_1} - f_1\frac{\partial f_2}{\partial x_1} \right\}$$ (F.24)

For the elements of the convergence matrix $\mathbf{G}'(\mathbf{x})$, we have

$$g'_{11} \equiv \frac{\partial g_1}{\partial x_1} = 1 - \frac{\partial}{\partial x_1}\left\{ \frac{f_1\dfrac{\partial f_2}{\partial x_2}}{D} \right\} + \frac{\partial}{\partial x_1}\left\{ \frac{f_2\dfrac{\partial f_1}{\partial x_2}}{D} \right\}.$$ (F.25)

$$g'_{12} \equiv \frac{\partial g_1}{\partial x_2} = \frac{\partial}{\partial x_2}\left\{ \frac{f_2\dfrac{\partial f_1}{\partial x_2}}{D} \right\} + \frac{\partial}{\partial x_2}\left\{ \frac{f_1\dfrac{\partial f_2}{\partial x_2}}{D} \right\}.$$ (F.26)

$$g'_{21} \equiv \frac{\partial g_2}{\partial x_1} = \frac{\partial}{\partial x_1}\left\{ \frac{f_1\dfrac{\partial f_2}{\partial x_1}}{D} \right\} + \frac{\partial}{\partial x_1}\left\{ \frac{f_2\dfrac{\partial f_1}{\partial x_1}}{D} \right\}.$$ (F.27)

$$g'_{22} \equiv \frac{\partial g_2}{\partial x_2} = 1 - \frac{\partial}{\partial x_2}\left\{ \frac{f_2\dfrac{\partial f_1}{\partial x_1}}{D} \right\} + \frac{\partial}{\partial x_2}\left\{ \frac{f_1\dfrac{\partial f_2}{\partial x_1}}{D} \right\}.$$ (F.28)

Armed with these values, we can calculate the eigenvalues of $\mathbf{G}'(\mathbf{x})$ from the defining equation $\det(\mathbf{G}'(\mathbf{x}) - \lambda\mathbf{I}) = 0$. This yields the following quadratic equation whose roots are the desired eigenvalues:

$$\lambda^2 - \lambda[g'_{11} + g'_{22}] + [g'_{11}g'_{22} - g'_{12}g'_{21}] = 0,$$

from which we get

$$\lambda_1 = \frac{(g'_{11} + g'_{22}) + \sqrt{(g'_{11} + g'_{22})^2 - 4(g'_{11}g'_{22} - g'_{12}g'_{21})}}{2}$$ (F.29)

$$\lambda_2 = \frac{(g'_{11} + g'_{22}) - \sqrt{(g'_{11} + g'_{22})^2 - 4(g'_{11}g'_{22} - g'_{12}g'_{21})}}{2}$$ (F.30)

Referring to chapter 13, we can write

$$f_1 = \alpha\beta - \mu$$ (F.31)

$$f_2 = \alpha\beta^2 - \sigma^2.$$ (F.32)

Simple algebra yields, using $x_1 = \alpha$, $x_2 = \beta$,

$$\frac{\partial f_1}{\partial \alpha} = \beta \qquad \frac{\partial f_1}{\partial \beta} = \alpha$$ (F.33)

$$\frac{\partial f_2}{\partial \alpha} = \beta^2 \qquad \frac{\partial f_2}{\partial \beta} = 2\alpha\beta \qquad\qquad \text{(F.34)}$$

Assume the given mean and standard deviations are $\mu = 1$ and $\sigma^2 = 2$. The analytical solution for the parameters α and β yield $\alpha = \mu^2/\sigma^2$, $\beta = \sigma^2/\mu$, which means $\alpha_\infty = 1/2$, $\beta_\infty = 2$. Using equation (F.21) the Jacobian determinant D is

$$D = \alpha\beta^2.$$

From equations (F.25) through (F.28), we further have

$$g'_{11} = 1 + \frac{\{2\beta\mu - 2\alpha\beta^2 - \sigma^2\}}{\alpha\beta^2} + \frac{\{\alpha^2\beta^2 - 2\alpha\beta\mu + \alpha\sigma^2\}}{\alpha^2\beta^2} = 0 \quad \text{(F.35)}$$

$$g'_{12} = \frac{2\left\{\dfrac{\sigma^2}{\beta} - \mu\right\}}{\beta^2} \qquad\qquad \text{(F.36)}$$

$$g'_{21} = \frac{\{\mu\beta - \sigma^2\}}{\alpha^2\beta} \qquad\qquad \text{(F.37)}$$

$$g'_{22} = 1 - \frac{\sigma^2}{\alpha\beta^2} \qquad\qquad \text{(F.38)}$$

Note the fact that since α appears linearly in both f_1 and f_2, the first term above is identically zero. After some simplification, substitution of equations (F.35) through (F.38) into equations (F.29) and (F.30) for λ_1 and λ_2, respectively, yields the following:

$$\lambda_1 = \frac{1 - \dfrac{\sigma^2}{\alpha\beta^2} + \sqrt{\left(1 - \dfrac{\sigma^2}{\alpha\beta^2}\right)^2 - \dfrac{8}{\alpha^2\beta^2}\left(\mu - \dfrac{\sigma^2}{\beta}\right)^2}}{2} \qquad \text{(F.39)}$$

$$\lambda_2 = \frac{1 - \dfrac{\sigma^2}{\alpha\beta^2} - \sqrt{\left(1 - \dfrac{\sigma^2}{\alpha\beta^2}\right)^2 - \dfrac{8}{\alpha^2\beta^2}\left(\mu - \dfrac{\sigma^2}{\beta}\right)^2}}{2} \qquad \text{(F.40)}$$

In view of equation (F.15), equations (F.39) and (F.40) are useful in the analysis of the convergence of this two-dimensional NR solution. It is interesting to plot these eigenvalues in the neighborhood of the known roots $\alpha_\infty = 1/2$, $\beta_\infty = 2$ to investigate how the NR scheme should behave around the solution. In essence, we would like to determine the maximum distance from the roots at which we still retain the condition $\max_i |\lambda_i| \ll 1$. This knowledge would go a long way toward instilling confidence in the corresponding uniform convergence of the NR scheme. Table F.3 is a data set for the region $\alpha \in [-2.5, 2.5]$ and $\beta \in [1.25, 3]$.

Table F.3
Spectral Radius Map of $G'(x)$

Alpha	Beta 1.25	1.5	1.75	2	2.25	2.5	2.75	3
−2.5	1.462	1.344	1.260	1.200	1.157	1.126	1.103	1.085
−2	1.566	1.427	1.324	1.250	1.197	1.157	1.128	1.106
1.5	1.735	1.565	1.431	1.333	1.262	1.209	1.169	1.139
−1	2.056	1.835	1.645	1.500	1.392	1.310	1.249	1.202
−0.5	2.931	2.627	2.283	2.000	1.779	1.608	1.476	1.372
0.5	1.358	0.629	0.231	0.000	0.140	0.226	0.281	0.314
1	0.679	0.463	0.249	0.753	0.521	0.217	0.646	0.609
1.5	0.453	0.210	0.554	0.667	0.734	0.779	0.813	0.839
2	0.339	0.507	0.668	0.750	0.801	0.836	0.862	0.882
2.5	0.272	0.619	0.736	0.800	0.841	0.870	0.891	0.907

Figure F.5 shows the same data graphically in the neighborhood of the point $\alpha_\infty = 1/2$, $\beta_\infty = 2$.[7]

Figure F.5 displays a fairly dramatic forbidden zone inside which we would expect the NR method to fail consistently. Conversely, relatively high (α, β) starting guesses should be safe, including the immediate neighborhood of the roots to the right of $\alpha = 0.5$. Note also the quite unexpected result that, with the chosen values for μ and σ^2, the method fails completely for any starting guess where $\beta = 1$, for then we have $g_1(\alpha, \beta) = 0$ identically, and it clearly fails for $\alpha = 0$, $\beta = 0$ as starting guesses.

Selections $[\alpha_0 = 4, \beta_0 = 4]$, $[\alpha_0 = -2.5, \beta_0 = 0.5]$, and $[\alpha_0 = 1.5, \beta_0 = 0.75]$ yield the convergence histories shown in Tables F.4, F.5, F.6, respectively. We would expect the first initial guess to more or less converge uniformly, the third to oscillate somewhat but still converge, and the second to

Table F.4
Convergence History for $[\alpha_0 = 4, \beta_0 = 4]$

N	α	β	$\max_i |\lambda_i|$	f_1	f_2
0	4.000	4.000	0.967	15.000	62.000
1	0.375	3.875	0.942	0.453	3.631
2	0.383	2.585	0.646	−0.010	0.558
3	0.474	1.994	0.000	−0.054	−0.114
4	0.500	2.000	0.000	0.000	0.001
5	0.500	2.000	0.000	0.000	0.000
6	0.500	2.000	0.000	0.000	0.000
7	0.500	2.000	0.000	0.000	0.000
8	0.500	2.000	0.000	0.000	0.000

Table F.5
Convergence History for [$\alpha_0 = -2.5$, $\beta_0 = 0.5$]

N	α	β	$\max_i |\lambda_i|$	f_1	f_2
0	−2.500	0.500	3.394	−2.250	−2.625
1	−4.000	−0.700	1.948	1.800	−3.960
2	−6.939	0.264	5.065	−2.834	−2.485
3	−21.066	−0.682	1.063	13.372	−11.805
4	−7.229	−0.496	1.988	2.583	−3.775
5	−12.179	0.201	5.170	−3.448	−2.492
6	−39.547	−0.534	1.084	20.111	−13.270
7	−10.765	−0.414	1.852	3.454	−3.843
8	−16.513	0.128	9.774	−3.115	−2.271

probably fail since it is deep inside the dark shaded area in Figure F.5. Let's see what happens in practice.

As expected, our second guess fails completely while the other two lead to somewhat well-behaved convergence histories. Note the oscillatory behavior in f_1 and β in Table F.5, indicating that the system is unable to dampen numerical error modes as would happen if the spectral radius of $\mathbf{G}'(\mathbf{x})$ were smaller.

At this juncture, a few comments are in order:

- It would be difficult to think of a simpler multidimensional NR iteration than the case presented here, which has no significant nonlinearity in the defining equations. Even with such trivial equations, we find a clear demarcation between the convergent and divergent regions. Evidently, the intricacies involved in multidimensional optimization are nonnegligible even in two dimensions.

Table F.6
Convergence History for [$\alpha_0 = 1.5$, $\beta_0 = 0.75$]

N	α	β	$\max_i |\lambda_i|$	f_1	f_2
0	1.500	0.750	2.095	0.125	−1.156
1	−0.889	1.861	1.647	−2.654	−5.079
2	0.497	1.777	0.201	−0.116	−0.430
3	0.492	2.029	0.020	−0.001	0.027
4	0.500	2.000	0.000	0.000	0.000
5	0.500	2.000	0.000	0.000	0.000
6	0.500	2.000	0.000	0.000	0.000
7	0.500	2.000	0.000	0.000	0.000
8	0.500	2.000	0.000	0.000	0.000

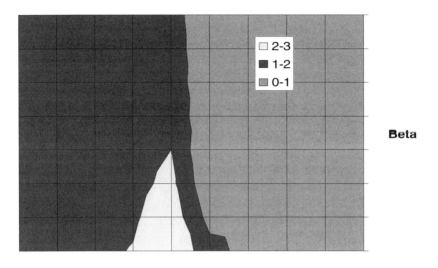

Beta

Alpha

Figure F.5. Mapping of $G'(x)$ by Spectral Radius (Newton-Raphson two-dimensional iteration)

- Whereas the scalar version of the NR method was relatively free from trouble (in the sense that we could use just about any starting guess without significantly affecting convergence), the probability of something going awry in a multidimensional case has increased dramatically.
- The method is somewhat forgiving in that even if the initial-guess vector is slightly inside the forbidden zone, it still finds its way out to the roots; however, this may not always happen.
- Higher-dimensional space often has many more surprises in store for careless analysts. Since the number of parameters in a serious model is usually four to seven, having a fairly good idea of the locations of the solution-roots is usually required to avoid failure. In the end, this is art as much as science.

Appendix G

Spline Function Interpolations

This section is a very cursory look at cubic splines. Over the past twenty years, splines have become somewhat of a staple of approximation in finance and economics. Rather than go over well-trodden ground again, our objective here is merely to guide structured credit analysts as to when to use and when to avoid these polynomial approximations in their work. For most problems in credit risk analysis, we find the direct use of cubic approximation functions to model interest rates and other basic parameters risky, usually unnecessary, and seldom warranted. In fact, it can often lead to erroneous judgments.

In general, splines find two main uses within numerical analysis. They are helpful when interpolating a continuous function at points other than the given set, and when the analyst has reasons to believe that the function in question satisfies certain a priori smoothness and continuity properties. (How often these requirements are overlooked is surprising.) But more importantly, they are used during the integration of partial differential equations in an attempt to limit the excessive growth of numerical errors. Since such integrations will seldom be relevant in structured finance, splines find their main purpose as subsidiary techniques of integration supporting the main goals of the analysis. Despite this secondary status with respect of structured finance, their current widespread popularity within financial analysis makes a discussion of implementation mechanics somewhat unavoidable.

What are Splines?

Spline functions are a class of piecewise interpolating polynomials that include the standard linear interpolation formula (the first-order spline, so to speak) as a special case. In all cases, the goal is to find an approximation to a real function y, given as discrete point pairs (x_i, y_i), $i = 1, 2, \ldots N$ in $\Re$, at locations other than the given points.

In practice, the problem boils down to finding a formula yielding the value of y between any two of the given points. The idea is to do this with functions possessing certain continuity properties. For the cubic spline, this means functions that have continuous first and second derivatives and that match the given points exactly.

This procedure is to be contrasted sharply with regression, where we attempt to fit a known function to a given set of points but without the requirement to match any of them. In other words, in regression the function is

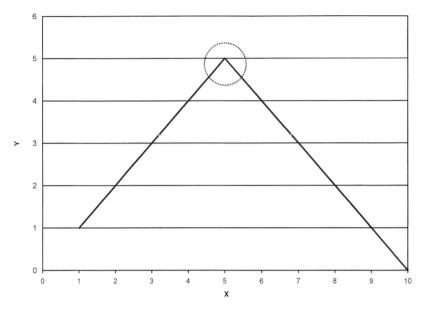

Figure G.1. A Very "Kinky" Function

known a priori but the data are unknown, whereas with splines, the *data* are known a priori but the *function* is unknown.

Continuity is required because the smoothness of a function is related to the order of its highest continuous derivative, and smoothness is one of the main goals of approximation theory. The underlying philosophy of approximation is based on the fact that natural phenomena are continuous and smooth, but our observations are not. Due to sampling inaccuracies, we have failed to account for a sufficient number of degrees of freedom, and so by requiring smoothness as a property of the approximating function, we deem it closer to the truth.

For example, a function like the one shown in Figure G.1 is itself continuous but discontinuous in its first derivative (slope) on either side of the kink. On the other hand, if we mandate that its first derivative be continuous everywhere, sharp kinks will not occur. However, the function could still be discontinuous in its second derivative somewhere, which would show up as an abrupt change in curvature. Such a function is depicted in Figure G.2. Although smoothness has clearly improved markedly, the function still appears somewhat awkward. The solution is to keep going and ensure that its second derivative be continuous at all points. By doing this to all orders, the approximating function becomes both visually and mathematically smooth to any required degree of accuracy.

Although this smoothing process can be continued ad infinitum, the smoothness benefits provided by increasingly higher orders of continuity are

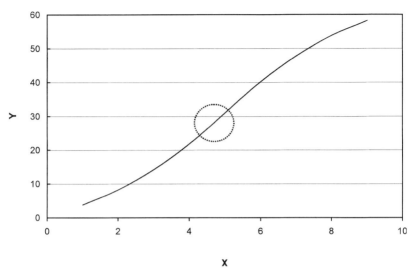

Figure G.2. A Less "Kinky" Function

usually not worth the trouble required to achieve them. Although smoothness is inherently desirable, it is rarely necessary beyond the continuity of the second derivative. The resulting function is the cubic spline approximation for the points (x_i, y_i).

The Cubic Spline Equations

As stated, suppose we are given a set of discrete functional pairs (x_i, y_i), $i = 1$, 2, . . N, and that we wish to build an approximating polynomial function that matches these values at the endpoints y_i and y_{i+1} of the ith interval. This can be done by a special case of equations (19.4) and (19.5), the Lagrange interpolation formulas from chapter 19.[8]

$$P_n(x) = \sum y_i L_i(x) \qquad (19.4)$$

$$L_i(x) = \prod_{\substack{j=0 \\ j \neq i}}^{n} \frac{(x - x_j)}{(x_i - x_j)} \qquad (19.5)$$

Equation (19.4) gives

$$y = Ay_i + By_{i+1}. \qquad (G.1)$$

Then equation (19.5) yields

$$A = \frac{x_{i+1} - x}{x_{i+1} - x_i} \qquad (G.2)$$

$$B = 1 - A. \tag{G.3}$$

Note that the x dependence of the approximating polynomial in equation (G.1) is hidden inside the respective definitions of the two coefficients A and B. Also note that coefficients A and B satisfy the two boundary conditions:

$$A(x_i) = 1 \tag{G.4}$$

$$A(x_{i+1}) = 0 \tag{G.4'}$$

$$B(x_i) = 0 \tag{G.5}$$

$$B(x_{i+1}) = 1 \tag{G.5'}$$

By construction, the approximating piecewise polynomial equation (G.1) matches the given functional values at the boundaries of any interval and varies linearly between such boundaries. Furthermore, the approximating function is continuous across the boundary between two intervals since y_{i+1} of one interval is simply y_i of the next.

Riding high on our success with functional values, we might be tempted to use the same trick with the second derivatives of the approximating polynomial and postulate a formula similar to (G.1) in terms of y'', its second derivative. We would begin by postulating

$$y'' = C''y_i'' + D''y_{i+1}''. \tag{G.6}$$

As we saw with equation (G.1), the parameters C'' and D'' would be linear functions of the independent variable x and the given abscissa x_i. Now the problem is that, by arbitrarily introducing a set of unknown free parameters y_i'', $i = 1, 2, \ldots, N$, we could have disturbed the original agreement between equation (G.1) and the given points. To see this, integrate equation (G.6) with respect to x twice, yielding

$$y = Cy_i'' + Dy_{i+1}''. \tag{G.7}$$

In equation (G.7), C and D are now *cubic* polynomials in terms of x and the given points x_i since they are twice-integrated functions of *linear* polynomials, and the generic formula for C (or D, for that matter) would be

$$C = \alpha x^3 + \beta x^2 + \delta x + \varepsilon. \tag{G.8}$$

Using equation (G.6) would allow us to match the postulated second derivatives y_i'' but not the functional values because of equation (G.7). Our problem is now to match both simultaneously.

The solution is clearly to add equation (G.7) to (G.1), while making sure that the addition of (G.7) does not upset the functional agreement already achieved via equation (G.1). Doing this while still ensuring the continuity of second derivatives using equation (G.6) would give us boundary conditions on C and D enabling us to find the values of the unknown coefficients in equation (G.8) and its equivalent for D.

First, to ensure that the functional agreement is preserved, we need the following:

$$C(x_i) = 0 \tag{G.9}$$

$$C(x_{i+1}) = 0 \tag{G.9'}$$

$$D(x_i) = 0 \tag{G.10}$$

$$D(x_{i+1}) = 0 \tag{G.10'}$$

Next, to guarantee that our postulated second derivatives are continuous across all interval boundaries, we have the analogues of conditions (G.4) and (G.5):

$$\frac{d^2C}{dx^2}(x_i) = 1 \tag{G.11}$$

$$\frac{d^2C}{dx^2}(x_{i+1}) = 0 \tag{G.11'}$$

$$\frac{d^2D}{dx^2}(x_i) = 0 \tag{G.12}$$

$$\frac{d^2D}{dx^2}(x_{i+1}) = 1 \tag{G.12'}$$

The eight conditions in equations (G.9) through (G.12') give us eight equations to define the values of the four parameters involved in equation (G.8) and their equivalents for D. We demonstrate the derivation for C only (the calculations for D being identical).

With respect to equation (G.8), conditions (G.11) yield the following two-dimensional linear system:

$$6\alpha x_{i+1} + 2\beta = 0$$

$$6\alpha x_i + 2\beta = 1$$

Using the definition $\Delta x = x_{i+1} - x_i$, Cramer's rule quickly yields the solution

$$\alpha = -\frac{1}{6\Delta x}, \tag{G.13}$$

$$\beta = \frac{x_{i+1}}{2\Delta x}. \tag{G.14}$$

Substitution of equations (G.13) back into equation (G.9) now gives the following two-dimensional system:

$$x_{i+1}\delta + \varepsilon = -\frac{x_{i+1}^3}{3\Delta x} \tag{G.15}$$

$$x_i\delta + \varepsilon = \frac{x_i^3}{6\Delta x} - \frac{x_{i+1}x_i^2}{2\Delta x} \tag{G.15'}$$

Cramer's rule again yields the solutions

$$\delta = -\frac{x_{i+1}^3}{3\Delta x^2} - \frac{x_i^3}{6\Delta x^2} + \frac{x_{i+1}x_i^2}{2\Delta x^2}, \tag{G.16}$$

$$\varepsilon = x_{i+1}\left(\frac{x_i^3}{6\Delta x^2} - \frac{x_{i+1}x_i^2}{2\Delta x^2}\right) + \frac{x_i x_{i+1}^3}{3\Delta x^2} \tag{G.17}$$

Finally, substitution of equations (G.3), (G.14), (G.16), and (G.17) into equation (G.8) gives, after some rearrangement,

$$C = \frac{1}{6\Delta x}\left\{-x^3 + 3x_{i+1}x^2 + \left(\frac{3x_{i+1}x_i^2}{\Delta x} - \frac{x_i^3}{\Delta x} - \frac{2x_{i+1}^3}{\Delta x}\right)x\right.$$
$$\left. + \frac{2x_i x_{i+1}^3}{\Delta x} + \frac{x_{i+1}x_i^3}{\Delta x} - \frac{3x_{i+1}^2 x_i^2}{\Delta x}\right\}. \tag{G.18}$$

Although equation (G.18) can be used as such, it is instructive to further rearrange its factors remembering equation (G.2), from which we derive

$$C = \frac{1}{6\Delta x}\{x_{i+1}^3 - 3x_{i+1}^2 x + 3x_{i+1}x^2 - x^3 - A[x_{i+1}^3 - 3x_{i+1}^2 x_i$$
$$+ 3x_{i+1}x_i^2 - x_i^3]\} + \frac{3}{6\Delta x}[-x_i^3 + xx_{i+1}^2 + A(x_{i+1}^3 + x_i x_{i+1}^2)]. \tag{G.19}$$

However, it is easily verified that the factor in the square brackets multiplying $3/(6\Delta x)$ is identically zero. Therefore, once equation (G.2) is compared to the remnants of equation (G.19), we have

$$C = \frac{1}{6\Delta x}\{\Delta x^3 A^3 - A\Delta x^3\} + 0 = \frac{\Delta x^2}{6}\{A^3 - A\}. \tag{G.20}$$

A similar derivation yields the analogous result for D:

$$D = \frac{\Delta x^2}{6}\{B^3 - B\}$$

Our equation for y can now be finally stated as

$$y = Ay_i + By_{i+1} + Cy_i'' + Dy_{i+1}''. \tag{G.21}$$

The reader can verify that, as expected, taking the second derivative of equation (G.21) yields

$$\frac{d^2 y}{dx^2} = Ay_i'' + By_{i+1}''. \tag{G.22}$$

As advertised, the second derivative of y indeed varies linearly between the given points and is continuous across each interval boundary.

Although the above arrangement works for any choice of the free parameters y_i'', it still does not guarantee that all such choices will also preserve the
continuity of first derivatives across interval boundaries. Guaranteeing this
property requires further work. First, taking the first derivative of equation
(G.21) and remembering that

$$\frac{dA}{dx} = -\frac{dB}{dx} = -\frac{1}{\Delta x}$$

$$\frac{dC}{dx} = -\frac{(3A^2 - 1)\Delta x}{6}$$

$$\frac{dD}{dx} = \frac{(3B^2 - 1)\Delta x}{6},$$

we find

$$\frac{dy}{dx} = \frac{y_{i+1} - y_i}{\Delta x} - \frac{y_i''(3A^2 - 1)\Delta x}{6} + \frac{y_{i+1}''(3B^2 - 1)\Delta x}{6}. \quad (G.23)$$

The cubic spline's essential trick is to choose the appropriate values for y_i''
by matching the first derivative of y across interval boundaries. This is allowable, since we introduced the free parameters y_i'' arbitrarily. Because they were
never part of the given data, we can select them as we please to achieve our continuity objective. We do this by setting the right-hand side of equation (G.23)
at the right boundary of one interval equal to the same value for the left boundary of the next interval, thus ensuring the continuity of the first derivative
across that boundary. Doing this for all $N - 2$ inside interval boundaries produces $N - 2$ equations for the unknowns y_i'', $i = 1, 2, 3, \ldots, N$. After some
rearrangement, the result is the following linear tri-diagonal system for the y_i'',
$i = 2, \ldots, N - 1$:

$$\left\{\frac{x_i - x_{i-1}}{6}\right\}y_{i-1}'' + \left\{\frac{x_{i+1} - x_{i-1}}{3}\right\}y_i'' + \left\{\frac{x_{i+1} - x_i}{6}\right\}y_{i+1}''$$

$$= \frac{y_{i+1} - y_i}{x_{i+1} - x_i} - \frac{y_i - y_{i-1}}{x_i - x_{i-1}} \quad (G.24)$$

The simultaneous solution of these $N - 2$ equations ensures that first derivatives of y are continuous at the inside boundary points, where they really
count. Note also that the first and last equations of tri-diagonal system (G.24)
refer to variables y_1'' and y_N'', respectively. As these are extra free parameters unnecessary to accomplish our goal, we are free to deal with them as we wish.
There are basically two alternative ways of setting their values:

- The *Dirichlet method*, whereby the missing y_i'' are set equal to given values at x_1 and x_N. If the value is zero in both cases, we have the natural
  spline.

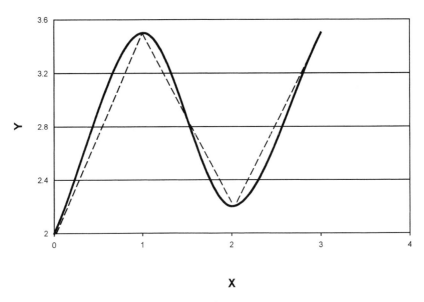

Figure G.3. Cubic and Linear Spline Interpolations

- The *von Neumann method,* whereby the first derivative of y is instead given values at x_1 and x_N. Using equation (G.23), these values are then turned into the corresponding y_1'' and y_N'' before back-substitution into equations (G.24).

Solving system (G.24) is not difficult. It can be done via the LU decomposition method described in chapter 17. Interested readers can consult *Numerical Recipes* for a full description of that process. For now, we want to turn our attention to the more important issue of why and when structured analysts would use cubic splines.

The Use of Cubic Splines in Structured Finance

Note that the difference between a linear and a cubic interpolation can be significant. For instance, Figure G.3 shows the difference between the linear and cubic splines on the same set of points. Before using cubic splines, analysts should ask themselves whether this behavior is truly representative of the phenomenon they are investigating. In many areas of economic modeling, there will be precious little data to justify departure from a purely linear interpolation.

As we mentioned earlier, cubic splines are special in that they maintain the continuity of the second derivatives of the approximating function across the inside points of the interval of approximation. This property takes on special meaning when solving second-order partial differential equations numerically, because discontinuities in derivatives involved in the original equations lead to the growth of errors in the numerical approximation to these derivatives. By ensuring that numerical approximations are free from such discontinuities, we tend to minimize the errors they cause.

It turns out that the natural phenomena that are the subject matter of mathematical physics are ruled by second-order partial differential equations. Hence, it makes perfect sense to use cubic splines in such numerical solutions. However, except for the so-called Black-Scholes differential equation (for which an analytical solution already exists), it will be rare for a credit analyst in structured finance to be asked to solve a second-order partial differential equation.

Unless there exist physical or economic justifications for a smoother behavior, there is no rationale whatsoever for preferring the cubic spline to the linear interpolation method when, in most cases, a piecewise linear fit is more than sufficient to achieve a physically acceptable result. (Observe from Figure G.3 that the cubic spline is unable to turn a sharp corner around a point, and that, characteristically, it behaves smoothly at each point x_i where the function behaves abruptly.) Yield curve modeling is a case in point. In our work, we have seen many practitioners use cubic splines to approximate the yield curve for maturities between those given by market data. Imagine for a moment that the abscissa and ordinate of Figure G.3 were the maturity and interest rate, respectively. Would anyone give credence to such interest rate behavior? Unless one could be reasonably certain that interest rates near maturity points where high volatility exists could not be better described as weighted averages of the preceding and following points, modeling the yield curve using a cubic spline would completely miss the point of interpolation. Cubic functions as links between successive points are credible only when there is intrinsic or extrinsic evidence for that behavior.

In structured finance, the danger of using the cubic spline is one of under- or overestimating interest payments collected or paid on a security, which could translate into a different credit rating for that security. This discussion becomes more than academic when a few basis points could mean the difference between an investment-grade rating and junk.

Cubic splines do have an indirect place in structured analysis—for example, in building subsidiary models where integration of a function is required and where the resolution required is finer than that delivered by the number of given points. In that case, assuming smoothness of the function to be integrated between the given points can be justified since we can assume that the true function is smooth to begin with, and that the given points are samples of an a priori smooth process. In the case of interest rates, no such assumption imposes itself at the outset.

In conclusion, cubic splines are wonderful tools of applied physics equipped with a philosophical interpretation that makes their use very appealing. In structured finance, they should be used sparingly when modeling critical deal variables, and then only after the problem has been carefully analyzed to find an appropriate justifying rationale.

Appendix H

Correlation Topics

In many applications of numerical methods to structured finance, analysts will be asked to simulate correlated instruments or variables. This appendix is aimed at clarifying some of the issues that may arise when doing so, and at avoiding mistakes when using Monte Carlo simulation techniques, which mistakes then result in higher credit enhancement requirements than would otherwise be warranted.

Correlation versus Conditional Probability

In the first instance, there seems to exist a certain confusion between the related, but by no means identical, concepts of correlation and conditional probability. Given the relatively high importance of correlation in credit analysis, the number of situations when the former is used as the latter is surprising. In what follows, we contrast these two ideas and discuss the conceptual and numerical differences between them in a real context.

The Pearson correlation coefficient or covariance between a variable x and another variable y is a measure of their linear association—no more than that. Define $E(x)$ as the mathematical expectation of variable x; in other words, set $E(x) \equiv \bar{x} = (1/n)\sum_i x_i$, $i = 1, 2, \ldots n$. For the covariance, we have formally

$$\text{cov}(x, y) = E[(x - \bar{x})(y - \bar{y})]. \tag{H.1}$$

Now, define σ_x and σ_y as the standard deviation of x and y, respectively, and the Pearson linear correlation coefficient ρ_{xy} as

$$\rho_{xy} = \frac{\text{cov}(x, y)}{\sigma_x \sigma_y}. \tag{H.2}$$

Also, note that the linearity of definition (H.1) along with those of σ_x and σ_y imply that ρ_{xy} will be invariant under any linear transformation of either x or y or both. To see this, set $z = ax + b$. We then have the following:

$$\rho_{zy} = \frac{\text{cov}(z, y)}{\sigma_z \sigma_y}$$

$$\sigma_z = \sqrt{E(z^2) - [E(z)]^2}$$

$$E(z^2) = a^2 E(x^2) + 2ab E(x) + b^2$$

$$E(z) = a E(x) + b$$

$$\therefore \sigma_z = a\sqrt{E(x^2) - [E(x)]^2} = a\sigma_x.$$

Since we have $E(z - \bar{z}) = aE(x - \bar{x})$, we finally obtain

$$\rho_{zy} = \frac{aE[(x - \bar{x})(y - \bar{y})]}{a\sigma_x\sigma_y} = \rho_{xy}. \tag{H.3}$$

On the other hand, the conditional probability of y, given x—written as $P(y|x)$—is a measure of the coincidence of two events and is quite different from correlation. By definition we have

$$P(y|x) = \frac{P(x, y)}{P(x)}. \tag{H.4}$$

These two concepts are different fundamentally and should never be confused. The correlation coefficient satisfies $\rho_{xy} \in [-1, 1]$ while $P(y|x) \in [0, 1]$. It is therefore not possible to simulate the full range of correlation coefficients using conditional probabilities, although in special cases a transformation function can be derived between the two over some range. However, in practically all cases, this correspondence will rarely lead to numerically identical values. This means, for instance, that one cannot attempt to simulate a correlation coefficient of 0.8 by using a condition probability of 0.8, and vice versa. As we shall see shortly, doing this can be quite misleading.

Relating Correlation to Conditional Probability

It is instructive to spend some time digging deeper into these concepts to get an idea of the range of errors one may be committing by using the concepts of linear correlation and conditional probability interchangeably. It may surprise many readers to find out that this is quite commonly done in credit analysis.

By inspection of equation (H.1), we conclude that the covariance between two variables is measured by how much time each variable spends above its average value with respect to the other. In cases where x and y are identically distributed, a zero correlation basically means that regardless of whether one variable is below or above its average value, the other spends as much time above as below *its* average value. By no means does this imply that the conditional probability of one given the other is zero.

We illustrate this point with a common example from structured finance. Assume that x and y represent two finite default processes we wish to simulate. To do this, we define both x and y as binary variables with the following interpretation:

$$x, y = 1 \Rightarrow \text{Default} \tag{H.5}$$

$$x, y = 0 \Rightarrow \text{No Default} \tag{H.6}$$

In this case, $x > \bar{x}$ means a default since x can take only two values, 0 or 1, and by assumption $\bar{x} \equiv E(x) > 0$ for any finite default process.

Assume for argument's sake that $E(x) = 0.05$ and $E(y) = 0.1$. Thus x will default, on average, five times in every 100 trials while y will average ten defaults in every 100 trials. Now, consider the following direct computation of the covariance between x and y using equation (H.1) for a hypothetical representative sample of 100 trials. Here we make an entirely reasonable assumption that two independent binary default processes yield their expected values precisely:

$$\text{cov}(x, y) = 0.01\{.5(.95)(.9) - 4.5(.95)(.1) - 9.5(.05)(.9) + 85.5(.05)(.1)\}$$

$$\text{cov}(x, y) = 0$$

As expected, the covariance as correlation between two independent variables is zero, but as we shall see below, the converse is not necessarily true. From the definition equation (H.4) of the joint default probability, we also have $P(y|x) = 0.5/5 = 0.1$ (i.e., out of five x defaults, y defaults 0.5 times on average). In this case, a zero correlation corresponds to a 10% conditional probability, which is just another reflection of the independence of x and y coupled with $E(y) = 0.1$. These numbers may have vastly different practical meanings in a transaction where the expected joint default rate is 0.5%. A relative error margin of this magnitude is clearly unacceptable.

Let us see what happens when we set $P(y|x) = 0.2$. By direct computation we now have, again assuming expected outcomes,

$$\text{cov}(x, y) = .01\{.95(.9) + 4(.95)(-.1) + 9(-.05)(.9) + 86(-.05)(-.1)\}$$

$$\text{cov}(x, y) = 0.005.$$

By definition, we also have the following:

$$\sigma_x = \sqrt{E(x^2) - [E(x)]^2} = \sqrt{0.05 - 0.05^2} = 0.218$$
$$\sigma_y = \sqrt{E(y^2) - [E(y)]^2} = \sqrt{0.1 - 0.1^2} = 0.3$$

Hence the linear correlation coefficient between x and y is

$$\rho_{xy} = \frac{0.005}{(0.218)(0.3)} = 0.076.$$

We conclude that a joint default probability of 20% corresponds to a correlation of 7.6%, and the difference between the two has grown from 10% at zero correlation to 12.4%. Let's play this game a few more times using various values of $P(y|x)$. The results are shown in Table H.1.

Among other things, Table H.1 shows that if we simulated corr(x, y) = 30% using $P(y|x) = 30\%$, we would in fact be simulating a 15.5% correlation between the variables x and y, a 50% discrepancy. An error of this magnitude is easily the difference between a good and a bad outcome. Depending on what x and y really mean, the transaction could be mispriced or overenhanced. Either way, someone is paying for the error.

Table H.1
Corr(x, y) versus P(y|x) for Binary x, y Variables

P(y|x)(1)	Corr(x, y)(2)	(1) – (2)	(2)/(1)
0.1	0.000	0.100	0.000
0.2	0.076	0.124	0.380
0.3	0.155	0.145	0.516
0.4	0.230	0.170	0.575
0.5	0.306	0.194	0.612

To properly simulate a joint default process with corr $(x, y) \approx 30\%$ is not difficult. Using Table H.1, one can deduce that x and y must be defaulted together five times chosen at random from among every set of 200 trials. The other fifteen y defaults would occur when x is not defaulting and the other five x defaults would occur when y is not defaulting. According to Table H.1, this corresponds to $P(y|x) = 50\%$ and could be modeled as such. The difference is that the correlation method allows the negative half of the correlation spectrum to be modeled while the conditional probability method is restricted to positive outcomes. Selecting a truly random sample of five out of every 200 trials can be done accurately and effortlessly using the low-discrepancy sequence technique described in chapter 13. It is well worth the effort in a world where significant sums are at stake.

In conclusion, credit analysis should be wary of the pitfalls that stem from mixing the concepts of linear correlation and conditional probability. Default processes are too important to credit analysis to risk being subjected to a potential 50% error rate.

Correlation versus Causality

A secondary, but important, aspect of correlation is the difference between correlation and causality often overlooked in analysis. The Pearson correlation coefficient between two variables is merely a measure of their linear association. As a result, an analytic function y with a relatively weak or nonexistent linear dependence on its independent variable x might display negligible correlation with the latter, despite the strong relationship between them. The statement cov $(x, y) = 0$ does not always imply that x and y have no relationship to each other. In point of fact, the absence of correlation between x and y could very well imply complete dependence, not independence. Consequently, a physical interpretation should never be ascribed to correlation. It should not be modeled automatically as a statistical random process without solid prior evidence of such randomness. Unfortunately, the latter requirement is often ignored in credit analysis.

To illustrate, consider the following simple analytical situation:

$$y \equiv f(x) = \cos(x), x \in [-\pi, \pi]$$

By direct computation using the pairs (x_i, y_i), $i = 0, 1, 2, \ldots, 50$ we arrive at the singular result $\text{cov}(x, y) = 0$. Yet, no one could seriously contend that x and y are not *related*; they are simply not *correlated* in the linear sense.

The interesting paradox, that tightly linked variables may not display correlation, could lead an analyst mistakenly to conclude that they have nothing in common and simulate their behavior using two independent random processes. To clear this paradox, we first have to introduce the notion of odd and even functions.

An even function $f(x)$ is defined by the condition $f(-x) = f(x)$. An odd function, on the other hand, is defined by $f(-x) = -f(x)$. The following three facts directly follow from these definitions:

1. When an odd function is multiplied by an even function, the result is odd.
2. When an odd function is multiplied by an odd function, the result is even.
3. When an even function is multiplied by an even function, the result is even.

Note also that $\cos(-x) = \cos(x)$. Hence the cosine function is even. And since $\sin(-x) = -\sin(x)$, the sine function is odd.

A graph of odd and even functions is shown in Figure H.1 using $\cos(x)$ and $\sin(x)$ in the interval $[-\pi, \pi]$ as examples. It turns out that the integral properties of even and odd functions provide a solution to the paradox. Note that as even functions are symmetric with respect to the x-axis, while odd functions are anti-symmetric, we have the following trivial results in the interval $[-a, a]$.

$$\int_{-a}^{a} f(x)\,dx = 2\int_{0}^{a} f(x)\,dx, \qquad f(x) \text{ is even.} \tag{H.7}$$

$$\int_{-a}^{a} f(x)\,dx = 0, \qquad f(x) \text{ is odd.} \tag{H.8}$$

From the respective definitions of oddness and evenness, all odd powers of x are odd functions and all even powers of x are even functions. Thus, the product $x\cos(x)$ is odd, being the product of an odd and even function, while $x\sin(x)$ is even, being the product of two odd functions. By equations (H.7) and (H.8), we conclude that $\int_{-\pi}^{\pi} x\cos(x)\,dx = 0$.

How does this help us? If, instead of using the small sample $i = 50$ to compute $\text{cov}(x, y)$, we had gone to the limit $i \to \infty$, $\text{cov}(x, y)$ would be defined as

$$\text{cov}(x, y) = \frac{1}{2\pi}\int_{-\pi}^{\pi} (x - \bar{x})(\cos(x) - \overline{\cos(x)})\,dx. \tag{H.9}$$

Since $\bar{x} = 0$ and $\overline{\cos(x)} = 0$ by definition, the integral in equation (H.9) yields the same result as for $\int_{-\pi}^{\pi} x\cos(x)\,dx$ alone (i.e., zero). By contrast, had we used $f(x) = \sin(x)$, the result would have been

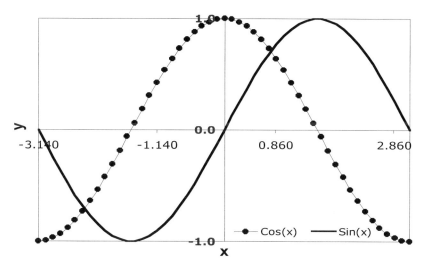

Figure H.1. Examples of Odd ($\sin(x)$) and Even ($\cos(x)$) Functions

$$\text{cov}(x, y) = \frac{1}{2\pi}\int_{-\pi}^{\pi} (x - \bar{x})(\sin(x) - \overline{\sin(x)})\,dx \neq 0.$$

In that case, simple integration with $\bar{x} = 0$ and $\overline{\sin(x)} = 0$ yields

$$\text{cov}(x, y) = \frac{1}{\pi}\int_{0}^{\pi} x \sin(x)\,dx = \left(\frac{1}{\pi}\right)[\sin(x) - x\cos(x)]_{0}^{\pi} = \frac{\pi}{\pi} = 1.$$

Our original sample of 50 data points yields $\text{cov}(x, y) = 0.979$ and $\text{corr}(x, y) = 0.756$.

For the function $f(x) = \sin(x)$, had we chosen the interval $[0, 2\pi]$ instead of $[-\pi, \pi]$, $\text{cov}(x, y)$ would have been -1 in the limit, and our discrete sample would have yielded $\text{cov}(x, y) = -0.9175$ and $\text{corr}(x, y) = -0.756$. In other words, simply by picking a different region of observation, the correlation coefficient has reversed itself completely.

If we pick the interval $[0, 4\pi]$ rather than $[0, 2\pi]$, we obtain $\text{cov}(x, y) = -0.988$ but $\text{corr}(x, y) = -0.3836$ due to increased x variance. From a rather simple functional relationship between x and y, we can apparently achieve just about any correlation coefficient we choose if we pick the right interval of observation, without any requirement for a change in the underlying process. Clearly, the concept of linear correlation leaves some of the physics by the wayside.

Digging more deeply, we note that the Taylor series expansion of the cosine function contains only even powers of x:

$$\cos(x) = 1 - \frac{x^2}{2!} + \frac{x^4}{4!} - \frac{x^6}{6!} + \dots \qquad \text{(H.10)}$$

As expected, the expansion for the sine function contains only odd powers of x:

$$\sin(x) = x - \frac{x^3}{3!} + \frac{x^5}{5!} + \ldots \tag{H.11}$$

The solution to our paradox therefore seems to lie in the properties of the given function as revealed through its Taylor series. By computing the first few Taylor series coefficients, we can give a more powerful and fruitful interpretation to the complete absence of linear correlation in the $\cos(x)$ case and the 75% linear correlation in the $\sin(x)$ case. In other words, the extent to which functions will be odd or even will depend on the relative magnitudes of the Taylor series' coefficients attached to odd and even powers of x, respectively. Sine and cosine functions are just extreme cases of functions with more or less oddness or evenness, respectively.

In the limit of the interval $[-a, a]$, $a \to 0$, equations (H.10) and (H.11) already tell us without computation that $\text{corr}(x, \cos(x)) \to 0$ while $\text{corr}(x, \sin(x)) \to 1$, since for small x, $\sin(x) \approx x$.

Hence, the leading behavior of functions can go a long way toward explaining their correlative properties. Depending on the interval under consideration, we would look to that behavior to motivate our level of relative acceptance or mistrust of correlation estimates. An even-powered leading behavior in x, such as $\cos(x)$, would cause us to pause and reconsider the meaning of a small linear correlation coefficient in light of what we just saw. By contrast, an odd-powered leading behavior like $\sin(x)$ could temper our excitement at the knowledge of high correlation, for changing the interval of observation could reduce or increase correlation almost arbitrarily without a corresponding physical basis.

When one is handed a time-series of two variables, it is therefore instructive to expand one of them as a function of the other and examine the relative magnitudes of the first few odd and even coefficients of the resulting Taylor series, even if only those recoverable from the available data points. This way, credit analysts can peek beneath the surface to better grasp the relationship between the correlation coefficient and the physics of the process, rather than read too much into the magnitude of the former without a valid understanding of the latter.

Given a relatively short and symmetric interval along the x-axis, it might be justifiable to interpret the complete absence of linear correlation between x and y as evidence, not of the lack of functional relationship between the two but, on the contrary, as a statistical proof of the exact opposite. As a simple application, note that the first derivative of an odd function is an even function and vice versa; this conclusion stems from the fact that derivatives of odd powers are even powers, and conversely.

Therefore, should one discover a total absence of correlation between x and y within a given interval, it would not be uncommon for the first derivative of the function y to exhibit a significant amount of positive or negative correlation with x. Via this technique, rather than concluding that there is "no relationship between x and y," a structured credit analyst with greater sophistication about correlation would be in a better position to identify relationships not immediately obvious from the raw data. This knowledge could then be put to use in devising a suitable invariant as input to a synthetic treatment of such data as discussed in chapter 11.

Final Remarks on Correlation

"Seek simplicity, and distrust it" is the motto of correlation analysis. One might reasonably assume that two uncorrelated variables have nothing in common, when in fact a zero correlation might stem from a highly predictable and reproducible process, hinted at precisely by the absence of correlation. Analysts also need to bear in mind the potential shortcomings of linear correlation coefficients in data analysis, and the paramount importance of the independent variable's domain of definition in drawing conclusions about relationships between variables. In practice, those bold enough to suspend preconceived notions to look beyond the immediately obvious are also those able to turn apparent chaos into order.

Throughout this appendix, we have been at great pains to warn credit analysts about the dangers of excessive reliance on appearances. Statistics don't lie, but statisticians do. Although the claims of statistical science are based solely on correlation, predictive power can only arise from the discovery of causal relationships among the data elements, and not from the coincidental interplay of statistical measures.

Notes

Chapter 1

1. In particular, the 144A market created by the Securities and Exchange Commission (SEC) in 1990 to allow the trading of privately placed debt among sophisticated investors who meet certain criteria and are known as *qualified institutional buyers* without SEC supervision.

2. Ann Rutledge, "Asian Securitizations: Moody's Analytical Approach." *Securitization: The Asian Guide. A Supplement to Asia Money* (December 1997/January 1998): 22.

3. The history of Thailand's securitization market is an anatomy of the risks of new-market investing, for example. Ann Rutledge, "Asian Markets Year in Review 1997/1998," *Outlook* (March 1998): 4–5.

4. True sale treatment is especially important to transactions originated in the United States, where bankruptcy courts have significant powers to adjust the claims of the bankrupt companies' creditors. It may be less relevant to transactions involving FDIC-insured deposit-taking institutions, whose receivership is handled under the Federal Deposit Insurance Act, and in many jurisdictions outside the United States with strong creditor traditions. In such cases, a legal opinion to the effect that the investor is in first position, and the perfection of the security interest, often suffice.

5. Not all true sale opinions are equally valid, and indeed the quality of legal reasoning can vary considerably. It is easier to articulate the principle of sale—an outright transfer of responsibilities and rights from one party to another—than to identify one, particularly when there are substantial incentives for stretching the truth. Safe treatment under the law is usually established with reference to one or more sale tests devised by the courts. No single outcome carries the day, but rather, a preponderance of sale-like attributes is desirable. An excellent summary treatment of true sale and substantive consolidation may be found in Peter J. Lahny IV, "Asset Securitization: A Discussion of the Traditional Bankruptcy Attacks and Our Analysis of the Next Potential Attack, Substantive Consolidation," *American Bankruptcy Institute Law Review* 9 (Winter 2001).

The choice of auxiliary verb is also significant. A "would" opinion is more committal than a "should" opinion, and "should" is as a warning to the investor that the true sale analysis is weak. "Should" also frequently appears in legal opinions from developing markets. Here it tends to mean that, although a sound legal argument for sale treatment may be constructed within the framework of the law, the outcome of a bankruptcy court is unknown or unclear. True sale reasoning is usually buttressed by arguments drawing on case history, doctrine, or other legal sources. However, as the true sale concept has never been successfully tested in a court of law in the United States, even a "would" opinion on a U.S. securitization is provisional in some degree.

6. Jason Kravitt, *The Securitization of Financial Assets*, 2nd ed. (New York: Aspen Law and Business, 1996); chapter 5.

7. Because in most cases, the transferor continues to be responsible for cash collection and distribution on behalf of the SPE, operational separateness is achieved only with active involvement of a trustee on behalf of investors.

8. Marty Rosenblatt, Jim Johnson, and Jim Mountain, "Securitization under FASB 140, Second Edition (Deloitte and Touche, January 2002): 71–77.

9. Please consult the next section for more institutional detail.

10. Marty Rosenblatt, Jim Johnson, and Jim Mountain, "Securitization under FASB 140, Second Edition" (Deloitte and Touche, January 2002), 11–18.

11. Moody's Global Asset-Backed Commercial Paper Market Review, third quarter 1999.

12. Sam Pilcer, "Understanding Structured Liquidity Facilities in Asset-Backed Commercial Paper Programs" (Moody's Investors Service, first quarter 1997), 4–5.

13. See, for example, two papers by Mary Dierdorff: "ABCP Market 1998 Overview and 1999 Outlook: Continued Explosive Growth in the Market Makes Liquidity the Hot Topic of 1999, Moody's Global Asset-Backed Commercial Paper Market Review, First Quarter 1999" (Moody's Investors Service, 1999), 16–17, and "Third Quarter 2001, Eureka Securitization Inc.," 610, 613–615.

14. In fully supported transactions, the sponsoring bank is liable for 100% of CP.

15. Bond Market Association, "Bond Market Statistics" (The Bond Market Association, July 2002).

16. See the Federal Reserve Board commercial paper statistics for 2002, at www.federalreserve.gov.

17. See, for example: Joseph C. Hu, *Basics of Mortgage-Backed Securities* (New York: Wiley, 1997); William W. Bartlett, *The Valuation of Mortgage-Backed Securities* (New York: Irwin Professional Publishing, 1994); and Frank Fabozzi, *Mortgage and Mortgage-Backed Securities Markets* (Boston: Harvard Business School Press, 1992).

18. The Bond Market Association, "Bond Market Statistics" (http://www.bond markets.com).

19. See, for example, Anthony Sanders, "Commercial Mortgage Backed Securities" (Columbus, Oh.: Ohio State University, June 1999).

20. William Goetzmann, "Global Real Estate Markets: Cycles and Fundamentals" (New Haven, Conn.: Yale School of Management, March 7, 1999).

21. Based on interviews with Patrice Jordan, managing director of structured finance for Standard & Poor's, and Tom Gillis, criteria and chief quality officer for Standard & Poor's Structured Finance Group, October 5, 2001; and on an interview with Douglas Watson, first head of Moody's Investors Service Structured Finance Group, August 3, 2001.

22. The Bond Market Association, "Bond Market Statistics (http://www.bond markets.com)."

23. Doug Lucas, "CDO Handbook" (New York: J. P. Morgan, May 30, 2001).

24. Conversation with Dr. Yu Jaejun of the Mirae Bond Corporation, April 2000.

25. The Bond Market Association, "Bond Market Statistics (http://www.bond markets.com).""

26. Maureen Coen and Claire Robinson, "Overview: Market Characterized by Growth and Evolution, Asset Backed Commercial Paper, Second Quarter 1994" (Moody's Investors Service, 1994), 8–9.

27. From the Association of Financial Guaranty Insurors (AFGI) (http://www.afgi. org).

28. Structurally they represented a line of innovation that had begun in the nineteenth century. See Peter Tufano, "Business Failure, Judicial Intervention, and Financial In-

novation: Restructuring U.S. Railroads in the Nineteenth Century," *Business History Review* (Spring 1997), 1–41.

29. For ABS and MBS market value structures the discretion remained with the issuer. In market value CDOs and ABCP, it resides with the collateral manager. As Douglas Watson has pointed out, cash flow CDOs that revolve can be subject to the same type of risks as market value CDOs in the substitution process and in collateral default scenarios. The more corporate the cash flow CDO is, in essence (i.e., the greater the amount of discretion and the longer the assets revolve), the less distinguishable its risk profile is from that of a market value CDO.

30. Isaac C. Hunt Jr., Commissioner, U.S. Securities and Exchange Commission. Testimony Concerning the Role of Credit Rating Agencies in U.S. Securities markets before the Senate Committee on Governmental Affairs, March 20, 2002.

31. Lawrence J. White, "The Credit Rating Industry: An Industrial Organization Analysis" (Boston: Kluwer, 2002). In R. M. Levich, C. Reinhart, and G. Majnoni, eds., *Ratings, Rating Agencies, and the Global Financial System* (Boston: Kluwer Academic, 2002), chapter 2.

32. Lawrence J. White, "The SEC's Other Problem," *Regulation* 25 (Winter 2002–2003).

33. Comments of Thomas Gillis, managing director of Standard & Poor's, interviewed October 5, 2001.

34. Comments of Douglas Watson, managing director of Financial Security Assurance, Inc., and first head of Moody's Investors Service Structured Finance Group, interviewed August 3, 2001.

Chapter 2

1. Within the corporate rating framework, a distinction is made between "issue" ratings and "issuer" ratings. The classic *issue ratings* apply to senior unsecured or secured debt of a public or private company, which take into consideration not only the issuer's fundamental debt capacity but also covenants and other forms of preferential access granted the investor through the structure. The classic *issuer ratings* are counterparty ratings that take "willingness and ability to pay" at face value. If these two varieties of rating are not identical, neither are they independent. Nothing in this discussion of the contemporary framework's analytical antecedents should be taken as a comment on the relative merits of issuer and issue ratings. Our comments on the corporate framework may be found in chapter 6.

2. Interview with Douglas Watson, first head of Moody's Investors Service Structured Finance Group, August 3, 2001.

3. Comments of Tom Gillis, managing director of Standard & Poor's, interviewed October 5, 2001.

4. Jason Kravitt, ed., *Securitization of Financial Assets*, 2nd ed. (Aspen, Colo.: Aspen Law and Business, 1996), chapter 7.02C: "[I]n analyzing [the] credit risk [of asset-backed securities that are not fully supported by third-party credit enhancement] the rating agencies employ two basic rating criteria: first, *they analyze the general credit risk inherent in the transaction*, and second, they assess the cash flow of the financial assets (and, in transactions that are structured in reliance upon liquidation or market value, the liquidation value of the financial assets), including risks inherent in the payment structure, and collateral composition and sufficiency" (emphasis added).

5. Interview with Douglas Watson, first head of Moody's Investors Service Structured Finance Group, August 3, 2001.

6. "During 1983–1985, the debate centered on how to handle the fact that structured finance deals very likely had a different profile of risk from industrial credits. It was felt at the time that the incidence of default would probably be higher, while loss-given-default would be lower. Remember that recovery data of 30–40% for industrial credits was not known to Moody's then, and would not be known until the late 1980s with the bond default work done by Chris Baldwin" (interview with Douglas Watson).

7. It sounds paradoxical but may be clearly illustrated with the example of an interest-only (IO) strip. Interest-only strips are paid from interest cash flows. Heavy prepayments will dramatically reduce the size of interest cash flows, even though the credit is not impaired—in fact, quite the reverse, since prepayments are early and safe return of principal. Carrying this scenario out to its logical conclusion, the investor returns on an AAA IO with high prepayments will take a bashing even though the underlying credit has not missed a principal payment.

8. In such cases, the rating analyst's evaluation is a classic "counterparty" analysis, which has qualitative and quantitative elements. The question is, "Does the institution have the capacity and the right motivation to stand by its performance promise?" The answer is based on data like the company rating, comments of rating agency analysts who follow the institution, and perhaps a back-of-the-envelope comparison between the dollar value-at-risk and the incentive. For more details on how this part of the analysis is conducted, please see step 4 of the actuarial method in chapter 3 of this chapter.

9. J. Fons and Christina Cotton, "Moody's Approach to Jointly Supported Obligations" (Moody's Investors Service, November 21, 1997). The variables are sourced as follows: default probabilities come from the default database and the correlation statistic is the result of a rating committee decision. The formula in the paper is attributed to Douglas Lucas, but the approach was in use during the 1980s.

The authors wish to note the identity of this formula with that given by Stephen Kealhofer in "Portfolio Management of Default Risk" (KMV Corporation, May 2001, 9) in his definition of *correlation*. In both formulas, the solution in the case $P(A \cap B) = 0$ is incorrect. Whereas the correlation statistic should be closer to -1 in this case, by the Moody's and Kealhofer formula, it can be equal to -1 only in the special case where the default probability equals its own standard deviation. To express the relationship as a conditional probability, the expression $P_{A \cap B} = P_{B/A} \cdot P_A$ would be technically more correct. However, the latter formula does not correspond as directly to the rating agency thinking process as the formula given in the text.

10. The method of constructing the latter-day Hong Kong benchmark pool for mortgages of single-A credit quality is described thus: "Moody's identifies the key financial characteristics of the residential mortgages and mortgage properties to construct an idealized or benchmark pool representing the market-mean. The benchmark comprises standard mortgages on geographically diversified, owner-occupied properties of average value in that market. Fundamental factors affecting pool performance are identified and examined for their variable impact under different future economic environments. The result of this scenario analysis is an estimate of loss, which is the basis for setting credit enhancement levels..." From Ann Rutledge, "Moody's Approach to Hong Kong's Residential Mortgage-Backed Securities Market" (Moody's Investors Service, November 1997), 2.

11. The fundamental factor analysis is seen to be vulnerable to methodological attack: do the factor adjustments bear a demonstrable empirical relationship to loss behavior? Or, since the factor adjustments are discontinuous, will they distort the incentives so that

the banks will tend to put in more collateral with 89% LTVs or 74% LTVs are most preferred?

12. Comments of Patrice Jordan, managing director of structured finance for Standard & Poor's, interviewed October 5, 2001.

13. Jerome S. Fons, "Corporate Bond Defaults and Default Rates 1970–1993" (Moody's Investors Service, January 1994), 9.

14. Richard Cantor and Jerome S. Fons, "The Evolving Meaning of Moody's Bond Ratings" (Moody's Investors Service, August 1999), 5.

15. David T. Hamilton, "Default and Recovery Rates of Corporate Bond Issuers: 2000" (Moody's Investors Service, February 2001), 19.

16. Standard & Poor's "Structured Finance Auto Loan Criteria," p. 3.

17. Mark Adelson, "Introduction to Moody's Analysis of Securitization Transactions and Structures" (Moody's Investors Service, June 29, 1995), 1.

18. Alan Backman, "Rating Cash flow Transactions Backed by Corporate Debt 1995 Update," (Moody's Investors Service, April 9, 1995, table 5, p. 11). Also see Alain Debuysscher, "The Fourier Transform Method—Technical Document," (Moody's Investors Service, January 23, 2003, appendix 4).

Chapter 3

1. The portfolio variance is expressed as $\sum_{i=1}^{N}\sum_{j=1}^{N}x_ix_j\sigma_{ij}$. The incremental increase in variance when a second pool is added can be seen in additional term, for the two-pool example: portfolio variance $= X_i^2\sigma_i^2 + X_j^2\sigma_j^2 + 2X_iX_j\sigma_{ij}$.

2. Paul Mazataud, "The Lognormal Method Applied to ABS Analysis" (Moody's Investors Service, July 27, 2000).

3. The observed mean ($\bar{x}$) and standard deviation (s) for a normal distribution are parameter estimates for the mean (μ) and standard deviation (σ). The standard deviation ($\bar{b}$) for a lognormal distribution is equal to $\sqrt{\ln[1 + (s/\bar{x})^2]}$, and the mean ($\bar{a}$) is equal to ln $\bar{x} - b^2/2$. Thus, increases in variance will decrease the corresponding mean.

4. Standard & Poor's, "Structured Finance Legal Criteria" (April 2000), 52–60, provides a good summary of the legal risks surrounding external credit sources.

5. Standard & Poor's, "Structured Finance Legal Criteria: Appendix D, Swap Agreement Criteria for CBO/CLO Transactions," 121–133, contains a good reference checklist of drafting issues.

6. Margaret Kessler and Laura Levenstein, "Credit Default Swaps versus Financial Guaranties: Are the Risks the Same?" (Moody's Investors Service, June 2001) provides a good overview of the risks of credit default swaps.

7. Standard & Poor's, "Global CBO/CLO Criteria: Appendix B, Structured Finance Interest Rate and Currency Swap Criteria" (Standard & Poor's, http://www.standardandpoors.com, 109–115).

Chapter 4

1. Standard & Poor's, "Global CBO/CLO Criteria," 24 (criteria); 32 (audit elements); 20–23 (ratings and rating proxies).

2. Various Moody's papers discuss the quantitative method: Alan Backman, "Rating Cash Flow Transactions Backed by Corporate Debt 1995 Update" (April 9, 1995); Arturo Cifuentes, "The Binomial Expansion Method Applied to CBO/CLO Analysis" (December 13, 1996); Arturo Cifuentes, Eileen Murphy, and Gerard O'Connor, "Emerging Market Collateralized Bond Obligations: An Overview" (October 23, 1996); Eileen Murphy, Gerard O'Connor, "Stopping for Yield: Moody's Approach to Evaluating Esoteric Assets in CBOs and CLOs" (December 3, 1999).

3. Standard & Poor's, "Global CBO/CLO Criteria," 33 (required variables for the default model); 21 (recovery values); 42–44 (stresses).

4. See note 2.

5. Typical stresses historically have been 1.5 for Aaa, 1.4 for Aa, 1.31 for A, and 1.23 for Baa, but these are subject to rating agency discretion.

6. Yvonne Falcon Fu, "Moody's Approach to Market Value CDOs" (Moody's Investors Service, April 3, 1998).

7. Arturo Cifuentes, "The Double Binomial Method and Its Application to a Special Case of CBO Structures" (Moody's Investors Service, March 1998).

Chapter 5

1. This summary draws extensively from Mark Adelson, "Asset-Backed Commercial Paper: Understanding the Risks" (Moody's Investors Service, April 1993).

2. Helen Remeza, "Moody's Approach to Rating Multisector CDOs" (Moody's Investors Service, September 15, 2000).

3. Sam Pilcer, "Understanding Structured Liquidity Facilities in Asset-Backed Commercial Paper Programs" (Moody's Investors Service, First Quarter 1997), 4–5.

Chapter 6

1. R. C. Merton, "Theory of Rational Options and Corporate Liabilities," *Journal of Political Economy*, 81 (May–June 1973): 637–659.

2. The pitch of two sounds, or the credit quality of two firms, will do just as well.

3. Most likely, this problem has arisen before at the rating agencies. In the beginning, rating designations were given as simple letter-grades like A or Aa. Over time, the number of designations increased by adding "notches" to compensate for a perceived insufficiency of resolution in the existing scale. The number of rating designations has tended to increase with the demand for transparency, the most recent instance being Moody's further notching of the Caa category in the late 1990s. This refinement process is likely to continue, even in corporate ratings, but it is much more critical in structured finance, where ratings are designed ex nihilo. Embracing the continuum hypothesis by a numerical credit scale is the easiest way to permanently remove the possibility of such contradictions and place structured credit risk measurement within a rational framework.

4. For example, if higher levels of a macro-index correspond to higher loss rates and static pool data have been collected during relatively good times, the average default propensities of all individual exposures would be adjusted by a factor greater than 1, and if static pool data originated in relatively bad times, the adjustment factor would be less than

1. In this manner, not only could the relative influence of both levels be quantified fairly accurately, but credit analysts would be operating within a transparent numerical world rather than one stemming from solipsistic qualitative speculations and subjective assessments, however well intentioned.

Chapter 7

1. Jerome S. Fons, "How and Why Do Structured Finance Ratings Change? Rating Transition Study for Single-Family Residential Mortgage Pass-Through Securities" (Moody's Investors Service, May 12, 1995), 5–6.

2. Jerome S. Fons, "Credit Shifts in Residential Mortgage Pass-Through Securities: A Rating Transition Study Update" (Moody's Investors Service, May 3, 1996).

3. Joseph Hu, "Structured Finance Special Report. Residential Mortgage Backed Securities: Strong Performance for U.S. RMBS Credit Ratings in 2000" (Standard & Poor's, January 2001).

4. "From 1987 through 1994, the cumulative number of ratings changed in the asset-backed market, as a percentage of the cumulative number of ratings outstanding during each year, was 6.6%, compared with 6.0% in the mortgage-backed securities market. Those figures were somewhat lower than for the traditional corporate bond market, where the percentage of ratings of issuers that were changed was 16.3% for the period between 1987 and the first half of 1993 (the last half for which data are available). Andrew Silver, "A Historical Review of Rating Changes in the Public Asset-Backed Securities Market, 1986–1995" (Moody's Investors Service, October 20, 1995), 1, 3.

5. "During 1983–1985, the debate [inside Moody's] centered on how to handle the fact that structured finance deals very likely had a different profile of risk from industrial credits? It was felt at the time that the incidence of default would probably be higher, while loss-given-default would be lower." Interview with Douglas Watson, first head of Moody's Structured Finance Group, August 3, 2001.

6. Joseph P. Snailer, "Rating Changes in the U.S. Asset-Backed Securities Market: First-Ever Transition Matrix Indicates Ratings Stability . . . To Date" (Moody's Investors Service, January 19, 2001), 1.

7. Joseph Hu, "Structured Finance Special Report. Asset-Backed Securities: Rating Transitions 2000—Resilient Credit Performance of U.S. ABS" (Standard & Poor's, January 2001).

8. For instance, see John Hull, *Options, Futures, and Other Derivative Securities* (New York: Prentice-Hall International, 1989), 81–83.

9. Borderline cases have been indicated by a slash between the two relevant rating categories.

10. Joseph Hu, "Life after Death: Recoveries of Defaulted U.S. Structured Securities" (Standard & Poor's, September 4, 2001).

11. The model does not address cases where a third party is providing the main form of credit enhancement, because the analysis of the third-party counterparty credit becomes substituted for the analysis of collateral performance in a structure as the focal exercise.

Chapter 8

1. The expression characterizes the "flowing" of cash through the tiered liability accounts.

2. If rates are quoted as annualized quantities in the P&S, the periodic rate is the annualized rate divided by the number of collection periods in a year. In most cases, a collection period is one calendar month.

3. In practice, the issue of servicing- or trustee-fee shortfalls is rather academic, as available funds will overwhelmingly far exceed these amounts.

4. See chapter 23 for more on triggers.

5. In transactions with more than two tranches, there would as many advance rates as there are classes of securities.

Chapter 9

1. Given interest rates, conditional prepayment models are quite accurate. However, absolute prepayment speeds are mainly related to interest rates (i.e., to fundamentally unpredictable quantities).

2. This argument clearly applies unchanged to pools of homogeneous loans.

3. Remember that defaults and prepayments are conceptually both "prepayments" for average-life computation purposes.

Chapter 10

1. For instance, see Murray R. Spiegel, ed., *Mathematical Handbook of Formulas and Tables* (New York: McGraw-Hill, 1968).

2. Note that in equation (10.10), the quantities $C_t(r)$ are the outputs from conditional prepayment models.

Chapter 11

1. J. M. Keynes, *The General Theory of Employment, Interest and Money* (New York: Harcourt, Brace, and World, 1936), 297.

Chapter 12

1. R. Nelson, *An Introduction to Copulas* (New York: Springer-Verlag, 1999).

2. The distinction between *pseudo-random* and *random* is rather academic. Since random numbers generated by a deterministic numerical algorithm can obviously be predicted in advance, they cannot truly be said to be "random." In a nutshell, *pseudo-random* means

that the numbers look random statistically while *random* means that they are the result of physical random processes to which no numerical algorithm can be associated.

3. Our discussion here parallels that found in W. H. Press, S. A. Teukolsky, W. T. Vetterling, and B. P. Flannery, *Numerical Recipes in C*, 2nd ed. (New York: Cambridge University Press, 1992), 276ff.

4. Press et al., *Numerical Recipes*, 275.

5. J. C. Van der corput, "Diophantische Ungleichungen: I. Zur Gleichverteilung Modulo Eins," *Acta Mathematica* (Stockholm) 52 (1931): 373–456; and "Diophantische Ungleichungen: II. Rhythmische Systeme," *Acta Mathematica* 59 (1932): 209–328.

6. J. M. Hammersley, "Monte Carlo Methods for Solving Multivariate Problems," *Annals of the New York Academy of Sciences* 86, no. 3 (1960): 844–873.

Chapter 13

1. The coordinates are simply the endpoint coordinates of the vector, the starting point being assumed to be the origin.

2. For more discussion, see Appendix F.

3. R. A. Horn and C. R. Johnson, *Matrix Analysis*, paperback ed. (New York: Cambridge University Press, 1990), 59ff.

4. Horn and Johnson, *Matrix Analysis*, 69ff.

5. Ibid., 33ff.

6. Ibid., 59ff.

Chapter 14

1. For instance, see A. A. Sveshnikov, ed., *Problems in Probability Theory: Mathematical Statistics and Theory of Random Functions*, Scripta Technica trans. (New York: Dover, 1978).

2. Kramer's rule can be found in any elementary mathematics textbook, e.g., M. H. Protter and C. B. Morrey Jr., *Modern Mathematical Analysis* (New York: Addison-Wesley, 1964), 287–288.

3. G. C. Chow, *Econometrics* (New York: McGraw-Hill, 1983), 38ff.

Chapter 15

1. Our formalism follows closely that of Chow in *Econometrics*.

Chapter 16

1. Press et al., *Numerical Recipes*.

Chapter 17

1. A monotonic function has nonnegative or nonpositive slope everywhere in the domain of interest.

2. Press et al., *Numerical Recipes*, 288–289.

3. For instance, the copula function approach described in David X. Li, "On Default Correlation: A Copula Function Approach," The Risk Metrics Group Working Paper no. 99-07.

Chapter 18

1. Press et al., *Numerical Recipes*, 864ff.

2. Ibid., 41ff.

3. Ibid.

Chapter 19

1. H. R. Schwarz, *Numerical Analysis* (New York: Wiley, 1989), 85ff.

Chapter 20

1. For example, see W. H. Press, S. A. Teukolsky, W. T. Vetterling, and B. P. Flannery, *Numerical Recipes in C*, 2nd ed. (New York: Cambridge University Press, 1992).

2. See chapter 9 for average-life calculations.

3. See http://www.statistics.gov.uk/statbase.

4. *Numerical Recipes*.

5. Frank J. Fabozzi, and Franco Modigliani, *Mortgage and Mortgage-Backed Securities Markets* (Boston: HBS Press, 1992), 171.

Chapter 21

1. To relax the assumption, we would simply have to alter the loss/cash flow dynamics without affecting the target reduction of yield. Thus, whether we assume zero or nonzero recoveries is moot.

2. For instance, see Stephen Kealhofer, "Portfolio Management of Default Risk" (KMV Corporation, February 11, 1998), 9.

3. The indices comprise seventy industry subgroups rolled up into forty industry groups, eighteen market sectors, ten macroeconomic sectors, and thirty-four countries including the major emerging markets. Dow Jones describes the time series thus: "Each index in the DJGI family is constructed and managed to provide consistent coverage of, and high correlation with its market" ("Guide to the Dow Jones Sector Titan Indexes," January 2001, page 10).

4. Remember that we are trying to simulate binomial processes at the tranche level using the IDFM method that requires a uniform distribution as its starting inputs in order to achieve correspondence with the desired binomials.

5. Press et al., *Numerical Recipes.*

6. Average life is a function of the assumptions concerning the timing of losses and principal proceeds; hence it is an input, not an output, of the binomial expansion analysis and must be determined via a cash flow analysis. However, as noted in chapter 3, the critical inputs into the structuring analysis (such as the average life, excess spread, and loss distribution) are in fact driven by the assumptions that are the prerogative of a rating agency—hence they are not genuine cash flow outputs, either. We have chosen simply to adopt the average life of the above analysis rather than replicate the cash flow portion of the BET analysis. We note that front-loaded stresses of the type presented in chapter 3 would serve to shorten the average life and reduce the credit for excess spread.

7. Alan Backman, "Rating Cash flow Transactions Backed by Corporate Debt 1995 Update," (Moody's Investors Service, April 9, 1995, table 5, p. 11). Also see Alain Debuysscher, "The Fourier Transform Method—Technical Document" (Moody's Investors Service, January 23, 2003, appendix 4).

Chapter 22

1. Martin Heidegger, "Modern Science, Metaphysics and Mathematics," in *Basic Writings* (San Francisco: Harper Collins), 247–282.

2. Although it bears Bernoulli's name, this equation was never found in his writings. As remarked in G. A. Tokaty, *A History and Philosophy of Fluid Mechanics* (New York: Dover Publications 1971), many believe that Leonard Euler is, in fact, the author of "Bernoulli's" principle.

3. This is not quite the whole story, but it will do for our purposes.

4. This constant is simply equal to the sum of both left-hand terms in the "free stream" (i.e., far away from the airfoil).

5. The liquidity facility was sufficient to pay interest on the bonds for eighteen months.

6. Seven notches above Baa3 equates to Aa2.

7. Formally, the *lease rate factor* is the monthly lease rate divided by the purchase price of the plane.

8. Note that this type of forecasting is an example of synthetic modeling discussed in chapter 11.

9. Martine Nowicki, "Moody's Structured Finance: An Update on Enhanced ETC's and Collateral Supported Debt" (Moody's Investors Service, October 1996); and Standard & Poor's Structured Finance, "Aircraft Securitization Criteria" (Standard & Poor's, 1999).

10. Ibid.

11. Standard & Poor's, "Aircraft Securitization Criteria."

12. Structured Finance Special Report, Fitch-IBCA, "Airline Generated Securitization Criteria" (September 1997).

13. Martine Nowicki, "Moody's Structured Finance."

14. Standard & Poor's, "Aircraft Securitization Criteria."

15. The "AeroFreighter Finance Trust" transaction (Moody's Investors Service: December 1999).

16. See the "Maintenance" section.

17. Ibid.

18. See chapter 11 on synthetic modeling for further information.

19. Note that a generalized year is not equal to a chronological year.

20. This is also available from fleet data.

21. Mark Tuminello and Zhidang Chen, "Moody's Approach to Pooled Aircraft-Backed Securitization" (Moody's Investors Service, March 1999).

22. If repossession time and expenses are counted separately, we have six parameters.

23. Mark Tuminello, Moody's New Issue Report, "Morgan Stanley Aircraft Finance," October 1998.

24. Ibid.

25. Rochelle Tarlowe, Moody's New Issue Report, *AeroFreighter Finance Trust*, March 2000.

26. Mark Tuminello, "Morgan Stanley."

27. CFM56 jet engines by SNECMA-GE, for instance, adding further credibility to the cycle-based method of aging aircraft.

28. Figures 22.6–22.8 were drawn from a randomly selected Monte Carlo scenario using empirical utilization distributions.

29. The "Airplanes Pass-Through Trust' transaction (Moody's Investors Service, April 1996).

Concluding Remarks

1. Thomas E. Copeland and J. Fred Weston, *Financial Theory and Corporate Policy*, 2nd ed. (Reading, Mass., Addison-Wesley, 1983).

Appendices A–H

1. For instance, Sveshnikov, *Problems in Probability Theory*, F. S. Hillier and G. J. Lieberman, *Introduction to Operations Research*, 3rd ed. (Holden-Day, 1980), 324ff.

2. Press et al., *Numerical Recipes*, chapter 9.

3. For instance, see A. N. Kolmogorov and S. V. Fomin, *Introductory Real Analysis*, ed. and trans. Richard Silverman (New York: Dover, 1980).

4. For instance, see Murray H. Protter and Charles B. Morrey, *Modern Mathematical Analysis* (Addison-Wesley, 1983).

5. A skew-symmetric matrix is equal to the negative of its transpose.

6. Horn and Johnson, *Matrix Analysis*, 167ff.

7. The lightly shaded region is the area where uniform convergences would be more likely.

8. From now on, our argument follows closely that of Press et al., *Numerical Recipes*.

Index